Rethinking Women's and Gender Studies

Rethinking Women's and Gender Studies re-examines the field's foundational assumptions by identifying and critically analyzing eighteen of its key terms. Each essay investigates a single term (e.g., feminism, interdisciplinarity, intersectionality) by asking how it has come to be understood and mobilized in Women's and Gender Studies and then explicates the roles it plays in both producing and shutting down possible versions of the field. The goal of the book is to trace and expose critical paradoxes, ironies, and contradictions embedded in the language of Women's and Gender Studies—from its high theory to its casual conversations—that relies on these key terms. *Rethinking Women's and Gender Studies* offers a fresh approach to structuring Feminist Theory, Senior Capstone, and introductory graduate-level courses in Women's and Gender Studies.

CATHERINE M. ORR is Professor and Chair of Women's and Gender Studies at Beloit College. Her work has been published in *Women's Studies Quarterly*, *Hypatia*, *NWSA Journal*, and *Feminist Collections*. She served as National Conference Chair for the National Women's Studies Association (2006–08).

ANN BRAITHWAITE is Associate Professor and Director of Women's Studies at the University of Prince Edward Island. She is co-author of *Troubling Women's Studies* (2004), co-editor of *Atlantis: A Women's Studies Journal*, and former President of the Canadian Women's Studies Association/*L'association canadienne des études sur les femmes*.

DIANE LICHTENSTEIN is Professor of English and former Chair of Women's Studies as well as of Interdisciplinary Studies at Beloit College. She co-edited a special issue of *Women's Studies Quarterly* (1999) focused on feminist activism and Women's Studies, and a cluster of essays on "locations" in the *NWSA Journal* (2005).

Rethinking Women's and Gender Studies

Edited by

Catherine M. Orr

Beloit College

Ann Braithwaite

University of Prince Edward Island

Diane Lichtenstein

Beloit College

Please visit the companion website for this book at:
www.routledge.com/cw/orr

First published 2012
by Routledge
711 Third Avenue, New York, NY 10017

Simultaneously published in the UK
by Routledge
2 Park Square, Milton Park, Abingdon, Oxon OX14 4RN

Routledge is an imprint of the Taylor & Francis Group, an informa business

Library of Congress Cataloging in Publication Data
Rethinking women's and gender studies / edited by Catherine M. Orr, Ann Braithwaite, Diane Lichtenstein.
    p. cm.
    1. Women's studies. I. Orr, Catherine Margaret. II. Braithwaite, Ann, 1961– III. Lichtenstein, Diane Marilyn.
    HQ1180.R48 2011
    305.407—dc23
    2011032010

ISBN: 9780415808309 (hbk)
ISBN: 9780415808316 (pbk)
ISBN: 9780203134719 (ebk)

Typeset in Adobe Caslon, Copperplate Gothic, and Trade Gothic
by EvS Communication Networx, Inc

Printed and bound in the United States of America on acid-free paper
by Edwards Brothers, Inc.

In loving memory of Margaret Moon Orr (1921–2010) and, for the loving memories we make every day, Gil and Wheaton

In loving memory of those I've lost ... and with much love to all those who continue to motivate and sustain me every day

In loving memory of Hyman Lichtenstein (1919–2008)

CONTENTS

PREFACE

The primary purpose of *Rethinking Women's and Gender Studies* is both to map and to interrogate foundational concepts and narratives associated with the field of Women's and Gender Studies (WGS) by focusing on its key terms. Each of its previously unpublished eighteen chapters offers an innovative path either to challenging assumptions associated with ubiquitous terms such as "feminism," "interdisciplinarity," "activism," and "institutionalization" or to questioning the silences around other terms including "secularity," "discipline," and even "sexuality." In each case, contributors consider what is at stake in the everyday uses of the language with which the field's practitioners both make knowledge claims and talk about WGS.

Rethinking Women's and Gender Studies offers a fresh approach to structuring Feminist Theory, Senior Capstone, and introductory graduate-level courses in WGS by focusing specifically on the language at the center of the field's most contentious debates, vexing histories, and enduring tensions. Each chapter provides a unique "jumping off" point by constructing genealogies of how these key terms are mobilized in WGS and then critically analyzing the consequences of their uninterrogated uses. Short introductions to each of the book's five sections further highlight the intersections and crossovers among chapters and pose questions to frame their reading. Additionally, "points to ponder" for all sections, some concluding questions, and a list of connected websites all combine to offer supplemental resources to elicit more inquiry and encourage discussion across and among chapters and sections.

Although it is in conversation with other recent texts that have similarly interrogated the routine practices of WGS, *Rethinking Women's and Gender Studies'* unique structure and its focus on the field's vernacular distinguishes it from these other texts. WGS practitioners at all levels will find in *Rethinking Women's and Gender Studies* much to contemplate about the field's current practices and future possibilities.

ACKNOWLEDGMENTS

No book is complete without giving recognition to the people who helped bring it to fruition. And there were many such people over the years of putting this book together.

We start by thanking our endlessly accommodating and generous contributors to this volume—for their enthusiasm and richness of ideas, their graciousness and unending willingness to work with us through multiple drafts, and their absolute patience with us as we all tightened the focus of the argument. Through conference presentations, campus visits, administrative side-projects, and, of course, the dozens and dozens of emails, you've all proven to be the kind of intellectual community that makes academia so worthwhile. Thank you all for your passionate involvement in this project!

All ideas require a thorough vetting—to try them out, to fine tune them, and to challenge them. Over the past few years, we have engaged in many conversations about these ideas with colleagues, students, and audiences at numerous panels and round tables. Thank you all for your enthusiastic engagement with this project which motivated us to continue to explore these questions in new and compelling directions.

Our immense thanks also to Carol Little for her close reading and copy editing skills. Funds provided by the University of Prince Edward Island's Dean of Arts (Don Desserud) and by Beloit College helped us put this manuscript together and are much appreciated. We would like to thank the readers of the manuscript—Suzanne Scott of George Mason University, Jane Caputi of Florida Atlantic University, Jennifer Wingard of University of Houston Clear Lake, Karen Booth of University of North Carolina Chapel Hill, Angelique Nixon of University of Connecticut, and Huma Amhed-Ghosh of San Diego State University—whose keen insights inspired us to think, and think again, and sharpen our arguments. Any many thanks also to Jodi O'Brien who championed our cause when it counted, and to Steve Rutter and Leah Babb-Rosenfeld at Routledge for supporting this project—and for suggesting a number of elements we wouldn't have thought of ourselves. The book is definitely better and much more user-friendly because of them.

Catherine thanks Gil and Wheaton for the caring, loving, and peaceful family life she always dreamed of. Thanks too, to the Orr, Moon, and Gribb clans for their love, support, and tolerance, not to mention their willingness to actually converse with her about what must seem to them the ultimate in academic navel-gazing.

Ann thanks all of those in her life whose presence motivates and keeps her going every day: her partner and friends who are always there with thoughts, ideas, and enthusiasm—and dinner and wine; and her dogs—who keep her on schedule and force her to step away from the computer—although they have no idea how much they contribute.

Diane thanks Steven, Paula, Rachel, and Carolyn for their unconditional support of this project and their patience with her many hours at the computer. She also thanks all of the friends and colleagues who worked with her as she developed her understanding of interdisciplinarity.

We also extend our deepest gratitude to our students, who may not always be aware of it, but whose presence and intellectual curiosity always compel us to explore new and provocative areas and ideas!

And last—but certainly not least—we editors want to thank each other for the wonderful experience over the past few years of working on this project! To say that we worked collaboratively is a profound understatement. We all read and commented on every draft of every chapter and on just about every email we sent to contributors. Every piece that is co-written in this book involved numerous rounds of edits, questions, comments, and rewrites—each of us taking a turn, and then another. Such a process embodies the spirit of working together that makes this kind of intellectual endeavour so energizing. That we would, without hesitation, do it all over again is probably the best compliment we could pay each other.

INTRODUCTION
WHY RETHINK WOMEN'S AND GENDER STUDIES

Catherine M. Orr, Ann Braithwaite,
and Diane Lichtenstein

Locating Ourselves: Why this Project? Why Now?

Passion ... Frustration ... Enthusiasm ... Disappointment ...
Ambivalence ... Relief ...

We start by locating ourselves in this book project, and in Women's and Gender Studies (WGS), through a list of emotions that all of us (editors and contributors) have variously felt about this field in which we work. As predominantly midcareer academics, and mostly full- or cross-appointed in WGS, we are all passionate about this field in which our professional and intellectual lives are very much imbricated.[1] In it, we have all found space to push boundaries of accepted knowledge, to pose difficult questions about the worlds in which we live, to engage in exciting new scholarship. Yet, at times, we have also experienced unease about this field. The frustration and disappointment we have so often felt at conferences and as conference panelists, at administrative meetings of our professional organizations, and even in our own programs, framed our subsequent conversations in conference hotel rooms and coffee breaks, in restaurants, in the hallways outside our offices, and through email exchanges and Facebook posts. Out of those conversations, and our attempt to make sense of the tensions in our range of reactions, the idea for this book arose.

1

For all of us, our lives in WGS have been framed by a period of radical questioning in the field—about its premises, subjects, and borders. A number of recent WGS texts, journals, and conferences speak to the importance of an intellectual project that has turned its gaze back on the field itself, offering not only a critique of knowledge produced elsewhere, but asking challenging, and provocative, questions about how WGS has produced its own knowledges. Yet we also noticed that this radical questioning that was so exciting to us, and becoming more vital to our own work, was not being widely embraced in the field. In fact, such questions seemed, at times, to be regarded by some as disloyal or as a repudiation of the field itself.

The more we went over these tensions with each other, the more we came to realize that the source of our unease had to do with the very language of the field itself. That is, we started to recognize that much of this radical questioning about WGS not only bumped up against what have become many of its central premises, but that those premises were deeply embedded in the very language of the field, especially in a number of commonly used key terms. It was in both the centrality of those terms, and the routine ways in which they were understood and mobilized within the field, that we came to see—or to locate—the resistance to some of this radical questioning.

At that point, we also began to think that something quite exhilarating might lie on the other side of raising some unpopular—even profane—questions about some of these terms, as well as the assumptions reflected in them. Why, for example, is a term such as "feminism" so easily assumed to be requisite for WGS—so much so that the centrality of that concept to our field is rarely, if ever, explained or questioned? Even while there are many definitions of that term mobilized in different contexts, and even while all of us now speak of "feminisms" in the plural, we seem to take for granted that feminism as a concept is compulsory to the field and rarely ask what it might also foreclose for how we do WGS. Likewise, we found ourselves wondering why we repeat so widely and often that WGS is "activist" yet seldom articulate exactly what we mean, or do not mean, by that term, or how it might function to propel the field in directions that should, at the very least, require further investigation. Or what exactly do we mean when we pronounce WGS to be "interdisciplinary," especially since most of us probably still operate on the I-know-it-when-I-see-it mode of defining this term? And the corollary question: why is it that so many of us refuse the term "discipline" to describe the field's place in the university? What are the consequences of this refusal in an institution that is so organized and powered by disciplines, and how does this refusal shore up particular understandings or versions of its institutionalization and status in the university? As these examples illustrate, our concern with the common language of the field is not so much with how those terms have been multiply defined, or with the different content of those definitions. Rather, our purpose in looking at them is to pursue a "meta" analysis—or a critical examination of the analytical frameworks themselves—that explores how the terms have *functioned* to establish and uphold particular versions of WGS that, in turn, determine what theories, approaches, institutional configurations, and even bodies become the proper subjects (in so many senses of that word) of the field. Most importantly, we want to ask: how does questioning any of these terms lead us to issues we may not want to face, stakes we might not want to acknowledge, conclusions that may challenge us too deeply?

As our conversations about the importance of this meta-analysis took in new participants, we identified other terms—"pedagogy," "methods," "sexuality," "community," "waves," "identity," "institutionalization"—as both ubiquitous in WGS and equally unquestioned and unquestionable. Of course, many of these terms have become foundational and taken for granted precisely because of what they have opened conceptually in WGS. Certainly our field's early challenges to accepted forms of knowledge production in the university, the development of feminisms across the disciplines, and the unorthodox and iconoclastic claims about methodological and pedagogical practices enabled new and dynamic modes of interrogating the world around us, in addition to new and exciting ways of being and working in the university. Through these terms, WGS interrogated and reconfigured many forms of knowledge in academe and transformed much of the "business as usual" of the institution. In no way has our project ever questioned the importance of these transformations. But as our discussions about these terms soon revealed, we could not settle for simply elaborating (or celebrating) the important and corrective roles of these new Women's-and-Gender-Studies-specific terms. Those terms, we realized (and our contributors here argue), have become so embedded in particular ways of talking in the field that they often function to silence other ways of knowing, other possibilities for the field. And even newer terms developed as "correctives" to previous conceptual shortcomings—"transnational," "intersectional," "queer," "trans"—have their own consequences to unpack. It became clear that we needed to return to the very language of the field to ask difficult questions not only about how WGS has come to think about itself but about how this thinking too narrowly dictated where we could go from here.

Many of our conversations were invigorating and made us feel as if we were doing the most wide-ranging, collaborative, and exciting theorizing of our academic lives. We wanted (and we still want) to impel ourselves, and all practitioners in WGS, to think more carefully and clearly about the terms we use to do the work we do. But there were also moments when even we, as editors, came up against the limits of our own understandings and abilities to engage certain questions. Those encounters were jarring and humbling, both for what they pointed out about our own assumptions and for what they told us about the difficulty of this kind of meta-level analysis. All three of us, for example, took for granted presumptions about the field's "secularity" (and that of academia more generally) and were thus initially flummoxed by one contributor's argument that WGS needs to rethink this precept if it wants to be more relevant to some of the very constituencies with which it claims to speak. Sure, we said, there are people who also do feminist analyses of Religious Studies of various kinds, but WGS is, and should be, secular ... right? Reactions such as this one (and there were others—about "sexuality," "institutionalization," "trans," for instance) forced us to recognize that we too were/are not immune to our own uncritical acceptance of the language of the field. Thus, even if we are impassioned by this self-reflective project, we also recognize that it must be an ongoing one in which we never stop identifying the varied ways in which the language of and about WGS can shut down just as many possibilities as it opens up.

In turning to these key terms, then, we want to make possible a way of doing WGS that models for ourselves (as well as for our students and colleagues) a version of the field that mandates the constant exploration of its core commitments *as well as* a radical doubt that emerges from those very same commitments. Our goal is to be as accountable as possible for how we "do" WGS—that is, for the ways in which our everyday practices in the field can unconsciously perpetuate precisely what we might claim to be challenging. Throughout this project, then, both in our ongoing conversations and the intense process of writing, we and our contributors have attempted to push WGS to a place where it has not been permitted to go (where it seemed it must not go) and then located ourselves precisely in that place. And we hope that readers of this volume will experience the same sort of astonishment and intrigue that we did to fuel their own passions for and about WGS.

Locating the Field: Doing Genealogical Work

In this book, our purpose is to re-examine the field's central premises through critical interrogations of a number of its key terms. The analysis offered in these chapters is more than a survey of different definitions or uses of particular terms in Women's and Gender Studies. In other words, chapters do not simply rehearse the debates around what WGS has meant by terms such as "methods" or "pedagogy" in an attempt to arrive at a more accurate or comprehensive use of those terms. Rather, each author here investigates a single term by asking how that term has come to be understood by the field's practitioners and then explicating the roles it plays in both producing and shutting down possible versions of WGS. Starting from her/his own scholarly or teaching practices, she/he investigates how this term functions intellectually, institutionally, and/or pedagogically in the field and asks: what is present in and what is absent from the narratives represented by the term? What is seen, what is not seen—indeed, what *must not* be seen—in the condensed understandings of the field the term has come to reflect? What has the term had to shunt aside in order to function the way it does, and to whose benefit, and whose loss? What practices in the field has the term unknowingly but inevitably allowed for? And what other possible ways of thinking about and within WGS open up by reconsidering the term?

To say that WGS is inadvertently caught up in its own silencings around key terms is not the same as saying that these terms only have one possible meaning. But, many of our contributors argue, even when elements of this everyday language of the discipline are held up as exemplars of contestation, multiplicity, and open debate (for example, by positing that there are many possible ways of understanding "activism," many approaches to "intersectionality," or many debates around "sexuality"), the possibilities potentially opened up too often get quickly overshadowed through other presumptions or unquestioned practices. Therefore, more than simply multiplying possible meanings and narratives for these key terms, our collective aim is to be cognizant of the ways in which *any* meaning or narrative can (must?) itself shut down others, including the alternate narratives offered in this book. Undoubtedly, there are debates and differences over the meanings of terms *and* the ways in which those terms are then mobilized. But as the chapters here make evident, there are nonetheless dominant or hegemonic uses of all of these terms—apparent through the narratives they signal and their implicit everyday uses in so many cases—that each author exposes and explores.

Readers will no doubt have noticed by now that the collective pronoun "we" has been used liberally so far in this introduction. The use of this "we" is a deliberate choice on our part as editors. Although we, of course, cannot and do not presume to speak for everyone in the field, its use here is a conceit that also allows us to implicate ourselves in the versions of WGS that we also seek to challenge. As our own reactions to some of these terms made clear (those "I-hadn't-thought-of-that!" moments), we cannot position ourselves completely outside of the field's hegemonic assumptions. But the recognition that there is a dominant WGS is also precisely what moves us to undertake, and to be excited by, the possibilities in this kind of rethinking project.

As such, our use of the term "genealogies" reflects our approach in the analyses of narratives and histories as diagnostic, as opposed to truth-seeking (Foucault 1977). Genealogies are always contingent and subject to change; they vary in their diagnostic function depending on starting points and choices made along the way. All of our contributors thus emphasize (or are at least indebted to some degree to) their own particular historical and cultural locations in their analyses, seeing those locations as an essential feature to be accounted for in this diagnostic project. What this focus on location means in practice is that the making evident of hegemonic perceptions of terms is (and must always be) taken up from particular locations: sometimes geographical, but also institutional, pedagogical, administrative—and always influenced by our own intersectional identities. Highlighting our approach here as genealogical also draws on the work of WGS practitioners who have expanded on its potential uses in the field. M. Jacqui Alexander and Chandra Talpade Mohanty, for example, outline a genealogical approach that is "an interested conscious thinking and rethinking of history and historicity … that compels Women's Studies to face head on the class divisions, racialization, heterosexualization operating within … [the] programs themselves" (1997, xvi). In focusing on the functions of particular terms in WGS, then, this is a project that is accountable from its multiple and varied locations. For Alexander and Mohanty, and for us, these functions must always be interrogated within a framework that both acknowledges and resists the hegemonic structures we inhabit, even when that framework has brought about important forms and facets of emancipation for so many. WGS is such a framework.

For the sake of consistency across chapters, we asked all of the contributors to address the same set of questions in their analyses:

- What is the genealogy of the term and its narrative(s) for the present moment in WGS? What alternate genealogies about WGS might we be able to trace if this term were reconsidered?
- What are some of the functions of this particular term within WGS? What have been the consequences of its uses—intellectually, institutionally, administratively, and/or pedagogically?
- What are some of the tensions within WGS generated by and/or manifested through this term? What has been or tends to be overlooked or even disavowed in that term, and how else might the term be understood and mobilized? What other versions of WGS might that term also point to?

While these questions lead to compelling conclusions, what interests us more here are the *paths* the authors take to reach them. The kind of mapping exercise signalled by these questions and undertaken by each author thus seeks to document which versions of WGS are represented and which versions are pushed aside in so many of the everyday conversations in and about the field. The "about" here signals an important caveat; none of us contends that our unpacking of any of these terms is the only one possible, or that the version of WGS to which it points is universal or uncontested. Because even if each author both starts from and ends up somewhere specific, depending on the particular location she/he has mapped, no author is completely "representative" of her/his locations. A genealogical approach emphasizes contingency, located-ness, and accountability in its diagnostic aims; as such, it offers us the opportunity to interrogate current conceptions of the field, and helps us imagine others. At the same time, it works against the seduction of simply offering "better" or more definitive accounts of these terms. Our goal, then, is to urge us all to think more genealogically about how and why particular definitions come to predominate.

One really trenchant example that illustrated clearly for us the complexities of this kind of accountability came with the issue of how to refer to the field in this text. Although many of us teach in programs that are called "Women's Studies," others are in places where the name has migrated—to Women's and Gender Studies, just Gender Studies, or Women's, Gender, and Sexuality Studies and other variations that arise out of the past few years of debate about the aligning of the field's objects of analysis with its moniker. Despite our attention to the contingencies of language everywhere else in this text, we also felt the need for some consistency across its chapters. We finally opted for "Women's and Gender Studies" (and its less cumbersome designation, "WGS") throughout, a name that cannot capture the entirety of the field's intellectual work[2] but one that we recognize as the preferred option for many institutional sites of that work at this point in time. This example illustrates both the importance of and concessions to language and locations in genealogical work *and* reveals our own attachments to and investments in particular versions of the field, even as we attempt to imagine alternatives.

Since all genealogies are "interested" re-tellings rather than roads to a singlular truth, it is important to note also that this approach contains its own tensions and limitations. Thus, all of the chapters in this collection operate from an awareness of the dangers of seeking to "correct" less intelligent, less informed, less savvy, or less chic versions of WGS. In other words, we want to avoid the tendency towards a WGS progress narrative that depicts the discipline's march forward from a stable and unquestioned past toward some idealized future.[3] It is sometimes hard to resist the impulse towards just such a redemption narrative, one which tells of how deeper insights will necessarily lead to better tomorrows for WGS; who doesn't want better (read: more revolutionary, more just, more compassionate, more dignified) tomorrows? But it is just such an impulse, we argue, that has too often kept us from seeing the contradictions, paradoxes, and tensions that thwart many of the field's stated goals and (however contingently) shared visions.

Locating the Conversation: Self-reflexivity and/in Women's and Gender Studies

As mentioned earlier, the self-reflective stance we take throughout this edited collection certainly did not start with us. Over the past decade or so, a number of Women's and Gender Studies scholars have turned their attention to the discipline itself, engaging a series of questions about the field's potentials and limitations in the changing Canadian and U.S. academy. *Rethinking Women's and Gender Studies* could not exist in anything resembling its current form without these volumes.

Joan Wallach Scott's collection, *Women's Studies on the Edge* (initially published as a 1997 issue of *differences* and republished as a different collection of essays under the same name in 2008), signalled a kind of permission to start down some new paths. "The Impossibility of Women's Studies," Wendy Brown's polemical essay contained in that volume, provoked many of us in the field, often in an attempt to rebut it, to rethink what counts as the focus or subject of WGS, its intellectual work, its parameters, and its connections to "feminist" and other critical languages and approaches. In that same issue of *differences,* Biddy Martin's "Success and Its Failures" compelled us to re-examine what is left out of or disavowed in stock narratives that have shaped the field's sense of its mission. A third essay in that 1997 issue of *differences,* Evelynn Hammond's interview with Beverly Guy-Sheftall titled "Whither Black Women's Studies," forced us to consider WGS's inability to "deal with difference" despite the discursive space and psychic energies devoted to expressing the field's embrace and incorporation of such (racialized) difference.

Probably no other scholar in the field's recent history has spearheaded a sustained body of work that demands the sort of rethinking we attempt here as Robyn Wiegman has. In her edited volume, *Women's Studies on Its Own* , she "ask[s] Women's Studies practitioners to think about the field *otherwise*" (2002b, 3). Her work encouraged us to listen to the unofficial discourses of the field as saying something significant about its core assumptions. As Wiegman puts it in her introductory chapter, titled "On Location": "I want the question of Women's Studies, along with the difficulties that are discussed at conference dinners, to be valued as crucial aspects of this thing that we are in the midst of: a historic project, to be sure, but whose political intervention into knowledge practices necessitates a challenge to every impulse of celebratory self-narration" (2).

Ann Braithwaite, Susan Heald, Susanne Luhmann, and Sharon Rosenberg's co-authored book *Troubling Women's Studies* (2004) came out two years later and took inspiration from Judith Butler's embrace of unstable categories (hence the term "troubling" in the title) to delve deeply into the stories that WGS tells about itself. The book's tendency to eschew easy answers or shore up one side of any given debate that rages in the field is one we replicate in this volume. A year later, Elizabeth Kennedy and Agatha Beins's anthology, *Women's Studies for the Future* (2005), urged us to consider ways in which WGS' institutionalization is experienced and negotiated at the program and department level at contemporary research universities.

Taken as a whole, these texts moved away from thinking that radical questions about the field itself constitute (only) its impossibility or signal its existential crisis. Rather, they demanded more complex discussions that launched a new era of self-reflexivity and self-examination about how WGS understands and reproduces its own intellectual and institutional power. They provoked a new set of queries that in turn trouble many of the presuppositions that form the basis of claims to knowledge in WGS; for them, as for us, this turn inward is both necessary and productive, embodying a challenge to the field from *within*.

We agree with the implication of these texts that to be critical of one's investment in an enterprise such as WGS requires both an identification with that enterprise at the same time that one embarks on the project of "disidentifying" with particular renderings of it. If, on some level, all of us in *Rethinking Women's and Gender Studies* are closely identified with WGS, we also all here strategically distance ourselves from it in order to ask new questions and gain alternative perspectives. This kind of project is very much an "inside job," generated by and intended for those with similar investments in WGS or related fields. We want to be clear about our own relationship to WGS in order to dissuade any misinterpretations by those who may be hostile to this field's mandates or overall orientation. Rather than a disavowal of the discipline, the shared aim of all the contributors to this volume is instead to look again—or otherwise—at WGS, refusing to become settled in the places we inhabit intellectually and institutionally. And, perhaps ironically, but certainly tellingly, this refusal derives precisely from the fact that we all embrace those places that we inhabit. We believe that such introspection at this moment in the development of the field is vital and that far from being tangential or too negative or even apocalyptic, it produces exciting new paths of inquiry that sharpen our vision and challenge us to interrogate our investments.

Locating the Reader: What Lies Ahead

The terms and concepts identified and investigated in this book are divided into five sections to highlight connections in the arguments that the authors make about them. While the placement of some of them may seem counterintuitive to some WGS veterans, their positioning here reflects specific tensions and paradoxes authors selected to highlight. The first section, titled *Foundational Assumptions*, identifies terms that constitute some of the primary intellectual claims of the field. "Feminism," "Interdisciplinarity," "Methods," and "Pedagogy" are all terms that have defined the intellectual premises of WGS since its inception. The second group of essays is collected under the title *Ubiquitous Descriptions*. "Activism," "Waves," "Besiegement," and "Community" point to narratives that have come to dominate how we in WGS talk about and position ourselves, especially in relation to others. As with the first group of essays, their employment is usually meant to reflect the idea that WGS is different from other academic fields. *Epistemologies Rethought* brings together the key terms of "Identity (Politics)," "Intersectionality," and "Queer," all of which, their respective authors suggest, have both pointed to absences in the field and generated new epistemologies for WGS' intellectual work. Yet, they argue, the ways in which these terms are mobilized too often overlook the very ways of knowing they were meant to include. In the fourth section, *Silences and Disavowals*, "Discipline," "History," "Secularity," and "Sexuality" bring to the fore assumptions that WGS practitioners have alternatively denied, renounced, or failed to recognize as part of the field. While often absent from the everyday talk in WGS, they nevertheless frame the field in important, albeit, unintentional ways. Finally, in the last section, *Establishment Challenges*, "Trans-," "Institutionalization," and "Transnational" speak to the organization of bodies and knowledges in the contemporary U.S. and Canadian academy generally and its impact on WGS practices. In doing so, these essays demand that we (re)consider both institutional arrangements and how we think about those arrangements lest WGS capitulate to the very systems it so often claims to oppose.

This collection of terms is neither encyclopaedic nor exhaustive of the possible terms that could have been included in such a volume. Other terms, such as "gender" or "women" or "women of color" or "masculinity" or "whiteness" (to name only a few) are equally significant to the field's language and everyday practices. But, we would argue, that is precisely the work of constructing genealogies: to capture a snapshot in a particular time and place, always partial and situated, always in process, always open to additions and alternations. The terms explored here, indeed this entire book, are that snapshot—not comprehensive, but making an argument nonetheless for how to make other WGS possible.

These essays represent for us editors the most serious and intense engagement with the project of WGS for which we could hope. To examine critically the terms we use and the assumptions reflected in those terms, to reflect upon the often unseen practices tied to common wieldings of those terms, to attempt to be accountable for the ways even our own rethinking can be further unpacked and questioned is, we passionately believe, to locate the field in places that make other versions of WGS possible. We hope you join us in this project, finding both inspiration and the desire to continue the ongoing work of identifying and unpacking more terms that frame the field, always asking both how they function and how their further exploration can move us in new directions, to think otherwise about WGS.

Notes

1. This book is the product of a series of continuing conversations among a group of people who have come to know each other over the past few years, rather than the result of an open call for submissions. Our connections have developed through formal and informal conference conversations, reading and discussing books and articles, reviewing each others' work, administrative networks in our respective professional organizations (NWSA and CWSA/ACEF), and more informal gatherings and retreats, all of which have pushed and prodded us in invigorating and exciting ways to keep thinking and rethinking this field.
2. After all, why should gender be the privileged category? What about race? Sexuality? Nation? Embodiment?
3. See Clare Hemmings's recent book, *Why Stories Matter: The Political Grammar of Feminist Theory* (2011) for a fascinating exploration of this kind of heroic narrative in feminist theorizing about itself.

PART 1
FOUNDATIONAL ASSUMPTIONS

The chapters in this first section focus on key terms that have defined the intellectual premises of Women's and Gender Studies (WGS) from its inception. "Feminism," "Interdisciplinarity," "Methods," and "Pedagogy" speak to the earliest claims about WGS' intention to stake out a different approach in U.S. and Canadian higher education. That WGS was feminist (as opposed to simply focusing on content about women or gender), that it was interdisciplinary (rather than working within a single traditional discipline), and that it had its own distinctive methodological and pedagogical approaches grounded in new epistemologies that asked new questions in both research and classroom contexts have all constituted the field's core assumptions for more than forty years. Contributors in this section, then, take up the legacies of these foundational assumptions, mapping their functions in the field at the same time as raising concerns about them.

Each of the terms in this section will be familiar to practitioners of WGS as central to the way we understand the field, so central, in fact, that we seldom stop to think about them anymore. The authors here suggest, however, that simply accepting the current usage of these terms without raising questions about the consequences of that usage has meant WGS has shied away from difficult dialogues about how the discipline might fall short of its own goals. Is feminism the most effective philosophical and political position from which to attain the social justice goals WGS claims as its core mission? Does the claim of interdisciplinarity really enable WGS to accomplish its critiques of knowledge production in the academy? What alternate possibilities might be opened up by critiquing methods of other disciplines as androcentric or marginalizing already disenfranchised peoples beyond simply advancing an alternative set of methods exclusive to WGS? And what kinds of uninterrogated assumptions about the experiences and identities of WGS students go along with a pedagogical mission aimed at certain kinds of conversion experiences?

In addition, to say that there are unique and important characteristics of WGS—i.e., that we are interdisciplinary, or feminist, or that we have methods and pedagogy specific to this field alone—sets up how we think, and don't think, about other terms and narratives in this book. As the authors here argue, to insist on feminism as central to WGS has often resulted in overlooking other structuring assumptions, such as the idea that WGS is "secular" (as is all of academia more broadly). Maintaining that we are interdisciplinary has too often meant that we don't challenge what we assume "discipline" to be. Likewise, positing that we have methods and pedagogies that are unique to this field has worked to control who and what gets included in WGS as part of this "community" and to overlook some of the costs of "institutionalization" (thus also belying our claims that WGS is not disciplined).

All of the terms in this section could have been combined in another configuration, with other terms from other sections of this anthology, resulting in different conversations and different snapshots of a contemporary WGS. By bringing them together as we have here, though, we want to draw attention to the ways in which these kinds of foundational assumptions both open up possibilities for establishing parameters for this field as well as shut down alternatives for thinking more deeply and widely about what we do in WGS.

1

Feminism

Layli Maparyan

When the Women's Studies[1] masters program at my university was launched in the mid-1990s by a group of women who had been working for this program at the university for over two decades, "History and Theory of European and U.S. Feminisms" became the first in a series of four required courses for the M.A. program; the others were "Globalization and Gender," "New Directions in Feminism," and "Feminist Methodologies." These courses, intentionally or unintentionally, represented a bridge between second wave and post-second wave academic feminist approaches. The course in question, "History and Theory of European and U.S. Feminisms" (nicknamed "Western Feminisms"), reflected a feminist history of consciousness whose center of gravity was decidedly, if not unwittingly, Eurocentric. Because most of the theories that were discussed at that time in academic feminist textbooks (i.e., Alison Jaggar and Paula Rothenberg's *Feminist Frameworks* [1978] or Rosemarie Tong's *Feminist Thought: A Comprehensive Introduction* [1989])—such as liberal, radical, Marxist, socialist, psychoanalytic, existentialist, and postmodern feminisms—were Euro-American in origin, it made a certain kind of sense to design a course with this focus. However, the mid-1990s was a time when "other feminisms"—such as black, Chicana, eco, and third wave feminisms, and even queer theory—were contesting this typology and positioning themselves for centrality within feminist histories of consciousness. Obviously, this process had begun much earlier, yet the mid-1990s was a time of the institutionalization of these shifts, often by women who had attained their feminist conscientization[2] in the 1960s or 1970s and had now gained enough institutional power to create Women's and Gender Studies (WGS) departments and programs. Students who had gained their conscientization during the 1990s were bringing a decidedly post-second wave mindset into the classroom, which influenced their expectations about the curriculum and put pressure on the "founding mothers" of WGS to make curricular updates and adjustments.

This generationally inflected "culture clash" is what led to my inheritance of this course in 2003. A white senior colleague nearing retirement—someone who had helped establish our masters program and who had been teaching the course since its inception—had experienced a "mutiny" of sorts in the classroom when a group of largely, but not exclusively, women of color students took issue with the Eurocentric focus of the course. Course title aside, these women contended that a Eurocentric platform was neither an accurate reflection of where feminism was at that time nor an appropriate introductory survey of feminist thought for a student body as diverse as that of my university. My colleague sympathetically agreed with the students, but did not feel prepared to overhaul the course so close to the time of her retirement. So, in an exhausted eleventh hour phone call, she asked if I would consider taking over the course, and I did, viewing it as an exciting opportunity to establish a completely different imprimatur for this course, if not our department's core curriculum as a whole. An important part of my strategy was to introduce an interrogation of the very "feminism" that these students had found so cognitively and socially dissonant.

Feminism is a foundational concept in WGS, so much so that it is treated as a *sine qua non* of the discipline. Yet the purpose of this chapter is to highlight and question assumptions about feminism. Why is "feminism" important, and how does it function for and in WGS? What have been the consequences of its use? What are the tensions generated by and/or manifested through the use of the term "feminism" in this field? How does temporal, spatial, or psychic context affect the ways in which this term and its related narratives might be understood or practiced? What is at stake when we normalize and naturalize feminism as the central organizing principle of WGS? And are there alternatives?

In this chapter, I interrogate a number of basic assumptions about the relationship between this field and feminism: (1) that WGS is (or should be) about feminism; (2) that WGS is (or should be) feminism-centered; (3) that women/people in WGS are (or should be) feminists; and (4) that WGS as a field, via feminism, directly impacts women's well-being worldwide. Ultimately, I argue that what's important is not feminism or WGS per se, but rather the transformative, liberatory impulse for which both feminism and WGS are two of many vehicles. Insofar as the nature of scholarly disciplines, or political communities, or ideological identities sometimes hamper the full and effective expression of this transformative, liberatory impulse, then what's at stake when we fail to question the centrality of feminism in WGS (or the field itself) is humanity's very survival and well-being. In these times of great threat—social, medical, ecological, spiritual—these questions are not moot.

Women's and Gender Studies as a Site of Convenience

From my vantage point, Women's and Gender Studies at this particular historical moment *appears* as a multivalent, poly-vocal *site of convenience* for multiple overlapping and at times contradictory conversations about social change, social justice, human empowerment, environmental restoration, and, increasingly, spirituality. By "site of convenience," I mean that people "show up" to WGS, as students and as faculty members, because they desire to talk about these things writ large, not simply because they desire to "study women" or "are feminists," and because they sense it is safe or even possible to do so there in ways that is it not in other sites. Thus, there is so much "going on" that WGS, like feminism, is very close to becoming an empty signifier, or at least one whose meaning can only be situational and constantly negotiated. This is the view from a global or national perch, however, and is not nearly as visible at the level of individual departments, or within the conferences, journals, or textbooks associated with WGS, all of which very often adopt some particular "feminist stance" with which they become identified, like a form of branding.

U.S. Women's and Gender Studies still idolizes particular versions of feminism to such an extent that it sometimes seems to limit the discipline's own consciousness of and self-realization about its necessarily polyform and dynamic attributes, which could be transformational and liberatory if they were better encompassed.[3] These versions are inarguably Western, highly secular, usually quite theoretical and/or ideological, and reflect the economic privilege of theoretical indulgence available to critical thinkers in economically developed nations, as compared with their counterparts in developing nations where feminists must, out of necessity, put a great deal of energy into intervening in dehumanizing social engineering projects (that usually originate in the West). Even though we discuss culture, globality, and the transnational[4] in U.S. WGS—in our classes, at our conferences, in our journals and books—our discussions typically remain highly academic and lack the inflections of a discourse built on close friendships with people who are radically different from ourselves. If our discourse were doing its job, I contend, not only would those close friendships be common and evident, intellectually as well as socially, but our discipline would actually embody a level of social equality and cultural plurality (whether racial, national, sexual, religious, class-based, or otherwise) much closer to what is idealized in our literatures and much less like what prevails in the mainstream (inside or outside academia). Since it does not, I can only reason that feminism isn't necessarily helping WGS, or WGS isn't necessarily helping feminism, even if both are, on their own terms, good and even necessary.

To be clear, I believe that feminism is the single most important cause of "shifting the center" in a progressive direction with regard to women's issues—equality, rights, ending violence, critiquing representations, questioning norms and standards for women, even destabilizing the notion of "woman" itself and making room for other liberatory possibilities of being, especially those that are related to sexual orientation and gender expression—over the last 60 years, if not the last 200+ years, in the United States and globally. However, I think that feminism has not been nearly as successful at transforming the engines of social inequality, violence, conflict, or hatred, which are rooted at a level of consciousness beyond the intellectual or political. Stated differently, feminism has contributed to a lot of important outer changes but not nearly as many essential inner changes. The reasons for this could consume another treatise.[5] Ever the optimist, however, it remains my desire that WGS, such as it continues to exist, lives up to its originating spirit and potential as

an agent of positive change in the world—including the world of academia. Crucial to the realization of this potential may be the ability of
both feminism and WGS to harmonize and coordinate with other social
movements, as well as to welcome spiritually-based perspectives into its
official discourse. My perspective on these questions is influenced by
womanism (Phillips 2006; Maparyan 2012), an evolving set of notions
arguably quite distinct from feminism, which has been the central organizing principle of my scholarly work since the mid-1990s. However, my
understandings have also been influenced by other self-identified feminist thinkers, particularly those with a spiritual orientation.[6]

(Dis-)Locating Feminism

The term "feminism" has been deployed and defined more than it has
been questioned in Women's and Gender Studies. While some practitioners have wondered what "feminism" is without really questioning its
existence or importance, others, both inside and outside the field, have
contested its level of inclusivity in ways that hint at the problematic
nature of placing it at the center of WGS. Yet to reject feminism as central and foundational to the discipline has largely been a method of eject-
ing oneself from WGS. This is one way that feminism has functioned
socially and politically in the field. More than serving the function of
unifying and connecting feminists, the project of definition has tended
to separate feminists, create conflict, and divert energy into semantic
and ideological debates and away from concerted social change action.
While terminological clarification has its place, in the United States at
least, these tendencies have caused, or at minimum paralleled, the now
well-established split between "feminism in the academy" and "feminism in the streets."[7] Globally, they now map onto a split that separates
U.S. feminism from feminism in developing countries. Furthermore,
the material realities and inequalities of the academy—everything from
the split between tenured/tenure-track and non-tenure track positions
to the differences in prestige and capital between elite, top-tier, mid-
tier, and lower-tier institutions, and even the subtle differences in treatment between faculty members or students who self-present as radical
vs. mainstream in terms of identity or appearance—continue to repro-

duce themselves within WGS and among feminists. These larger contexts of power relations separate us, too.

My understanding of and relationship to feminism arose from what I had read on my own (not in school), beginning while I was an undergraduate student, and continuing until through my current position as a professor in WGS.[8] As a self-taught WGS scholar whose own *entre* into the field had been through black feminist and womanist texts from the early 1980s to about 1990, I had not really been exposed to high theory academically, except when I sat in on a colleague's lesbian and gay studies course during the early 1990s. A brief period of fascination notwithstanding, I had never really grown to love high theory, strongly preferring the grittier, more personal, and more accessible style of writing out of which my own feminist conscientization had been birthed. However, I developed a new relationship with high theory when I read Chela Sandoval's captivating and provocative text, *Methodology of the Oppressed* (2000) in early 2001. Sandoval's book was the text that made all those literatures come into conversation for me, and I wanted to share that with my students, many of whom were struggling with high theory themselves but who at the same time had keenly developed theoretical sensibilities that had evolved out of simply living in and navigating postmodern society. Sandoval's text was the ultimate outsider-within trick, using high theory language to tell "homegirl" truths to an audience that would not otherwise listen or pay attention. For ten years, *Methodology of the Oppressed* served as the core text in a course I taught called "New Directions in Feminism," a required graduate seminar serving as the capstone of our M.A. program.

Even though I had to read the book (including its copious footnotes) twice to "get it," these readings eventuated in a set of epiphanies that would guide my navigation of feminism as well as my WGS teaching from there forward, even as my own womanist sensibilities expanded and solidified. Although Sandoval's theoretical scheme has not gone uncontested as a way of positioning women of color discourses in various liberatory movements (see, for example, Paula Moya's compelling critique[9]), Sandoval's useful construct of "the differential" (2000) (a coordinating mechanism that allows one to shift between gears) offered a new, non-linear way of cognizing both critical theories (feminism being just one) and social movements (feminism being just one) that superseded more prevalent histories of feminist consciousness that focused on temporal linearity (this came before this, and so on), and reflected entrenched geo-ethnic hierarchies privileging narratives and politico-economic objectives of the white and wealthy. Even schools of thought within feminism (such as liberal, radical, Marxist, postmodern, etc.) could be viewed in terms of the differential, relating not as temporal successors to one another but rather as different gears in the same gearbox or different tools in the same toolbox, each best suited to a particular terrain or task.[10] Sandoval's identification and contrast of two distinct strands of human social evolution, namely, "neocolonizing postmodern globalization" and "democratic decolonized globalization" (also known as "alternative dissident globalization") (2000), clarified the stakes associated with continued unchecked capitulation to the politics of domination and privilege (in feminism or elsewhere) vs. individual and collective liberation of the psyche from these organizing principles (within all critical theories and across all social movements). By appealing to "democratics" (a type of ethical compass) and "love" (the spiritual or energetic *movidas* of all liberating social change), Sandoval set the stage for a new understanding of not only feminism, but of all similarly oriented critical theories and social movements. Linking these insights to the "interstitial" social change work and identity constructions of an "eccentric cohort" of U.S. third world feminists (operating primarily between 1968–1990) and other (de-)colonized/ing scholars (for example, Frantz Fanon and Roland Barthes), Sandoval showed an undeniable connection between so-called lived theory in the streets and so-called high theory in the academy. Using the privileged tools of high theory—genealogy, archaeology, and jargon—to import a non-privileged "homegirl perspective" into an academic community that had previously been impermeable to it, Sandoval accomplished a feat of integration and illumination that resonated with my own academic, political, and identitarian sensibilities.

When I brought this perspective to my students, often in translated form, many of them, too, resonated with it. Sandoval and her text created a platform for questioning feminism and its centrality, and even necessity, within WGS. Most of my students responded to their whirlwind tour with Sandoval first with complete disorientation and later, sometimes years later, with deep appreciation for the ways in which our engagement of *Methodology of the Oppressed* helped them make sense of paradoxes that could otherwise have caused them to dismiss both the field and feminism and walk away from their studies with a sense of alienation. For example, Sandoval helped students contextualize such aggravating oddities as feminist imperialism, on the global scale, and the lack of collaboration (or even conversation) between WGS and African American Studies departments or faculties, on the local scale. They came to understand why it sometimes feels as though like-minded people who ought to be collaborating on the larger project of libera-tion, at our university or on the planet, are often living out their politi-cal aspirations in separate universes. They reached a place where they could, like seasoned meditators, "observe the flow" without judging it, and make autonomous decisions about how to relate to it. "To be or not to be a feminist" was no longer a life-or-death question, and students learned that "the feminism that has been 'deployed' in the field must be dislocated for other perspectives to flourish."[11]

What's at Stake?

What is at stake when we normalize and naturalize feminism as the central organizing principle of Women's and Gender Studies? Let me begin by saying that while I use feminism here in the singular, femi-nism is, of course, also multiple, itself demarcated by multiple vectors of ideological and historical difference that are extremely meaningful to their respective constituencies. Think, for example, how different liberal is from radical feminism, or socialist is from postmodern feminism, or Marxist is from third wave feminism. Nevertheless, these various forms have somehow created a hegemonic cluster based on preexisting vectors of inequality (especially race, class, and nation) that have shaped their emergence and perpetuation. By virtue of its social power, this hege-monic cluster has locked many non-hegemonic forms of feminism (e.g., black, Muslim, African feminisms) into its orbit due to the tensions it maintains with them. For people "outside the orbit," feminism seems less like the marketplace of ideas that academic feminists imagine it to be and more like a modern-day version of the Tower of Babel.

Thus, the biggest risk of putting feminism at the center of WGS is that we exclude from the global movement to improve the lives of women and girls and all who are associated with them the masses of humanity who do not self-define as feminist or who do not wish to identify with feminism. WGS plays a key role in the direction and definition of this movement because of the power and capital invested in academia by the general public. Regardless of whether feminism is central, WGS as a field will continue to be relevant and necessary as long as structural gender inequality, violence against women and girls, and the need for various forms of women's and girls' empowerment continue to exist in the world, because, to enlarge on a quote made famous by the Combahee River Collective, "We realize that the only people who care enough about us to work consistently for our liberation are us" (1983, 275). Given the trajectory of the field's evolution over time, however, the question becomes "who is 'us'?" The "us" of WGS now encompasses women, men, and trans people who have come together around a plethora of issues, including, but not limited to, social change, social justice, human empowerment, environmental restoration, and spirituality, in a context where sex, gender, and sexuality are among the privileged topics. Yet, ironically, despite this great attractiveness to an increasingly diverse array of people, as WGS becomes, by virtue of its content or methods, more and more removed from other sites of the global movement to improve the lives of women and girls, its relevance decreases, and a certain kind of rift widens. Where it could serve as a forum for dialogue, for harmonizing and coordinating diverse perspectives, it paradoxically becomes a site of exclusion that reproduces existing conflicts, polarities, and elitisms, all in the name of "liberation."

Let me offer three examples of groups whose relationship with feminism or feminist theory (in the U.S. academic sense) is tenuous enough to warrant concern about how feminism is positioned within WGS: men, women from the developing world, and religious activists. Even though there are today numerous self-defined male feminists, historically, many men have felt ambivalent about claiming or aligning with feminism, and women feminists have contributed to this ambivalence by sending mixed messages about whether men feminists are welcome or even possible. Even though most programs can claim a male student or two, WGS cannot yet claim gender parity. Although this may be for reasons other than the centrality of feminism to the curriculum, the role of feminism in structuring or gatekeeping men's involvement in and integration within the field should be examined carefully.[12]

Women of the developing world raise a different set of questions with regard to feminism as the central organizing principle of WGS, where the issue isn't belongingness—"is she or isn't she a feminist?" More germane is the fact that feminist issues in the developing world and the developed world (often?) bear little resemblance to each other. In addition, feminism as a supposedly global construct has failed to erase the hierarchies of power and wealth that define the political and economic relationships between developing and developed countries' populations, including women. After 200+ years of feminism proper and nearly 60 years of feminism in its contemporary form, why are feminists and WGS scholars in the developing world still focusing on food, water, jobs, education, maternal health, infant survival, and ecological preservation, while feminists and WGS scholars in the developed world are focusing on identities, performativity, pop culture, media representations, body image, symbolic violence, and, more generally, "theory?" While I certainly oversimplify the field of feminist topics in both contexts, I identify trends to make a point: there are (at least) two distinctly different (arguably incommensurable) feminist conversations taking place at the same time on the same planet, so when we say "feminism" is at the center of this field, our next question must be, whose feminism, and whose WGS? So far, we do not have a single "feminism" capable of encompassing both feminist universes simultaneously. To me, that suggests a flaw in maintaining feminism as the central organizing principle of WGS.

A third group to consider is religious activists. U.S. academic feminism has been markedly antireligious in its contemporary incarnation and, further, has tended to cast religion as oppressive to women.[13] Outside feminist theological circles, which rarely intersect with WGS proper, the liberatory and progressive dimensions of religion have scarcely been considered. The exception is women of color feminisms, where religion, whether institutionalized or indigenous, occasionally makes a notable appearance; the spiritual dimensions of this work, however, tend to be ignored in favor of the secular content. It is ironic that, in recent times, religious activists, particularly religious women activists, have been responsible for embodying and manifesting many of the forms of positive and progressive social change that secular feminism (including academic feminism) has envisioned. Over the last half century, parallel with the formation and ascent of feminism and other similar critical theories and social movements, missionary work, whether local, national, or international, has transmuted into a kind of service-based progressive social activism that rivals anything that nonreligious feminists have done within the same time span. Furthermore, new, nonmissionary forms of social change work and even consciousness transformation work have sprung up among religious people working as individuals or in groups. Much of this work addresses the same social problems that feminists and feminism address. Books such as Katharine Rhodes Henderson's *God's Troublemakers: How Women of Faith Are Changing the World* (2006) showcase this work by reporting on interviews with twenty "socio-ethical entrepreneurs" who use progressive forms of religion as the basis for their activism; some identify as feminists, while others do not. WGS has not caught up with the new realities of activism by people of faith, and some people who consider themselves religious are alienated from the field for this very reason. Part of the problem lies in the fact that feminism, in its contemporary incarnation, rests heavily upon a Marxist and New Left genealogy, effectively disallowing and overwriting other "feminist" genealogies that could offer different organizing mechanisms for WGS and the global movement for women's wellbeing more generally. From my perspective, womanism is one such "different organizing mechanism."

Locating Womanism

In 2006, I published *The Womanist Reader*, which was the result of over a decade of concerted research on the womanist idea and its many manifestations across academic disciplines as well as outside academia. The objective of this volume was to document the first quarter century of womanist thought (1979–2004) as well as to outline the operative parameters of womanism, which had unfortunately been mischaracterized and ultimately written off as just a version of feminism or, more particularly, black feminism. The conclusion I came to is distilled in the following characterization of womanism: "Womanism is a social change perspective rooted in black women's and other women of color's

everyday experiences and everyday methods of problem solving in everyday spaces, extended to the problem of ending all forms of oppression
for all people, restoring the balance between people and the environ-
ment/nature, and reconciling human life with the spiritual dimension"
(Phillips 2006, xx).

I discerned five core attributes of womanism, namely, that it is anti-
oppressionist, vernacular, nonideological, communitarian, and spiritualized. Womanists are concerned with humanity as a whole, and the
elimination of all forms of oppression, whether named or unnamed;
the focus is not the oppression of women, but rather women's perspectives on ending all forms of oppression and violence. Womanism has
a grassroots spirit; it focuses on everyday life and that which connects
all people, regardless of social status or identity, in terms of common
humanity. Womanism refrains from requiring among those who identify with it the type of inflexibility that defines ideological systems and
postures, which tend to create insider/outsider lines and thus potentially
reproduce exclusions and create violences.

As I discuss at length in *The Womanist Idea*, womanism is a "spirit"
or a "way" or a "walk" whose objective is inclusion, harmonization, and
coordination of diverse beings, including people, animals, plants, spiritual entities, etc., and whose method is basically love-based. Womanists are holistic in orientation, focusing on the well-being of the
collective—not just the human collective, but the human-ecological-
spiritual collective, with full recognition of the importance of individual well-being and self-actualization in the creation of commonweal.
Finally, womanism is spiritualized; that is, it is a spirit-infused understanding about life and change. The term "spirit" (or "Spirit") here
is removed from any religious connotations so as to free it to accommodate different kinds of understandings about the divine, cosmic,
or transcendental underpinnings of all life and existence. Womanism acknowledges that, even if this perspective has been articulated
and in many respects stewarded by women of color, it welcomes and
includes people of all genders and cultural backgrounds. By virtue of
this brief synopsis of womanism, it should be obvious that womanism
and feminism are things of a different sort, yet each has specific and
valuable social change implications that can be coordinated to amplify
the impact of social change work.

From my perspective as a womanist teacher, the purpose of discussing feminism is to help students through a process of no-holds-barred inquiry that offers up feminism as one potentially helpful discourse alongside many others that may also inform them meaningfully. My objective is to deepen students' commitment to personally making the world a better place in some way or another and heighten their ability to do so from a place of conscious awareness about multiple viable strategies in the context of deep introspection about themselves and awareness of the relationship between self-change and world-change. The choice to work through the theoretical and practical implications of challenges of feminism in the classroom, as well as other relational, face-to-face environments, such as various community settings, is informed and inspired by my womanist sensibilities and is an active rejection of the solipsistic immersion in theory (and its concomitant withdrawal from grassroots engagement) that has dominated Women's and Gender Studies for the last two and a half decades.

Womanism is an interesting site of integration for people who claim, "I'm a feminist and a womanist," "I'm a womanist but not a feminist," and "I don't believe in labels but I do believe in women's empowerment." In other words, womanism easily accommodates people who hold each of these perspectives. When I teach courses on womanism, we deal explicitly with the reasons why people might: reject or embrace feminism; reject, embrace, or switch labels; reject, stick to, or mix and match ideologies; take logically consistent or inconsistent actions; claim or hide an identity; participate or not in a movement; commit to something wholeheartedly, half-heartedly, or not commit to anything, etc. Womanism allows us to focus on the self and one's own lived experience of politics—emotionally, spiritually, intellectually, physically, socially, environmentally—and to begin to view oneself as the organizing principle of one's own life rather than some external set of recommendations. I encourage my students to assert, "I AM the organizing principle of my own life"—a notion quite different than "feminism (or even womanism) is the organizing principle of my life" that a feminist-centric WGS tends to covertly produce. The idea that social change begins with self-change is introduced as a tenet of womanism with implications regardless of whether one calls oneself by any label or explicitly endorses any particular political ideology or identity. This practice in the classroom inherently evokes questioning the necessity of feminism (or even womanism) as the central organizing principle of WGS.

In my womanism courses, my students and I examine scholarship, and even nonacademic writing, that wrestles with questions about feminism, the self, and putting it all together—from a variety of disciplinary and nondisciplinary angles. For example, in a special topics seminar I taught called "Womanist Perspectives on Spiritual Activism," we read five memoirs by spiritually-oriented women activists from around the world: *Learning True Love: Practicing Buddhism in a Time of War,* by Sister Chan Khong (2008); *Left to Tell: Finding God Amidst the Rwandan Holocaust,* by Immaculée Ilibagiza (2006); *It's Always Possible: One Woman's Transformation of India's Prison System,* by Kiran Bedi (2000); *Love and Courage: A Story of Insubordination,* by Pregs Govender (2007); and *Unbowed: A Memoir,* by Wangari Maathai (2007). We spent a great deal of time examining the social change praxis of these women, as well as applying different frames, from feminist to womanist to esoteric, to understand the methodology and effectiveness of these women in their work. In the process, we found our concepts of and our attachments to feminism, womanism, and various other forms of identity and political or religious ideology dissolving, even at the same time as we were able to continue to appreciate the value and efficacy of each. What these texts highlighted more than anything was that the condition of the self is inseparable from the execution of politics and the nature of the conditions present in the external world; in other words, oppression and violence exist outside us because they exist inside us, individually and collectively, even if we call ourselves feminists, womanists, progressive, spiritual, or whatever. In this class, students were steered to expose their inner workings and bring themselves to account. While some degree of privacy in this process was observed, the imperative itself was situated within an academic setting, making this class novel and in certain ways challenging. Quietly, this course disrupted the notion that WGS has to be about or centered in feminism, without negating the value or relevance of feminism or womanism. Indeed, fueled by the spiritual, metaphysical, and contemplative aspects of this class, students were left questioning identity, ideology, and activism all around.

What Is Women's and Gender Studies?

All of this conceptual mobility forces us back to the question: What *is* Women's and Gender Studies? If feminism is not at the core, and womanism is not at the core, and, arguably, women are not even at the core, what gives the discipline meaning or coherency? What has become evident to me and perhaps to many WGS scholars is that virtually all of the liberation discourses (be they critical theories or social movements per se) have become so interpenetrated and interpellated within the last sixty years that they are no longer conceptually or ideologically distinct. This point is well articulated in Paul Hawken's book, *Blessed Unrest: How the Largest Movement in the World Came into Being and Why No One Saw It Coming* (2007), which argues that the world's democratic (including feminist), indigenous, and environmental movements have all converged into a common, as yet unnamed, global movement. I view this morphing, this dissolution of boundaries, this movement into inchoate space, as a form of "progress" and self-actualization for feminism as well as all other similarly progressive movements. Ultimately, in my view, what holds WGS together is not women or feminism or womanism but, rather, the liberation impulse itself. Early "Women's Studies" began, spurred by the women's movement, with a focus on women's liberation. Over time, the recognition that women's liberation is tied to many other kinds of liberation, as well as the recognition that that category "woman" is too limited to encompass all of the aspirations that had become part of WGS, led to a widening of issues beneath the WGS umbrella. Today, we describe this field as being about ending sexism, racism, classism, heterosexism/homophobia, xenophobia, ableism, ageism, human domination of the natural environment, and a host of other injustices. Womanism suggests that, in the final analysis, we may simply speak in terms of the movement to liberate all humanity and the Earth from all forms of violence, domination, oppression, subjugation, suffering, harm, unwellness, and even unhappiness—all with methods as basic as love and the recognition of our own, others', and all creation's innate divinity.[14]

Conclusion

How does a liberation movement morph? That is, how does it become a different version of itself? It does so by integrating its own evolving insights perpetually as it continues to address its central objective, namely, liberation, i.e., improving life through increasing justice and happiness, and reducing violence and suffering. When a movement is going well, more and more people—more and more *different* kinds of people—become a part of it. It loses its exclusive, exclusionary, boutique quality, and becomes "the new normal." Feminism as a movement and Women's and Gender Studies as a field, however painfully and fitfully, have done just this, in a fashion that has been almost too rapid to cognize. WGS remains one site—an attractor point, an energy organizer—where this confluent location of change discourses can be examined, unpacked, and further developed. This remains the value of WGS, by any name. Even if feminism, despite protestations, is dissolving (along with many other critical theories and social movements) into a larger, more diffuse, yet more pervasive movement for all humanity and the earth, WGS remains one portal through which one can enter that movement and participate in the related discourse. In my view, this is a lovely kind of success story, a story of a metamorphosis and transcendence into a site just past the horizon of its original dream.

Notes

1. Although this volume is talking about the name of the field as Women's and Gender Studies, in our case at Georgia State University, the program is called Women's Studies.
2. The term "conscientization" is an Anglicization of the Portuguese term *conscientizaçao*, which appears frequently in Paulo Freire's classic text, *Pedagogy of the Oppressed* (1970).
3. See, however, the special issue of the online journal *The Scholar and Feminist*, edited by Julie Kubala and Mandy van Deven, titled "Polyphonic Feminisms," which addresses this issue of feminism's polyvocality directly and with cultural and critical sensitivity. http://www.barnard.edu/sfonline/polyphonic/index.htm.
4. See Parisi's chapter on "Transnational," this volume.
5. This issue is treated fairly extensively in my book, *The Womanist Idea* (2012).
6. AnaLouise Keating, Gloria Anzaldúa, and M. Jacqui Alexander have all been highly influential in this regard, as have Akasha Gloria Hull, Pregs Govender, and Chela Sandoval.

7. This split is identified and theorized in *The Revolution Will Not Be Funded: Beyond the Nonprofit Industrial Complex* by INCITE! Women of Color Against Violence (Incite! 2009).

8. Texts such as Moraga and Anzaldúa 1983, Smith 1983, Hull, Scott, and Smith, 1982, Walker 1983, Davis 1984, Lorde 1984, Anzaldúa 1987, Collins 1998, Hemphill 1991, and hooks 1995 formed my feminist consciousness, such as it was.

9. See Paula M. L. Moya, *Learning from Experience: Minority Identities, Multicultural Struggles* (2002).

10. See also Henry, this volume, who questions the wave metaphor, and thus the notion of temporal succession of feminist ideas.

11. I am thankful to Catherine Orr for this wording, taken from her comments on one of my drafts of this chapter.

12. See, for example, Gary Lemons' memoir, *Black Male Outsider: Teaching as a Pro-feminist Man* (2008), which deals with these issues in a revealing and thoughtful way.

13. See Crowley, this volume, who addresses secularity. The issue of religion is also discussed in Johnson's chapter.

14. The question of whether "womanism will be more resistant to the very strong forces of academic institutionalization and elitism than 'feminism' or 'WGS' has been" (I thank an anonymous reviewer for this wording) is an important one to consider. In the field of religious studies, where womanist scholarship has its longest history and its best developed institutional structures, there is evidence that it is not completely resistant. However, I continue to believe, based on my research on womanist spiritual activists (see *The Womanist Idea*), that womanism, at least as I understand it, contains the seeds of various kinds of social formations, practices, and forms of consciousness that do actively neutralize, transform, and overwrite the kinds of structures of oppression that plague academia (as well as most social institutions), such as hierarchization.

2

INTERDISCIPLINARITY

Diane Lichtenstein

In the fall of 2001, I began preparing for my upcoming duties as Chair of Interdisciplinary Studies at my liberal arts college. I plunged into texts such as William Newell's edited collection, *Interdisciplinarity: Essays from the Literature*, Julie Thompson Klein's *Crossing Boundaries*, and Newell and William Green's article "Defining and Teaching Interdisciplinary Studies." I naively believed that this homework would be primarily review because I had always identified as someone "in" the interdisciplinary field of Women's and Gender Studies (WGS), although my disciplinary department is English. I had taught not only the introductory course and senior seminar in Women's and Gender Studies but also had team-taught as well as worked on numerous projects with colleagues across disciplines at a small, U.S. college where multidisciplinary collaborations (in teaching, governance, and scholarship) prevail. Despite my experiences, I had been "liv[ing] with casual and unexamined understandings of interdisciplinarity," to use Marjorie Pryse's phrase (2000, 106). To no surprise, I was forced almost immediately to confront my very real and very deep ignorance; in reality, I could not have articulated a substantial definition of interdisciplinarity or any of the significant issues being raised by interdisciplinary studies' practitioners.

Since its inception in the 1970s, the field of WGS in the United States and Canada has imagined itself to be interdisciplinary. Judith Allen and Sally Kitch observe that "feminist scholars usually think of 'interdisciplinarity' and 'women's studies' as inherently and inextricably linked" (1998, 275). The current National Women's Studies Association website states, "Women's studies is comparative, global, intersectional, and interdisciplinary" (June 5, 2011). The Canadian Women's Studies Association/ l'association canadienne des études sur les femmes announces that its purpose is "To develop and support Women's Studies as an interdisciplinary field within the academic community" (June 5, 2011). WGS' commitment to interdisciplinarity is a commitment to revealing (what it believes are) the limitations of disciplines as well as to creating new knowledge outside (and among) those disciplines.[1]

But *why* has WGS needed to believe it is interdisciplinary? Perhaps the answer is simple: because those identifying as practitioners of Women's Studies in the early 1970s saw themselves as doing transgressive work. By articulating and attempting to solve problems, and calling into question the arbitrary mapping of knowledge in disciplines, these graduate students, professors, and scholars believed passionately that they needed to challenge academic structures in order to devise a new vocabulary as well as new approaches to pedagogy, methodology, epistemology, and institutional structures. That "interdisciplinary" quickly became an assumed, uncontroversial, and positive term is not surprising. It *did*, and still does, contain within it promises of innovation, integration, unbounded possibility, and even of progress—from less to more "correct" questions and answers.

WGS has sought to challenge not only disciplinary borders and disciplinary rules of conduct but the very idea of boundaries as well as the institutional structures that maintain those boundaries. But to assume that these challenges *are* in and of themselves interdisciplinary obscures very real questions about how our field now functions as a discipline and does and does not contest systems of knowledge production. Reliance on the narrative that "the field is interdisciplinary" conceals a deep tension—that an intellectual project can be pursued in institutions whose structures function as obstacles to that project. For individual practitioners, as well as WGS itself, the task is to "work simultaneously in disciplines and in opposition to them" (Klein 2005, 192). And, as Ann Braithwaite points out in "Discipline," in this volume, "The absence of engagement with" questions about disciplines (and interdisciplinarity) is also "a refusal ... to ask what is counting as WGS, and how, in particular contexts," as well as a way not to ask "about the field's subject, about its borders and parameters, and about its relation to other fields of inquiry (or disciplines)." We cannot simply use "interdisciplinarity" as a basket in which we place "subjects" that do not seem to fit into what we perceive to be well-bounded disciplines.

In the pages that follow, I will focus on the following three sets of questions: (1) What is/are interdisciplinary studies, and is there a common definition of, or process for doing, interdisciplinary work in WGS?; (2) Why has WGS valued interdisciplinarity so highly and needed to believe in its own interdisciplinarity?; and (3) How has interdisciplinarity functioned in WGS, and what have been the consequences of telling the story of the field's interdisciplinarity for forty years?

Definitions and Assumptions

Interdisciplinarians, or those who identify with interdisciplinary fields and programs but not Women's and Gender Studies, have invested deeply in formulating definitions. The Association for Integrative Studies even includes a definition in its mission statement: "Interdisciplinarity combines the insights of knowledge domains to produce a more comprehensive understanding of complex problems, issues, or questions ranging from comparison to fully realized integration" (AIS, June 6, 2011). And the essay first published in 1982 by Newell and Green, "*Defining* and Teaching Interdisciplinary Studies" (emphasis mine), has become a touchstone for interdisciplinarians. The authors define interdisciplinary studies as "inquiries which critically draw upon two or more disciplines and which lead to an integration of disciplinary insights" but also convey uncertainty about "what the appropriate relationship is between interdisciplinary studies and the academic disciplines themselves. Should interdisciplinary studies try to overthrow the disciplines, or reform them, or stand alongside them?" (1998, 24). This last question was tacitly answered by Klein and Newell in "Advancing Interdisciplinary Studies." They write, interdisciplinarity is:

 a process of answering a question, solving a problem, or addressing a topic that is too broad or complex to be dealt with adequately by a single discipline or profession. Whether the context

is an integrated approach to general education, a women's studies program, or a science, technology, and society program, IDS
draws on disciplinary perspectives and integrates their insights
through construction of a more comprehensive approach. In this
manner, interdisciplinary study is not simply a supplement but
is complementary to and corrective of the disciplines. (1998, 3)

This formulation declares that interdisciplinarity both derives from and
complements disciplines' perspectives and insights and thus answers
Newell and Green's earlier question. It also hints at the need to challenge the structure of disciplinary knowledge in the phrase "corrective
of the disciplines," although that phrase could be interpreted as elucidating the supplemental and complementary functions of interdisciplinarity rather than as subversive. This definition should also remind us
that (1) WGS' interdisciplinarity looks very different when perceived by
scholars in other fields; (2) from some of those scholars' perspectives,
WGS is just one example of a "context" in which interdisciplinary work
gets done; and (3) interdisciplinarians and WGS practitioners have different investments in the "advancement" of interdisciplinarity.

In the December 2007 issue of the Association for Integrative Studies *Newsletter* (now named *Integrative Pathways*), Newell presents "Six
Arguments for Agreeing on a Definition of Interdisciplinary Studies."
Student learning and program viability are the goals for the "agreement."
Nowhere does Newell articulate a desire to challenge disciplines; he
actually states that "Interdisciplinary studies draw explicitly on the disciplines" for information, data, techniques, tools, perspectives, concepts,
theories, and methods (2007, 4). According to Lisa Lattuca, Newell
concurs with other interdisciplinarians who tend to want to integrate,
and maintain, disciplines. In contrast, Latucca explains, "feminists …
espouse an interdisciplinary perspective that redresses fragmented and
dichotomous viewpoints by recognizing the interconnectedness of reality" (2001, 16) and seek to redefine knowledge by "dismantling disciplinary perspectives, not maintaining and integrating them" (2001,
15).[2] She then surmises that for feminists,

Disciplinary approaches to research and teaching result only in
partial and thus distorted knowledge that serves to keep those

> who have power in power and those without power subordi-
> nate. Interdisciplinary approaches result in less distorted forms
> of knowledge and thereby redistribute power to individuals who
> would otherwise be powerless. (2001, 16)

As Lattuca shrewdly notes, "In this view interdisciplinarity is therefore
both a means to an end and an end in itself. In comparison much of
the literature on interdisciplinarity views interdisciplinarity as a useful
approach to answering social or technological questions and not as an
end in itself" (2001, 16).

Lattuca's conclusion, that many WGS' scholars seek to "dismantl[e]
disciplinary perspectives, not maintain ... and integrat[e] them" (2001,
16), might be *the* difference between interdisciplinarians' and WGS
scholars' approaches to interdisciplinarity. For many interdisciplinarians, the goal is not to dismantle disciplines but to integrate their
knowledge in ways that produce new knowledge—to achieve *synthesis*,
while WGS' practitioners seek to "redress fragmented and dichotomous
viewpoints" (2001, 16) produced by disciplinary knowledge. This comparison might also suggest an explanation for the lack of definitions of
interdisciplinarity from WGS' practitioners[3]; if WGS' investment is in
calling structures into question, then it is possible that, in Klein's words,
"Interdisciplinarity ... has no inherent meaning" (2005, 63) and does
not require defining. This might explain why the debates among practitioners have not produced definitive claims about how exactly WGS'
interdisciplinarity, per se, challenges old, and forges new, knowledge, or
even what constitutes interdisciplinary work.

So how have the assumed meanings of interdisciplinarity developed
in WGS? To answer this, I turn to two early statements about the field.
The first is the editorial in the premiere issue of *Signs*, published in
1975. The editors, Catherine Stimpson, Joan Burstyn, Domna Stanton,
and Sandra Whisler, proclaim that the journal has as its "purpose" "to
be interdisciplinary," and they offer "three patterns" for interdisciplinary work: (1) a single person "skilled in several disciplines, explores one
subject"; (2) a few people, "each skilled in one discipline, explore one
subject together"; and (3) "delegates of several disciplines" simply "publish in more or less random conjunction with each other in a single journal" (1975, v). Although the editors do not delve into the implications

of the definition they provide, their statement of purpose boldly claims that the field will be interdisciplinary. Three years later, Greta Hoffman Nemiroff also devised a taxonomy, but hers distinguishes among inter-, multi-, pluri-, and transdisciplinarity. In "Rationale for an Interdisciplinary Approach to Women's Studies," published in the first issue of *Canadian Woman Studies/les cahiers de la femme*, Nemiroff argues for interdisciplinarity as an antidote to the fragmentation of students' education although she acknowledges how difficult it will be for faculty to move beyond the privileges and reward systems of disciplines. She also notes that "the newness" of Women's Studies "requires inventiveness, research, and discovery. There is the challenging need for conceptualization and the creation of a methodology" as well as "the need to pursue and unearth more information.... In accordance with these criteria, Women's Studies is an appropriate field for interdisciplinary work" (1978, 61). Nemiroff recognizes the privileges associated with disciplines, the potential for Women's Studies to be interdisciplinary because of its newness, and the implied relationship between Women's Studies and interdisciplinarity—the former could both use and achieve the latter on conceptual, methodological, and informational levels. Yet what seems to be missing in both Nemiroff's essay and the *Signs'* editorial is a challenge to the arbitrariness of disciplinary boundaries and the need to call those boundaries into question.

Newell and Green published their "Defining and Teaching Interdisciplinary Studies" at the same time numerous scholars were reflecting on the relationship between disciplines and Women's Studies; Newell and Klein published "Advancing Interdisciplinary Studies" when Women's Studies practitioners were raising significant questions about an interdisciplinary Ph.D. Might our field have benefitted from the insights of these interdisciplinarians? Nancy Grace's 1996 "An Exploration of the Interdisciplinary Character of Women's Studies" provides a response. Curiously, few WGS scholars seem to have read or refer to this article. Is it because it appeared in *Issues in Integrative Studies* rather than a WGS journal? Grace herself identified as a Women's Studies practitioner who attended an Institute for Integrative Studies in 1993–94. After participating in the Institute, she surveyed Women's Studies syllabi from 1976 through 1994 (with a majority from 1988 to 1990) which were included in a 1991 NWSA report. To assess these syllabi for their interdisciplinarity, Grace used the Association for Integrative Studies' "The Guide to Interdisciplinary Syllabus Preparation." Recognizing that a syllabus tells only one story about a course, Grace nevertheless concludes that such courses fall into seven categories, with "single discipline with feminist perspective" at one end of a spectrum, and "feminist transdisciplinary/disciplinary" at the other. In the mid-1990s, when Grace conducted her research, the majority of courses fell into the first category. They were "strictly disciplinary offerings which present a single disciplinary perspective combined with feminist analysis. The topic of the course is not investigated through more than one disciplinary lens ..." (1996, 68). I doubt that Grace's findings would be very different if she conducted her study again, now. Those findings seriously call into question whether or not WGS is functionally interdisciplinary, if we use the criteria for interdisciplinarity developed by interdisciplinarians.

The National Women's Studies Association was established in 1977, and the Canadian Women's Studies Assocation/l'association canadienne des études sur les femmes in 1982. In between, in 1979, the Association for Integrative Studies was founded. Given WGS' investment in interdisciplinarity, it is striking how little attention the field has paid to the only academic association dedicated to interdisciplinary studies. In contrast, interdisciplinarians always include WGS in their histories of the development of interdisciplinary studies. According to these narratives, WGS grew out of the civil rights movements of the 1950s and 1960s and developed with, or as part of, the feminist movement. Allen Repko tells the story this way: "... the confluence of three major developments in the 1960s: the Vietnam War, the student revolution, and dramatic changes in social mores" contributed to the process of critiquing the disciplines. That confluence:

> served as a catalyst from which emerged new thinking about how the Academy should relate to society.... The disciplines and the scholarship that they produced had failed to explain, or even ignored, the great social movements and struggles that characterized the period.... By contrast, interdisciplinarity became a programmatic, value-laden term that stood for reform, innovation, progress, and opening up the university to all kinds of

hitherto marginalized publics. The radicalism of the 1960s produced new fields such as African American studies, women's studies, and ethnic studies, and new definitions of culture and politics. (2008, 36)[4]

In this history, interdisciplinarity is associated with "reform, innovation, progress, and opening up the university" (moves that WGS has claimed for itself) and was the catalyst for monumental changes in the academy. According to this narrative, WGS, a product of 1960s' radicalism, has been not so much the cause of change as one of the outcomes.

In *Creating Interdisciplinarity: Interdisciplinary Research and Teaching among College and University Faculty,* Lattuca also narrates the history of interdisciplinary studies in the United States. She points out that as early as the turn of the twentieth century, "faculty and administrators began to worry … about the fragmentation that might accompany disciplinary divisions" (2001, 6), and "… concerns about haphazard course selection and overspecialization by students" (2001, 6) led to "distribution and concentration requirements" that "directed study" but "did not reinstitute a unified view of knowledge" (2001, 7). As for specific interdisciplinary initiatives, the Social Science Research Council was established in the United States in the 1920s "to promote integration across the social science disciplines," area studies in the 1930s "signaled an attempt to focus multiple disciplinary perspectives on a single geographic area" (2001, 8), and "World War II encouraged interdisciplinary research applications in service of military and political ends" (2001, 8). Twenty years later, "Interdisciplinary curricula … gained prominence during the social transformations of the 1960s" (2001, 9), structuralism in the 1960s and 1970s "defied disciplinary boundaries" in its "search for underlying systems or forms," and poststructuralism in the 1970s and 1980s "rejected the search for unity, systems, and underlying forms as illusory and futile" (2001, 10). Also in the 1970s and 1980s, "Feminist theory trained attention on how difference, reflected in the form of gender, ethnicity, class, and power, influences the social world" (2001, 10), while "Postmodernists … repudiated scholarly attempts at objectivity, neutrality, universality, and generalizability" (2001, 10). Repko's and Lattuca's historical interpretations emphasize not only the ways in which *interdisciplinarity* evolved from particular trends and values in

U.S. higher education and culture but also suggest that the history of WGS cannot be easily separated from those trends and values, and that WGS developed fairly directly from *higher education* trends that embodied tensions between disciplines and interdisciplinarity as well as from political and social trends.

Believing in Interdisciplinarity

Elaine Showalter observed in 1971 that "Radical feminists see Women's Studies … as a potential revolutionary force within the university and society," while "traditionalists" view Women's Studies "as a new academic discipline, and are concerned with establishing its legitimacy in terms of research, lectures, papers, exams, and grades" (quoted in Messer-Davidow 2002, 120). Showalter identifies a terrain that would only become more intensely contested in the decade to follow. Observing that "radicals" (activists) were already lining up against "traditionalists" (academics), Showalter implies that interdisciplinary was opposed to "disciplinary" and even that "radical" meant interdisciplinary, while "traditional" meant "disciplinary." Ellen Messer-Davidow notes that Showalter and other "feminists who launched women's studies … started out with cross-disciplinary … aspirations, but they met up with disciplinary and institutional limitations" (2002, 157) such as the need to "assemble the curriculum from courses based in disciplinary departments. By the mid-1970s, feminist studies had formed with internal tensions—between disciplinarity and interdisciplinarity, orthodoxy and heterodoxy, routinization and innovation—that still characterized it in the 1990s" (2002, 158). Messer-Davidow's implied equation, between "feminist studies" and interdisciplinarity, heterodoxy, and innovation, also suggests a cause and effect relationship—and that Women's and Gender Studies has held onto an interdisciplinary identity in order to remain heretical and perhaps even revolutionary.

Florence Howe and Carol Ahlum observe in their "Women's Studies and Social Change" that "Women's studies is part of a broad effort to develop interdisciplinary studies" (1973, 401) and values "interdisciplinary" as a corrective to "the narrowness of traditional training" (399). Recognizing both the disciplinary expertise of Women's Studies faculty and academic structures, Howe and Ahlum acknowledge that "For some time to come, team-taught courses will have to compensate for" that narrowness "and provide interdisciplinary approaches to curriculum" (399) and that "Of necessity a women's studies curriculum assumes an interdisciplinary approach" since it will be "difficult, if not impossible to consider sexual stereotyping, status, and social change without reference to multiple aspects of women's lives ..." (1973, 404). Without feeling the need to define interdisciplinarity, Howe and Ahlum jump to the political conclusion that Women's Studies has to be interdisciplinary in order to challenge knowledge structures such as disciplines that prevent a meaningful study of women. Almost by default, or without significant alternatives to those seemingly limiting disciplines, Howe and Ahlum rely on a vocabulary that pitches interdisciplinarity as the solution to the problems caused by the disciplining of knowledge and that had already begun to set the terms of the "autonomy vs. integration debate," as Braithwaite discusses in this volume in "Discipline."

Stimpson, in "What Matters Mind: A Theory About the Practice of Women's Studies," also recognizes that, "interdisciplinary work ... will give the most spacious possible view of women and society, adequate knowledge, and rich conceptual models" (1973, 43). But, she notes, "The tributes to interdisciplinary work are more odes to an ideal than analyses of practice," and Women's Studies' "actual interdisciplinary feats" have "so far" been "tame," consisting of "remarks about the same subject ... made at one time by persons from several disciplines," "the resurrection of old practices within certain disciplines ...; or a simple blurring of strict disciplinary lines" (1973, 43). Stimpson does not blame "Women's Studies practitioners" but "the extreme specialization of American scholarship" for the obstacles in the way of "cross-fertilizing disciplines" (1973, 44). Forty years later, we might ask, has WGS (still) failed to confront and remove the obstacles that prevent disciplinary "cross-fertilizing?"

By the 1980s, WGS sought to locate itself as an avowedly interdisciplinary academic field in a disciplinary university world. Marilyn Boxer, in "For and About Women: The Theory and Practice of Women's Studies in the United States," characterizes "interdisciplinary" as an "ill-defined term" which describes "a practice that has been for the most part multidisciplinary and interdepartmental" (1988, 91). She proceeds to summarize the department/mainstreaming debate as a "choice between establishing a separate department that could ... be forgotten or eliminated ... or of creating a decentralized program as a base from which to reach out" (1988, 96). On one end of the spectrum is autonomy, recognition, and abandonment of "the energy-draining ... effort to transform the established disciplines" (1988, 92). On the other end of the spectrum is the position that "rejects disciplinarity itself as fragmentation of social experience, a male model of analysis that cannot describe the whole of female—or human—existence. By stressing the indivisible nature of knowledge, women's studies could become a force for liberation from a dehumanizing overspecialization" (1988, 92–93). Sandra Coyner, in "Women's Studies as an Academic Discipline; Why and How to Do It," also asked, can Women's Studies effect more change if it functions on college and university campuses as its own department, with tenure lines, budgets, and a discrete curriculum, or as a program with faculty dispersed throughout traditional disciplines? As her title announces, she favors the former. One of her arguments centers on the often-cited criticism of traditional disciplines as rigid. Her response is, "We need to imagine boldly a discipline organized solely around our own priorities" (1983, 65). And, of course, those priorities include interdisciplinarity. The relationship between an intellectual interdisciplinarity and institutional disciplinarity developed as a contentious one in Women's Studies' first years. Could it have been otherwise? Probably not, I would maintain, since interdisciplinarity so quickly became associated with challenges to disciplinary structures and limitations.

Susan Stanford Friedman also struggles with the tension between WGS' interdisciplinarity and its location in disciplinary institutions as she analyzes the need for a Ph.D. in Women's Studies. In "(Inter)Disciplinarity and the Question of the Women's Studies Ph.D.," Friedman sets up opposing camps: "those who see women's studies as a discipline," and "those who see women's studies as an interdisciplinary field." For the former, "the formation of doctoral degree programs in women's studies is a logical next step and a professional necessity," while for the latter, such programs "pose serious intellectual and pedagogical problems" (1998, 311). Friedman admits that she feels caught between a "desire for the survival of an intellectual rigorous women's studies within an economically strapped academy" and a continued "reimagining [of] the formations of knowledge and the structures of the academy" (1998, 322).

Allen and Kitch, in their *Feminist Studies* article, "Disciplined by Disciplines? The Need for an *Interdisciplinary* Research Mission in Women's Studies," also ponder the implications of establishing Ph.D. programs in WGS. "Without departmental structures," they write, "women's studies is ... unlikely to generate autonomous Ph.D. programs, which we believe are essential to the production and support of interdisciplinary women's studies scholarship. And without Ph.D.'s in women's studies, there will continue to be few opportunities for women's studies scholars to acquire training in interdisciplinary methods and fewer potential faculty positions in which interdisciplinary scholarship is an asset" (1998, 291–2). Friedman, as well as Allen and Kitch, struggle to solve the problem of locating interdisciplinary work in a disciplinary institutional world. But the terms of the debate make a solution impossible to articulate. By the 1990s, WGS would have no way to reconcile its goal of dismantling disciplines in higher education's infrastructure.

In her contribution to *Women's Studies for the Future*, "Disciplining Feminist Futures? 'Undisciplined' Reflections about the Women's Studies Ph.D.," Vivian May points to "the repeated characterizations of women's studies' interdisciplinarity as undisciplined, illogical, and ill-conceived" (2005, 198).[5] Each of these adjectives makes obvious what has been problematic about not examining interdisciplinarity meaningfully. May hypothesizes that those characterizations "signify a continued inability to imagine difference as productive of anything akin to knowledge ..." (2005, 198). In her chapter "Institutionalization" in this volume, Aimee Carrillo Rowe argues that "The discourse that naturalizes Women's Studies' institutionalized status as an accomplishment" has made it difficult, if not impossible, to discern and then scrutinize the field's "formation through ongoing relational practices" which themselves obscure the functions of privileges produced by race, class, and family constructs.

Deborah Rosenfelt observed in "What Women's Studies Programs Do That Mainstreaming Can't," that "in an economically uncertain world ... Women's Studies may not be allowed to continue its evolution toward ... disciplinary status" (1984, 174). She then concludes, "Only the existence of autonomous programs can guarantee the maintenance, let alone the development, of Women's Studies in this era of retrenchment" (1984, 174). Fifteen years later, other Women's Studies practitioners were still claiming that interdisciplinarity was a goal to strive toward, rather than an accomplishment. For example, Domna Stanton and Abigail Stewart expected readers of their *Feminisms in the Academy* to "engage in the kind of self-conscious pluridisciplinary and cross-disciplinary activities that may be a precondition for interdisciplinarity" (1995, 7). That Women's Studies would someday be interdisciplinary remains a powerful belief and is inseparable from the expectation that academic structures will change. This is evident in the research conducted by Elizabeth Bird in 1998–99. Bird interviewed sixty feminist academics who had helped establish Women's Studies programs about their "engagement in the curriculum" from 1970 to 1995. All of those interviewed worked in England, Wales, Scotland, Northern Ireland, Canada, and the United States, in institutions of higher education. The "interviews suggest that rather than overturning the system, either inside or outside the academy, knowledge was reined in and brought back into the intellectual and physical spaces that constitute traditional disciplines" (2001, 474). But there is hope: "the established disciplines and the organisational structure that embedded political power in those disciplines resulted in the disciplines themselves changing their character, rather than the emergence of a new discipline" (2001, 475). If "changing their character" means becoming less invested in their own constructs and more eager to engage meta-questions about integrative pedagogies, methods, and concepts, then it seems reasonable that interdisciplinarity will continue to function as an important goal. The questions with which scholars have approached interdisciplinarity and its significance for WGS reveal how deeply the field has believed itself to be a catalyst for change that has pushed higher education to rethink fundamental questions about knowledge.

Functions and Consequences: Is Women's and Gender Studies Interdisciplinary?

Scholars reflecting on the field's interdisciplinarity have focused primarily on whether or not Women's and Gender Studies should be a discrete academic discipline or an interdisciplinary field in continual dialogue with disciplines and on how either or both might be formulated. Allen and Kitch note that WGS' "interdisciplinary intellectual aspirations" had not been met in the late 1990s not only with respect to faculty but also with respect to "core intellectual frameworks and paradigms" (1998, 293). To help move the field toward fulfillment of those aspirations, they asked significant questions about WGS as an *interdiscipline* that would be "a new, intellectually coherent entity built upon a common vocabulary and … an understanding of the epistemologies and methodologies of various disciplines," that would reveal "important 'missing linkages' among aspects of human life, social structures, and motivations," and that would enable epistemologies to be "mutually enhanced" as well as "multiple aspects of reality [to be] interconnected" (1998, 277). But is it possible for an "interdiscipline" *not* to function as if it were a discipline, with respect to U.S. and Canadian higher education expectations and restrictions? And if the interdiscipline of WGS functions as if it were a discipline, what does it gain from maintaining its interdisciplinary identity?

Mary Romero confronted the issue of academic systems and noted, "many of the problems surrounding attempts toward interdisciplinarity that Women's Studies has encountered are structural issues resulting from the imperfect fit of an interdisciplinary program located within the matrix of a traditional disciplinary institutional structure" (2000, 151). Would calling WGS a discipline resolve this dilemma? Even if the enterprise we identify as WGS could be made to fit within the container that is a discipline, would that container stack up neatly alongside other disciplines? Romero concludes that "the further institutionalization of Women's Studies increases the multi-discipline structure rather than 'interdisciplinarity'" (2000, 158). I believe that this is due in part to the fact that as we move farther away from WGS's earliest forms, we become more attached to our assumption that multi- means inter- with respect to disciplines. We also run the risk of sentimentalizing those origins as mythically radical or of lamenting the "fall" from a radical interdisciplinary origin.

Boxer concludes her "Unruly Knowledge: Women's Studies and the Problem of Disciplinarity" with five pragmatic "suggestions": (1) "cease worrying about whether Women's Studies is a discipline—and call it that if we like"; (2) "pursue the goal of establishing ourselves within disciplinary departments … and … participate in interdisciplinary units of whatever kind best fits our current intellectual interests and our specific institutional histories and structures"; (3) "attend carefully to the work of our colleagues in Women's Studies whose disciplinary and methodological approaches differ from ours"; (4) "participate in and support both disciplinary professional associations and NWSA"; and (5) "develop graduate programs" (2000, 126). By asking us to worry less about labels and more about the actual work we do and the knowledge we seek, Boxer advocates a "both/and" approach.[6] Diane Elam also believes that WGS can move beyond this debate. In her analysis, Women's Studies is an "'interdisciplinary discipline'" that draws its strength from "multiple disciplines without being simply reducible to any one of them" (2002, 220). But if by "interdisciplinary" we mean, among other definitions, the dissolution of disciplines, how can WGS be both interdisciplinary and disciplinary? And how can it secure its location in the academy, producing Ph.D.s, for example, and still reap the benefits of functioning as if it were a free agent?

Eloise Buker answered the title of her essay, "Is Women's Studies a Disciplinary or an Interdisciplinary Field of Inquiry?," by admitting the costs of disciplining WGS, but deciding that, yes, WGS needs "to declare itself a distinctive field of inquiry, a discipline" (2003, 88). Buker is persuaded by WGS having built an intellectually strong "body of knowledge" and by the need for departmental status "to acquire sufficient resources to continue to flourish" (2003, 88). Yet, she declares, "Women's Studies must sustain its intellectual roots in an open interdisciplinary epistemology" (2003, 88). Buker's title raises additional questions: Can knowledge be simultaneously disciplinary and interdisciplinary? Does conceptualizing WGS as an interdiscipline get us any closer to methodological, pedagogical, and knowledge-producing syntheses? What would synthesis provide? And, will crossing a disciplinary boundary result in the type of interdisciplinary knowledge WGS seeks?

An Ending, If Not a Conclusion

Women's and Gender Studies' presumed interdisciplinarity rests on a number of assumptions: interdisciplinarity is "universal" (and would not look different if examined from multiple interdisciplinarians' perspectives); interdisciplinarity is a necessary component of "transgressive scholarship"; defining interdisciplinarity is unnecessary; a synthesis of disciplinary knowledge, methods, and conceptual frames can be achieved; transcending the limitations imposed by disciplinary knowledge, methods, and frames is possible; since disciplines define the parameters of knowledge production, interdisciplinarity must challenge the disciplines in order to make new knowledge production possible; interdisciplinarity is a process, as Lattuca suggests, and producing knowledge through this process is a worthy goal; WGS *will develop* into a fully interdisciplinary field; and, perhaps most importantly, interdisciplinarity, even as it continually recedes from our horizons, will save WGS from the institutionalization of academia's disciplining.

If we continue to assume that interdisciplinarity and disciplinarity are distinctive, and different, and the former is superior to the latter because it challenges the presumed limitations of the disciplines, and if WGS is a discipline, then we need to ask why we would hold onto an interdisciplinary identity. And if universities are beginning to embrace interdisciplinarity—even to use it as a marketable commodity—do WGS' claims to transgressive knowledge production through interdisciplinarity become less meaningful? If WGS has used interdisciplinarity to remain "outside" the institution, but interdisciplinarity becomes "inside," where are we located? As a field, WGS has needed to proclaim over and over again that it is interdisciplinary in order to continue to tell another story: that it radically trespasses onto and around regular academic structures, including disciplines. This narrative has enabled WGS teachers and scholars to accomplish brilliant and even radical work. But it has also made us self-satisfied and prevented us from seeing our field in the context of higher education as well as from learning from interdisciplinarians who have also been studying interdisciplinary knowledge, pedagogy, methodologies, and structures.

Irene Dolling and Sabine Hark reminded readers of *Signs* that disciplines and departments are different constructs, and that "inter" and "multi," as well as "disciplinary" and "departmental," are categories with messy and uneven boundaries. In "She Who Speaks Shadow Speaks Truth: Transdisciplinarity in Women's and Gender Studies," they propose renewed emphasis on what they call "transdisciplinarity": "a continual examination of artificially drawn and contingent boundaries" (2000, 1197) as well as "a critical evaluation of terms, concepts, and methods that transgresses disciplinary boundaries" and can "be a means to [a] higher level of reflexivity" about WGS' "modes of knowledge production" (2000, 1195). Dolling and Hark project an energized and positive future for not only defining but also for doing transdisciplinary work. Their "higher level of reflexivity" directs us to produce transgressive knowledge as well as to incorporate and expand upon interdisciplinarians' approaches.

Interdisciplinarity seems to provide a way for WGS to use the privileges of institutionalization while maintaining a defensive distance from that institutionalization. It is also an ever-receding horizon, an unachievable destination. But it has functioned as a catalyst and as a place toward which to travel. WGS teachers and scholars still need to tell the interdisciplinary story because it justifies our work and our goals—we need to believe that we are challenging the old and forging the new. But if interdisciplinarity is always in the future, what is it in the present? And what will we do now, when interdisciplinary studies in their myriad variations are becoming marketable commodities, at least in U.S. and Canadian higher education? *If* (and I realize that this is highly speculative) the academy has changed (at least partly) as a result of WGS' forty-year efforts, what new stories will we tell ourselves? If we are not as interdisciplinary as we have thought, and if we are no longer transgressive with respect to institutional structures such as disciplines, then what are we? What new narratives will motivate and sustain us?

Notes

1. As Braithwaite discusses in her chapter "Discipline" in this volume, we must also challenge assumptions about disciplines.
2. See Maparayan's "Feminism" and Braithwaite's "Discipline," among other essays in this volume, for discussions of "feminists" as Latucca uses the word.
3. Of course, a number of Women's and Gender Studies' scholars do provide definitions. See, for example, "(Inter)Disciplinarity and the Question of the Women's Studies Ph.D." (Friedman 1998, 310).
4. See Orr's chapter on "Activism" in this volume for a discussion of the relationship between "activism" and "Women's and Gender Studies."
5. Unlike May, I do not read the historical meta-narrative of Women's and Gender Studies' interdisciplinarity as being so deliberately critical.
6. May describes the "both/and" as "an either/or oppositional stance" in "Disciplining Feminist Futures?" (2005, 200). Klein also refers to Women's Studies' "'both-and' strategy" with respect to disciplines and interdisciplinarity (2005, 192).

3
METHODS

Katherine Side

Feminists have nothing to fear from healthy internal debates about methods and their epistemological antecedents.

(Fonow and Cook 2005, 2215)

Despite Mary Margaret Fonow and Judith Cook's assertion that feminist academics have nothing to fear, there are relatively few healthy internal debates about methods and their epistemological antecedents, and the ways they discipline, and establish the discipline of, Women's and Gender Studies (WGS). I, too, am guilty of this limited engagement. A graduate of a freestanding Ph.D. program in WGS, and a faculty member who holds a full appointment in WGS and serves as Department Head, even I hesitate to engage in these internal debates because of my anxieties about how my involvement in WGS contributes to the construction of unquestioned spaces in the discipline. This hesitation was made obvious when a colleague telephoned me, last summer, to discuss the development of a new graduate program in WGS at her university. She asked me: Which courses are essential to include in the curriculum? Which courses should be required, and which ones optional? What are graduate students in WGS required to know? During our conversation, I worried that the program with which she was involved would simply replicate an already well established pattern, particularly at the graduate level, of defining WGS without engaging in the debates advised by Fonow and Cook. The graduate curriculum would likely include a required course in feminist theory, another course in methods, a graduate seminar to prepare students to write theses, and elective courses drawn from across the university. This pattern has become expected in WGS programs, without careful interrogation about how it constructs the discipline, builds on its strengths, and replicates its limitations. But, I argue, without engaging in questions about curriculum, and especially in questions about methods, which is my concern here, we are avoiding critical examinations of WGS as a bounded field of study, or more contentiously, as a discipline.[1] In hindsight, I wish I had challenged my colleague and urged her to think critically about curricular choices, and I wish that I had done so too. Why I didn't do this forms the backdrop for my argument in this chapter.

In this chapter, then, I question the term and the role of "methods" as one way into these debates. I consider how this term operates to construct dominant narratives about WGS and about other academic disciplines. Some of the central questions that frame my concerns include: What is the genealogy of the term "methods" in WGS? How does this term function in the discipline, and the disciplining, of WGS and in its assumptions about other disciplines? How does it reference and construct normative narratives and practices? Which narratives and practices are disavowed to maintain our loyalties to particular accounts of methods and their importance? What is this discipline that we are creating, and avoiding, through its uses?

Because the term "methods" often stands in for various other concepts, including methodology and epistemology, I adopt Sandra Harding's use of this term (1987) to refer to tools, techniques, modes of inquiry, and research designs for identifying, collecting, and analysing research evidence and data, although it is likely that I slide into uses that elide methods with the terms "ontology" and "epistemology," and with stated and unstated assumptions and principles about research more generally. I do not outline here which tools, techniques, modes of inquiry, and research designs are suited, or not suited, to WGS, as a project that this analysis questions. My main argument is that the term "methods" is imagined, from within WGS, as a corrective to uncontested assertions about the limitations of methods in other disciplines, which are presumed to be specific, unique, and recognizable. Methods in WGS function simultaneously as everything and nothing: everything that other discipline specific methods are not, and nothing because WGS claims no specific method as its "own." This position—WGS methods as everything and nothing—is a source of intellectual and institutional anxiety that is questioned, even by its own practitioners. It is also, paradoxically, the foundation of invigorating possibilities for the intellectual and institutional future of the field.

Constructing a Genealogy for Methods

Narratives about Women's and Gender Studies methods constitute part of a larger repertoire of tales about its origins and ancestry. Some of these tales evoke familiar accounts that carve out unique roles and specific contributions by some of its practitioners. They document sites of struggles, and at the same time they embed the legacy of these struggles in present articulations of the discipline, and its disciplining, and frame expectations for its future. Some individuals are committed to reproducing tales about WGS methods as significant for the discipline's past, present, and future, while others, including me, harbour considerable anxiety about their consequences.[2] What have we, all of us, come to expect by using the term "methods?" And, what might scholars in other disciplines expect from us? Which possibilities are expanded by the idea of WGS methods, and which are contained by its use? What does the term mean for what Robyn Wiegman repeatedly refers to as "Women's Studies as an academic enterprise" (2008)? How do our accounts about methods produce and reproduce particular versions of WGS, to the exclusion of other possibilities?

Some self-proclaimed "founders" and "inventors" of the earliest Women's Studies programs are secure in their claims that they developed new methods where none existed previously. Many of the contributors to anthologies edited by Florence Howe (2000) and Wendy Robbins et al. (2008), *The Politics of Women's Studies* and *Minds of Our Own* respectively, articulate the invention of WGS and its methods, while marking its distinction from other academic disciplines and their alleged gaps. Educated prior to the establishment of WGS, they received their education in other, discipline specific methods. Taught "to value the intellectual genealogies of particular scholarly niches," their own thinking and experiences also led them to consciously resist these niches (Blee 2002, 178).[3] Their scholarship questioned, and sometimes rejected, other discipline specific research methods, methodologies, and epistemologies. By virtue of this history, they designated themselves as critics of discipline based methods and as inventors of WGS methods. For example, contributors to *Minds of Our Own* were directly involved in establishing what was then called Women's Studies in Canada, in the 1970s. By their own accounts, they established "new forms of criticism" (Thomas 2008, 43), uncovered women's histories (Zemon Davis and Ker Conway 2008, 80), and explicated the "political aspects of women's lives" (Robbins et al. 2008, 35), often beyond the university (Levine 2008, 56). Contributors to *The Politics of Women's Studies* similarly asserted they put women first (i.e., Arenal 2000) and positioned "women's experiences" as evidence of a shared commitment to "participatory democracy" in methods (Buhle 2000, xix).

These scholars interrogated methods, methodologies, and epistemologies in disciplines by questioning "the presumed objectivity and value neutrality of the natural sciences" (Martin 2008, 13), the "maleness of philosophy" (Bordo 1999, 29), and "the evidence of experience" in historical research (Scott 1999, 79). They used critiques of disciplines and their essential epistemological and methodological foundations, and the discovery of these "new" methods, to assert their belief in interdisciplinarity as a key identity for early versions of WGS. As Diane Lichtenstein points out in this volume, they often did so without questioning the arbitrariness of disciplinary boundaries, or whether interdisciplinarity was possible.

These first constructions of WGS methods, though, did more than outline how particular groups of individuals, in specific locations, became involved with the development of the discipline. They also cast WGS methods as novel, and necessary, for their abilities to correct the limitations of other discipline specific methods. They established normative practices, and then referenced these normative practices for teaching and employing WGS methods, *without* ever explicating clearly what was included in and what was excluded from them. Collectively, they have continued to uphold this version of WGS methods by granting the role of overseer to current teachers and scholars in the field, who imply that the telling of a particular version of the discipline's origins is actually more important than critical examinations of its specific tools and techniques for understanding.

Arguments for a distinct WGS method, though, have often required that methodological commonalities amongst other disciplines be collapsed, that uniform language and understandings be adopted, and that their differences, and distance, from WGS be exaggerated. All disciplines (other than WGS), despite diverse ontological and epistemological bases, are assumed to share continuously employed, and even static, methods and methodological flaws. Debates about the discipline's scholarly distinctiveness animated discussion at the 1982 National Women's Studies Association meetings and subsequent to this, a 1984 special issue of *Women's Studies International Forum*. In an article included in this issue, "Varieties of Women's Studies," Peggy McIntosh and Elizabeth Karmack Minnich cite a program brochure that reiterates the assertion that methods in WGS offer something different: "Women's Studies provides the impetus toward re-examining each of the traditional scholarly disciplines to identify and correct misinformation and unexamined assumptions about 'women's place' in history. In doing so, we have also learned to look at men's lives in new and more humanistic ways, bringing to bear on each discipline an awareness of the interplay of gender, race and class" (1984, 146).

Jacky Coates, Michelle Dodds, and Jodi Jenson, in their 1998 co-authored article that asks, "Isn't Just Being Here Political Enough?," advocate for a distinct "action-oriented" approach in WGS that breaks the "rules" that are expected in other disciplines (1998, 333). Sandra Kirby, Lorraine Greaves, and Colleen Reid adopt, as the subtitle for their 2006 methodology textbook, "methods beyond the mainstream." Even Fonow and Cook, in their review essay on the topic of feminist methodology in a 2005 special issue of *Signs*, present an analysis that highlights distinction rather than one that questions its constructions.

A cursory examination of methods in other disciplines calls into question their alleged shortcomings. Without suggesting that sexist attitudes and behaviours have never existed in colleges and universities, there is a paucity of evidence to support assertions that methods in other disciplines ignored the specific areas that WGS methods address. Writing about the ways that graduate students in WGS are challenged by "the still-present emphasis of disciplinary training," Pamela Caughie and Jennifer Parks conceive, problematically, of disciplines as coherent and fixed entities. WGS, they argue, contrasts this fixity because it is "decidedly undisciplined insofar as it is an interdisciplinary field emerging out of challenges to traditional disciplinary knowledges and methodologies" (2009, 33). But, has it ever been the case that WGS methods were so different from methods in other disciplines? And, has it ever been the case that other disciplinary methods were premised, even partially, on shared understandings and practices? Changes in discipline specific methods that have responded to complex social and intellectual phenomena cannot be attributed solely, and/or partially, to the influence of WGS. Decades onward, these may be uncomfortable realizations about the limitations of our intellectual influence. Yet the continuity of these assertions indicates how invested we are in them as normative tales, and in their retelling.

In some instances, there are significant investments in assertions about the centrality of experience for WGS methods and their presumed political outcomes. Linda Christiansen-Ruffman contends that methodologies in the field "were designed to build from the experiences and perceptions of women in their specific context... and they were oriented towards change both within scholarship and society" (2007, 114). But, Alison Jaggar, in *Just Methods*, argues that WGS scholars still "need to develop better accounts of the relationships between experience and knowledge" (2008, 271). She argues that we have paid too little attention to analyses and translations of experiences and their meanings (2008, 269). The relevance of experience for methods has been more heavily scrutinized by those located, institutionally, outside of WGS, than those who are located within it. Claims about the necessity of WGS methods to enact social and political change require closer scrutiny. Christiansen-Ruffman contends that the political orientation of the field is necessary, and that it is, "many years later, more important than ever" (2007, 114). Political purposefulness remains amongst the most identifiable hallmarks used to distinguish these methods and their importance. Yet some scholars question the wisdom of change as a necessary crucible for these methods. In her 2004 essay, "Where We've Been and Where We're Going," Ann Braithwaite points to the lack of clarity in accounts of the women's movement as it is evoked in WGS and questions the assumed connections between (past) women's movement and (contemporary) WGS. It is this particular narrative, about political change, that led Wendy Brown to charge the field with being incoherent and to question the relationship between its overt political mission and what she regards as its elusive intellectual mission (2008, 17).

One of the questions with which I am concerned, then, is why, four decades onward, and in a very different historical moment and institutional space, this particular claim about WGS specific methods continues to be so vigorously defended by some scholars, and so hotly contested by others. Why is this claim still contentious and a frequent source of division in WGS? What exactly is at stake in these debates?

Consequences of Normative Narratives

Judith Kegan Gardiner cautions Women's and Gender Studies scholars not to be naive about early beginnings. Referring to a version of "the success story" that traces and highlights a tale of progress, she advises: "It is a story no longer to be taken naively. It needs to be historically situated and re-evaluated for its meaning for the present, for its political investments and potential dangers, including the danger of continuing with an old story when new conditions have rendered it obsolete" (2003, 410). Narratives about the political purposefulness of WGS methods bind it to a nonspecific past and circumscribe the significance of an uncritical category of "women" onto it. These narratives also establish a falsely singular and unexamined purpose: women's individual and collective advancement toward the liberal goal of equality. By defining equality as a shared goal, they also assume that WGS students and scholars will serve as its obligatory ambassadors. Often, this occurs in internships, practicums, and service-learning requirements for students, and activist and action oriented research and participation for scholars. But in doing so, these narratives also actively construct other intellectual contributions to WGS, including critiques of patriarchy, progress, linearity, liberalism, and Eurocentrism, as apolitical contributions, sometimes with a level of antagonism that David Rubin suggests is "aimed at their suppression" (2005, 249).

A significant limitation of this political imperative is that it does not enhance understandings of methods. If it is the case there are no methods that are specific to WGS, how is it possible that transformative outcomes are specific to this discipline? Rubin, in "Women's Studies, Neoliberalism and the Paradox of the 'Political,'" identifies the paradox that results from assumptions about politics as normative practice: "The quandary here is that in seeking to be political, a field such as Women's Studies can potentially reproduce practices that much of its political energy has been dedicated to critiquing, practices that establish various hierarchies and perpetuate the inequalities that they generate" (2005, 249). This paradox constricts critical analyses of WGS methods and forecloses opportunities to interrogate the bases of its assumptions.[4]

Some scholars, whose methods were once marginalized within their own disciplines, have, ironically, positioned themselves as overseers of methods in WGS. They enact this role in various ways, from narrating origin stories about "Women's Studies" and its inclusion in curricula, to the dismissal of specific theoretical perspectives as unwelcome incursions that risk unravelling utopian ideals. Overseers conveniently ignore the way that narratives, as normative practices, function as ideology and establish their own hierarchies, inequalities, and exclusions, and discipline thinking in accordance with ideological expectations. These limitations exist, despite Caughie and Parks' claim that, "Women's Studies has developed a particular awareness of structures of power and how they affect marginalized persons" (2009, 36).

Kathleen Blee, in "Contending with Disciplinarity," examines the limitations of feminist theory in WGS in ways that are easily extended to methods. As I have noted, courses in theory and methods comprise key requirements in many WGS degree programmes, but neither, Blee argues, is carefully scrutinized for its content, pedagogy, intention, or implications (2002, 179). Teaching theory and methods in WGS is heavily indebted to other disciplines for content, discussion, and debate, which may be counterproductive because it undermines its own tenuous claims: "In practical terms, the attention to traditional—and disciplinary—theories [and methods] that is required to understand the [interdisciplinary] genealogy of contemporary feminist theorizing may bolster students' understandings of disciplinary traditions at least as much as it provides a sense of the intellectual possibilities of operating outside of these tradition" (Blee 2002, 179).

Asserting WGS methods as a necessary corrective to methods in other disciplines reinforces another set of fictional narratives about methods in other disciplines as identifiable, cohesive, and bounded. As Marjorie Garber argues, methods in other disciplines certainly appear clear and straightforward to those who are positioned outside of them (2000). But methods in other disciplines may, in fact, be no clearer than methods in WGS. They appear clear because of the intellectual and institutional legitimacy that disciplines construct and claim, and which buffers them from critical interrogations, especially from amongst their own scholars. It may be assumed that the uncertainty associated with methods in WGS leads to the possibility of superficiality, but education in other discipline specific methods is only assumed to confer methodological mastery. Discipline based scholars are also unable to clearly articulate the distinctiveness of their methods. For example, Deborah Gorham, in her defense of discipline based scholarship, questions whether WGS actually "creates new methodologies for research or teaching" (1996, 60). Gorham argues that WGS is incapable of producing methods that exist elsewhere and that have been developed over "years of discussion and debates" (62). In making her case, Gorham accepts, at face value, that recognizable and unquestionable methods exist in the discipline of History, with "some degrees of accuracy and better and worse pieces of history" (61). Unfortunately, she offers no evidence to substantiate this claim. She suggests that knowledge claims are best established and challenged from within disciplines, and not from outside of them, but she cannot explain why this might be the case, if it is the case at all.

In much the same way, Brown is certain about the transparency and clarity of methods in Political Science. In her often-cited 1997 article, "The Impossibility of Women's Studies," she suggests that she has remained open to being convinced that WGS exists like any other discipline, or more specifically, that it exists like Political Science. Despite her open mindedness and (perhaps) her "limited traffic" in the program at her university, she finds no convincing evidence that it exists on comparable terms. "Where," she asks, "are the boundaries that define [Women's Studies] and differentiate it from other kinds of inquiry?" (2008, 18). Forms of inquiry must, she presumes, clearly distinguish WGS from other disciplines. But the delineation of methods as forms of inquiry in Political Science remains unclear, even to Brown. In a 2008 reprint of this article in *Women's Studies on the Edge*, she outlines the "fundamentals" of knowledge in Political Science, even while acknowledging their "fictional character" (36). Brown, however, seems at a loss to identify the forms of inquiry or the methods through which these fundamentals are acquired. She states, "[T]his is a contestable list, and it does not specify how this basic grasp is to be procured" (36). If methods, as forms of inquiry, distinguish Political Science and serve to construct even its fictional boundaries, she should surely be able to identify and name them; however, this is not the case.

What exactly are the methods specific to the disciplines of History and Political Science? If discipline specific methods exist, how can the vast differences in methods that are employed and observed within disciplines be explained? Are discipline specific methods elusive enough that even their own scholars cannot readily identify and name them? What are the specific knowledge claims that methods generate? There is far more scrutiny about the legitimacy of methods in some fields and disciplines, especially newly established ones, than there is within long established disciplines. And it seems that there is greater latitude and tolerance for employing a variety of methods within a discipline than there is tolerance for employing methods across disciplines.

It would be unfair to imply that these particular tales about WGS methods were only ever recounted in uncritical ways. They are questioned by scholars who examine the field's knowledge, knowledge claims and practices, and their implications.[5] But scholars who question narratives about WGS methods, including me, also tolerate these incomplete and flawed tellings for wholly strategic and pragmatic reasons. From within the discipline, we participate in the project of making methods in *other* disciplines appear lacking so that we can acknowledge their limitations and justify the inclusion of discipline-specific WGS methods as essential to our curricula. WGS methods are also held up to demonstrate collective resistance to disciplinary strictures, albeit resistance that Sally Kitch says mimics, curiously, the position of those who are opposed to the inclusion of WGS in colleges and universities (2002). In some locations, the language of interdisciplinarity is purposefully enacted. This can be an intentional strategy to secure the resources necessary to sustain WGS programs, including cross-listed courses, faculty members who teach in but are not appointed to the program, and student enrolments.

These shared resources support WGS, but they also solidify disciplinary hierarchies and undermine the field's ability to acquire its own resources. WGS can simultaneously establish, and disrupt, professional identities for scholars by providing an institutional location, affiliation, and identity and, at the same time, calling these into question. Under these conditions, WGS is established as a space that can help to evade, or at least delay, important questions about methods and their implications. It can become both the space where methods are produced and reproduced, and the space that lacks identifiable, discipline specific methods. As difficult as this may be to acknowledge, this may also be the case for other disciplines as well.

Possibilities of Indeterminacy

Indeterminacy and discomfort can be understood as places of possibility rather than signs of Women's Studies' dissolution.

(May 2005, 186)

Although a distinct set of methods is questionable at best, Women's and Gender Studies programs and departments continue to act as if they exist in ways that convey expectations for the discipline. Caughie notes that courses in methods are designed to teach students how to be future WGS scholars, how to occupy the professional identity of scholars, and how to distinguish themselves from other scholars (2003b). Faculty members, in their teaching and scholarship, are expected to reiterate a coherent narrative about discipline specific methods, regardless of their professional identity, and regardless of their adherence to, or rejection of, an array of beliefs and positions. These expectations require that we disavow some important possibilities, with likely detrimental consequences. For example, if we leave dominant versions about the invention of WGS methods unquestioned, we must disavow the complexities and contextual specificities of our own histories, a possibility that is almost certain to result in distortions and exclusions. If we adhere to unsubstantiated beliefs that other discipline specific methods are clear and transparent, but inherently flawed, we miss opportunities to recognize their important intellectual engagements and influences, and we limit opportunities to engage with them. If we become complacent in our certainty that WGS has methods that are distinct from, and perhaps even superior to, other disciplines, we miss out on occasions to have conversations across disciplines. Disavowing the limitations of our methods renders us oblivious to the risks they pose, including the ways they inscribe normative narratives and practices, impose intellectual and institutional rigidity, stifle creativity, and curtail bodies of knowledge and ways of exploring them. But, isn't it also possible that if WGS interrogates the specificity of its methods, other disciplines might do the same, or be required to do the same? In this scenario, of course some disciplinary-based scholars might resist, but others might be relieved to relinquish the supposed cohesiveness and certainties of their methods.

Assertions that methods partially define disciplines are not unique to WGS. Scholars from across disciplines profess to be educated in methods that are foundational to specific knowledge claims. These claims delineate divisions of labour in universities and secure credibility and legitimacy for their adherents. They construct and maintain hierarchical arrangements that connote legitimacy and security for some disciplines, often at the expense of others. WGS, if it expects to continue to generate knowledge, cannot afford to be seduced by the allure of legitimacy; rather, it must take risks. For example, it can be strengthened by advancing a position that rejects the rigidity of discipline specific methods, for itself, and for other disciplines. It can be strengthened by exposing their production and reproduction. WGS can benefit from questioning dominant narratives about its unique methods, and by retiring its now standardized origin stories as well-worn clichés. The same is also true for other disciplines. What would it mean if WGS existed as a discipline without having to stake out and claim a specific method as its own? If no discipline specific methods were required for the field, would they (could they) be required for other disciplines? How could possibilities for knowledge across disciplines be reshaped? What are the exciting intellectual possibilities?

These questions reveal some interesting ways that processes of disciplining (or constructing disciplinary boundaries) operate. Based on the premise that WGS cannot identify its own method, I proposed (in a department where I formerly taught) that Majors acquired their credit in research methods by completing undergraduate courses in the discipline most relevant to their proposed research topic. This idea was considered briefly but ultimately rejected because it limited students' exposure (which remained unquestioned as necessary) to feminism. As an act of disciplining, this decision raises the types of questions that Ann Braithwaite takes up, in this volume, about the relationship between WGS and academic feminism. Subsequently, I proposed that the term "methods" be removed from the course title. This proposal was deemed unacceptable to the university's Undergraduate Curriculum Committee, whose members argued that the identification of methods was necessary for all disciplines. Both instances point to how WGS is constituted, how other disciplines are constituted, and the ways in which unspoken assumptions and academic conventions are prioritized over critical inquiry and questioning.

I am not arguing here that there are no observable or discernable ways of conducting research or investigating scholarly topics, or even that we do away with considerations of methods altogether. Instead, I argue we should use the term "methods" more critically and question the extent to which particular methods "belong" to disciplines. Just as Claire Hemmings, in "Telling Feminist Stories," advises that feminists question rhetorical accounts of the development of Western, second wave thought (2005a), we should also question rhetorical accounts about WGS methods. This is not an entirely apolitical endeavour. A project that confirms that the discipline does not have its own methods, and that it should not have them, could still privilege some subjects of analyses and some knowledge projects over others. For example, disavowing methods for WGS, but retaining unexamined and uncritical assumptions about the significance of women and/or feminism, could still shape understandings of the field in limited and problematic ways.

The possibilities of this argument, though, merit serious further consideration. Admitting that, as scholars of WGS, we are not indebted to a particular set of ideas about methods could generate approaches and knowledge projects that have been previously unconsidered. Intellectual space to question our claims about methods could come as a relief to course instructors, including me, who struggle over what can, and should, be taught as WGS methods and in methods courses. Advancing a position of indeterminacy and discomfort requires that we think carefully about how methods function, whose purposes they serve, and the need to question their alleged distinctiveness.

Looking back, I realize now that the conversation that I had with my colleague, about the development of her graduate program, should have proceeded quite differently. Instead of concerning ourselves, as we did, with institutional structures, conventions, and expectations, we could have used our conversation to engage in generative intellectual debates. It could have been an opportunity to question some of the assumptions, knowledge claims, and practices that remain embedded in WGS curriculum. It could have been an opportunity to think through possibilities for the field. Having thought more carefully about this now, I would ask very different questions of her. I would ask her whether or not she intended to include a course in methods as part of the graduate WGS curriculum. How would the term "methods" be used, and how would it be challenged? Which practices, assumptions, and ideologies would the term "methods" reference, and which ones would it interrogate? How would these difficult discussions be problematized for WGS, and how would they be problematized beyond it? These questions and an openness to engage with them, I would suggest to her, are challenging, but essential, requirements for any graduate program in WGS and, indeed, for all of us.

Notes

1. See Braithwaite in this volume for more on this refusal of "discipline" in WGS to describe or talk about the field.
2. For example, as an increasing number of WGS PhDs are produced, concerns about their methodological "soundness" are also surfacing. These concerns are almost certainly juxtaposed against an unquestioned "soundness" of methods in other disciplines, a point I take up later in this chapter.
3. See also Jayarantre, Epstein, and Stewart 1991.
4. See Orr in this volume for a longer exploration of how the refusal to explore assumptions about "activism" actually (and ironically) shuts down the political claims of WGS.
5. See, Braithwaite et al. 2004; Hemmings 2005a; and Side 2005.

4

Pedagogy

Susanne Luhmann

We sought to achieve democratic, egalitarian, communal, empower-
ing, non-hierarchical, antiracist, antisexist, antihomophobic, and anti-
imperialist relationships in teaching and learning that would act within
the classroom as foretastes of an alternative university and, ultimately, a
better world.

(Kegan Gardiner 2002, 192)

Judith Kegan Gardiner's account, here, of the heady aspirations that
fuelled the founding of academic Women's Studies, as it was then
known in Canada and the United States, may strike contemporary readers as both wistful and ironic—perhaps even exhausting. Such a range
of affective responses stems from the joining together of the field's political commitments and its pedagogy. Conceived by many people, though
not everybody, as "the educational arm" of the women's liberation movement (Duelli-Klein 1991), early Women's and Gender Studies invested
teaching and learning with political significance.[1] Tellingly, however,
Kegan Gardiner's statement devotes far more language to describing
the political, as compared to the pedagogical, complexity of the project.

In this chapter, I reflect upon the political desires that the field of
Women's and Gender Studies (WGS) inherits from its early history,
particularly its desire to educate for social change, as pedagogical problems, or, more precisely, as a problem of learning and for the learner.

This orientation towards the complexities of learning differs significantly from the more common reduction of pedagogy to a concern for *teaching* (and its techniques). Thus this chapter will not discuss classroom strategies—a wealth of other feminist pedagogy literature already does that. Instead, I suggest that the pedagogical consideration of learning's unpredictable effects (and affects) might better enable us to understand the limits of, and give us renewed purchase on, the political possibilities in and of WGS. To think about WGS' political ambition pedagogically might prove productive for (re)locating the field in the twenty-first century.

From the beginning, WGS has asked us to think differently about education, even if it has not always lived up to its own promise. If WGS, as Marilyn Boxer, one of the field's chief chronologists, describes, was not to be just a new field of academic inquiry, but aimed to "effect transformation in individual and social consciousness" (1998, 80), then adding women and feminism to the post-secondary curriculum and integrating WGS into the university as a new field of study could only be a beginning. Teaching and learning would also need to be reinvented so as to create the transformative environments that the founders imagined WGS classrooms would be. Teaching had to become feminist, so that learning could be too.

Thus, in 1987, in her much cited article, "What Is Feminist Pedagogy?," Carolyn M. Shrewsbury proposed that feminist pedagogy be "a theory about the teaching/learning process that guides our choices of classroom practices" (6). For her and for many others since, feminist pedagogy meant *feminist teaching strategies* that matched the liberatory and emancipatory goals of the field. Here, the implicit assumption is that different (namely feminist) content and teaching practices will readily translate into different and transformative learning, learning that is feminist. This assumption, as we will see later, underestimates the complex processes at stake in learning. Indeed, the assumption was that feminist learning would follow somewhat directly from, and be the result of, feminist teaching. However, learning turned out to be a more complex intellectual, to say nothing of affective, process, the results of which cannot be presumed in advance.

In her 1990 text by the same name, Linda Briskin defined feminist pedagogy boldly as nothing less than "teaching and learning liberation."[2] The promise was that teaching in WGS would foster learning that personally empowered women and contributed to the social transformation of the world into a more (gender-) just place. To conceive of this teaching as personally and socially transformative was deeply compelling, and many of us got swept up in the momentum of that promise, which was still alive and well when I began teaching as a graduate student in 1991. Certainly, this narrative, central to most critical education discourse from the 1970s onwards, motivated many of us to be interested in education and WGS in the first place—and continues to draw many still today.

Yet, the ambition to teach liberation raises some vexing issues: What if the classroom does not feel liberatory to the teacher and/or to the students? Indeed, what do we make of students who complain of the "oppressiveness" of WGS? How do we make sense of students who refuse the emancipation WGS teaching proffers? Is this the sign of the failure of the teacher, the curriculum, the students, the institution, or of all of us? Or, perhaps more perplexing to me these days: what if students claim to have been transformed (or "personally empowered as women") by a WGS class that was neither about empowerment nor women? To ponder these dilemmas in a more fundamental way, we may ask: what is at stake when the desire for politically transformative teaching meets the complexities of learning? By way of this question, I signal that, rather than offering advice on *how to teach* social transformation, this chapter considers the difficulties at stake in *learning* aimed at social change—a topic that, I argue, continues to be badly under-theorized in much of the WGS literature. To think about the complexities of learning in the field, I have found psychoanalytically inflected work on learning most helpful. This work considers in detail the unconscious and affective dynamics at stake when we are asked to make an attachment to ideas and knowledge that asks us to reconsider ourselves and the world around us.

I approach my argument by revisiting some of the debates that have been central to the emergence of early WGS literature. In these early texts (from the 1970s and 80s), practitioners sought to revision the role of students, teachers, and relations of power in the feminist classroom. Moving through, and commenting upon, these debates, I draw out the central role identification plays in this literature. Assumptions about

processes of identification were central—and arguably still are today—
to the field. Indeed, identification with the material, as women and with
other women, and/or as feminists emerges as a requirement for what
counts as successful teaching and learning in WGS.

When Pedagogy Became Liberatory

While Shrewsbury's initial definition of feminist pedagogy as "a theory
about the teaching/learning process" (1987, 6) was useful, her subsequent reduction of the term to an evaluatory function—of whether
teaching strategies and techniques are *sufficiently* feminist—unnecessarily limited pedagogy discourse. Beyond limiting pedagogy to a question
of teaching strategies and techniques, sufficiently feminist or otherwise,
it might be more productive to consider the difficulties at stake when
students attach to new knowledge, knowledge that challenges their subjectivity. Questions of subjectivity and subject formation are central to
all learning, but perhaps nowhere more so than in WGS because the
field tends to measure its success in the ways students change their sense
of self: do they come to identify with feminism or not? A related, but
perhaps even more difficult, question to ask is: what is at stake in WGS'
aspiration for a liberatory education? Might the unintended outcomes of
this aspiration be that the kinds of conflicts and crises (which learning
in WGS necessarily entails) are too easily (mis)read as signs of failure?
To further consider this question, I first describe how the field came to
understand its work and its pedagogies as liberatory.

Elaine Showalter opined that if WGS were to be a "revolutionary
force within the university and society" (1971, vii), then its teaching
had to move beyond merely offering a critique of patriarchal or male
centred educational institutions. Instead, it needed to demonstrate new
ways of learning, which, at the same time, were to "directly speak to
women's special needs and experiences" (vii). This orientation towards
the experiential in the curriculum was at once highly productive and
visionary, and often personally compelling, but it was also, ultimately,
rather problematic for the field.

The emergence of a focus on women's experiences tied in with a larger
critique of what were termed androcentric teaching practices. Jane Gallop polemically compared the latter to pederasty, where a "greater man

penetrates a lesser man with his knowledge" (1982, 63). Gallop's polemic critically gendered what Brazilian liberation theologist Paulo Freire had criticized as "the banking model of education" (1970). Taking inspiration from the founder of the critical pedagogy movement and from his critique of teaching as mere knowledge transfer from teacher to student, critical and feminist pedagogy literature began to reflect a rethinking of the role of teachers and students.

Students were no longer to be "empty vessels" waiting to be filled with the teacher's superior knowledge, but were to become active producers of knowledge. Incorporating the consciousness raising practices of the women's movement into WGS classrooms was one way in which students became knowers. Attending to the experiences of women students certainly challenged the androcentric orientation of both mainstream curricula and the critical pedagogy movement, but as we will see in a moment, the curricular attention to "women's voices" and to experiential narratives as alternative sources of knowledge about "women's reality" had their own problems.

From the late 1980s onwards, writers such as postcolonial theorist Chandra Mohanty (1987) and, a little later, poststructuralist feminist historian Joan W. Scott (1992) spoiled "experience" as an unproblematic source for authentic knowledge about women's "reality." Mohanty critiqued the homogenization of women's "experiences," so that these were only ever narratives of women as victims or "truth tellers"—never as oppressors or beneficiaries of social inequality. She proffered a more complicated understanding of "experience" as fragmented and discontinuous, and argued for its need to be historicized and theorized with attention to specific geopolitical locations of women. Scott went even further, suggesting that subjects don't have experiences, but, rather, are constituted by them (1992). Focussed on the individual narrating experiences, cultural studies scholar Valerie Walkerdine suggested that telling experiences, reading about and learning from them, always already entails acts of interpretation (1990).

The attention to women's voices and experiences had successfully reoriented teaching. It was no longer primarily about transmission, and students were no longer just rational or passive receptors of knowledge. Yet, the substantive critiques of "experience" proffered by theorists such as Mohanty, Scott, and Walkerdine, while influential in feminist theory circles, did little to unsettle the claim to an experiential grounding of WGS pedagogy. Yet, the field's own commitment to seeing students as producers of knowledge, for example about their own lives, also opened up the possibility that students might (and do) produce knowledge that challenges what in feminist terms has come to count as "liberatory" or "empowering" in the WGS classroom. However, such knowledge is often read as wilful ignorance or resistance to knowledge. I will return to this point later and suggest a different understanding. For now it might suffice to conclude that liberating the classroom from the mere knowledge transfer between teacher and student proved highly productive, but raised complex new issues, with which we are still grappling today.

Theorizing the Feminist Teacher

If feminist education were to exceed knowledge transfer, and if students were to be active producers of knowledge, then the Women's and Gender Studies classroom also had to be liberated from the repressive (paternalistic) teacher. No longer the sole conveyor of knowledge, the feminist teacher was variously conceptualized as "facilitator," "midwife" (Belenky et al., 1986), or "birthhelper" to the knowledge produced by students. This, however, effectively silenced women instructors as their specialised scholarly expertise was regarded as being of little use for this process. Accordingly, subsequent metaphors—such as "respected role model" (Shrewsbury 1987) or "nurturing mother" (Morgan 1987), sought to reinstate teacher authority, though on different terms. These new metaphors couched the teacher-student relationship within narratives of a special bond between the woman teacher and women students, presumably grounded in a shared gender status.

These narratives reflected certain mid-80s feminist discourses that re-valued maternalism. Terms popular at the time, such as "respected role model" and "nurturing mother," today seem rather prescriptive, not just of the behaviour expected of a "good feminist" teacher (aka mother), but, also of the good feminist student (aka daughter). The latter is presumed to develop a (positive) identification with the teacher. Any attempts to transform WGS classrooms in light of the feminist commitments to mutuality, connectedness, and egalitarianism that fuelled its pioneers must grapple with complex identificatory (and disidentificatory) relations between students and teachers. If early formulations presupposed the student's respect for the teacher's maternal attention and her modeling herself after the teacher, such renderings of intergenerational relations among women left little room for the messy feelings that mark student/teacher, and, even more so, mother/daughter dyads. These formulations also ignored the ways in which many women became feminists by modelling themselves not *after*, but *against* their mothers or mother-figures—teachers. And they overlooked the possibility that becoming a feminist might just as likely be a formation fuelled by desire for, rather than identification with, the feminist teacher. At minimum, the (false) assumption was that the "feminist mothering" of the teacher would not set off intergenerational resistance in the next generation. (Astrid Henry's discussion, in this volume, on feminist "waves," sheds much light on the complexities of intergenerational dynamics among feminists.)

By the 1990s, the maternal metaphor was falling out of favour. Kathleen Martindale, for example, critiqued the nurturing model-teacher as deeply entrenched in bourgeois assumptions that pathologized more confrontational methods of mothering (and teaching) and denied the conflictual nature of learning (and parenting) altogether (1992). In light of heightened analytical and political attention to social differences (racial, sexual, class, gendered, generational, etc.) among students, the teacher increasingly became theorized as the "interrupter," as the one who interferes in unequal or discriminatory classroom relations (Lather 1991; Manicom 1992). Here, like the return of the repressed, the feminist pedagogue's open claims to authority re-emerged, now framed in terms of an "emancipator authority." This led Ellsworth to critically remark that feminist authority likes to see itself as exclusively operating in the service of the greater goal of liberation and social justice but is rarely willing to reflect upon the exclusionary or regulatory effects of its practices (1992).

If the mother-teacher metaphor is rare today, the assumption of some kind of commonality between a woman teacher and women students, while weakened, lingers. We might no longer assert that students and teachers interact simply "as women," and we certainly may notice that students may not identify as women at all. But that often vexes WGS

practitioners. Such vexation is a sign of the lingering power of a discourse of "woman identification" as a condition for WGS learning. Students of color, trans, or bio-male students were not the audience that
these early writers had in mind, nor did they anticipate male-identified
instructors in the WGS classroom. Indeed, a pedagogy premised upon
identification of (daughter) students with their teacher (mothers) makes
categorically unintelligible the sons of the "Women's (Studies) Movement"—and many of its daughters as well (Creet 1991; Noble 2006).

Theorizing Power

A central preoccupation of these early pedagogy debates was with
oppressive social structures and hierarchical classroom relations, and
how to change them. As early as 1989, however, Constance Penley
warned that "the risk of aiming toward or claiming the eradication of
power relations is that the force and pervasiveness of those power relations may be overlooked, 'out of sight, out of mind'" (138). Jennifer Gore
offered a more extensive critique of how Women's and Gender Studies pedagogy literature vacillated between, on the one hand, equating
power and authority exclusively with patriarchy and oppression (and as
something to be rejected), and on the other hand, reclaiming authority as feminist assertiveness and empowerment (1992). Underlying
both of these conceptions was a repressive model of power, according
to which—as discussed earlier—women's knowledge and voices were
understood as historically having been silenced. In this logic, to speak
and seek authority became a form of resistance and a force of subversion;
feminist power was regarded as nonrepressive, empowering, and oppositional to existing power relations. Power was condemned when put
to work for domination, but embraced when used to strengthen individuals and political opposition. Thus, dominance and repression were
always outside of feminism, while feminist power was about assertiveness, empowerment, and subversion. As Gore rightly points out, this
view cannot see the regulatory and normalizing power of feminist discourse and WGS classroom practices.

From a very different perspective, but similarly critical of an easy
dichotomy of subversive versus repressive power in (progressive) education, some WGS scholars became interested in the psychoanalytic

implications of education.[3] They considered power as not only institutionally present but also "psychically embedded in the social relations of education" (Finke 1993, 7). Rather than wanting to rid education of the powerful affective dynamics at stake in the pedagogical encounter—as if that were even possible—these theorists focused on the "interplay of desire and power among teacher and student" (Finke 1993, 8). They sought to understand the unconscious processes at stake in learning. Beyond merely asserting or shirking authority, which assumes that power is a possession, the task of the teacher, they argued, is to be mindful of unconscious dynamics, and to attend to the kinds of affective histories of learning that both students and teacher bring to the classroom.

Theorizing Identification

I have already discussed some of the ways in which experiences and identification were central to the revisioning of student-teacher relations and for students' relationships to curriculum materials. Indeed, the enthusiastic voice of an early student captured this when she claimed that "because course material addresses the experiences of women in our society, women students have to strain *not* to identify" (Rutenberg 1983, 72).

While learning involves attaching to knowledge, and while reading as learning certainly works through processes of identification, Walkerdine reminds us just how unpredictable such processes are. She argues that textual positions are "not just grafted on to a cognate and waiting subject, who can easily be changed. Rather, the positions and relations created in the text both relate to existing social and psychic struggle and provide a fantasy vehicle which inserts the reader into the text" (1990, 89). Because subject positions are not determined by the text, but are actively (though unconsciously) created by the reader/learner in complex psychic dynamics of identification and disidentification, texts do not just change the reader. If we take seriously the role of fantasy in learning, pedagogical attention necessarily must shift from what is being taught and how it is taught to the readers' or learners' responses and to the kinds of meaning students produce.

At first glance, a pedagogical orientation towards meaning as actively produced by the learner may seem reminiscent of the goals of learning in Women's and Gender Studies discussed earlier. However, the difference is that much of the early thinking about feminist pedagogy was invested in seeing existing knowledge about women as having been distorted or repressed. The assumption was that knowledge produced by women about women, as compared to knowledge produced by men about women, would more accurately reflect "the real experiences of gender," as Briskin had put it in 1990. Indeed, the very process of uncovering in the classroom, experientially, the extent of gender injustice was assumed to transform students.

Thus WGS' aspirations have historically been quite different from those of more traditional disciplines; rather than fill students with information *about* something, we practitioners have aspired that our students learn *from* the content so as to "craft and alter" (Britzman 1998) themselves—by developing feminist consciousness, becoming liberated and politically active subjects. However, measuring successful teaching and learning in these terms poses several problems. First of all, students may make meaning from the material studied that differs significantly from what the teacher wants them to understand. But even if the student learns the "right thing," this does not necessarily lead to the "right" action. Knowing about date rape, domestic violence, eating disorders etc., sadly does not mean that women will not suffer from them, as Laurie Finke (1993) has pointedly remarked. Thus knowledge in itself is not liberatory for the knower. Moreover, knowing about social injustice does not necessarily lead to an attitude of empathetic identification with those who suffer. Instead, processes of identification are inherently unstable and ambivalent; they always risk the possibility of *dis*identification, the refusal of a position that is "too saturated with injury" as Judith Butler (1993, 100) has suggested.

Alice Pitt offered a pointed critique of WGS' aspiration to contribute to social justice through students' attachment to feminist knowledge and their (trans)formation into feminist subjects when she observed that in WGS classrooms, "female students' capacity to recognize themselves as women within the terms of the course is a significant measure both of the course's success and of students' success in the course" (2003, 26). Defining successful teaching and learning in terms of "successful" feminist (and female) identification tends to conflate two different modes of identification: auto- and allo-identification (Sedgwick 1991,

62). WGS wants students to identify *as women* (or gendered beings) *with other women* who are similarly or differently socially located. Or, to put this differently: to identify with the material studied should lead to an identification as woman and feminist in the terms laid out by the curriculum, and to an identification with other, often less privileged, women.

This certainly is a prescriptive pedagogy. Under its terms, successful learning involves students prioritizing certain identities and identifications over others. It requires that students give up their identification with men, or at least make this less primary, in order to identify as and with women. Such reorientation may make critical sense for white, straight, and middle class identified students, who accrue privileged status from their heteronormative relations and alliances with men of their class and race. But the demand to identify "as women with other women" resonates differently for women who may feel more commonality (and political allegiance) with men similarly minoritized along racial, ethnic, religious, or class lines, than with the (often privileged) women they are asked to identify with. And it becomes even more complicated for female bodied, but not female identified students, and for male-identified (bio or non-bio) students.

Eve Sedgwick noted the long history of conflating identification with/as women within feminist thought and its political effectiveness. Yet, its consequence, she argued, has been that "intimate dissonances" (1991, 61) between/within one's gendered identity and one's social/ political identifications with others are lost, denigrated, and disavowed. Indeed, as I just outlined, the mythical conflation of identifying as/with women may re-inscribe normative forms of gender identity, sociality, and politics—even while WGS seeks to otherwise unsettle these.

Understanding feminist learning as identifying with/as women also informed the curriculum focus on "women's experiences" in WGS, discussed earlier. More recently, this has meant curricula that reflect women's diversity. While such diversification is preferable to all white, heterosexual, able bodied, and middle class representations, it still presumes that identifications follow neatly from social identities: i.e., black female students will recognize themselves in the images and representations of black women, or lesbian students are supposed to find their experiences validated in the curricular representations of lesbians. The assumption is that students will learn from the representations proffered because they identify with the described experiences.

Within such logic, students' refusal to identify as women with other women as set forth in the course comes to be viewed as a problem, a sign of an insufficient feminist or/and woman identity and of failed teaching and/or learning. And, I wonder, what about male students who find themselves more drawn to identify as women than with women? The crux of such identification pedagogy is that if "woman" (or, by extension, all gender) is a coercive fiction and the outcome of profoundly regulatory and disciplinary practices, as Butler pointed out over twenty years ago in *Gender Trouble* (1990), then we may want to seriously query the emancipatory potential of affirming gendered identities and making them the centre of feminist learning. Moreover, defining the goal of WGS and its pedagogical efforts along narrow identity lines also means that the field risks having no relevance to all those whose identities do not fit neatly into, or who refuse to identify accordingly with, those identity lines, including, but not limited to: effeminate men, women racialized as non-white, transfolk, and so on. An even more serious consequence of such mandatory identification pedagogy is that despite its strong moral commitment to "diversity" and intersectional analyses, WGS programs are often not successful in attracting (and retaining) scholars and students whose identities are most painfully marked by intersecting vectors of power.

Thus, I do think that students' disidentification, be it against feminism and/or WGS, or the identities on offer, or, their refusal to identify *properly* (as set forth by the feminist curriculum) can tell us something about the complex process that is learning (that is, if we understand learning as exceeding the realms of both the sociological and of consciousness). While learning certainly works through identification, as Walkerdine and others cited earlier suggest, we may also want to consider Sedgwick's contention that identification is "fraught with intensities of incorporation, diminishment, inflation, threat, loss, reparation and disavowal" (1991, 62). Thus refusing identity and identification may be a sign of resistance to the regulatory regime that WGS teaching can be implicated in.

In the mid to late 1990s, a body of feminist theorizing further foregrounded the aggressive underbelly of processes of identification.

Exploring the (psychic) harming of the object of one's identification, this literature pointed to the appropriative, violent, and narcissistic elements of identification, wherein the other variously becomes an extension of the self, is resented, and/or disavowed.[4] Diana Fuss concluded that, psychoanalytically speaking, identification involves "a degree of symbolic violence" (1995, 9) and posed a question that seems critically relevant to WGS' pedagogical efforts, namely "how can the other be brought into the domain of knowledge without annihilating the other as other...?" (4).

While earlier feminist theory posed identification as/with women as a solution and the road to feminist empowerment, in the 1990s, the above mentioned theorists cautioned against the colonizing, aggressive, and potentially destructive impulse in identification. Identification with another, they argued, is not necessarily benevolent. Instead, proclaiming identification may involve the disavowal of the other in the name of empathy. Accordingly, we must ask: is identification truly an outcome that feminist learning in WGS should aspire to? The feminist theorists cited above certainly spoil, or make more complex, identification as a viable political (and pedagogical) strategy for social change. On the other hand, while identification cannot be demanded, it can also not be avoided. If we believe Hélène Cixous, then "one never reads except by identification" (cited in Diamond 1992, 390). Similarly, one also never learns without identification. So where does that leave us?

Pedagogy of/as Affect?

I suggest that pedagogical thinking requires close attention to the complexities involved in learning, understood now as attaching to knowledge. And attachment learning is not only a cognitive and rational process, but also an emotional and erotic moment, which involves *fantasy*. One such fantasy may be that feminist knowledge is liberatory. Another, quite common fantasy, is the fear of being destroyed by feminist knowledge. We encounter both in the classroom.

Affects such as love and hate are central to learning according to psychoanalytic theory. Psychoanalysis calls the attachment of the student to the teacher or the material "transference." Shoshana Felman has argued that the student must authorize the teacher (though it can also be a text or an idea), and she or he does so by way of the fantasy that the teacher knows (1987). Psychoanalysis considers this attachment a form of love.

If learning is indeed conditioned on loving the subject who is presumed to know, then the question arises under what conditions such transference does or does not occur. For Women's and Gender Studies pedagogues, obstacles to learning are often described as being of a social nature: a repressive institution, insufficient curricular representations, a patriarchal knowledge culture that silences women's voices, experiences, feminist critiques, and so on. These external conditions are understood to prevent certain forms of learning. And, identification, as a response against those external forces, was presumed to be based upon sameness or similarity as women. But the inner psyche—affects such as love and hate—and their histories, also affect how students attach to knowledge. This is not to deny that cultural conditions may play a role in who is presumed to know and who is not: for example, are women culturally recognizable as knowers? It is widely acknowledged that students have quite different expectations of their male and female professors. Similarly, racialized women, young women, women with disabilities, effeminate men, masculine women, and visibly queer and transfolks may not be presumed by students to know anything of relevance. (Though, the opposite may also be true.) Certainly, to reduce transference entirely to identity categories would be simplistic. But to not consider the force of social differences in processes of transference would be naïve.

The fundamental difference between the early feminist pedagogy literature and a psychoanalytically informed approach lies in how each thinks about learning and about what learning does to students. WGS pedagogy literature has largely been invested in positing feminist education as empowering and affirming of the (female) self. Psychoanalytically informed feminist approaches to education are much more cautionary; they see learning as potentially threatening to the self. In the remainder of this article, I linger a little more on this understanding of learning as threat.

Knowledge as Crisis

Psychoanalytically speaking, knowledge poses a threat to the self. Learning potentially entails being disturbed by knowledge in two different ways: if the student falls in love with the knowledge that the feminist teacher and the feminist curriculum represent, s/he may fear being lost in the process; and/or, the knowledge produced in the feminist classroom may threaten to shatter the student's established sense of self. Both disturbances may result in repression and resistance to learning. But this means that student refusal and resistance to WGS may indicate not (or not always) a too small, but rather a too large, attachment. Resistance may be a form of self-preservation, of protecting the self from (what may feel like an unbearable) disturbance. The "I do not want to know" may actually mean "I cannot bear to know," because the implications feel too overwhelming. The claim that learning in the field is "empowering" to students does not adequately prepare students—and teachers—for the challenging experience, the tug and pull, that learning about and from the field represents.

But to think of learning in WGS in terms of transference—or love—may also encourage us to reconsider those students (and teachers too) who wholeheartedly embrace the knowledge being offered, who "love" WGS just a little too much. Such an embrace may seem to be a validation of the field and of the teacher, as well as evidence of the "empowering" effects of our teaching. But at stake in this "love" might actually be disavowal.

Moreover, if we want to avoid indoctrinating students who then merely parrot the loved subject—as much as processes of imitation may be an important step in learning, feel personally confirming for the teacher, and seem like successful recruitment into the discipline—eventually, this "love" needs to be resolved. If WGS is to do what it claims already to be doing, namely producing critical and independent thinking, then students must move from loving and imitating the teacher or the text to loving the processes of thinking and learning instead.

The challenge is to resolve the illusion of knowledge, which the teacher represents. That is no small feat, but it is an important one if we do not want our graduates to turn away from WGS knowledge after graduation, because it turns out to be failing to give them all the answers. For transference to be resolved—assuming for a moment that this is even possible—the binary between teacher and student needs to be dissolved. The student needs to grapple with the limits of knowledge, her/his own, the teacher's, and feminism's.

The dissolution of transference may actually pose the biggest challenge to WGS teaching, both for the teacher as well as for the student.
The challenge for the teacher is to forgo embodying the "imaginary illusion" of being the subject of knowledge.[5] In so doing, the teacher must
forgo the narcissistic pleasure derived from gaining authority, tradition-
ally denied to her and to feminist knowledge. Such dissolution of transference also means the end of students' identification with the teacher.
The teacher is no longer the students' idealized role model. Students
finding their own voices seem to confirm a central WGS goal. But as
Finke reminds us, a successful end to transference might mean that the
student does not identify any longer with the teacher's political vision
and commitment (1993). And this might actually feel like pedagogical
(and political) failure, especially in a context where feminist conversion
and consensus count as the litmus test for successful teaching in WGS.

Furthermore, and this may be the most difficult knowledge for the
field and for us practitioners to bear, it may also require of the teacher
to accept that feminism and WGS offer no final answers, only more
questions, and that students need to chart their own way through their
attachments to feminism.[6] The successful resolution of transferential
relations between students and teachers (and feminist knowledge) might
be worth it, though, considering the dire effects of unresolved transferential demands, such as feelings of betrayal and grief, so common in
intense (and unresolved) teacher/student relations and in attachments
to (and subsequent detachments from) the feminisms WGS represents.

Conclusions: Or, More New Questions?

I began this chapter with the wistful narration of feminist teaching's
political ambition, which fuelled the founding of Women's and Gender
Studies and produced the energy required to establish and maintain the
field, often against intense institutional and public hostilities. Throughout the chapter, I described some of the ways that the WGS pedagogy
literature has sought to rethink relations among teachers, students, and
the material to bring to life its vision of a transformed and egalitarian
classroom. Certainly, WGS teaching must be credited with enormous
visionary zeal and creativity.

Yet, as the field matures in the twenty-first century, it seems a good time to take a closer look at the field's own transferences—for example, that its teaching is liberatory—and to acknowledge the complexities at stake in its political pedagogy. This involves, as I argue throughout, paying attention to the (unconscious) identifications, their appropriative and assimilative dynamics, and the crises at stake in learning, particularly learning about/for social injustice. We may also want to rethink what counts as successful teaching and learning in WGS, now no longer defined, or not exclusively, in terms of students' "successful identifications." In the face of the categorical instability of the term "woman" and its regulatory function, it becomes increasingly politically and intellectually unintelligible to assume that WGS is about women, or that we know what "women" are. Similarly, if WGS were no longer, or at least not primarily, about producing women who identify as feminists, what then? Posing this may feel rather dangerous to the kind of collective politics that the field has understood itself to be participating in. But, letting go might open up the field, and our teaching, to entirely new and exciting questions, questions for which we don't have answers yet.

Notes

1. The origin of this long-standing albeit controversial mandate for WGS is somewhat murky. Roberta Salper (1971) argued that Women's Studies, "like Third World Studies, is the academic arm of a broader movement" (cited in Elaine Showalter 1971, iii). Linda Gordon speaks of Women's Studies as "the academic wing" (1975, 566). This view of the field was not shared by all as some sought to establish a new and legitimate academic discipline, while others wanted to be a "revolutionary force within the university and society" (Showalter 1971, vii). See also Boxer (1988).
2. See also Weiler 1991 and Welch 1994, 2006.
3. See also Finke 1993, Penley 1989, and Pitt 1996, 2003.
4. See Butler 1993, Diamond 1992, and Pellegrini 1996.
5. To my knowledge, the teacher's transferential relations with her students, or the desire to be loved, with the exception of Gallop's (1995) edited collection, have remained largely unaddressed in the radical and feminist pedagogy literature.
6. As Maparyan reminds us in this volume, however, "feminism" as the center of Women's and Gender Studies is itself a problematic notion—and one in need of further questioning.

Foundational Assumptions

Points to Ponder

1. What are some other ways in which "Feminism," "Interdisciplinarity," "Methods," and "Pedagogy" are evident in the everyday talk of WGS? What assumptions about the field do they point to? Given the arguments of these chapters, how might those be challenged—and changed?
2. How might Luhmann's complication of "Pedagogy" as (feminist) liberation converse with Maparyan's idea that WGS might organize itself around a "liberatory impulse" rather than an ideological rendering of feminism?
3. Does the "ignorance" associated with Lichtenstein's reading of "Interdisciplinarity" and the "anxiety" associated with Side's reading of "Methods" shape a WGS curriculum that undergirds the primacy (and thereby power) of more traditional disciplines? Why or why not?

PART 2
UBIQUITOUS DESCRIPTIONS

This section brings together key terms that have come to dominate how we in Women's and Gender Studies (WGS) describe ourselves, especially in relation to others. "Activism," "Waves," "Besiegement," and "Community" point to narratives that are central to how the field consistently positions itself both historically and institutionally. For example, we may (and do) debate what counts as activism or whether and how it is and isn't recognized as part of our work in the university, but we don't usually question its role in establishing a unique identity for the field compared to other disciplines. Likewise, we may discuss where a wave begins and ends or even who and what gets included, but we rarely challenge the concept itself as a useful one for talking about differences in generations or historical moments in WGS.

The authors of these chapters argue that there are costs or consequences to how particular versions of these concepts have become acceptable while alternatives have not. How does the activist mandate actually work against the political engagement of WGS in the world outside of its disciplinary borders? What narratives of the field's historical foundations does the wave metaphor reinforce and which ones does it push aside? What understandings of the field's institutionalizaton and position in the academy, to say nothing of its intellectual work, does the besiegement narrative foster? How do the expectations of community— both within and outside of WGS—denigrate the work that WGS practitioners actually do?

As the authors in this section indicate, these are all narratives of the field that have an interlocking relationship with terms unpacked in other sections. Saying that we are described by our (unique to us) activism means that we often haven't looked closely at other ways in which our institutional presence is defined, or at how this term might buttress particular versions of "feminism" over others. Describing the field's past and present through such a well-known concept as waves means that we often don't think clearly enough about the role that "history" does, and, especially, does not, play in our self-descriptions or in our intellectual work. Similarly, telling a story about the field's constant besiegement, whether from outside the university or from other locations within it, has too often allowed us to make assumptions about ourselves as a community and then to overlook some uncomfortable questions about the "institutionalization" of WGS in academe and the complexities of differences within WGS, as outlined by terms such as "identity (politics)," "intersectionality," and "trans." What the authors for all of these terms are taking up are the ways in which, again, what we have assumed are common sense understandings of these terms might actually limit the types of questions we ask and, thus, other ways of thinking about (and doing) WGS.

5
ACTIVISM

Catherine M. Orr

Upon my first encounter with Women's and Gender Studies (WGS), the discipline appealed to my desire to see social justice done. It invited me to *do* something, be politically active, and embrace the revolutionary mandates of the movements from which it emerged. Becoming credentialed in WGS, I thought at the time, would in some measure both legitimize and brand my nascent activism as sufficiently "radical" and enhance my abilities to make the world a better place. And while wading further into WGS meant learning theories, reconstructing histories, and debating perspectives on power, privilege, and identity formation that provided me with a number of intellectually euphoric moments, I was not feeling like what I was doing actually met that revolutionary mandate. Rather, my social justice work seemed transformed into an object of analysis to be considered from a distance.

Despair, feelings of failure, and a well-received dissertation followed. What did not follow, I confess here, was any deeper understanding of the existential features, behavioral characteristics, comparative effects, or definitional constraints of something called "activism" in WGS. The best I could do was to claim to know it when I saw it, and follow up with a series of assertions, authors, citations, and it-feels-so-true declarations about activism's centrality to the discipline. This approach held up through a number of publications and a successful tenure application. All this is to say that when I speak of an absence of analysis or a lack of interrogation on the part of others, it is not from the position of one who has always known better. Rather, I am speaking of the discipline along with a WGS career I call my own.

Like others in this volume, I seek to uncover how a key term functions to both open up and foreclose certain kinds of knowledges and understandings about our own identities, investments, and research agendas in WGS. As such, a quick account of the ways in which activism has been mobilized by various WGS scholars will reveal both similarities to other chapters on "community," "feminism," and "history" as well as some unique historical and rhetorical features. However, I also seek to make the case for the *political* value of excavating what cultural studies scholar John Mowitt calls "antidisciplinary objects." Such objects foment crisis in disciplinary contexts by raising profane questions about our most sacred—in an ideological sense—terms. In short, I offer up the productive potentials of crisis as intellectually necessary for what WGS claims as fundamental.

Mapping the Absences

Any cursory survey of how activism has been conceptualized within Women's and Gender Studies immediately reveals a number of problems. First, activism is rarely, if ever, defined, let alone qualified for content or approaches unique to WGS.[1] Rather than delimiting and/or analyzing the term in the field's discourses, activism's presence and subsequent importance are frequently asserted along chains of signification that include recurring elements: public demonstration, articulating grievances, often against some state policy or protocol, on behalf of gendered/sexualized/raced subjects, who are innocents or victims and thus circumscribed as the authentic—read: "real"—objects of WGS's analysis. A recent special issue of *Women's Studies Quarterly* titled "Activisms" makes the point. The cover art features (in the words of the artist) "images ... of women in states of extremity: in the process of being arrested, moments before, during, and after confrontations with the police; women outside the domestic sphere, in public, speaking and demonstrating" (Rothenberg 2011). Yet in terms of content, the editors can only seem to point to the current "dazzling multiplicity of acts and actions" and the "profusion of projects" (Katz and Miller 2007, 10) as opposed to any review of past scholarship on activism in need of reread-ing or rethinking.

Variations on this theme of public protest have proliferated over the years since the field's inception and include, if not most recently then certainly most publicly, the critique of Judith Butler by Martha Nuss-baum in *The New Republic*, titled "The Professor of Parody." In it, Nuss-baum stresses her disagreement with Butler in *moral* terms by dividing feminist academics into two camps: those whose work in the academy is done in service to women outside of it and those complicit in "the vir-tually complete turning from the material side of life, toward a type of verbal and symbolic politics that makes only the flimsiest of connections with the real situation of real women" (1999, 38). In eschewing what Nussbaum considers to be the moral imperative of academic feminism writ large, Butler, in Nussbaum's terms, "collaborate[s] with evil" (1999, 45). For Nussbaum, "real" women are more "practical" in their femi-nist orientations, with an unnamed and dislocated group of academic feminists from India standing in as those who, unlike Butler's devotees, "have thrown themselves into practical struggles, and feminist theoriz-ing which is closely tethered to practical commitments such as female literacy, the reform of unequal land laws, changes in rape law" (1999, 38).

When activism is the focus of analysis in WGS contexts, the issue under scrutiny is almost always about activism's demise at the hands of academic excesses.[2] In other words, activism is that which WGS is not doing (but should be)—a sort of definition of the field in the negative. And this position of the negative has a tremendous amount of disciplin-ing power even as the term itself goes uninterrogated.

Without an affirmative definition or clear limits—but most assuredly with high moral stakes—activism is frequently mobilized in a man-ner that speaks to its centrality in WGS at the same time as it lacks coherence. Almost *anything* can be activism. Some examples include psychologist Jayne Stake's survey work on undergraduate WGS courses. Through a number of survey instruments, Stake seeks to document both the enthusiasm for and lasting impact of "activism" for WGS students. For her, activism constitutes everything from "[keeping] informed of women's rights issues" and "talk[ing] with others to influence their atti-tude" to "attend[ing] a meeting for women's rights" and "contribut[ing] time to a women's rights cause" (2007, 49).

But as the research contexts shift, so too does that which activism comes to represent. In her pioneering work, *Black Feminist Thought*, sociologist Patricia Hill Collins offers a set of conceptualizations of activism that are very different from Stake's. Collins argues that the various forms of ideological resistance performed by African American women from slavery to present day constitute "Black Women's activist tradition" (1990, 139). She uses the story of domestic workers to illustrate her point: "Sara Brooks is not typically seen as a political activist. Her long hours as a domestic worker left her little time to participate in unions, community groups, demonstrations, or other forms of organized political activity" (1990, 139). For Collins, then, the struggle to survive is a political act, and thus "activism" for generations of African American women has been just about everything they do to maintain the health and well-being of themselves and their families.

My point is not to quibble with either Stake's or Collins's notion of activism as it applies to their research agendas. Rather, I am attempting to call attention to the endless elasticity of a term that nevertheless serves for so many in WGS as that which the field has and should continue to embrace as its *raison d'être*.

Yet, Collins's attempts to articulate meanings of "activism" in African American communities over time provoke questions about still more absences in WGS scholarship, specifically *historical* absences. Which "pasts"—in the way Wendy Kolmar speaks to them in this volume's "History" chapter—of activism are called up to support disciplinary coherence and which are orphaned or outside the stories we tell? What is the history of activism in WGS? Here especially I think the obviousness of the question can be deceiving. The origin stories of those early WGS programs and departments that began in the 1970s and early 1980s, not to mention the personal narratives of those who populated them, are, not surprisingly, replete with references to second wave activism. It is this history that is called upon to ground activism's foundational status within the discipline and informs frequent calls for WGS to rededicate itself to this activity.[3] Yet even this historical activism is not investigated, theorized, or in any way evaluated to make sense of its relationship to the discipline. This historical activism, nevertheless, is mobilized to great nostalgic effect for WGS practitioners.

Drawing from Katie King's work on "origin stories" and the role of "magical signs," Ann Braithwaite argues that for many in the WGS founding generation, "'the women's movement' comes to act … as a new magical sign, a new place of condensation, displacement and reduction" (2004, 105). Rather than analyzing the relationship between WGS and what each author experienced (or did *not* experience) as "The Women's Movement," most of the early founders of WGS programs assume, through narrative form, a kind of automatic intersection of the two. The problem here is that the version of WGS that emerges is one that is circumscribed as *the* authentic WGS and one that, by definition, subsequent generations cannot experience. This WGS of the past—the "real" WGS—thereby becomes that which is always already lost to this generation. Nostalgia indeed![4]

One final attribute circulated in the discipline's narratives about activism references its uniqueness. Without promoting and engaging in activism on behalf of oppressed peoples, the argument goes, WGS would be like any other discipline that simply produces knowledge for knowledge's sake. English and WGS scholar, Marjorie Pryse, puts it directly: "What has differentiated Women's Studies from other disciplines since its beginning in the 1970s is the interconnection between academics and activism" (2000, 112). Using the National Women's Studies Association's organizational structure and conference programming as a model for this interconnection, Pryse argues for a forging of methodologies that, like activism, are unique to WGS.

In fact, during my time as National Conference Chair for NWSA (2006–08), the relatively low number of "activists" in the conference program was a perennial lament in conference evaluations and among some board members. As I discerned over the years, the assumptions behind such comments include: (1) one cannot be an activist if one identifies as an academic; (2) when nonacademic activists are not present, it is because of WGS academic excesses (e.g., specialized language, assumptions that conference attendees hold the historical/theoretical knowledges core to WGS training) as opposed to the myriad of reasons nonacademic activists might have for spending their limited time and resources elsewhere; and (3) WGS is not legitimate if nonacademic activists are not present.

My attempt here thus far has been to briefly trace the extent to which WGS has demurred in defining, delimiting, or in any way offering a sustained interrogation of a term that is arguably foundational to the discipline's understanding of itself. Even so, this ill-defined, endlessly-elastic term is used in punitive ways to chastise the WGS practitioners whose scholarly projects or theoretical orientations stray too far from the practical—and thereby political (following Nussbaum)—applications that activism is said to represent.

Analyzing the Functions of Activism: Sacred Objects and the "Real World"

In his book *Text: The Genealogy of an Antidisciplinary Object*, John Mowitt (1992) takes up Michel Foucault's (1975) treatise on the exercise of disciplinary power. As a specific formation of disciplinary power, Mowitt argues, academic disciplines do not merely constitute the objects they claim to study (say, "culture" or "the past") but the subjects that claim an identity under their sign (say, "anthropologist" or "historian," respectively). Disciplinary power, in other words, produces things, including subjects' understanding of their own agency to act within particular domains ("feminist academic" in the larger academy, for example). One of the implications of this basic idea for Mowitt is that rather than toiling away in isolation (à la "the ivory tower") from the rest of society and its fundamental social arrangements, vis-à-vis the state, education, economy, and so forth, academic knowledge production actually *reflects* and takes place within these larger formations of institutional power. This means that our understandings of disciplinary practices are located within larger cultural and institutional environments and, therefore, any analysis of academic disciplines and their objects of analysis must move beyond either the shaming and blaming of individual academics or the confessions of personal failure for not being, say, "more relevant." As such, Mowitt is taking aim at that tired trope of the academic-"real world" divide.

From this broader insight about disciplinary power, Mowitt then traces the ways in which academic disciplines' frameworks, social contexts, and activities *displace* their object of analysis as part of the same dynamic that marks the disciplinary object's *formation*. Commenting on a number of insights from philosopher René Girard's essay, "From Mimetic Desire to Monstrous Double," about the sacred roles of objects, Mowitt extrapolates a series of claims about relations between disciplinary objects and their subjects, "a process which [for Girard] is predicated upon [the object's] initial displacement and its subsequent misrecognition." Mowitt continues: "what is crucial here is that we recognize that disciplines cannot know what they claim to know, and what substitutes for this lack of knowledge is a bureaucratically articulated policing of fidelity" (1992, 40). In other words, as disciplines form from newly "discovered" or emerging objects of analysis, other kinds of disciplinary activities begin to take over. This paradoxical dynamic, which is at the heart of what he refers to as "disciplinary reason," provides a rather stable set of relations between knowers and the objects they claim to know about. Put another way, what keeps "us" together in a discipline like Women's and Gender Studies is not a common knowledge of the objects around which we organize ourselves (such as activism), but rather the social and institutional formations that result from our surveillance of those objects' "proper" uses by our fellow disciplinary practitioners.

At this point, I want to highlight the language of "sacred objects," the "disciples" those objects produce, and the "policing of fidelity" that occurs within disciplinary contexts. This overlay of religiosity onto academic practices provides especially valuable insights into the punitive uses of activism along with its general lack of interrogation in WGS. In particular, I am thinking about how activism is cast in positive *moral* terms to "call out" WGS practitioners who are said to not directly engage in activism vis-à-vis their scholarship or whose work does not have an immediate and practical application to an activist community outside of the discipline. Ultimately, I don't think this is just about intellectual disagreements, political divides, or even subtler distinctions between strategy and tactics. Rather, as I hear the evocations of activism in WGS narratives, I sense a *ritual* practice, an exercise that, to be sure, expresses and reinforces particular values among members of our community, but does not easily lend itself to reflections about the practice by those members engaging in it. In other words, if activism is a "sacred object" within the field, it means that we evoke it repeatedly but in a manner that leads to the "displacement and subsequent misrecognition" that Girard speaks to. Yet this doesn't necessarily get us to the question of function in the sense that it still doesn't reveal how such displacement is achieved in all this talk about activism. For example, how can all of those early program founders' memoirs that evoke an activist ethos as a foundation of an indispensible component to the discipline at the same time constantly avoid any analysis of it?

In her book, *Ritual Theory, Ritual Practice*, religious studies scholar Catherine Bell speaks to the basic dynamics at work in this kind of ritu-alization within community-based narratives. These dynamics include a "construction of schemes of binary oppositions, … the orchestrated hierarchization of these schemes, … [and] the generation of a loosely integrated whole in which each element 'defers' to another in an end-lessly circular chain of reference" (1992, 101). In other words, ritual-ized narratives reify certain dualistic meanings that circulate within a community and, in turn, suspend any examination of those mean-ings by referencing yet another set of binary terms. Thus, the power of the narratives about activism in WGS draws on specific sets of terms that resonate throughout the field's complicated and multifaceted his-tory—practice/theory, political/intellectual, practical/esoteric, modern/postmodern, materialist/poststructuralist, town/gown, and, of course, activist/academic—and are then coordinated through various discur-sive locations. The result is a kind of mutually-reinforcing and reductive coherence that, as Bell claims, "simultaneously facilitates the emergence of some symbolic terms in a dominant relation to others … [and creates a] sense of general identity of the whole [that] naturalizes such hege-mony. This," she contends, "is the heart of the not-seeing, the oversight, of ritualization" (1992, 104).

If "activism" is a symbolic term that stands in a dominant relation to other terms in WGS through ritualized practice, then the lack of intel-lectual interrogation begins to make sense. Insofar as activism is a term that dominates the field's sense of its own identity and distinguishes it from other disciplines, the term itself is simultaneously and necessarily absent—or displaced—as an object of the field's analysis. As a disciplin-ary artifact, it becomes not just untouchable but, in almost every sense, un-seeable. But this then begs the question: What is it about activism that is "not see[n]?"

Before I respond to this provocation, I want to return to Mowitt for just a moment to establish some grounds for further argument. After all, Mowitt is not taking pains to explicate the dynamics of disciplinary reason simply to declare our inability to see our way out of it (and, by implication, neither am I). Rather he is most interested in how some disciplinary objects take on what he refers to as "antidisciplinary" functions. An "antidisciplinary object," among other things, is characterized as that which by its very inclusion within the discipline provokes instability and uncertainty within that discipline. He argues that "[w]hat is distinctive about an antidisciplinary object … is its aim to institutionalize a form of inclusivity that actually encourages curricula to undergo legitimation crises—and not simply at the local level of a particular institution, but at the level of the borders that distinguish the local from the global" (1992, 220). In other words, while an antidisciplinary object constantly and frustratingly escapes, or even confounds, our disciplinary reason, it simultaneously offers us an opportunity to "think otherwise"[5] about how our activities as scholars (the local) can link up with the larger social world (the global) we desire to transform. Antidisciplinary objects offer paths to rethink the ritually codified binaries such as the ivory tower and the real world or academic and activist.

Registering the Effects of "Activism" for Women's and Gender Studies

In her extensively sourced history of U.S. Women's and Gender Studies, *When Women Ask the Questions*, Marilyn Jacoby Boxer (1998b) traces the tensions and anxious debates around activism—in particular, its loss—in an increasingly institutionalized Women's and Gender Studies. Two sections, "Academics *versus* Activism" and "Academics *and* Activism" (emphasis in original), summarize the basic debate she takes up. Despite the primacy of "academics" in the section titles, however, it is quite clear given the authors and texts Boxer cites that one can privilege activism *over* academics or one can practice activism *along with* academics, but activism must always be primary. She cites only one dissenting source on this matter: feminist anthropologist Judith Shapiro who in 1981 spoke rather unequivocally of the "danger" of activism's primacy in WGS, highlighting, "the limits it places on intellectual inquiry... [as well as the] implication that our activities as social, moral, and political beings are dependent on what we are able to discover in our scientific research." She argued further that "[l]oosening the tie would have liberating consequences ... [for scholarship] and for feminism as a social movement" (in Boxer 1998b, 174). As Boxer notes, Shapiro's statement to publicly call for WGS practitioners to decenter activism's place in the discipline was "a rare act" (1998b, 174), and certainly such calls have remained rare. But echoes of Shapiro have begun to mount in the past decade or so.

For example, Wendy Brown's (in)famous 1997 essay, "The Impossibility of Women's Studies," makes a sustained and influential contribution in that it calls attention to a number of negative effects that accrue to a discipline organized around the emancipation of a single identity category, women, through *political* struggle. Brown notes that while WGS was at one point politically and intellectually vibrant, it now "may be politically and theoretically incoherent, as well as tacitly conservative" (2008, 21). More than just the march of time or the influence of external circumstance, Brown attributes what she sees as WGS's lack of vibrancy to its insistence that it is a "political project." By "privileging the political over the intellectual and ... by effectively conceding that these operate on separate planes," she argues, we "affirm the status of Women's Studies as something distinct from the rest of the university's intellectual mission for research and teaching" (2008, 33). What distinguishes WGS is, to Brown, exactly what will be the discipline's unmaking in the eyes of the larger academic community.

While not evoking impossibilities, "The Past in Our Present: Theorizing the Activist Project of Women's Studies," Bonnie Zimmerman's (2002) essay raises still other questions about the goals of maintaining activism's centrality in the field. She notes that the twenty-first century manifestation of the field's early activism is often comprised of degree requirements for acts of volunteerism, service learning, and civic engagement projects in the nonprofit world. She wonders about the outcomes of an activist zeal that is channeled into battered women's shelters and rape crisis centers: "the emphasis within Women's Studies on volunteer activities, whether in the public sector or in the nonprofit agencies that employ so many of our graduates, may actually reinforce current power structures and relations by taking on some of the work that used to be considered the responsibility of the state" (2002, 188). In other words, Zimmerman, like Brown, sees a political conservatism that results from the discipline's attempt to maintain its activist orientation as central, but her concern is not so much the primacy afforded activism within the field but its misapplication in the current undergraduate curriculum of so many WGS programs and departments.

Also in 2002, Wiegman begins her article, "Academic Feminism Against Itself," with a similar assertion that a desire to form a disciplinary mandate around activism is, itself, an impossibility. But she goes further than Brown or Zimmerman by contending that an emphasis on activism—more than dooming the discipline's status in the academy or smoothing over impulses to protest a lack of state responsibility—actually limits the potential of WGS to operate on *either* an academic *or* an activist register:

> I question the assumption that the political future of Women's Studies as a field can be guaranteed by repairing the distinction between academic institutionalization and feminism as a world changing social force. Indeed, I worry more about the implications for Women's Studies of refusing altogether the distinction between the academy and activism than about the difficulty of repairing the distinction between them. (2002a, 18)

In other words, Wiegman is troubled by conflating WGS's academic aspirations with an activist mandate because *as a disciplinary imperative*, allegiance to activism offers no guarantees when it comes to quelling the anxieties brought about by feminism's institutionalization in the academy, nor does it necessarily prove to be counter hegemonic in its effects, a point convincingly echoed in Aimee Carrillo Rowe's "Institutionalization" chapter in this volume.

It is actually the discipline's desire to engage in political protest that suffers at the hands of activism's primacy. Wiegman argues that calls to recenter WGS around an activist mandate produce the compulsion to focus our disciplinary energies on what she calls "the live subject." This live subject is the idealized "other," an oppositional construct "whose self consciousness, political agency, and distance from academic professional culture functions both representationally and epistemologically as *the* privileged political link between academic knowledge production and the goals and effect of social movement" (Wiegman 2002a, 26). Following this logic, then, WGS, as an activist project, is executed in the name of those who are "respresentationally and epistemologically" *not* WGS.

We can see in Wiegman's assertion of the live subject as manifestation of activism yet another disciplinary artifact that, according to Bell's formulation of dualisms, is part of that "loosely integrated whole in which each element 'defers' to another in an endlessly circular chain of reference" (1992, 101). In addition, this rendering of the live subject echoes Mowitt's earlier discussion about (disciplinary) objects and the subject identities they produce. Wiegman puts it this way: "To the extent that the practitioner of Women's Studies encounters a demand to produce this object of study [the live subject]—because it is the object that functions as the authentic and authenticating source for feminism's present political commitment—*the practitioner must be understood as the object's disciplinary effect*" (emphasis hers) (2002a, 30). Thus, it is the object we in WGS claim, make sacred, and subsequently displace, that in turn disciplines us; it is the object that becomes the source of, not the salvation from, the limitations of the present moment.

Ultimately, I think this conclusion means that we need to rethink the *political* project of WGS within a framework beyond that of the university itself. Activism's lack of definition and interrogation means that the discipline becomes vulnerable to complicity with other kinds of political agendas. As we police one another's activist credentials or use activism to claim disciplinary uniqueness or to stave off anxieties about a particular narrative of institutionalization in the academy, we are not seeing the political effects (or lack of effects) our ritualized narrative seems to promise. The key locations we should be considering, I think, are not just a social movement (which may or may not be operating) outside the academy and the institutionalization of that movement within it, but about local versus global contexts as sites where WGS becomes meaningful and indeed politically *useful*. By seeing WGS as that which must be an activist project with immediate and tangible impact on "real" women's lives, as opposed to a strategic intellectual one that might better see and account for its complicities with agendas far beyond university politics, we may very well be not only "selling out," but doing so on a much grander scale than we realized.

To recount, the primary problem with activism as a foundational disciplinary artifact in WGS is not its lack of definition, delimitations, or historical grounding. That much, as Mowitt tells us, is merely an effect of disciplinary reason, and therefore should be regarded as symptom rather than as cause. Instead, the primary problem is that a disciplinary mandate centered on activism disciplines WGS practitioners in a way that limits our focus to a narrow set of intellectual *and* political engagements that might otherwise be contemplated and strategized. What substitutes for a less-bounded, open, un-inhibited contemplation and strategizing within the discipline, to use Mowitt's words, is "bureaucratically articulated policing of fidelity" (1992, 40). Put another way, activism's centrality in narratives about WGS's unique contributions or moral imperatives cuts off important questions that might otherwise be raised about everything from the nature and extent of our activist pasts to the ways we might want to articulate both the boundaries and frontiers of our intellectual and political engagements in the present to, most importantly for me, how we might imagine WGS's futures as the discipline struggles to remain relevant in an increasingly globalized web of power, cultural contexts, and social forces that do not always begin or end with a "live subject." In other words, we lose opportunities to engage complexities that may not offer obvious or immediate political solutions, what Wiegman calls "a non-instrumentalized relation to knowledge production" (2002a, 33).

Certainly there are the obvious questions that follow from the absences I documented in the first section: What is activism? Who is an activist? Which sort of activism are we talking about when we mobilize it in the name of WGS? Which gendered/sexualized/raced subjects are central to the discipline's understanding of itself? To respond to such questions in ways that are less about "policing fidelity" or making declarations of authentic or inauthentic disciplinary investigation, I want to return to activism for the purpose of contemplating different functions of the term. I want to explore the possibilities that might be available to the discipline if we were to recast activism as, in Mowitt's terms, an "antidisciplinary object."

Chronicling Consequences and Contemplating Change

Again, an antidisciplinary object is one whose aim is "to institutionalize a form of inclusivity that actually encourages curricula to undergo
legitimation crises—and not simply at the local level of a particular
institution, but at the level of the borders that distinguish the local from
the global" (Mowitt 1992, 220). Following this logic, if we were, say, to
directly interrogate what actually constitutes activism, either contem-
porarily or in the field's origin stories, we would find ourselves quickly
grappling with the consequences of not just the borders, limits, and
definitions of a key term, but more importantly, questions of all sorts
about what sorts of borders, limits, and definitions we can or should
draw around WGS itself.

By way of example, I offer American Studies scholar Rosalyn Baxandall's (2001) article, "Re-visioning the Women's Liberation Movement's Narrative: Early Second Wave African American Feminists,"
that documents a series of histories of what could be called "feminist
activism" outside the parameters of what we think about as the history
of "The Women's Movement." In putting together a documentary book
about 1970s feminism, Baxandall traveled the United States and sought
out archival materials and interviews away from the more well-known
hot spots in New York City, Boston, Chicago, or Berkeley. Based on
what she found, she concludes that the activism of the early Women's
Liberation Movement is too narrowly conceived by scholars who do
not include the great variety of work done in that epoch, especially by
women of color, many of whom were organizing well before 1968.

Baxandall describes the work of Mothers Alone Working (MAW),
which started in 1965 in San Francisco. It had about 200 black and
white, working class, single moms as members, and "organized summer
camps, daycare, and sports days," pairing children of single mothers
with university students, and hosted speakers on women's organizing,
preventative medical services, job training, and food stamps (2001, 231).
Another group, The Damned, which began even earlier, in 1960 in New
Rochelle, New York, was made up of exclusively African American
women and led by Pat Robinson, a social worker and follower of Mal-
colm X. The group's primary focus was teen pregnancy, and it worked
through a practice that seemed to be for all intents and purposes, femi-

nist consciousness raising. Baxandall argues that "[t]he Black women in groups like MAW and [the Damned] were far more centered around their role as mothers and the responsibility and power that goes along with motherhood than their counterparts in the predominantly white women's liberation groups" (2001, 238).

Although the women in these groups certainly seem "feminist" (especially in terms of the "liberatory impulse" that Layli Maparyan uses to characterize that term in this volume), and they certainly seem activist, and they certainly are emerging from the same historical context as what Women's and Gender Studies narratives usually cite as a founding social movement for the field, what they did is not, according to our field's histories about this period, activism in the name of Women's Liberation, the second wave, or The Women's Movement. Baxandall wonders, "[p]erhaps if scholars expanded their definitions of feminism to include women engaged in self-help and neighborhood action, MAW and the Mount Vernon/New Rochelle women would be considered among the pantheon of feminist foremothers" (2001, 241).

For me, Baxandall's history raises compelling and productive questions about what counts as activism, let alone feminist activism, and thereby the activism that makes WGS unique. Again, this is not to argue that the activities that MAW members engaged in were the same (or perhaps even significantly different) sorts of activities with the same sorts of outcomes and effects of, say, New York Radical Women or Cell 16. We don't know because, at the present moment, the configurations of our disciplinary mandate do not assist us in raising those kinds of questions. What I am attempting to highlight here is that, perhaps, the current assumptions, impressions, and images of activism we draw from to ground our discipline's history have only included that which made its way into universities via the privileged (mostly) white women for whom that institution was relatively welcoming. And making activism sacred, instead of investigating its limits, means that we are not seeing its potential to falter as disciplinary artifact; it is this faltering that could push us to provide alternative explanations of our disciplinary mandate. Likewise, investing ourselves in exploring activism's limits might also call into question those nostalgic pleas to return to an activist past; after all, the narratives we have constructed about the field have mediated that past.

Baxandall's research is just one small example that helps us see how uninterrogated terms like activism may actually work in tension rather than in harmony with the antiracist values the discipline claims as central. Indeed, the histories unearthed in just this one article stress the need for more "global," in Mowitt's terms, and less "instrumentalist," in Wiegman's terms, approaches to what constitutes legitimate disciplinary artifacts for scholarly investigation in WGS. For while the "live subject" in the form of women like Pat Robinson may help us in initially raising questions about this discipline's limits, ultimately the work of both investigating and reworking the boundaries that place her outside of them may require scholarship that operates in the abstractions and esoteric spaces of language play and, what might be to some, theoretical excesses. In short, our discipline's *political* mission may necessitate that we eschew activism's undue influence.

Conclusion: The Making of an Antidisciplinary Object?

Perhaps it is because activism, as a disciplinary artifact that both launched the discipline and grounds its current claims about Women's and Gender Studies' uniqueness, has promised so much, that interrogating its power to discipline the field's practitioners has been so energetically resisted. As one who has built a career on making these sorts of claims, I understand its risks. Undertaking an interrogation of activism has the potential to force a productive sort of legitimation crisis onto WGS's collective agenda. Providing this sort of potential is the basic function of an antidisciplinary object: it shakes things up and compels us to think in fundamentally different ways about our taken for granted assumptions. To be antidisciplinary—through activism or any other sacred term that circulates through WGS contexts—means that we seek the knowledge that is currently unrecognizable in the discipline's current configuration. It does not mean becoming any less oriented around, for example, the WGS social justice mandate. Rather, as I hope I have demonstrated here, it can very well mean rededicating ourselves to that mandate by interrogating the limits of the discipline's current terms of engagement and being curious about what we are "over-seeing" as a result of our disciplinary allegiances.

Notes

1. Looking for activism's presence in the indexes of Women's and Gender Studies anthologies and monographs has become an exercise in ritual frustration for me. Examples abound, but a case in point is Boxer (1998b). She takes up the "academics *versus* activism" and "academics *and* activism" debates specifically in a chapter titled "'Knowledge for What?'" and more generally assumes an unproblematic linkage between activism and Women's and Gender Studies throughout the book. Yet "activism" does not appear in the index.

2. See, WMST-L archives: "Women's Studies programs' commitment to feminist activism" (July 10, 2006), Rogers and Garrett (2002), and Ralston and Keeble (2009), especially the first two chapters. For an extended treatise on this topic, see Messer-Davidow (2002) as well as my own dissertation, Orr (1998).

3. Memoir-based anthologies are especially replete with such calls. See for example Mari Jo Buhle's introduction to Howe (2000) and the editors' afterward in Robbins et al. (2008).

4. See Orr 1999 for extended discussion on misplaced nostalgia.

5. See Wiegman's plea to WGS "practitioners to think about the field *otherwise*" (2002b, 3) in *Women's Studies on Its Own*.

6
WAVES

Astrid Henry

The term "waves" has been central to Canadian and U.S. feminisms' narratives and histories since the late 1960s, when feminists began describing themselves as "second wave" and articulating a relationship to their "first wave" predecessors. The rise of a "third wave" of feminism in the early 1990s—and crucially, its insistence on using the term "wave" to name itself—has only helped to solidify the use of the waves metaphor as Canadian and U.S. feminisms' dominant model of organizing its history into three discreet eras: the first wave of the nineteenth and early twentieth centuries, the second wave of the 1960s and 70s, and the third wave of our present era. While many feminist scholars, particularly over the last decade and a half, have rightly criticized the waves metaphor for its reductive effects on chronicling feminism's history, the metaphor has remained entrenched within feminism's lexicon.[1]

As a college student in Women's Studies (as the field was still known then) classes in the late 1980s, I didn't give much thought to why feminism's history was narrated in waves. From my women's history classes I learned that there had been a "first wave" in the nineteenth and early twentieth century and that we were now in a "second wave" of feminism that began in the 1960s. I didn't question why Women's Studies scholars used "waves" to describe these two historical periods, nor, as I recall, was this question posed by my professors or the class readings. Feminism's "waves" were simply part of its history; the language of "waves" was part of what it meant to be a Women's Studies student and scholar.

It wasn't until I started reading books and articles by self-proclaimed "third wave" feminists in the mid-1990s that I began to think about the effects of the waves metaphor on feminism and, in particular, on feminist intergenerational dialogue. Educated to think of myself as part of feminism's "second wave"—inasmuch as this term described the late twentieth century—I was surprised to find that others of my generation felt the need to argue for a new, "third" wave distinct from the second. It was at the moment when some of my peers were employing "waves" to suggest that we were part of a new feminist movement based on our youth that the metaphor itself came into relief, showing its rhetorical power and conceptual limits. In retrospect I can see that it took the presence of two simultaneously existing "waves," both of which I identified with, for me to see the problems inherent in the wave structure.

As a way of quickly marking chronological periods, generational cohorts, and ideological trends, the term "wave" undoubtedly provides a useful shorthand for describing the history of women's movements, feminist identities, and Women's and Gender Studies (WGS) as an academic field. Yet, the conceptual problems that accompany the waves metaphor's use warrant a critical examination. In this chapter, I will explore the metaphor's: (1) conflation of demographic generation and ideology; (2) homogenization of beliefs and identities within an historical moment; (3) slippage into a mother-daughter familial structure; (4) representation of temporal change; and finally, (5) reinforcement of the Western, and particularly English-speaking, context from which feminism's "wave" structure emerged. While the waves metaphor does seem to reflect something true about historical, political, and generational change, it also imbues that change with a particular set of associations and meanings.

The use of the waves metaphor to describe U.S. feminism's history first occurred in the late 1960s when those involved in the women's movement of the era began to refer to themselves as "second wave," while simultaneously designating the women's rights activists of the nineteenth and early twentieth centuries as feminism's "first wave." In an article for the *New York Times Magazine*, entitled "The Second Feminist Wave," Marsha Weinman Lear first put into print the term "second wave" to describe the then-burgeoning movement. Lear's early use of the waves metaphor—one that would quickly be adopted by both activists in the movement and journalists reporting on it—relied on an image of oceanic waves to stress the ebbs and flows of the object being described. In Lear's description, the "first wave"—the period between 1848 (the Seneca Falls Convention) and 1920 (the gaining of the vote)—had not just "ebbed" but was completely gone in 1968, "disappeared into the great sandbar of Togetherness" (1968, 24). Without having to contend with feminists from the past movement, the "second wave" could thus confidently assert its difference and its superiority, seeing itself as the sole representative of the contemporary feminist scene.[2]

By contrast, when Rebecca Walker declared "I am the Third Wave" in an article in *Ms.*, she did so at a time when the second wave was still very much alive (1992, 41). Walker's use of "wave" signaled an important shift in meaning, as "wave" now came to designate an age-based generation. While admittedly Walker cannot be said to represent all of the feminists who would describe themselves as third wave in the 1990s and 2000s, she illustrates the generational themes that would mark the third wave's use of the waves metaphor. First, Walker spoke as a young woman—she was still an undergraduate at Yale when the *Ms.* article was published—who had grown up with feminism all around her. Second, Walker spoke as the daughter of a well-known second wave feminist, Alice Walker, thereby establishing a "mother-daughter" relationship between the second and third waves. Third, Walker addressed women her own age, challenging them to take up the banner of feminism in their own way. Fourth, by calling herself "third wave" rather than solely "feminist," Walker stressed the perceived newness and difference of her feminism from that of her second wave predecessors. Finally, Walker developed her vision of third wave feminism through a critique of the second wave, specifically its dogmatism and lack of complexity (Walker 1995).[3]

Whether in memoirs, retrospectives, or scholarly analysis, the waves metaphor has been used to mark time: "second wave" serving as the name of feminism's past (in both positive and negative associations), and "third wave" signifying its present (again, both positively and negatively). The ubiquity of the wave structure in contemporary feminist discourse makes it seem as though "waves" are a necessary component of chronicling the history of feminism and of WGS. Yet the metaphor of the wave is just that: a metaphor, a transfer of meaning between two things that do not have a necessary connection. Thus, while "waves" may, in fact, capture something about feminism's movements, its divisions, and its ebbs and flows, the waves metaphor may also impose certain arbitrary meanings upon feminism and its history. The waves metaphor, therefore, is both descriptive and prescriptive, simultaneously offering a representation of feminism's history and constraining our imagination of that history.

Generation and Ideology

The first, and perhaps most obvious, problem with the waves metaphor comes from its being used to designate a generational cohort. When Lear first coined the term "second wave" to describe the women's liberation movement in 1968, she was describing activists of many different ages. The conflation of "wave" with "generation" in our contemporary era is even more apparent when we look to the multiple generations who participated in what we now call feminism's "first wave." Only with the emergence of feminism's third wave does the term come to signify a single demographic generation—and consequently, a much more rapid vision of generational replacement. Because they initially spoke as members of Generation X (born between 1961 and 1981), third wave feminists grouped the second wave into a similar generational cohort. Second wavers became increasingly conflated with Baby Boomers (born between 1946 and 1960), when in fact many second wave leaders were born prior to the end of World War II. Thus ideological differences between feminists were defined as generational differences, and every member of a certain demographic generation was seen as sharing the same beliefs.

Lisa Marie Hogeland has argued, "The rhetoric of generational differences in feminism works to mask real political differences—fundamental differences in our visions of feminism's task and accomplishments" (2001, 107). In describing ideological differences primarily (or even exclusively) as generational differences, the waves metaphor obscures the diversity of feminist thought within any age-based "wave," presumes that people of a particular age and generation share a singular ideological position, and denies the possibility of cross-generational identification across political lines. As Meryl Altman asks, "Was the metaphor of a 'wave' meant to name a historical period in which, if one happens to be a certain age at a certain time, one has no choice but to swim? Or, is a 'wave' a set of principles and commitments, to which a person of any age might freely subscribe at any time—or might choose not to subscribe?" (2003, 7).

Within Women's and Gender Studies programs and departments, we can see how age and historical moment might not always line up neatly. Suppose we take two students in a WGS Ph.D. program in 2012, one is 24 years old (born in 1988) and the other is 52 years old (born in 1960). From a demographic point of view, these two scholars-in-training are not part of the same generation: the younger is a member of the Millennial Generation, the older is a Baby Boomer. Yet, as members of the same cohort group of Ph.D. students, they are experiencing WGS at the same moment—studying the same texts, the same theories, the same history of the field. If their experience of WGS is generational, it is institutionally so, based on the year in which they enter and leave their Ph.D. program. In other words, these two students, twenty-eight years apart in age, share the same "birthdate" as scholars in the discipline.[4]

Even established WGS scholars can be difficult to situate within a specific "wave" based upon their biological age. Take, for example, Judith Butler, arguably one of the most important theorists within the field today. Born in 1956, Butler is a Baby Boomer, demographically speaking; she earned her Ph.D. in 1984, before most third wavers had started college, and she is in the same age group as many of the well-known feminist theorists who developed the then emerging field of Women's Studies. If one's age determines one's wave, Butler would be second wave. Yet, Butler's prominence as a theorist began in 1990 with the publication of *Gender Trouble*; her career thus coincided with the rise of feminism's third wave, and many writers have cited Butler as a major influence on third wavers' thinking. In addition, Butler's contributions to feminist and queer theories, particularly her critique of the naturalness of gender difference, also make it difficult to classify her as a "second wave" theorist.[5] Butler exemplifies how a feminist's ideological or academic "generation" can be distinct from her demographic one.

The conflation of one's age with one's wave has led some writers to define themselves as a numerical proportion of a particular wave. Altman, for example, describes herself as "wave 2.5" (2003, 8) since she is younger than the feminists who developed Women's Studies in the late 1960s and early 1970s, but older than the third wavers of Walker's generation.[6] Recently, I have heard my students use the term "wave 3.5" to describe the generation a decade or two younger than the original third wavers. Yet while these "half waves" offer other options for generational identification, their fine tuning of the waves structure ultimately keeps us trapped within its reductive strictures.

Rejecting the equivalence of biological age with ideology, Rory Dicker and Alison Piepmeier write that "the third wave has less to do with a neat generational divide than with a cultural context" (2003, 14). This "cultural context" is explained by Leslie Heywood and Jennifer Drake when they state that "young feminists who grew up with equity feminism, got gender feminism in college, along with poststructuralism, and are now hard at work on a feminism that strategically combines elements of these feminisms, along with black feminism, women-of-color feminisms, working-class feminism, pro-sex feminism, and so on" (1997, 3). Defining the term "wave" as a cultural context that produces a particular form of feminist consciousness, rather than as an age-based generation, would necessarily mean that anyone in the same cultural context could belong to the wave associated with it. Thinking about "wave" in this way would suggest that all feminists living in our contemporary cultural moment could potentially share similar feminist values.[7]

Homogenization

The redefinition of "wave" as a cultural context seems to broaden the group included in any wave. Yet merely replacing "generation" with "historical moment" demonstrates the second problem with the waves metaphor, namely the way that it ultimately homogenizes the group belonging to the wave. Differences of political ideology and strategy, as well as of lived experience, are minimized under the banner of a single wave in which a diverse range of individuals, events, and ideas are transformed into a monolithic group with the same public face. The waves metaphor thus reduces complex *intra*generational differences in the name of stressing a singular *inter*generational identity.

In the third wave's sometimes hostile portrait of the second wave, we can see examples of the reductive effect of generational identity, such as when certain white, "anti-sex" feminists, such as Andrea Dworkin, are used to represent the entirety of the second wave, eliminating the racial, sexual, and ideological diversity of this wave. This strategy has also been used to indict the second wave for its exclusionary politics. For example, Patricia Justine Tumang argues that "The predominantly white and racist feminist movement of the 1970s ignored the relationship between racism, classism, and homophobia." Stressing what makes her "wave" different, Tumang continues, "In the growing emergence of 'third wave' feminism, feminism isn't reduced to one English-speaking white from North America" (2002, 379). The creation of a monolithic second wave against which to position themselves has emboldened third wave writers, allowing them to represent the diversity that they claim was missing in second wave feminism. Paradoxically, by homogenizing the portrait of the second wave in order to critique its racism and homophobia, third wavers actually obscure the important role that women of color and queer women of all races played in second wave feminism. In *Colonize This!*, Rebecca Hurdis asks, "Is it possible to construct a feminist genealogy that maintains inclusivity?" (2002, 287). Indeed, the wave model seems to make such inclusivity difficult, since the need to stress difference *between* the waves can erase important differences *within* each wave.

In contemporary histories of Women's and Gender Studies as an academic field, there has been a similar homogenizing tendency, with second wavers involved in building the field almost uniformly described as "seasoned political activists [who] were ready to transfer techniques of organizing from the community to the campus" (Buhle 2000, xx).[8] The editors of *Is Academic Feminism Dead? Theory in Practice* begin their book by describing the moment in which, "activists took feminism into the university in the 1970s," providing just one example of what has become a ubiquitous narrative of the field's history, one in which feminists moved "into the university" in order to transform higher education (The Social Justice Group 2000, 1). This version of WGS history, while undoubtedly containing some truth, effectively erases the role of feminists (and soon-to-be-feminists) already "in the university" at the time of this great influx into the academy, while also leaving activism itself unexamined, as Catherine Orr discusses in this volume. Many of the authors included in *The Politics of Women's Studies: Testimony from 30 Founding Mothers*, for example, were already located inside the academy well before "activists took feminism into the university," and their essays describe what these careers were like before and after feminism's arrival. Mary Jo Buhle notes that "The founders of Women's Studies more often than not *became* feminists through the process of teaching courses, organizing programs, and developing the curriculum" (2000, xx, emphasis in original), suggesting a more complicated history of the relationship among feminism, activism, and academia than the singular narrative of the nonacademic feminist activist who brings feminism into the university. Like the third wave's self-portrait as racially and sexually diverse, the second wave's representation of itself as the activist generation provides another example of how generational differences have been constructed in the service of self-flattery; by representing themselves first and foremost as activists (and only secondarily as academics) some second wavers have been able to critique what they describe as younger scholars' "increasing focus on professionalism" by eliding the professionalism of their own generational peers (Robinson 2002, 203).

We can also see the influence of the wave structure's homogenizing effects in the institutional histories of WGS programs and departments, which are also discussed by many of the other contributors to this volume. To argue that "Women's Studies" was "born" in the 1970s—and therefore is "second wave"—ignores the heterogeneity of Women's and Gender Studies programs, many of which didn't begin until the 1980s and 1990s, while others were mere infants in the early twenty-first century. As Shirley Yee notes in her article reflecting on WGS in the late 1990s, "While some programs are celebrating twenty-fifth anniversaries and expanding their curricula to include graduate study, others are still struggling to get off the ground, operating on miniscule budgets in order to offer undergraduate classes" (1997, 47). Even given the reality described by Yee—something that anyone working in WGS today is undoubtedly aware of—many histories of the field focus on its emergence in the 1970s, discounting the changes in the field brought by subsequent decades. Take, for example, Buhle's introduction to *The Poli-*

tics of Women's Studies, in which she says of the 1970s: "The first ten years of Women's Studies were extremely heady ones. Not only did well over half the growth in the field to date occur during the first decade, but all of the basic institutional structures were put in place" (2000, xvi). *All* of the field's basic institutional structures were put in place in the 1970s? While I don't fault Buhle for celebrating the incredible achievements that occurred during this decade, it is historically inaccurate to suggest that the field has a single creation story, a single moment of birth. As programs and departments emerged in the 1980s and 1990s—as well as in the 2000s—their institutional structures and their sense of the discipline were undoubtedly shaped by myriad changes and developments within WGS since the 1970s. A case in point is Leora Auslander's discussion of the Center for Gender Studies at the University of Chicago, which was founded in 1995, two decades after the field's "heady days." As Auslander describes the mission of the Center's founders, "we hoped that … *we would avoid three of the major pitfalls of the Women's Studies programs created during the 1970s*: the marginalization of work on sexuality (particularly gay and lesbian sexuality), an inadequate attention to questions of race, and sectarianism" (1997, 3, emphasis added). Auslander's comments point to what was missing in 1970's Women's Studies—what *wasn't* in place—thereby demonstrating how the field (including, undoubtedly, those programs that originated in the 1970s) has changed and thus cannot be equated to any one particular wave.

A Mother-Daughter Relationship

The use of terms like "foremothers" or "founding mothers" of early Women's Studies leads to my third point: the slippage between the generationally-defined wave structure and the familial structure of the mother-daughter relationship. As I have discussed elsewhere, contemporary discussions of feminist generations have often used the mother-daughter trope to describe relationships between the waves, turning the second wave into a mother and the third wave into a daughter.[9] This "matrophor," to use Rebecca Dakin Quinn's term for "the persistent nature of maternal metaphors in feminism," has been ubiquitous within the writing on generational differences between feminism's two current waves (1997, 179). Of course, in some notable cases, such as Rebecca

Walker, third wave feminists are the actual daughters of second wave feminists. Yet, the use of the mother-daughter trope within feminist discourse on generational conflict has extended far beyond its literal use. With its implied sense of connection and aggression, the mother-daughter relationship is a particularly rich metaphor, affect-wise, and has often exacerbated the generational tensions and conflicts between the waves—as well as kept feminist generational relationships trapped in "heterocentric and repro-logical paradigms," as argued by Jennifer Purvis in this volume.

Contemporary writing about the discipline of Women's and Gender Studies also makes use of this "matrophor." As one contributor to *Women's Studies on Its Own* writes: "It's hard to avoid the maternal metaphor for those of us who were there at the beginning of Women's Studies" (Robinson 2002, 202). Likewise, Florence Howe's anthology on the history of the field takes as its subtitle "testimony from thirty founding mothers" (2000). But using the maternal metaphor to describe the "birth" of the field also structures the relationship between the "founding mothers" and the "child," so that changes in the discipline are viewed through a generational and familial lens. Seen in these terms, WGS scholars in the 1990s are always necessarily different from those of the 1970s, with this difference measured in the mother's pride, envy, or ambivalence. Additionally, the passage of time only emphasizes the mother's distance from the birth, provoking her sense of aging or possible alienation from the "mature child." In her introduction to *Women's Studies on Its Own*, Robyn Wiegman highlights this alienation when she poses the question, "Have the emergent generations of professionally trained feminists abandoned their foremothers' tradition by making of feminism an academic career?" (2002b, 3). As this "mother-daughter" pair gets mapped onto the field's other reigning duo, the activist-academic pair, the "daughter's" careerism is seen as causing a separation from her "mother," whose reason for being in the academy, it seems, was to promote activism, not to make a career. Countering this view, third wave academic Devoney Looser writes, "Haven't such senior academic women's lives to some small degree made such 'careerist' feminist desires possible? The stereotyping of third-wave feminists as more 'careerist' than their predecessors seems more than a little suspect for this reason alone" (1997, 40). Looser points to the ways in which the "mother" generation makes possible the very desires they critique in their "daughters."

An interesting use of birth language can be found in a recent essay by third wave scholars Stacy Gillis and Rebecca Munford, who write that "the powerful activism and scholarship of Women's Studies over the past thirty years *gave birth* to third wave feminism—just as second wave feminism had *given birth* to Women's Studies" (2003, 5, emphasis added). As such, the field of WGS serves as a kind of midway point between the second and third waves, making the field that which connects the two groups of feminists. While Gillis and Munford rely on familial language to make their point, they potentially provide a way out of the mother-daughter structure and move toward a recognition of how WGS serves as an institutional point of connection for multiple age-based generations of students and scholars.

Temporal Change

Putting aside the generational and familial associations of the waves metaphor, I would now like to examine the language of "feminist oceanography," which creates its own problematic vision of temporality, movement, and continuity (Siegel 1997, 52). Flora Davis, for example, uses the rise and fall of an ocean wave to describe the history of the U.S. women's movement:

> The wave analogy is helpful because it … reminds us that major social changes tend to happen in waves. First, there's a lot of intense activity and some aspects of life are transformed; then, when the public has absorbed as much as it can stand, reaction sets in. Stability reigns for a while, and if there's a strong backlash, some of the changes may be undone. Eventually, if vital issues remain unresolved, another wave of activism arises. (1991, 11)

Davis's language is emblematic of how "waves" have been used to narrate feminism's history, and in many ways the metaphor *does* capture how social justice movements operate and how social change occurs. But the metaphor's oceanic origins also brings with it a certain set of assumptions about historical movement: namely, that progress will always be followed by movement backward, just as the tide recedes back into the ocean.[10]

Furthermore, in its use as a metaphor the wave seems to exist as a discrete entity, and only "if vital issues remain unresolved" will another wave will emerge. Curiously, the ocean motif seems to ignore the experience of anyone who has actually stood on a beach watching waves— namely, that multiple waves crash on the shore at the same time. In its vision of a singular wave in time, the use of the metaphor tends to isolate the women's movement from other movements, other currents in the water. As Kimberly Springer has noted, the waves metaphor can obscure the role of race-based movements "as precursors, or windows of political opportunity, for gender activism" (2002, 1061). In focusing our attention on singular gender-based political movements, she continues, "The wave model perpetuates the exclusion of women of color from women's movement history and feminist theorizing" (1063), and thus furthers a narrow, hegemonic white vision of feminism.[11] Similarly, if Women's and Gender Studies is understood as the result of a single wave—one in which "Feminists of the Second Wave have built Women's Studies into the academy as a legacy for the Third Wavers"— the impact made on the discipline by other social justice movements, as well as other academic movements, are obscured (Boxer 1998b, 23). In other words, the singular wave model of narrating the field's history makes it difficult to trace out other activist and intellectual precursors to—as well as contemporary influences on—its development, including the Civil Rights Movement and critical race studies, the gay and lesbian movement and queer studies, and the numerous disciplinary traditions that have shaped the "interdiscipline" of WGS. Returning to the beach to remind ourselves of the simultaneous and overlapping nature of oceanic waves may allow us to reconceptualize the waves metaphor so that it can account for plurality and multiplicity.

The oceanic understanding of waves brings with it a sense of continuity between the waves and the notion that each wave will rise and fall in a similar manner. Yet the enumeration of "new waves" within feminist discourse creates a sense of teleological progress, with each successive wave improving on the previous one. Jane Newman has described this logic of progress as "presentism," in which the present is "the culmination of a narrative of the victors ... a narrative of progress whose hero(in)es inhabit only the present" (2002, 145). Such presentist discourse is easily found in much third wave autobiographical writing, in which young women describe themselves as "the daughters of feminist privilege" who "walk through the world with a sense of entitlement that women of our mother's generation could not begin to fathom" (Morgan 2000, 59). These young "heroines inhabiting the present" can be read as a sign of feminism's success. But the implied "fall" of each ocean wave also suggests, as Davis does in her use of waves, that "some of the changes [made by an individual wave] may be undone" (1991, 11). As a way of narrating the history of feminism and of WGS, the ocean wave is paradoxical: feminists are destined for inevitable progress and inevitable regress.

The waves metaphor's built-in paradox may explain why many of the recent books and articles on the field of WGS written by generationally second wave authors question whether it is, in fact, moving forward. Such texts often recount the history of the discipline with clear nostalgia for the past—the 1970s in particular, "a golden age for Women's Studies and the women's movement in general" (Howe 2000, 15). Turning to the past to reflect on the future of WGS seems to have led to a focus on the "supposed failures of Women's Studies" in the present (Kennedy and Beins 2005, 1). As "nostalgia for an increasingly idealized past" came to dominate the discussion of WGS' present and future, "second wave" came to serve as a repository for all that was good about the field (Scott 2008, 3). "The heroic days of Women's Studies are now in the past," sighs Buhle (2000, xxvi). Reading third wave memoirs alongside second wave institutional histories leaves one with a strange conclusion: these are the best of times for women, the worst of times for WGS.

One of the most jarring problems in evaluating the "teleological" narrative with the "nostalgia" narrative is that both are correct. Second wave feminism *did* represent a high point of activism and social movement; it also inaugurated the field of Women's Studies. As such, the second wave seems superior to the third wave in terms of collective action and creating social and legal changes. Yet, looking at the field of WGS, one would have to acknowledge the success of its current moment, as Alison Piepmeier discusses in her chapter in this volume: thousands of programs around the globe, including in a majority of U.S.

and Canadian universities and colleges; Master's and Ph.D. programs, with an increasing number of doctorates in the field; thriving scholarship within the "interdiscipline" and within its many disciplinary branches; and continued (and, in many places, growing) enthusiasm for, and interest in, the field from students, whatever their age or wave.

Ednie Kaeh Garrison has proposed that we retain the waves metaphor but reconceptualize it by replacing the "feminist oceanographic" understanding of waves with the "electromagnetic wavelengths we call radio waves" (2005, 239). Such an understanding of waves, argues Garrison, "allows us to see how things happen cyclically and chronologically at one and the same time," since multiple radio waves exist simultaneously, overlapping and interfering with each other (238). While "ocean waves infer a movement that carries us along," radio waves "infer a kind of intentionality and purposefulness" (243–244). In other words, in any given moment we will encounter multiple concurrent radio waves, making deliberate our decision to tune in and pick up a frequency. Garrison's "radio waves" provide a useful way of understanding how ideas function in WGS: multiple "waves" of scholarship, schools of theory, and disciplinary (and interdisciplinary) perspectives exist simultaneously, not just the two waves reinforced by our current binary model. In pursuing our research and designing our courses, we choose to tune in to certain frequencies and not others. As such, in our actual practice of the field we already experience the cacophony of ideas suggested by the radio waves metaphor. Garrison's "radio waves" model, like a more plural view of oceanic waves, gives us a way of seeing the diversity and multiplicity of feminist thought and activism in any given moment, past or present. While she does not provide a way out of the waves metaphor, she suggests that it can be reimagined to better capture the ways in which knowledge production and social justice movements operate.

U.S., Canadian, and European Context

Finally, the waves metaphor reinforces a Western and often English-speaking vision of feminism, based on the U.S., Canadian, and European contexts from which feminism's wave structure emerged. "The common rhetoric of feminist 'waves'," writes Susan Stanford Friedman, "misleads in many ways. It is insufficiently global, in the first place, using the feminist movements in the West, especially Britain and the United States, as the defining periodization for all" (2002, 431). Friedman's point is clearly visible in the ways in which "third wave feminism" is currently being used in various places around the world, particularly in Australia, Britain, Canada, and the United States. The concept of third wave feminism as it has developed over the last decade and half is a product of postindustrialized Western democracies that have experienced earlier periods—or waves—of feminist activism and that have led to at least some level of success in advancing the cause of gender equality. Central to this definition of the "third wave" is that it comes after an earlier period of women's activism which is historically located in the 1960s and 70s.

To provide an example of how third wave feminism is specific to postindustrialized Western democracies, we can turn to the case of Poland. In a recent article, feminist scholar Agnieszka Graff describes how the waves metaphor falls short in describing Polish feminism, which never experienced a women's movement in the 1960s and 70s. Younger feminists today in Poland do not identify as third wave feminists since to do so would require a second wave against which to define themselves. Indeed, Graff describes contemporary Polish feminism as a combination of third wave modes of activism (the use of drag performance, for example) and second wave demands (reproductive rights and pay equity, in particular). As Graff writes, "If we were to apply American chronology to this particular moment [in Poland], we would probably have to call it a third wave form for a second wave content in a backlash context" (2003, 103).

As Women's and Gender Studies becomes increasingly transnational, as discussed by Laura Parisi in this volume, we need to be wary of the ways in which we use the waves metaphor to structure our syllabi and curricula. In describing the history of Canadian and U.S. women's movements and feminist theories, the waves metaphor is undoubtedly useful. Yet, as we continue the important work of making our programs and our courses more global in scope, we need to develop alternative genealogies of feminist thought, as new models of narrating the history of our field and of the women's movements that inform it.

As Ann Braithwaite reminds us, "Telling a story about the past of Women's Studies is not only to remember 'what was'; it is also an 'imagining'—not only of 'what was' but also of 'what is' and thus also of 'what will be.' How one thinks about the past, and the narratives one tells about that past, demonstrate how one thinks about the present and what one hopes for the future" (2004, 9). The waves metaphor has played a powerful role in shaping the story of WGS and of feminism generally. Yet, "as an epistemological tool it sets limits on the way we can articulate feminist history, consciousness, and praxis" (Garrison 2005, 243). Imagining the past as a sequence of discrete waves, each ideologically homogenous and generationally unified, reduces the present and the future to a series of familial squabbles and Manichean conflicts. Instead, to welcome what Elizabeth Grosz calls "the surprise of the future" (2000, 29), we need to think outside of the wave structure and all its attendant restraints. And when we get a glimpse of that future, to paraphrase Katha Pollitt, "Let's just not call it the fourth wave" (2009, 10).

Notes

1. For example, see Laughlin et al. 2010, 76–135.
2. For more on the generational relationship between U.S. feminism's first and second waves, see Henry 2004, 52–87.
3. Interestingly, a simultaneous use of the term "third wave" defined it as: "a new feminism that is led by and has grown out of the challenge to white feminism posited by women of color" (Short 1994, 14). The text often cited for this use of the term is *The Third Wave: Feminist Perspectives on Racism*, an anthology that was developed in the early 1990s but was never published. In this collection, the term "third wave" was meant ideologically, as a cross-generational, anti-racist movement. This non-generational understanding of the wave metaphor basically disappeared in the 2000s as the generational meaning exemplified by Walker became omnipresent. See Dicker and Piepmeier 2003, 7, 8; Heywood and Drake 1997, 1; Orr 1997, 30; Short 1994, 14, 16; and Springer 2002, 1063.
4. For more on how the waves metaphor is inadequate to capture the reality of academic generations, see Aikau et al. 2007.
5. Interestingly, one of Butler's first published essays, "Lesbian S & M: The Politics of Dis-illusion," can be found in the anthology *Against Sadomasochism: A Radical Feminist Analysis*, published in 1982. Butler's essay exists alongside articles by Robin Morgan, John Stoltenberg, Kathleen Barry, and other "anti-sex," second wave feminists with whom she would never be associated today.
6. See also Kinser's use of the term "Mid Wave" to describe the location between the second and third waves (2004, 124).

7. For more on cross-generational identification, see Siegel 2000, 3 and Garrison 2000, 145.

8. See also Auslander, who writes, "Essentially all of the women behind the creation of Women's Studies programs in the 1970s, and most of their students, had a past if not a present in the women's movement" (1997, 18-19).

9. See Henry 2004. For more on the use of the maternal metaphor within feminism, see Luhmann 2004.

10. For more on oceanic waves and their use as a metaphor, see Aikau 2007 and Laughlin et al. 2010.

11. See also Laughlin et al., in which the authors argue that the "waves metaphor entrenches the perception of a 'singular' feminism in which gender is the predominate category of analysis" and "highlights periods when middle-class white women were most active in the public sphere" (2010, 77, 82).

7

BESIEGEMENT

Alison Piepmeier

At a meeting of the faculty, staff, and students of one Women's Studies program with which I was involved, senior faculty members spent much of the scheduled time expressing fears that the university would abolish Women's Studies. Naturally alarmed, I asked questions that met with murky, paranoid answers until I, too, felt half-certain that we were doomed. Later I set up a meeting with the administrator. "Why," I asked her, "do they think that the program is going to be abolished?" She replied, after much reflection, "There's nothing specific, really. It's just that Women's Studies is always under fire."

(Looser 2002, 214)

In January 2009, a discussion took place on the WMST-L listserve, an international email forum for Women's and Gender Studies (WGS) faculty, about "the future of Women's Studies." This is a conversation that could have gone in a number of different directions: for instance, list members might have considered new material to incorporate into curricula, articulated the key theoretical models in use in the field, or proposed ways in which the discipline should market itself. Instead, the conversation quickly became a sort of defense of WGS, as if what it meant to discuss the future of the field was to affirm repeatedly that the field *has* a future. One thing that struck me was that, throughout the discussion, the language of battle was used. "We fight back, we always have, even if some put their heads down in the hopes of muddling through. Sometimes we die fighting," wrote one discussant. Another wrote, "we have specific struggles to fight within the academy," and another, "I feel very strongly that hard-fought ground is being unnecessarily ceded."[1]

This kind of expression isn't confined to online discussions. As early as 1972, a position paper by Catharine Stimpson, scholar and founding editor of the feminist journal *Signs*, illustrated this rhetoric in full force: "The people who resist women's studies are so numerous, the affection for intelligent women so frail, the self-destructive impulses within women's studies so tempting, the unanswered questions so complex, that it seems obvious that women's studies is in a position of weakness" (1988, 49). She argues, "Women's Studies has too many enemies outside of the movement who can and will hurt it. The dangers out there demand vigilant attention. The resistance to Women's Studies has grown, not shrunk, as Women's Studies has grown. Its modes range from passive skepticism to active hostility..." (Stimpson 1988, 45). In a recent publication about the history of the field, Florence Howe refers to "women's studies battlegrounds" (2002, 27). In the epigraph to this essay, Devoney Looser recounts one administrator claiming that "Women's Studies is always under fire" (2002, 214). In all these venues, from the origins of the field to the present day, as WGS practitioners debate the focus of the field, recount its history, or plan for its future, they present themselves as fighters and the discipline of WGS as under fire—besieged.

Although we don't typically speak of "besiegement" per se in the field, this term points to a familiar narrative: the story of our programs as under constant attack from our university administrations and faculty colleagues, as well as struggling with backlash from the larger community and fighting for recognition and legitimacy. This narrative frames WGS programs as academic outlaws, or at least outsiders, battling with large, well-funded foes, who decry our legitimacy and constantly undercut our efforts, and it's a narrative that arises regularly in WGS conferences and publications. Indeed, the narrative is so pervasive that when I presented a version of this chapter—a chapter in which I call into question the accuracy and function of the narrative of besiegement—at a WGS conference, the conversation afterward quickly devolved into questioning how we could respond to the many attacks facing our programs. In other words, conference participants began unselfconsciously reiterating the besiegement narrative.

This is the story under which I was mentored as a WGS administrator: I was taught by one predecessor to see the work we were doing as oppositional, as if every move we made—even scheduling classroom space—was potentially under attack. I went along with this narrative in my work as a junior administrator, but it began increasingly to feel artificial, inadequate, and potentially damaging. "How," I wondered, "can we be such outsiders when our classes immediately fill, we have a large cohort of affiliated faculty, and we're able to find funding to host some of the most successful events on campus?"

Evidence of Besiegement

The origins of this narrative of besiegement aren't mysterious. They emerged in response to the tenuous status of Women's and Gender Studies programs in the early days of the field. The fact is, WGS programs have historically been subject to attacks from inside and outside the university. When the field emerged in the late 1960s, it was greeted with negative responses on campus ranging from skepticism to outright hostility.

More recently, the attacks seem predominantly to have come from outside of the academy, since WGS programs are an established part of the curriculum at many colleges and universities. Indeed, it's arguably the success and proliferation of such programs that has led to scrutiny from conservative organizations. Martha McCaughey has documented a number of these attacks over the last decade from conservative groups in the United States such as the Washington, D.C.-based Independent Women's Forum, North Carolina's John William Pope Center for Higher Education Policy, and the David Horowitz Freedom Center (McCaughey 2008). In 1999, an Arizona state senator proposed cutting all state funding to all WGS programs. A *Newsweek* feature that aired in 2000 claimed that these programs offer "ideological browbeating and indoctrination passing as teaching" and "are more about solidarity than scholarship" (Begley 2000, 70).

In 2005, the Pope Center targeted WGS programs in North Caro-lina, calling them "sickly" and arguing that "they leave themselves wide open to charges of intellectual laziness, bias, and irrelevance" (Vick-ers 2005, 1, 16). In 2008, Roy Den Hollander filed a lawsuit against Columbia University for having a WGS program that he claimed vio-lated the First Amendment, "by aiding the establishment of the religion Feminism" (Docket No. 08-7286-CV, 2008 U.S.). David Horowitz has specifically targeted WGS programs, including those in the state of Kansas in 2006, as well as specific classes and professors. His 2009 book, *One Party Classroom* (Horowitz and Laskin), purports to identify the 150 worst courses in higher education, and 59 of them are WGS courses.

So it's not delusional thinking on the part of WGS scholars and administrators that has led to this pervasive narrative in the field. WGS programs have been and, in some cases still are, under attack. Program directors, especially those who were instrumental in initiating programs in the early days of the field, often had to learn to operate in hostile environments. They developed besiegement mentalities as a self-pres-ervation strategy, and the narrative of the field as "always under fire" began to emerge.

As we've seen, WGS programs have actually been, and are still, vulnerable to attack from inside and outside the academy. This situa-tion, though, doesn't, to my mind, fully explain the pervasiveness of the besiegement narrative. Indeed, even as they recount the challenges they faced in founding early Women's Studies programs, their direc-tors note the support they received and the successes they experienced. Tucker Pamella Farley observes that in New York in the early 1970s, "we were growing fast, functioning very successfully, and doing exciting educational and scholarly work; at the same time we were under attack, driven to defend ourselves, and struggling to survive. It was a complex moment" (2000, 272).

The evidence of success is present even in many narratives of besiege-ment. For instance, in the 1997 NWSA Backlash Report, written to address attacks on Women's and Gender Studies, many of the descrip-tions of attacks contained information about the success of the programs. One campus reported a faculty member trying to dissuade students from taking WGS courses, but the administrator noted that the courses filled immediately. Another person shared the story of a campus paper attacking the program, but followed with, "the pro-Women's Studies response was so huge that the newspaper had to devote 4 editorial pages to printing 'some' of the responses in favor" (Scully and Currier 1997, 34). The authors note, "the majority of administrators reported that their [WGS] programs and faculty had not experienced problems and, of those who did report problems, the majority indicated the damage had not been very serious" (Scullly and Currier 1997, 86–87). Other examples: when an Arizona state senator tried to cut all funding to WGS programs, she withdrew the proposal after it generated a great deal of opposition. Den Hollander's lawsuit was dismissed in April 2009 by a judge who said, "Feminism is no more a religion than physics, and at least the core of the complaint is therefore frivolous" (1:08-07286-CV-LAK-KNF, 2009 U.S.). Even those who view WGS as endangered often recognize this complexity. Joan Wallach Scott says of the 1980s, "We were embattled, yet on the verge of success" (2008, 3). Even when attacks are happening or are perceived, there is evidence that the field is resilient and well-protected.

As with the above examples of complex experiences of success and embattlement, my own experience as a second-generation WGS director has also made me skeptical of the besiegement narrative as the only one to tell. By the time I came to administration in WGS, the programs at the schools where I worked were quite successful—successful enough to have an associate director, or to do a national search for a full-time director. They were not in danger of being shuttered. My experience has been that the upper administration at the universities were supportive of the programs, even enthusiastic about them, because these programs had high enrollments, strong student satisfaction, active faculty involvement, and often a great deal of support from the community. Further, I've experienced WGS as a field that's quite firmly established nationwide. It is not an academically tenuous or an outsider field. We are, in fact, academic insiders, with all the trappings of maturing disciplines.

Although Farley notes how complex the moment of the 1970s was, I want to argue that the point is that all of our moments are complex. WGS programs are often operating in somewhat hostile climates—hostility that's related to feminism, or to the liberal arts, or to academia in general—but they're also experiencing a great deal of success. Why, then, has the narrative of besiegement become such a prominent—even a default—way of describing and discussing the field? It seems that the narrative has become "naturalized," a story that's taken for granted in the field and that's deployed in particular, often seemingly unconscious, ways. I contend that the besiegement narrative serves a number of functions for WGS faculty and administrators, functions that are practical as well as ideological, and that play out at the intellectual and administrative levels. This narrative serves as a tool for heightening marginality, intellectual and generational claim staking, and absolution. These functions often overlap, and I don't offer this as a comprehensive list. In addition, there is some slippage between WGS and academic feminism in the works I'm examining. The two are clearly not the same thing, but there are lines of connection, and so both appear in my mapping of the besiegement narrative.

I don't mean to collapse all narratives of besiegement or attack into one another. Besiegement, of course, is often a lived reality for certain populations in certain locations. One of the strengths of this discipline is that we (are supposed to) recognize this; we examine systems of privilege and hierarchy, how they're constructed and solidified, and how they might be challenged. Further, as essays in this volume note, there are identity categories that are marginalized within the academic locations of WGS (as noted in the "Trans-" and "Sexuality" chapters). My point, then, isn't that the besiegement narrative is uniformly used in problematic ways and that WGS scholars and practitioners should always be skeptical of it. Instead, I'm examining—and calling into question—a particular set of ways in which scholars frame the field itself as besieged. This narrative has leverage because, as scholars, we're inclined to see it as plausible.

Heightening Marginality and Activism

Framing Women's and Gender Studies programs as under attack implies that these programs are marginalized or alienated, and because this is a field that's often already activist-identified, this supposed outsider status leads to the programs being framed as resistant. The battle metaphors that crop up in conversations such as the online discussion of January 2009 speak to this: WGS faculty and administrators often use the besiegement narrative to identify their programs as outsiders to the academic community. The besiegement narrative, then, can be used to create or heighten a sense of the field's marginality or to call for its rejection of academic insider status. In her history of the field of WGS, *When Women Ask the Questions*, Marilyn Jacoby Boxer observes the ambiguous appeal of marginality when she notes, "Existing both inside and outside traditional academic structures, feminist scholars now ponder 'how to be or not to be marginal at one and the same time'" (1998b, 76). Other scholars also call into question efforts to incorporate the field fully into the academy. For instance, linguistics professor Robin Lakoff, argues, "feminism, once a stance of radical external critique, can only be compromised by admission to insider status. How can it attack authority when it speaks in the voice of authority?" (quoted in Boxer 1998b, 172).

Myra Dinnerstein speaks of the founding the "Women's Studies" program at the University of Arizona. "At the same time that we worked hard to get accepted within the university, I always felt it crucial to maintain a sense of alienation from the institution" (2000, 300–301). The editors of *Out of the Margins: Women's Studies in the Nineties* promote the institutionalization of WGS in Britain, but only because, they ask, "do we have a viable alternative?" They explain, "Some would say that the attempt to establish within the academy a feminist intellectual space is in itself a problem, that in institutionalizing Women's Studies we are taming feminist knowledge: that it leads to ... our defeat," and they encourage programs to "resist incorporation" (Aaron and Walby 1991, 1–2). They identify WGS' success as dangerous for the field; indeed, according to them, its success, paradoxically, may even be what causes it to fail. They offer a variety of warnings, suggesting that the field must maintain its marginality, and implying that it is inevitable, and that its "embattlement ... will not change" (Aaron and Walby 1991, 8).

Why this emphasis on marginality? There are a number of answers to this question, but it seems that the reason that is most closely linked to the besiegement narrative is that marginality can provide a sense of meaning by keeping the programs linked to activism. As Biddy Martin observes, "Righteousness accrues to positions with apparent claims to marginality" (2008, 171). If WGS is marginalized, then its faculty and administrators can see themselves as embodying a righteousness, even a political purity, which the rest of the academy threatens. University administrators—and, indeed, other disciplines on campus—can be identified as the opponents, the entities against which the field is supposed to struggle. As Catherine Orr notes in this volume, activism becomes a kind of "sacred object" that asserts moral power over the field. By virtue of being besieged, WGS programs automatically become sites of resistance and therefore of activism.

Perceptions of marginality are a necessary prerequisite for activism. Activists are those on the margins; they aren't the ones firmly and comfortably housed in institutional authority. Framing the field as besieged defines the field as marginalized and therefore eligible for activist credentials. Indeed, this aura of activism that results from declared marginality is often quite appealing to many WGS faculty, offering a link to the field's activist past. This is another reason for the prevalence of the besiegement narrative: since WGS as an academic field emerged from and remains in many cases wedded to feminist activism, the besiegement narrative provides a kind of activist credentialing for programs which are firmly housed in the academy and may not participate directly in activism. Boxer offers a typical origin story of the field as activist: "If the idealism of the 1960s was one parent of women's studies, its other parent was activism" (1998b, 26). Many early program directors associate their work to establish the field with the women's movement. In the volume *The Politics of Women's Studies: Testimony from 30 Founding Mothers* (Howe 2000), several of the founding directors emphasize the political origins of their work in the field. The history of WGS affects its present day, and that history wasn't very long ago, so that program founders—those who, like Catharine Stimpson, saw it as at risk from "the dangers out there"—often view the field today through the lens of its origins. Being besieged can mean being activists, and that's something that's prized within many programs. This often undertheorized celebration of activism is another potentially problematic narrative in WGS, as Orr discusses, and that narrative is bolstered by the besiegement narrative. For programs that still frame themselves as the academic arm of the women's movement, the besiegement narrative can be validating, suggesting that the work being done is important enough that it's subject to attack.

Indeed, there can be a certain satisfaction to this sense of being besieged. Founding directors remember the excitement of their work:

"These first feminist courses were unlike any I've taught before or since. It was truly a revolutionary period: everything was being questioned: everything was experimental. We had the sense of being on the threshold of a new world. The excitement and energy were overwhelming" (Donovan 2000, 96–97). Younger WGS scholars recognize that this excitement may be missing from the field as they experience it. In *Not My Mother's Sister*, Astrid Henry notes,

> In looking back on this period in feminism's history [the second wave], I have often found myself feeling envious of the enthusiasm and confidence with which feminists of the early second wave were able to write about their own historical moment. One can't help but notice a great sense of exuberance in these early second-wave texts, a feeling of being part of something larger than oneself, of being an agent in history. (2004, 73)

Karla A. Erickson explicitly links this excitement to the threat of attack, when she writes in a narrative describing her graduate work in WGS, "In spite of the many benefits of a feminist-friendly learning environment, I at times felt less inspired—conducting feminist research without a fight did not have quite the same thrill as it had had in a more toxic setting" (2007, 337). By maintaining a sense of besiegement, then, scholars and administrators may perpetuate the activist thrill as well as a sense of purpose and moral authority.

Staking Intellectual/Generational Claims Within the Women's and Gender Studies "Community"

The previous discussion suggested some of the generational components that may play into deployments of the besiegement narrative. In this section I want to examine ways that the narrative can be used to stake generational and intellectual claims, which means that these attacks often come from within a space defined as Women's and Gender Studies. This function has intellectual and administrative components, and in this context it is often applied to dissent within what we might identify as the WGS community, particularly in relation to the debates between versions of activist and theoretical feminism that took place in the field in the 1990s. Martha McCaughey's essay in this volume alerts us to the fact that, while WGS often wants to function as an informal, welcoming community, we are in fact part of the academic establishment, so our "community" may well be shaped by debates such as this one. My concern is less with the content of these debates than with the way that theoretical and generational changes in the field were seen, in some quarters, as evidence of besiegement. For instance, at a National Women's Studies Association conference in the early 2000s, a woman stood during the question and answer period of the major keynote address and asked, "How can we get these postmodernists out of our departments?" Although I perceived her question as a bizarre non sequitur, many others in the audience applauded. This WGS practitioner and those who validated her question by applauding were framing postmodernist scholars as interlopers whose presence in the field was damaging the programs. Their scholarly work alone made them threats whose attacks justified a besieged response. The besiegement mindset thus becomes a tool that not only differentiates between the discipline and "the outside world" but that is used within the discipline to police its boundaries and ultimately hold it back from certain kinds of academic change.

Susan Gubar and Robyn Wiegman's debate in the journal *Critical Inquiry* in 1998 and 1999 shows how the besiegement narrative can be used to stake out intellectual and generational territory. In her article, "What Ails Feminist Criticism?," which initiated the debate, Gubar argues that feminist scholarship is suffering because of the rise of new intellectual approaches. She frames her essay using the metaphor of illness. Although this metaphor is softened from the "who killed feminism" rhetoric of her initial version of this essay, both are versions of the besiegement narrative. In this essay she uses besiegement to stave off changes in the discipline of WGS, in particular changes resulting from poststructuralist criticism and from scholars who are women of color. Rather than addressing theoretical issues on their merits, the bulk of her argument rests on framing these forms of criticism as dangerous because of the dissension they provoke and the fact that they have destabilized the term "women." Although she attempts a lighthearted tone, her essay continually draws on and invokes the besiegement narrative. She refers to the particular theoretical approaches she criticizes as "maladies" that "threaten the relationship feminists within the academy have sought to maintain with one another and with women outside it" (Gubar 1998, 881).

This essay, and Wiegman's response, also demonstrate how the intellectual and generational functions of the besiegement narrative can overlap. Gubar denies the generational component, explaining early in the piece that her argument could easily "be misunderstood as a self-serving generational account, in which early feminist critics (prominent in the seventies) felt beleaguered by attacks of their successors (in the eighties and nineties), a group that just happened to be comprised of theorists of color and of lesbianism. Oh dear!" (1998, 879). Nevertheless, the essay does seem to be doing the very work she denies. Wiegman, too, identifies Gubar's concerns as generational, when she frames Gubar's complaints as "a tension emerging within academic feminism between one generation's critique of patriarchal masculinism and another's interest in a self-reflexive articulation of differences among women" (1999, 363).

Gubar is not the only one identifying poststructuralist theories as agents of attack. Historian Joan Hoff goes so far as to compare post-structuralists to pornographers, seeing them as people who "assert male dominance over women by literally and figuratively silencing them by deconstructing (or hacking) them up into smaller fragmented pieces" (quoted in Boxer 1998b, 145–146). Indeed, Wendy Brown discusses the reluctance within the field to accept new theoretical models in terms of a metaphor of military maneuvering. She notes that, for those who resist change in WGS, "Theory that destabilizes the category of women, racial formations that similarly blur the solidarity of the category—each of these must be resisted, restricted, or worse, colonized, to preserve the realm" (Brown 2008, 21).

The generational component plays a part institutionally, as well. In the last decade, an increasing number of WGS programs have been directed by younger faculty who did not found these programs. These new directors have had the opportunity to grow and develop already-existing programs. In *Women's Studies on Its Own*, Wiegman notes that "those of us trained by the founding generation have the opportunity to carry something forward, and to do so from within the positions of power that feminism in the academy has made possible for us" (2002b, 2) which the "founding generation" fought for but did not necessarily get to enjoy. These administrators are likely to experience these programs as academically rigorous, influential, and central to shaping the curricula of departments around campus. For this cohort, of which I am a member, WGS is an exciting enterprise, academically cutting-edge, popular, and influential—and this has always been the case for our work with the field. In other words, I experience WGS as a discipline—as Ann Braithwaite argues in this volume, "an integral institutional site and intellectual project in the university"—not a marginalized movement.

My argument here follows Devoney Looser's observations in "Battle Weary Feminists and Supercharged Grrls: Generational Differences and Outsider Status on Women's Studies Administration" (2002). She notes that WGS is a field in which new—often young and untenured—administrators regularly direct programs in the presence of those programs' founders, and those founders often have experienced it as a battlefield, as a hard-won fight. This experience of the past is the lens through which they may experience the program's present day affairs. She recounts one experience in the epigraph to this essay, an experience in which the besiegement narrative was so enthusiastically repeated by WGS faculty members that Looser became convinced of its validity, despite a lack of actual evidence. The besiegement narrative became a way that earlier faculty and administrators of the program could attempt to keep the program operating in a particular generational mode; in other words, it became a tool for staking a generational claim, for keeping Looser's generation of faculty and program directors from having the leverage to move the program in different directions.

Absolution

Finally, the besiegement narrative can be used to try to achieve a kind of absolution. The narrative often functions as a way for individual scholars or administrators to absolve themselves of negative behaviors and ideologies without actually addressing or changing those behaviors or ideologies. The besiegement the field is suffering can serve as an excuse, as if the field's vulnerability precludes responding to critiques. Joan Wallach Scott, in the introduction to *Women's Studies on the Edge*—a book offering multiple critiques of Women's and Gender Studies—chooses to embrace the besiegement narrative and its absolution function in order to frame her volume's critiques. She notes, "We recognize that this is a difficult moment in which to seem to criticize women's studies programs. They are under siege from the right....And the attack on feminism goes beyond the borders of the academy" (2008, 6). She goes on to list, for the second time in only five pages, the kinds of attacks WGS is facing from various quarters. By so doing she validates the besiegement narrative but uses it to present her own volume not as further besiegement but as a defense of academic feminism that is under siege.

I see this absolution function happening in particular in relation to racism within Women's and Gender Studies. Using besiegement to absolve the field, or individuals within it, from being identified as racist is clear in Susan Gubar's, "What Ails Feminist Criticism?" (1998). One of the two significant threats Gubar identifies to academic feminism is, "the barrage of diatribes directed against white feminists" (886) by scholars who are women of color. She repeatedly frames the work of these scholars in the language of attack, arguing that they are damaging academic feminism by hurting white feminists. For instance, Gubar writes, "White feminists began to feel beleaguered by blatantly imperative efforts to right the wrong of black female instrumentality" (1998, 889). She continues, not only calling white women beleaguered, but using the language of attack: "The politics of racial authenticity may be experienced as an attack on feminism's endorsement of all women's right to self-expression" (1998, 891). Rather than addressing the substantive critiques that scholars have made about racial politics within feminist scholarship, Gubar deflects these using the besiegement narrative. In her essay, then, the real problem is that feminists are being divided, not that racism permeates the practices of academic feminists. Wiegman notes that Gubar is claiming the identity of "injured whiteness," strategically framing white feminists as victims because this framing allows her to avoid responding to critiques: "From this victimized position, all analytical moves made by feminists of color are assaults against feminism, not crucial contributions to its self-examination and articulation" (1999, 377–378). In other words, the besiegement narrative allows Gubar to absolve herself and the field of racism. She dismisses criticism that argues that feminist scholarship and WGS are replicating racist practices and operating within white privileged frameworks; for Gubar's argument, racism is irrelevant, as the real "threat" to academic feminism comes not from racist white scholars but from the "assaults against feminism" made by feminists of color.

Although Gubar's essay is a particularly clear example of this use of the besiegement narrative, many other WGS scholars have invoked besiegement for similar absolution purposes. In her history of the field, Boxer recognizes that many white feminists, like Gubar, interpreted the critiques of women of color as an assault on the field: "At the very time they were braving personal and institutional hostility to bring forth new women's studies programs or to bring those programs through their early formative stages, they found themselves dealing with attacks from within" (1998b, 112). Marilyn Boxer, too, seems to identify these critiques as "attacks from within"; she does not contradict this language. To her credit, however, Boxer reframes this interpretation of critiques by women of color: "Quickly, however, they recognized that their ignorance was no claim to innocence but rather proof of privilege" (1998b, 112).

Consequences

There are many consequences of the various uses of the besiegement narrative. When this narrative is used to keep Women's and Gender Studies locked into anachronistic modes of operation, both administratively and intellectually, one consequence is that people who are doing rigorous academic work will not see WGS as an appropriate academic home. This, of course, would be—and in some cases already is—to the field's great detriment. Many of the authors in *Women's Studies on the Edge* observe that the most cutting-edge feminist scholarship is emerging from sites outside WGS programs. In that volume Biddy Martin identifies this problem when she argues, "If feminist studies of gender are to remain vital, or even take the lead in reorganizing our approaches to knowledge and learning, we have to recognize and resist defensive refusals to be moved out of entrenched positions" (2008, 195). The defensiveness that Martin refers to operates on multiple levels; scholars and administrators who believe their field is under siege may feel themselves to be more literally than psychologically defended. Wendy Brown, too, notes the consequences of a besieged mentality for feminist scholarship: "Each [theory] ... is compelled to go elsewhere, while women's studies consolidates itself in the remains, impoverished by the lack of challenges from within, bewildered by its new ghettoization in the academy—this time by feminists themselves" (2008, 21). Indeed, Brown notes that this reluctance to embrace new theoretical and scholarly models, and the condition of seeing this new scholarship as threatening to the political mission of WGS, risks making the field anti-intellectual: "anti-intellectualism…is increasingly codified as the spirit of women's studies work" (2008, 35). Ironically, the besiegement mentality in this case could lead to the field's diminishment—the besiegement narrative itself could become the thing that is endangering WGS programs and that we need to guard against.

Devoney Looser recognizes, as do I, that WGS programs are often truly under fire. But she notes, too, that the *belief* that one's program is under fire—especially in the absence of evidence—can have negative consequences: "Worrying about our survival (which I came to believe was never in question) prevented us from discussing what we wanted or needed—putting us in an entirely reactive rather than proactive mode" (2002, 215). Indeed, according to the besiegement narrative, success can be seen as evidence of selling out. There's an ideological purity demanded by the besiegement mentality that can work against strategic program administration. And within a besiegement mentality, an insistence on ideological purity makes sense: every compromise seems a concession, one step closer to letting the walls crumble and the enemy in. This is another practical implication of the besiegement narrative: it can drag our programs down administratively, draining energy that could be used in other, more productive, ways. By locking us into a mode of behavior that might have been more appropriate for a previous generation, it detracts from our ability to define the field. By demanding that we operate as endangered outsiders, it limits our ability to appeal to students or to faculty affiliates, not to mention university administrators. To the extent that this narrative encourages us not to function as academic insiders, it may damage our institutional standing. Again, the danger is that the besiegement narrative can become a self-fulfilling prophecy.

Aimee Carillo Rowe effectively problematizes the notion of institutional standing in her chapter in this volume on "Institutionalization," and her work might be used to bolster the besiegement narrative. I'd like to argue that the narrative of besiegement as it's commonly deployed doesn't address the white heterosociality Carrillo Rowe has identified. Instead, the besiegement narrative more often functions to keep existing power structures in place, with particular emphasis on white women's power. There's room for meaningful disagreement about what to make of WGS' institutionalized status, but it is clearly the case that as a field we are experiencing increasing institutional success. What this volume is asking us to do is move away from uncritical acceptance and interrogate our narratives, with attention to what is visible and to the places we have "not been permitted to go." Carrillo Rowe's essay notes that feeling comfortable in a site of institutional success may make certain things invisible (such as the power structures of academia that enable white heterosociality). In the context of the narrative of besiegement, then, WGS is not permitted to go to institutional status and power. The tension between our two narratives is productive.

There are losses when we give up the besiegement narrative. We lose the idea of ourselves as automatically and always activists. We lose a sense of uniqueness when we recognize that we're part of the academy rather than being heroic outsiders; we lose the "purity" and "righteousness" that can be associated with marginality. This can also lead to a loss of a sense of identity, an identity around which people have easily and consistently rallied. And yet, importantly, these losses make meaningful opportunities visible. When we let go of this narrative, what we're faced with is the need to define our field by something other than negation: what we're not or who we're fighting against. We're faced with the opportunity to respond to critiques from within, and to allow the field to grow and change in response to generational and intellectual shifts in the academy. We have the chance to recognize our institutional power, and to make use of it. I am arguing that it is time for WGS to seize these possibilities.

Notes

1. See https://listserv.umd.edu/cgi-bin/wa?A1=ind0901e&L=wmst-l#16.

8

COMMUNITY[1]

Martha McCaughey

Why Examine "Community?"

This chapter explores a series of beliefs about the identity, role, and mission of Women's and Gender Studies (WGS) that revolve around assumptions about "community." A series of often unspoken understandings about community manifest themselves in the administrative and pedagogical decisions, debates, and daily practices in WGS. Our field does not have one agreed upon definition of community, but rather is characterized by competing assumptions about to whom and what community refers. The term is implied as often as it is directly invoked, and its definition, purpose, and desirability are largely taken for granted rather than articulated or defended. In exploring the history of the often painfully loaded and conflicting notions of community in WGS, I trace the tensions over community back to the founding of the field in academe and our uneasy relationship to our institutional success. In so doing, I show that some of the tensions in WGS are rooted in these unresolved, often unexamined conflicts over the meaning of community.

Community in WGS is imagined and used discursively in two specific ways. In the formative years of the field (before my time in academe), the word community quite clearly referenced a group outside the walls of the proverbial ivory tower, a community which presumably spawned early Women's Studies programs and to whom the academic enterprise would remain accountable—the "activist roots" so often championed in written histories of the field. Today, however, we find community implicitly and explicitly referring to those of us who are WGS faculty (and sometimes our students) inside the academic world. The gestures and implications of WGS scholars as a community, I suggest, ultimately serve to deny the ways in which we've become part—albeit (and revealingly) *uncomfortably* part—of the academic establishment and less directly accountable to "the community" outside the academy.

Reconsidering the uses and meanings of the term "community" in WGS is especially timely now for several related reasons. First, the field in the United States is under a well-organized attack by particularly well-funded right-wing groups such as the Independent Women's Forum, Concerned Women for America, and the Pope Center for Higher Education Policy (McCaughey and Warren 2006). These conservative groups argue for a traditional curriculum in colleges and universities, and criticize WGS for being political rather than "truth-based." Second, the emerging consumerist mentality about higher education prompts people—from the aforementioned groups to students and taxpaying citizens—to approach professors, our classrooms, and our knowledge "products" as consumers who are paying for our services. Hence, WGS programs are increasingly faced with letters from taxpayers, alumni, and others who are offended by, for example, a queer film series or the program website's omission of links to anti-abortion organizations. Third, public appreciation for the kind of work done in the humanities and in fields like WGS has waned because these fields have little cash-in value relative to degrees in business, technology, and health sciences (Michael 2000, 170–171).[2] Finally, given the increasing diversity of identities, research methods, pedagogical styles, and political commitments of WGS practitioners, we can more easily see that community feels different for the many people involved in the field.

During my first semester as a WGS faculty member in 1996, I became keenly aware of the centrality of the concept of community, its competing definitions, and its symbolic value to different groups of people when I was asked to attend a meeting at the campus Women's Center to justify the position I was taking in a talk I'd proposed for the Women's History Month celebration. Hoping to ease the committee's concerns about my presentation and underscore my feminist credentials, I invoked my official position as a WGS professor who was, I explained, writing a book about the topic in question. One committee member, an instructor in the university's math department and long-time feminist activist on and off campus, simply stated, "You're not an activist just because you wrote a book." Didn't she realize, I thought to myself, that I would not, and could not, write such a book had I not been an engaged participant in the very movement about which I was writing? Didn't she see, I wondered, that as a WGS professor, I was about as legitimate a feminist as she could hope would join her campus?

At that point, of course, I realized the difference between us—and that this difference mattered: I was a professional feminist scholar. I was squarely inside the white-male-dominated bourgeois system that had created sexist knowledge claims and that had been the object of grass-roots feminist challenges. She, on the other hand, performed her feminist activism in her spare time, as a labor of love. Her activities seemed steeped with a purity of motive, whereas I was perceived as making my living off "the community." The very things that I thought would establish my legitimacy actually called it into question. My position as a feminist academic professional hardly established me as a true feminist, in Barbara Smith's sense of struggling "to free all women" (1982, 48). Instead I appeared to some as engaged merely in what Smith calls "bourgeois female self-aggrandizement" (1982, 51). As with "activism," so "community" is often invoked or implied as the opposite of, or antidote for, the elitist excesses of the academy.[3] I had embraced my position as a feminist inside the system—I "inhabit institutional power in the name of feminism" (Wiegman 2008, 51), whereas others are attending to those who have "real" problems. Because I was inside the power structure, I could not claim a position that was innocently oppositional. Moreover, my relationship to feminism and its political agenda was one of professionalism, as opposed to the volunteerism that characterized the relationship many others had with feminism.

My own sense of legitimacy came, by necessity, from my academic peers in the WGS profession who would judge my work worthy, or not, of publication and who would assess my professional progress toward tenure. None of the people who called me in to question my presentation for Women's History Month would have been qualified judges in this sense. And yet, on another level, I had a strong desire to connect with the people sitting at that table: the feminist activists, the volunteers at the Women's Center, those who believed in organizing Women's History Month, and the people both on and off campus whom the events reached. I had read accounts of the field being rooted in the feminist movement; thus I saw my own hire as a score for the cause—and I had planned to do my part by performing public service as a feminist academic and by writing a book that was "relevant" to women's lives.

As I will show, however, the attempt to speak to or for a community of women *outside academia* inappropriately frames women as the group from whom we in WGS organically emerged and whose concerns we are capable of, and should be, capturing in our work. At the same time, the concept and goal of a WGS community *on campus* hides the experiences of marginalization felt by some of the very people the label is assumed to include or represent. Even when feminist scholars have issued challenges to other feminist scholars aligned with WGS to think of women who are situated differently from themselves in terms of their race, sexuality, nationality, age, or physical ability, they often presume that "we" are women and that "we" have a particular purpose with our academic work—that "we" are ideally setting about to "free all women." By considering both senses of community in WGS in turn, I argue that neither a WGS community nor a community of women who is presumably freed by WGS work can be sustained, politically or intellectually, when in our field we have so successfully dispelled the notion of a common history, political position, or identity among women.

The Community Out There: There is No There There

One of the earliest mentions of "community" as a group that exists outside academia came up in 1977 at the very first National Women's Studies Association convention—which included numerous panels to accommodate academics and nonacademics alike—when a group of nonacademics charged the university women with "[taking] much more from the Women's Movement than they have to date returned" (in Boxer 1988, 84). The preamble to NWSA's original Constitution of 1977 embraced nonacademic perspectives, "refus[ing] to accept sterile divisions between academy and community" (National Women's Studies Association 1977). "Community" here referred to where we came from and whom we served, but not the academics themselves. This idea is still part of Women's and Gender Studies, insofar as some of us may still involve ourselves, and encourage students' involvement, in activities outside the university: e.g., service-learning, grassroots theatre, or giving seminars in prisons. When WGS partners with people (usually women) outside the academy to engage in, for example, fundraising for a local women's shelter or the transformation of the local secondary school culture, we proudly proclaim our connection to that community.

This original incarnation of "community" in early Women's Studies is exemplified by Catharine R. Stimpson, founding editor of *Signs*, in her essay, "The New Feminism and Women's Studies," when she asks questions about "the relationship between a Women's Studies program and women in the larger community" (1975, 80). Stimpson points out tensions between WGS institutionalized as part of academe and the women and/or feminists outside of academe when she asks, "If a women's liberation group in town helps to set up a Women's Studies program at a local university, should it have a say in that program? Should it have a veto over faculty hiring?" (1975, 80).

The important and transformative criticisms of WGS leveled by feminists of color in the academy also invoked "community" as something out there and to which feminists scholars did, or did not (but ideally did), belong. For example, Barbara Christian writes of her concern that many feminist scholars

> do not have a visceral connection to *communities outside the university* and for whom feminist literature is not so much a prod to change as much as it is an artifact. For one of the academy's major strategies of containment is not only excluding some, but discouraging others who might disrupt and transform it by attempting to incorporate them into an exclusively academic culture so that they become increasingly *cut off from the other cultures and communities* which nourish them. (1990b, 60, emphasis added)

This tension, then, over to whom and where feminist scholars belonged, was present in the early stages of the field. As Marilyn J.

Boxer notes in her relatively early history of the field's beginnings, the responsibility to a larger feminist community was debated from the start: how best can we connect "the work of the academy to the concerns of the world?"[4] The worry that WGS would lose its radical edge and be co-opted by the academy has also been expressed since the field's beginning (Boxer 1988, 83).

I am arguing, though, that we must critique the notion of community as a group *from* which we hail in WGS—that such programs stem from and respond to the needs of a specific group (namely, women)—in order to recognize what that conception masks: the diversity of those who formed and work in the field and the way in which the very practitioners of WGS have deconstructed the idea of unitary identities. In addition to how the field will come to terms with the differences among women and the plurality of sex/gender categories, several other intense current debates are themselves partially rooted in unspoken assumptions about community: whether WGS should be defined by its intellectual mission or by its political mission (see Wiegman 2008; Brown 2008); whether WGS scholarship can legitimately be highly theoretical or instead must be accessible to our "sisters down the street";[5] whether to rename "Women's Studies" programs "Gender Studies"; and whether to require our students to engage in community service.

While WGS has become successfully institutionalized, with paid faculty lines, operating budgets, minors, majors, and certificates, we find ourselves having to justify our work whilst carefully characterizing its nature and value. One way to do this, as John Michael (2000) points out in his book on academic professionals and the culture wars, is to seek some sort of connection with the public, or with communities outside academia. If we are not, or cannot be, the technocrats, then we can, just as some of our colleagues in the arts, humanities, and social sciences have done, champion a position as critical or public intellectuals who "address a wider audience and claim to speak for or to represent excluded, silenced, or oppressed groups, criticizing the dominant order in the interests of a more egalitarian, just, or democratic society" (Michael 2000, 3). This move, however, demands that WGS academics be well liked by students and acceptable to everyone who believes they have a right to criticize and reshape academic programs today. The very desire to be accountable, then, while understandable and even commendable, is a double-edged sword. It thus demands that we sort out the tensions inherent in our understandings of the community we say our work addresses, represents, or liberates.

WGS scholars have long struggled over whether we are part of the academic elite or those activist groups whose struggles presumably led to the formation of the field. The idea of a community out there assumes that WGS professors emerged from, and speak for, women "out there" in "the real world." But those women "out there" are not out there to be addressed or represented; rather they are a creation of intellectuals in the first place (Brown 2008). It is as arrogant to assume that we as researchers can tell others what is best for them as it is to pretend that our scholarship reflects their needs. When we admit that our relationship to people outside academia is not as simple as representing, reporting to, or freeing them—that we seek to shape thinking and not simply reflect the views of women in "the community"—we see that the political mission of our scholarship involves influence, argument, and conflict (the very ideas often thought to be anticommunitarian). Moreover, theoretical work in WGS can have an impact on policies and practices even if "sisters down the street" do not read it. WGS scholars ultimately do not, and cannot, represent women as much as we seek to *shape* policy and people's thinking on issues of gender and inequality.

A Haven in a Heartless Academy: There is No There Here

While we may have become more mindful that there is *no there there*, Women's and Gender Studies scholars have, perhaps in reaction, come to regard a there *in here*—a WGS community in academia itself.[6] WGS might offer scholars and students a significant sense of belonging, especially if they feel alienated from the work, norms, and social lives of those in other academic units. Victoria O'Reilly refers to "community building" as the development of discipline-specific scholarly practices such as publications, conferences, and other professional activities centered on WGS (1998, 130). Here, efforts toward "community building" in WGS do not mean, for instance, developing women leaders in a rural community or empowering female residents in public housing complexes. They are about institutionalizing WGS, about building alliances in the academy.

Miranda Joseph uses the term "community" to indicate the group of academics who come together on campus as WGS, when she describes the embattled search for the faculty position she was hired to occupy at the University of Arizona: "The search process itself became a battle over candidates who were imagined to be … more or less willing to participate in the norms of the Women's Studies community" (2002b, 277). Similarly, Betsy Eudey uses the term to refer to the feminist scholars on her campus when she states that "the Women's Studies community supported the inclusion of males in Women's Studies courses…." (2007, 458). Jean O'Barr's history of the program in Women's Studies at Duke University, *Feminism in Action*, invokes community in the subtitle: *Building Institutions and Community Through Women's Studies*. The word "community," however, rarely comes up in the book and when it does, it refers mainly to those scholars teaching and studying WGS on the campus. For instance, in her acknowledgements, O'Barr thanks "the Duke University community" (1994, xiii), while in her introduction, she refers to the physical, psychological, and intellectual spaces of/for feminist scholarship in the academy. The word does not arise again until her book's final three pages, where it is mentioned in three different contexts: she refers to the "critical and supportive community" of WGS and also "the feminist community surrounding Women's Studies," which is "a moral community, a group of *faculty and students* united by a cluster of beliefs and committed to a set of goals" (1994, 282, emphasis added). Finally, O'Barr writes that WGS "*crosses the ivy boundaries into the communities where it is located*, insisting that the relationship between theory and practice is at the center of all its concerns" (1994, 282, emphasis added).

To create a sense that we are a community of scholars united by either a common identity or a change-oriented mission, a number of practices that paid particular attention to the spaces we occupied and how we conducted ourselves in those spaces were championed as ways to create community in/as WGS. Despite the complexity and diversity of the historical formation of the field, it nevertheless made sense, or simply felt right to some, that WGS hold faculty meetings in people's homes, share meals at our meetings, and create homey environments on campus. These gestures and preferences can be seen as dominant expressions of the way in which WGS was fashioned as its own community, where lines between private/public and personal/professional were easily and sometimes productively blurred.

The notion that WGS is a unique, even special, kind of academic group—a "community"—also accounts for a number of practices in programs where I've worked or visited, such as a reluctance or downright refusal to follow Robert's Rules of Order, and the offering of hugs instead of handshakes. These gestures reference a sort of anti-authority style common for a variety of countercultural movements of the 1960s.[7] Given their rejection of the arrangements and tone of both the overall society and the leftist political groups of the 1960s and 1970s, many feminists have expressed "an emphatic aversion to hierarchical and authoritarian organization" (Frazer and Lacy 1993, 118). So, it is no surprise that WGS would forge an organizational structure that is markedly different from the elitism and hierarchy that characterize academia; to do so was to make it communitarian, or a "community" (Frazer and Lacy 1993, 118). It's what makes us change-oriented or feminist.

The more recent and common understanding of community as WGS practitioners, though not necessarily articulated as such, helps position the field as oppositional. Just as other communities form as a respite from traditional or dominant values in society,[8] WGS sees itself as a community necessary for a broader critique of the academy and for opposing patriarchal norms and practices within it. It is not surprising, then, that we would reference "the WGS community" instead of calling ourselves a field, a discipline, or a group of scholars. (Revealingly, I have never heard anyone refer to "the physics community" or utter anything about "the economics community"). Precisely because those in WGS have often wanted to distance themselves from academic professionalism and the elitist, racist, and patriarchal norms of the academy in general, referring to ourselves as a "community" reveals an ambivalence about our institutional position.

Sociologist Ray Oldenburg argues that people need three places—the home, the office, and the social hangout or public gathering place (1991). He argues that Americans are losing this third place, and thus are losing a sense of community and opportunity to create the social bonds required for a functioning democracy. In WGS, we find a merger of home and work places to, in effect, feel like a third place. For many people, WGS is indeed a different (though not necessarily better) place to be. WGS programs craft a "third place" through unconventional practices and an emphasis on the importance of the physical space they occupy. The atmosphere at many WGS events has been championed as a break from the norms within faculty members' home departments and the stuffy relations of university life more generally.

In the foreword to Jean O'Barr's history of the WGS program at Duke University, Kristin Luker describes O'Barr's commitment to creating a warm atmosphere:

> Instead of the dreariness and shabbiness typical of university offices (even in fine private universities such as Duke), the Women's Studies Program offices are filled with sunlight, plants, and carefully chosen art. In the entryway, greeting the visitor is a display of ten years of T-shirts from various national Women's Studies conferences, all striking for their bright colors and clever puns.... (in O'Barr 1994, ix)

Luker applauds the way in which WGS links this atmosphere to teaching and scholarship: "O'Barr's particular contribution to feminist theory is in realizing that ... there is a deep (although rarely articulated) connection between the plants, coffee, and T-shirts on the one hand and new ways of teaching and of doing scholarship and the general work of the academy on the other" (in O'Barr 1994, ix–x). For the personal is not only political (and vice-versa) in WGS, it's downright warm and fuzzy.

The idea that we are a comfy and cozy community leads to unstated demands that all who affiliate with it feel and act "at home" in WGS. While I have experienced moments of joy and comfort in this particular atmosphere, I also question the ways in which the often unspoken, unexamined, and conflicting notions that WGS offers a community structure both the field and the experiences many have in it. It is hard for some WGS faculty members to imagine that a more professional atmosphere—the very elitism the field did not want to replicate—would actually feel better to some of its members. I did feel like I was, indeed, still at work when at WGS meetings, and I was aware of a number of other faculty who, because of their identities, lifestyles, political beliefs, or work/life balances, did not feel at home in these third spaces either. Professors situated differently along racial, class, and generational lines often experience the putative intimacy and comfort of WGS events differently. Being part of the so-called "WGS community" could be what Carrillo Rowe (in this volume) argues is a style of belonging that white women have cultivated not just with each other but also with powerful white men in the academy—an intimacy in the institution—as the condition for their institutional advancement. Lacking the option to cultivate white-on-white intimacies, feminists of color have felt like "outsiders within"—not just in the white- and male-dominated academy at large but in WGS, too (Collins 1998, 5).[9]

The methods by which Women's and Gender Studies scholars struggle, often painfully, over their political and other differences reveal the assumption that community should be a place that is comfortable in all senses. The idea of a "there in here" troublingly presumes that hierarchies, arrogant perceptions, and symbolic violence are all outside, rather than also inside, WGS. The assumption of WGS as an oppositional academic community also underlies tensions over who can teach, and how they teach, in the field. WGS professors have too often engaged in a problematic "quality control" that smacks of policing,[10] in part because we are invested in doing things differently. But considering one's academic group a community conflicts with the necessary value of academic freedom, which in some ways is ultimately individualistic and therefore in tension with some ideals of community (Frazer and Lacey 1993). Our hard-won academic legitimacy means that affiliating with WGS can no longer be loose or based in feminist political identity or commitment. Instead, accreditation and other requirements demand that WGS faculty members be reviewed and credentialed. This academic legitimacy, and the standards for inclusion that necessarily come with it, have been painfully felt by those who still think of the field as community-based in the original sense of the term.[11]

O'Barr describes the importance of the plush parlor that greets all who enter the WGS offices at Duke University (1994, 1–4). She acknowledges the way its Victorian- and French-antique décor "symbolized the demonstrated wealth, prized delicate movements, restricted interactions to stylized exchanges, displayed ornamental objects, required the labor of other women to clean and maintain them, idealized past times as essentially good times, and claimed such spaces as the embodiment of women" (1994, 2). And thus, because "in the parlors we felt constrained to an idealized and abstract model of womanhood in which women were more a part of the decoration than of the action" (1994, 2), O'Barr moved the most fragile furniture to the rooms' corners and recovered the other furniture with more durable fabric. Most importantly, she and her WGS colleagues in 1988 added to the parlor walls a series of framed portraits of women who were "firsts" at Duke. Despite these efforts, however, the atmosphere might still be experienced as stuffy rather than inviting, as bourgeois rather than comfortable, as European rather than multicultural.[12]

Even though most WGS programs decorate with much lower budgets, commonly using others' discarded furniture or rugs held together with duct tape, the idea of a "comforting third place"—an intimate setting in which we will find "coffee, community, camaraderie, [and] connection" (quoted in Klein 2000, 135)—could be the motto of almost any WGS program; that is, however, the promotional phrase of the Starbucks coffee franchises. While the institutional success of WGS can hardly be paralleled to the cannibalistic market-expansion strategy of Starbucks,[13] the contradiction in Starbucks' folksy self-definition could be compared to the increasingly institutionalized, formalized academic programs in WGS. Indeed, as we expand we formalize and do the same competitive things other academic units do: we deny or grant tenure, we disagree with one another's work, and we comply with various employment laws. We thus cannot be a comforting third space for affiliated scholars without, at best, some irony.

The idea of a WGS community disavows our institutionalized success and signals our putative difference from traditional academic units. It offers those within it an imagined political legitimacy by accentuating a sort of purity of political accountability even though our institutional position means that we are not, and cannot be, accountable to communities of women, feminists, or others in some fundamental ways. After all, people without formal scholarly credentials cannot teach in our programs, hire and fire faculty, play a role in evaluating professors for tenure, or review papers we need to get published. Depending on how we write, they might not even be able to understand what we publish. If they do understand it, as my own experience showed me, they do not necessarily agree with it or see it as useful to them. They might still be invited to our conferences, but even those have become increasingly professionalized. Calling ourselves a community, and acting as though we are a special sort of community that is different from other academic units on a campus, denies the fact that we are academic professionals who disagree, evaluate one another, and earn a living doing this work. The label also functions to, or at least expresses the hope that we will, retain the anti-establishment roots of early Women's Studies and activist elements emphasized in the dominant narrative of the field's history and mission.[14]

Just as feminists pointed out that the popular idea of the home as a haven in a heartless world denied the very politics of the private sphere (Goldsack 1999), so I would insist that it's equally problematic to conceptualize WGS as a haven in a heartless academy. Doing so denies the politics inside the field, and the painful lateral violence done inside this community of scholars and students. Positioning WGS as a special community "distinct from the university's intellectual mission for research and teaching" also enables the accusations of anti-intellectualism leveled by outsiders (Brown 2008, 33). The cost of succumbing to the seductive label of "community" for the group of academics doing feminist scholarship is the erasure of the differences in identities, motives for engagement with the field, research methods, teaching styles, and political perspectives—and the intellectual impact WGS scholars can make. Troubling the notion of community prompts us to re-envision WGS work.

Other Kinds of Belonging

The very success of Women's and Gender Studies forces us into a conflict with our own understanding of the kind of community that we originally sprung from and formed—and the community to which we are ostensibly responsible. In order to embrace the many forms of diversity that exist in WGS, and make room for competing perspectives that will fuel our field's success, we will have to give up the idea that we agree on political issues, teaching styles, or professional goals. This means giving up the idea that WGS will offer a retreat from all that we dislike about the university. We will also have to give up our romantic ideal that we are academic outsiders.[15] We will need to abandon the simplistic notion of WGS exceptionalism—as if we were the only field born of political incentives, the only field that encourages students to engage in service-learning and internships, or the only interdisciplinary field where scholars from a variety of disciplines come together for intellectual or other camaraderie. Entire university mission statements include the goal of engaged scholarship, championing the importance of using knowledge in the service of society/the community/the public. Indeed, many individual scholars outside of WGS also do purpose-driven research, harnessing the potential of their theories, methods, and analyses to make an impact in an area or on an issue they feel passionate about. Whether these public economists, public sociologists, public historians, and public architects (to name a few) label their work engaged, applied, translational, public, activist, or popular scholarship, many academic professionals frame their research as necessary for, or directly involved in, the process of understanding and alleviating social problems.

While we can protect and enhance the value of WGS by showing how we fit that mission of the university, the increased need to do so, especially in light of shrinking university budgets and declining public support for higher education, can lead to public demands for scholars' accountability. While professors tend to be all for public scholarship when it engages people and projects that they support, we might not want to envision the Starbucks Corporation, the conservative Koch Foundation, or the local group of hog farmers as our public to whom we must be accountable in our research. Indeed, at those times we bemoan the "corporatization of the university" and attempt to reduce "outside influences" on our teaching and research.[16]

The more successful and the more diverse WGS has become, the harder it has been to sweep under the rug, plush or duct-taped, our actual diversity. I suggest, then, that recourse to the term "community" as a self-identification of the field is a problem—not the solution—and hope WGS professionals will reconsider the place in which we work, the people for whom we speak and write, and our relationships to notions of difference, theoretical and political certainty, and authority. We do not have a superior truth based on our identities, our theories, or anything else. Indeed, the truths and values we hold are often in conflict. As professional WGS scholars we are, like other professional intellectuals, embedded in conflictual contexts. We persuade our students and colleagues, both inside and outside of the field, to adopt our beliefs by engendering uneasy reflections in them about their actions and beliefs in relation to more commonly held principles (Michael 2000).

The tensions still surrounding the intellectual and institutional commitments of WGS, on the one hand, and its political and identitarian bases, on the other, are not easily solved. While we should probably avoid unifying tropes for community in our field, and reconceptualize what community means in and for WGS, I do not pretend to have a simple solution or prescription for what to do instead. As many have noted, some of the most important intellectual questions that have come out of the field emerged as a direct result of the very contradictions inherent in it (Wiegman 2008). Indeed, precisely because of our unique history, and because we are intellectuals who at our best do not avoid intellectual or political paradoxes, we need not be threatened by a reconceptualization of community in WGS. But in order to build on our differences in strategic and productive ways, we must resist nostalgic and unifying tropes for conceptualizing our scholarly work and identities. Thus we might consider Carrillo Rowe's vision of "radical belonging" across "power lines" that connect people who are differently invested (2008). We might also apply the insights of queer theory to see community as a concept that can be queered, and WGS as a field that we can intentionally, and professionally, destabilize by welcoming strangers and strange theories. Rather than expect our intimacy to come from a harmonious absence of conflict, we might develop another sort of intimacy that acknowledges and moves through the alienation and distance we experience when trying to connect with people from whom we feel truly different or with whom we have long-term disagreements.

Notes

1. I wish to thank Kelly Coogan-Gehr, Lisa Johnson, John Michael, and the editors of this volume for valuable suggestions on earlier drafts of this essay. Of course all remaining errors and lapses in logic are my own.
2. I find John Michael's (2000) book very helpful for assessing tensions in WGS even though it does not directly address the WGS field or feminist intellectuals.

3. See Orr, this volume, for more on the idea of activism's role in WGS.

4. This is the self-described mission of Mount Holyoke College, the oldest of the "seven sister" colleges in the U.S. Northeast. "History of Mount Holyoke College" http://www.mtholyoke.edu/inauguration/history_mhc.html. Accessed February 9, 2011.

5. These are the words of the widely read feminist author Naomi Wolf, who implored me, as I was writing my first book in the mid-1990s, to "please write your book for your sisters down the street, not your colleagues down the hall."

6. "There is no there there" is a famous Gertrude Stein quote which has been appropriated by many writers since. And, of course, others have appropriated this by substituting "here" for "there," as I have done (e.g., Baker 1981).

7. See Binkley (2007) for an excellent history of the everyday practices and lifestyles that emerged out of the 1960s counterculture in the United States.

8. See Little (2002) for more on this.

9. Collins describes the outsider-within as "the location of people who no longer belong to any one group," and the "social locations or border spaces occupied by groups of unequal power" (1998, 5).

10. Brown reflects on these tense debates over which/whose courses can count as WGS when she asks, "How did we become cops anyway?" (2008, 23).

11. One woman, for example, applied to be a member of the WGS faculty on my campus and cited her credentials as being a feminist, a woman, and a mother of daughters.

12. See http://womenstudies.duke.edu/parlors for images of these parlors today.

13. See Klein (2000) for a discussion of Starbucks' marketing and growth strategies.

14. As evidence that WGS has emphasized its activist mission over and above a scholarly one, I want to point out that the Southeastern Women's Studies Association actually voted at their 28th annual meeting (in 2005) to add scholarship to the activism in its mission statement. The SEWSA mission statement now includes the following sentence: "The organization is committed to activism *and scholarship* that works towards eliminating oppression and discrimination on the basis of gender, race, age, religion, sexual orientation, ethnic background, physical ability, and class. Member states in the southeastern region include Alabama, Florida, Georgia, Mississippi, North Carolina, South Carolina, Tennessee, and Virginia" (emphasis added).

15. As Piepmeier argues in this volume, the WGS community can be built on a victim mentality or *narrative of besiegement*. This shows the ways in which WGS scholars can be invested in being academic outsiders. If we acknowledged ourselves to be inside the academic system, it might feel as if we are no longer a different type of place, no longer a community. And,

some might worry that being just another academic program at the university would cost us our street cred—and our identities as activists.

16. See Washburn (2005) for a disturbing example of the hog industry trying to stop a University of North Carolina epidemiology professor's research, and for other examples of corporate influence on university research.

Ubiquitous Descriptions

Points to Ponder

1. How do the assumptions outlined in the chapters about "Activism," "Waves," and "Community" together ground ideas about what WGS is or should be about? What (and who), according to these authors, might be left out of WGS because of those assumptions?
2. What are some ways in which the "Besiegement" narrative solidifies or feeds into related narratives about the need for "Community" inside of the academy and/or "Activism" on the outside of it? What happens to WGS if these narratives of "Community" and "Activism" are relinquished?
3. Is there a construct we might devise to understand the history of WGS that does not use "Waves," perhaps another metaphor that more accurately or less-problematically describes its history? What might be some possibilities—and limitations—in any new metaphor?

PART 3
EPISTEMOLOGIES RETHOUGHT

"Intersectionality," "Identity (Politics)," and "Queer" are terms identified here as posing deep challenges not only to how knowledge in Women's and Gender Studies (WGS) has been produced, but to how the field has accounted—or not—for complex and intimate sets of relations between identities and knowledges. Through their use in WGS, these terms have worked to draw our attention to the idea that starting from the experiences of particular groups of people, especially those who are marginalized by particular forms of structural inequalities, reveals that there are different "truths" about the world, and different ways of knowing. Thus, these terms have highlighted the idea that knowledge is always partial, situated, ever changing, and most of all, subject to relations of power. As such, these are terms that have both helped raise a number of questions about the assumed subject(s) of the field and demanded that we think more carefully about what, or more particularly who, is overlooked, ignored, or lost in any claims to knowledge, especially knowledge produced in WGS contexts.

Asking questions such as "which women?," "who are women?," and "why focus only on women?," all identified perceived absences in early WGS, and challenged the field to rethink how it conceptualized knowledge all together. However, what intrigues the authors in this section is that even these terms that signal both difference from and inclusion in more recent WGS practices too often continue to render some knowledges overlooked or unintelligible. These authors thus turn their gaze back onto WGS itself, noting how its own attempts to correct past oversights require further investigation. When are claims to thinking intersectionally not actually inclusive? Why are the knowledges that emerge from the recognition (and politicization) of certain identity formations so often oversimplified in the field's renderings of itself? How do the most radical questions grounded in the field's pasts become all but incoherent to current WGS practitioners?

More than simply being *about* absented points of view in WGS, these chapters also challenge us to consider how we are all implicated in the production of knowledge as both inclusive and exclusive in WGS, even when we are consciously attempting to overcome absences and oversights. As such, many other terms could have also been included in this section, terms such as "trans," "sexuality," "history," and "discipline," and other points of intersection revealed and highlighted. And we invite readers to identify those other crossover moments, and the kinds of broader arguments they make or reveal about knowledge production in WGS.

9

INTERSECTIONALITY

Vivian M. May

Though the late twentieth century marked the emergence of inter-sectionality in the critical lexicon (specifically by Kimberlé Crenshaw [2000] in her 1989 essay, "Demarginalizing the Intersection of Race and Sex"), many insights encompassed by the term had been developed and articulated by women of color for over a century. Beverly Guy-Sheftall traces nearly two centuries of intersectional theorizing[1] by black women in *Words of Fire* (see especially her essay, "Evolution" [1995b]). As Barbara Smith emphasizes, "History verifies that Black women have rejected doormat status, whether racially or sexually imposed, for centuries" (1983, xxiii). While U.S. black feminist thought is not the only place where intersectional thought has been developed (e.g., there is a strong thread of intersectional analysis within Latina feminism(s), and Indigenous feminists have long asserted analyses informed by interde-pendence and interconnection), intersectionality's beginnings in black feminist theorizing are noteworthy. Unfortunately, this longer history is often overlooked.

For instance, in the 1830s, Maria Stewart anticipated many aspects of intersectionality in developing "the beginnings of an analytical framework within which to understand the lives of black women" and, at the same time, establishing a "political framework that could prove useful for challenging many of the oppressive structures confronted by black women" (Jordan-Zachery 2007, 255). As Julia Jordan-Zachery underscores, a "liberation framework" has long been central to inter-sectionality (256), meaning questions concerning positionality, knowl-edge, and freedom are interconnected and must be considered together.[2] Likewise, as I have previously argued,[3] late nineteenth-century black feminist educator, intellectual, and activist Anna Julia Cooper devel-oped intersectional analyses and methods in two major works: her 1892 volume, *A Voice from the South by a Black Woman of the South* (1988), the first book-length example of black feminist theorizing in the United States, and her 1925 Sorbonne doctoral thesis, *L'Attitude de la France à l'égard de l'esclavage pendant la révolution*, in which Cooper examines the transatlantic dynamics of the Haitian and French revolutions.

Unfortunately, this longer history of intersectional thought is not as widely recognized as it should be in much of the Women's and Gender Studies (WGS) literature even though, at the same time, intersectional-ity has impacted curricular, pedagogical, methodological, and theoreti-cal work in the field. As an epistemological approach, intersectionality offers tools to examine the politics of everyday life (e.g., the lived expe-riences of privilege and oppression, the implications and structures of marginalization, and the phenomenological and political meanings of identity). It is equally pivotal in analyzing social institutions, systems, and structures. Intersectionality exposes how conventional approaches to inequality, including feminist, civil rights, and liberal rights models, tend to: mistakenly rely on single-axis modes of analysis and redress; deny or obscure multiplicity or compoundedness; and depend upon the very systems of privilege they seek to challenge.

While intersectionality's meaning is neither static nor unified, conti-nuities have emerged over time. Intersectional analyses have been devel-oped as a means to foreground race as a central factor shaping gendered experience, emphasizing that addressing racism is fundamental to femi-nism and vice versa, and to contest the false universalization of gender as monolithic, as with the false universalization of race and racialized experience. Intersectional analyses highlight and address erasures and silences in historical and political records resulting from false universals. By starting from the premise that systems of power and lived identities can be best understood as intertwined and not merely as plural, intersec-tionality entails alternative notions of subjectivity (Alarcón 1990) and consciousness (Sandoval 2000). Crenshaw's naming of intersectionality is important because the term provides a means to identify longstanding intellectual and political projects examining the workings of power and privilege, underscoring the politics of location, and refashioning notions of personhood at work in the body politic.

Yet it is also the case that intersectionality has (and has had) quite a varied role in WGS. For many, it is analytically, pedagogically, and politically central. Some view intersectionality as one among many choices in the marketplace of feminist ideas, whereas others see it as an historical stage whose time has passed. Intersectionality has also been characterized as intangible under an "impossibility thesis"—i.e., doing intersectional teaching, theorizing, research, or politics is regarded as an ideal but *not actually achievable*. As Stephanie Shields documents, "In conventional social and behavioral research, intersectionality frequently becomes redefined as a methodological challenge…. [For instance,] psychological scientists have typically responded to the question of intersectionality in one of three ways: excluding the question; deferring the question; limiting the question" (2008, 305).

The unevenness of intersectionality's uses, approaches, and conceptualizations demonstrates WGS' complex terrain. I maintain, however, that the field's future does not lie in tokenizing intersectionality, treating it as an obligation, or pushing it aside as an impractical vision or intellectual relic. As a result of my time spent researching Anna Julia Cooper, I have become convinced of the need for more nuanced understandings of intersectionality: repeatedly, I found that an inadequate understanding of intersectionality, even in its contemporary iterations, means that Cooper's innovative ideas and complex analyses are widely misunderstood. While Cooper articulates how race, gender, class, and region (and later, nation) interdepend and cannot be examined as isolatable, many of her contemporaries and later scholars examining her work could not seem to fully grasp her arguments—in large part because Cooper's words and ideas were examined via single-axis frameworks, either/or models of thought, or measures of rationality that could not account for multiplicity. The precepts used to interpret Cooper have often run counter to the ideas she was developing.

An inability to fully understand the philosophical and political worldview that intersectionality entails is not unique to assessments of scholars such as Cooper. Intersectional analyses frequently have been received as illogical, lacking, or incomprehensible, as Audre Lorde's query suggests: "We find ourselves having to repeat and relearn the same old lessons over and over.... For instance, how many times has this all been said before?" (1984, 117). Therefore, intersectionality's recursiveness should not simply be characterized as recycling as Nash suggests (2008, 9), because the ongoing need to reiterate points about how engaging with intersectionality requires a major shift in thinking.

The struggle to comprehend and implement intersectionality is epistemologically and politically significant for WGS, and suggests a problem of understanding that must be accounted for. As Susan Babbitt describes it, unpacking a problem of understanding entails first examining how "dominant expectations"—about rationality, subjectivity, narrative style, or form—tend to "rule out the meaningfulness of important struggles" and impede their ability to be understood (2001, 298). Some discourses "are not able to be heard" (300); they seem unimaginable because of power asymmetries and injustices (308). Moreover, this implausibility is rarely questioned. Often, "people *think* they have understood ... when they have not in fact understood what most needs to be understood" (303), so that, any difficulty in understanding (i.e., that there is something important that is still *not yet understood* from a normative stance) and the fundamental differences in worldview are thereby put to the side. The alternative way of seeing becomes characterized merely as different or illogical: its meaning is flattened. I would argue that intersectionality's recursiveness signifies the degree to which its practices go against the grain of prevailing conceptualizations of personhood, rationality, and liberation politics, even in WGS.

Problems of Understanding and Nominal Use

To better illustrate how elusive this shift in thinking can be, and because I am interested in well-intended applications of intersectionality that fall short, I first turn to two texts that are widely taught in Women's and Gender Studies. One is Marilyn Frye's essay, "Oppression"—regularly included across the WGS curriculum because Frye's delineation of systemic "double-binds" (1983, 2) is useful. A companion text is Alison Bailey's article, "Privilege," wherein she asks why "students who otherwise embrace Frye's analysis become reluctant to extend it to cover their own unearned advantages," suggesting they may not fully "understand oppression as the product of systematically related barriers and forces not of one's own making" (1998, 104).[4] Both Frye and Bailey seek to examine gender oppression as interlocking with other systems of oppression and privilege. As Bailey explains, since "oppression is not a unified phenomenon," in order "to understand how oppression is experienced …, it is not necessary for social groups to have fixed boundaries" (106). Yet despite their important contributions to examining oppression, and notwithstanding their intent to focus on how gender is interwoven with race, class, and sexuality, both authors (differently) slip away from developing the multifaceted analyses they set out to undertake.

For example, Frye concludes her essay with a gender-universal analysis of patriarchy that posits the divide between men and women as primary, since, she argues, "men" are never denigrated or oppressed "as men." Frye explains, "whatever assaults and harassments [a man] is subject to, being male is not what selects him for victimization; … men are not oppressed *as men*" (1983, 16). To be taken up, Frye's analysis requires a form of "pop-bead" logic (Spelman 1988, 136, 186), wherein the gender "bead" of masculinity can be pulled apart from race, sexuality, social class, and other factors. Masculinity seems, therefore, not to be impacted by or intersected with disability, race, sexuality, or citizenship status, in an inextricable, dynamic way.

This atomization of multiplicity is also evident in that Frye is confident, in analyzing the politics of anger or of the smile, that "it is [her] being a woman that reduces the power of [her] anger to a proof of [her] insanity" (1983, 16). Perhaps Frye can presume it is her "being a woman" alone that is causal because she is white, able-bodied, and middle class—since people who are marked as "different" by means of race, disability, and social class, for instance, are also often stereotyped as more irrationally "angry" than are members of privileged groups. Some women are perceived as "angrier" (or as inappropriately angry) in comparison to other women; likewise, some women are expected to show docility or compliance via smiles or silences to other women because of intertwined factors of (and asymmetries of power related to) race, class, sexuality, and ability.

Additionally, Frye's analysis of how women's dependency (4, 7–10) is derogated (while structurally reinforced) obscures how different forms of gendered dependency are differently derogated because gender is not isolatable from other facets of identity. Some forms of dependence (heteronormative, middle class) are more idealized (e.g., women's dependence on men who are their fathers or husbands for protection and care), whereas others are stigmatized as deviant and in need of remediation (e.g., poor women's dependency on the state via welfare). Both types of institutionalized dependency can be understood as oppressive, but differently so; one carries social stigma, the other social approval (even if, as feminist scholars, we may think it should not). Throughout her analysis of the workings of oppression, Frye includes reference to (and seeks to acknowledge) differences among women (of race, class, and sexuality), yet reverts to statements about women as a general group and to analyses of gender processes as not only homogenized but also isolatable from other factors and processes.

Like Frye, Bailey also falls back at times on gender universals when referencing group dynamics. She claims "men" are automatically granted the unearned privileges of protector status, authority, and credibility, and are therefore more likely to be perceived as better leaders (1998, 116). Bailey obscures how other aspects of one's personhood (and of other systems of privilege or oppression) mitigate "men's" authority and credibility. To be a male who is nonwhite, working class, disabled, gay, and/or a noncitizen means one is *not* automatically perceived as an authority figure. As Devon Carbado explains in examining his own unearned privileges as a black, heterosexual male, his "relationship to patriarchy is … not the same as for a working class Black male," a middle-class white male, or a queer male, black or white (1999, 430). However Bailey's return to a gender binary between "women and men" in her analysis of oppression and privilege obscures such nuances.

Other forms of slippage away from intersectionality are evident in Bailey's analysis, even as she astutely shows how unearned privileges and earned advantages are interrelated (e.g., in redlining practices in real estate) (1998, 109). She also underscores how some *earned* advantages are more easily acquired if accompanied by *un*earned gender, race, class, able-bodied, or heterosexual privileges, hence the "wildcard" quality of "additional perks" inherent to unearned dominant group privileges (108, 114–116). Yet this complex view of the matrices of privilege and oppression is undermined in Bailey's reference to an Andrew Hacker teaching exercise she finds "particularly effective … to illustrate the extent to which whites unconsciously understand the wild card character of white privilege" (114). As Bailey explains, Hacker:

> asks his white students to imagine that they will be visited by an official they have never met. The official informs them that his organization has made a terrible mistake and that according to official records you were to have been born black. Since this mistake must be rectified immediately, at midnight you will become black and can expect to live out the rest of your life—say fifty years—as a black person in America. Since this is the agency's error, the official explains that you can demand compensation. Hacker then asks his white students: How much financial recompense would you request? The figures white students give in [Bailey's] classes—usually between $250,000 to $50 million—demonstrates the extent to which white privilege is valued. (114)

Unfortunately, Bailey does not address the exercise's fundamental assumptions—e.g., to be black is so negative as to require compensation. Not only does this exercise reify the notion of blackness as horrifying, homogenize the experience of "being black," and implicitly require the emotion of pity (which usually combines with power asymmetries in poisonous ways) to function cognitively as a teaching moment, it also implies that black students would need to consent to the horror of their own being to participate in the exercise.[5] Moreover, Bailey's discussion of Hacker's exercise ignores positive ways to "be black" in this country: longstanding cultural traditions, faith practices and theological views, community practices, and artistic and literary legacies are excluded from the exercise's parameters. Paradoxically, it reinforces a white imaginary, one predicated on dominance, to try to teach about (and attempt to undo) white privilege.

Such slippages away from intersectional analysis are sites of epistemological struggle. In other words, the dynamics I have discussed in Frye's and Bailey's essays are not unique, though they illustrate a wider set of practices; many important texts used (and useful) for introducing and teaching key concepts in WGS (such as oppression as a systemic and social factor) simultaneously aim to employ a multiplicative analysis and to examine compoundedness, yet take up a "pop-bead" approach instead. Examples of such slippage are equally prevalent in recent debates concerning intersectionality and research methods where, unfortunately, researchers often use intersectionality nominally rather than analytically.

By *nominal use*, I mean when a study is intersectional in name only, intersectional primarily at the level of the descriptive, or, even worse, when intersectionality is simply a "dummy" factor or faddish signpost. Rather than being employed to guide feminist research, shape theoretical questions, develop claims, or interpret data, much research utilizes intersectionality merely for descriptive or demographic factors. As Shields discusses, "Moving from the description of difference/similarity to explanation of processes is a challenge.... It is neither an automatic nor easy step to go from *acknowledging* linkages among social identities to *explaining* those linkages or the processes through which intersecting identities define and shape one another" (2008, 304). Shields underscores that, too frequently, "The end result is to mention the newer view of difference, but to continue to work in the same way as always" (306).

Catherine Harnois examines similar dynamics in studies that employ gender universalism to explore "women's relationship with feminism" across racial groups. She finds that researchers assume this relationship to be "the same for women of different racial or ethnic groups," and that "a woman's relationship with feminism can be measured by a particular set of indicators that themselves do not vary across racial groups" (2005, 810). Several studies exclude "the possibility that particular characteristics and life experiences might affect women of different racial and ethnic groups in different ways.... [such that] generational differences, income and educational levels, family forms, and involvement with the paid labor force might shape women's feminist identities differently, depending on their race and ethnicity" (810). Differences related to age, family structure, social class, and sexuality are thereby elided. Harnois concludes: "Each of these studies includes race only as a dummy variable, and in none of these studies is race allowed to interact with any other independent variable" (810). Moreover, unstated assumptions about gender and feminism obscure how predictors for "the salience of feminism in women's lives" were off target vis-à-vis black women: "self-identification," a commonly used measure of feminist identity, turned out to be an unreliable "indicator of how 'feminist' Black women are" (819). Likewise, using "attitudinal or ideological variables to measure the salience of feminism in women's lives is also problematic" because feminism does not have only one meaning or history (812).[6]

Another form of nominal use occurs when researchers try to employ intersectionality, but do so selectively, such that the research design contradicts many of intersectionality's key ideas.[7] In analyzing qualitative studies about black lesbians (including her own previous work), Lisa Bowleg exposes common errors in identity research. Although intersectionality highlights how identities are interconnected and cannot be ranked or isolated, researchers seeking to understand complex identity tend to rely on interview methods predicated on singularity not compoundedness. Bowleg concludes: if you "ask an additive question, [you] get an additive answer," in which participants rank or separate out identities in order to answer research questions (2008, 314). Additive approaches in research design suppress the ability of participants to discuss and analyze the "interdependence and mutuality of identities" (316).

Reflecting back on her earlier research, Bowleg remarks: "It is obvious now in retrospect that a truly intersectional question would simply ask the respondent to tell about her experience without separating each identity"; as Bowleg had done when she asked participants the following: "what would you say about your life as a black person?; Woman?; Lesbian?; and Black lesbian woman?" (2008, 315). Similarly, Ange-Marie Hancock contends: "an intersectional approach would not simply expand to a typology of discrete racial/ethnic groups within the category. Most importantly, intersectional approaches to collecting and analyzing data would attend to issues of hybridity or multiraciality recognizing the contingency" of both group and individual identity (2007, 73).

Moreover, as Bowleg demonstrates, if the focus is on intersectionality as relevant primarily to demographics, then key "dimensions of experience," including "meaningful constructs such as stress, prejudice, [and] discrimination," are not engaged with by researchers (2008, 316), and the contexts of lived experience (both micropolitical and macropolitical) are positioned as beyond the scope of research (320). Julia Jordan-Zachery agrees that leaving out background contexts remains a problem in current intersectionality research, despite intersectionality's focus on the contextual and the lived. Like Bowleg, Jordan-Zachery critiques the use of additive models of identity and the reliance on apolitical views of intersectionality that curtail its potential impact both in terms of knowledge production and social change. Jordan-Zachery contends that the implied separation of knowledge from power falsely characterizes intersectional analysis as divorced from social transformation, which is troubling given its roots in liberation politics (2007, 261).

Thus, despite notions that intersectionality is widely (and adequately) used in WGS scholarship, these examples—illustrating depoliticized notions of intersectionality, analyses obscuring interaction across (and the simultaneity of) systems of power, and slippages to (falsely) universalized or "pop-bead" notions of identity that suppress the mutual interaction of identity categories—suggest otherwise. I am not proposing one "right" way to read intersectional theories or devise intersectional methods, nor am I advocating that the field have a singular or "core" set of principles revolving around intersectionality (especially as intersectionality questions universalizing impulses). My concern is that intersectionality is being tokenized, evaded, or characterized as outmoded before its full impact has unfolded. I am also troubled by ahistorical interpretations and acontextual uses of intersectionality, and find myself asking: why does it seem that intellectual innovations (such as intersectionality) devised in large part by women of color continue to be treated casually?[8] Why are the intellectual histories behind such theoretical innovations (or interventions) regularly bracketed or ignored?

A Snapshot of Intersectionality

Rather than assume "everyone understands intersectionality," I want to pause to summarize some of its central insights. Intersectionality calls for analytic methods, modes of political action, and ways of thinking about persons, rights, and liberation informed by multiplicity. It is both metaphorical and material, in that it seeks to capture something not adequately named about the nature of lived experience and about systems of oppression. Intersectionality adds nuance to understanding different sites of feminism(s) and the multiple dimensions of lived experience, it lends insight into the interrelationships among struggles for liberation, and, as Maparyan indicates elsewhere in this volume, it shifts what "counts" as a feminist issue and what is included as gendered experience. Intersectionality offers a vision of future possibilities that can be more fully realized once a shift toward the multiple takes place. Its critical practices include:

- *Considering lived experience as a criterion of meaning*: Intersectionality focuses on how lived experience can be drawn upon to expose the partiality of normative modes of knowing (often deemed neutral) and to help marginalized groups articulate and develop alternative analyses and modes of oppositional consciousness, both individually and collectively.[9]
- *Reconceptualizing marginality and focusing on the politics of location*: Intersectionality considers marginalization in terms of social structure and lived experience and redefines "marginality as a potential source of strength," not merely "tragedy" (Collins 1998, 128). Lugones and Price insist that the marginalized, "create a sense of ourselves as historical subjects, not exhausted by intermeshed oppressions" (2003, 331). While hooks characterizes the margins as a "site of radical possibility, a space of resistance" (1990, 149), Lugones describes marginality as a site of the "resistant oppressed" wherein "you have ways of living in disruption of domination" (2006, 78, 79). Methodologically, attending to the politics of location entails accounting for the contexts of knowledge production (Bowleg 2008, 318; Jordan-Zachery 2007, 259) and thinking about the relevance of the knower to the known—factors usually considered outside the realm of knowledge "proper."[10]
- *Employing "both/and" thinking and centering multiracial feminist theorizing*: Moving away from "dichotomized" thought (Lugones 1990, 80) and "monolithic" analyses of identity, culture, and theory (Christian 1990a, 341), intersectionality theorizes from a position of "simultaneity" (Nash 2008, 2; V. Smith 1998, xv).[11] Bridging the theoretical and empirical (McCall 2005, 1780), and using "double vision" (Lugones 2006, 79), intersectionality "refers to both a normative theoretical argument *and* an approach to conducting empirical research that

emphasizes the interaction of categories" (Hancock 2007, 63). While it is *not* merely the descriptive for which intersectionality was developed, it is often reduced to this.[12] As Shields explains: "Most behavioral science research that focuses on intersectionality ... employs [it] as a perspective on research rather than as a theory that drives the research question.... [Intersectionality's] emergent properties and processes escape attention" (2008, 304).

- *Shifting toward an understanding of complex subjectivity*: Alongside an epistemological shift toward simultaneity and both/and reasoning is a shift toward subjectivity that accounts for "compoundedness" (Crenshaw 2000, 217); critiques of unitary knowledge and the unitary subject are linked (McCall 2005, 1776). Rather than approach multiple facets of identity as "non-interactive" and "independent" (Harnois 2005, 810), an intersectional approach focuses on indivisibility, a "complex ontology" (Phoenix and Pattynama 2006, 187) conceptualized as woven (Alarcón 1990, 366), kneaded (Anzaldúa 1990e, 380), and shifting (Valentine 2007, 15). This approach "denies any *one* perspective as the only answer, but instead posits a shifting tactical and strategic subjectivity that has the capacity to re-center depending upon the forms of oppression to be confronted" (Sandoval 2000, 67).

- *Analyzing systems of oppression as operating in a "matrix"*: Connected to complex subjectivity are analyses of domination that account for relationships among forms of oppression. As Pauli Murray aptly put it, "The lesson of history that all human rights are indivisible and that the failure to adhere to this principle jeopardizes the rights of all is particularly applicable" (1995, 197). The Combahee River Collective insists on "the development of an integrated analysis and practice based upon the fact that the major systems of oppression are interlocking" (1983, 261).[13] A "single axis" approach "distorts" and "theoretically erases" differences within and between groups (Crenshaw 2000, 209–17); multiple systems of power must therefore be addressed simultaneously.

- *Conceiving of solidarity or coalition without relying on homogeneity*: Rather than sameness as a foundation for alliance, Lorde attests, "You do not have to be me in order for us to fight alongside each other" (1984, 142).[14] Intersectionality pursues "'solidarity' through different political formations and ... alternative theories of the subject of consciousness" (Alarcón 1990, 364). Mohanty advocates thinking about feminist solidarity in terms of mutuality, accountability, and the recognition of common interests as the basis for relationships among diverse communities. Rather than assuming an enforced commonality of oppression, the practice of solidarity foregrounds communities of people who have chosen to work and fight together.... [It] is always an achievement, the result of active struggle (2003, 78). This requires acknowledging that marginalization does not mean "we" should "naturally" be able to work together. Lugones urges us to "craft coalitional gestures" both communicatively and politically, since there is no guarantee of "transparency" between us, even margin to margin (2006, 80, 83).

- *Challenging false universals and highlighting omissions built into the social order and intellectual practices*: Intersectionality exposes how the experiences of some are often universalized to represent the experiences, needs, and claims of all group members. Rather than conceptualize group identity via a common denominator framework that subsumes within-group differences, creates rigid distinctions between groups, and leads to distorted analyses of discrimination, intersectionality explores the politics of the unimaginable, the invisible, and the silenced. Intersectionality understands exclusions and gaps as meaningful and examines the theoretical and political impact of such absences.[15]

- *Exploring the implications of simultaneous privilege and oppression*: In addition to focusing on the "relational nature of dominance and subordination" (Zinn and Dill 1996, 327)[16] and breaking open false universals, intersectionality focuses on how personhood can be structured on internalized hierarchies or "arrogant perception" (Lugones 1990); thus "one may also 'become a woman' in opposition to other women" not just in opposition to "men" (Alarcón 1990, 360).[17] Normative ideas about identity categories as homogenous "limit[s] inquiry to the experiences of otherwise-privileged members of the group," and "marginalizes those who are multiply-burdened and obscures claims that cannot be understood as resulting from discrete sources of discrimination" (Crenshaw 2000, 209). Intersectionality seeks to shift the logics of how we understand domination, subordination, personhood, and rights.

- *Identifying how a liberatory strategy may depend on hierarchy or reify privilege to operate*: Intersectionality offers tools for seeing how we often uphold the very forms of oppression that we seek to dismantle.[18] For instance, Crenshaw identifies how the court's normative view of race and sex discrimination means that the very legal frameworks meant to address inequality require a certain degree of privilege to function (2000, 213). She lays bare the court's "refusal to acknowledge compound discrimination" (214) and highlights the problem Lugones characterizes as a collusion with divide and conquer thinking (2006, 76).

Conclusion: Intersectionality and Women's and Gender Studies' Future

Ubiquitous reference to intersectionality in Women's and Gender Studies curriculum and scholarship suggests the field has shifted fully to the multidimensional ways of thinking about gender and systems of oppression that are key to intersectional thinking—e.g., that gender is inherently interwoven with the politics, structures, and epistemologies of race, sexuality, social class, disability, and nation. The current literature includes soaring rhetoric about intersectionality and WGS. For instance, Kathy Davis asserts: "At this particular juncture in gender studies, any scholar who neglects difference runs the risk of having her work viewed as theoretically misguided, politically irrelevant, or simply fantastical" (2008, 68). Yet, I maintain that one could: (1) readily find well-regarded venues for WGS scholarship that do not adequately attend to or take up "difference"; and (2) that it would be seen as good work by many rather than dismissed outright as "misguided" or "irrelevant," much less "fantastical." Despite widespread reference to intersectionality in WGS scholarship, it is often employed cursorily. One tendency is to posit intersectionality as something scholars should acknowledge (i.e., an obligation), but a contextualized understanding of the concept is not requisite. Alternatively, intersectionality can be seen as positive but unrealistic—to be achieved in the future, but at present impossible. Thus, even laudatory reference to intersectionality can be fleeting or superficial, which underscores how far the field has to go to fulfill much of intersectionality's pedagogical, analytical, theoretical, and political promise.

We must ask some difficult questions. Do nods to intersectionality in WGS provide a "conceptual warrant" to avoid, if not suppress, multiplicity? Has intersectionality's critical lexicon, forged in struggle, been co-opted and flattened rather than engaged with as an epistemological and political lens? We must address the common notion that "everyone" already "does" intersectionality; even if one agrees, for the sake of argument, that "we" all "do" intersectional work, the question remains, *how*? Does intersectionality shape research, pedagogy, or curriculum structure from the start, or is it tacked on or tokenized? How does intersectionality translate into methodology, be it qualitative, quantitative, literary, or philosophical? Is it reduced to a descriptive tool or conceptualized as impossible? Do its key insights slip away, even in well-intended applications? Statements about intersectionality's having "arrived" beg the question Collins raises when she wonders whether it is being adopted primarily as the latest "overarching" terminology to explain both the matrices of identity and of systems of oppression, but in a way that obscures complexities. She writes: "If we are not careful, the term 'intersectionality' runs the … risk of trying to explain everything yet ending up saying nothing" (2008, 72).

Finally, as Laura Parisi also argues in this volume, it is important to consider whether an evasion of intersectionality can occur by focusing on the transnational. Attending to global feminisms, theorizing transnational politics, and forging comparative practices is pivotal to WGS given the complex flows of global capital, the porosity of borders, and the dangers of "reified nationalisms" (Giddings 2006, v), yet there are cautionary tales; a shift toward the global can frequently take place alongside a sanctioned historical amnesia about localized imbrications of race and gender. As Karla Holloway notes, "U.S. feminist studies goes looking for transnational bodies while local body-politics are under-interrogated" (2006, 1). Not only do domestic politics of race risk being displaced onto the politics of global gender "elsewhere," but whiteness itself as "an embodied and gendered politic is effectively disappeared from the interrogative terrain as feminism's focus on colored bodies goes global" (3). Holloway reiterates: "Although race matters and evidence of ethnicity seem to occupy our academic and political projects, Black folks themselves disappear from view and white folk are protected from analysis…. In transnational paradigms, local bodies seem not to interest U.S. women's studies" (14). Holloway suggests that an age-old racialized gender politics of U.S. white nationalism seems operative in some of the recent turns to globalization in WGS; this "new" nationalism (in the name of transnationalism) turns on an economy of fear and plays out in the public domain via narratives of danger on the one hand, and the idealization of white womanhood on the other.

Thus, Alexander and Mohanty's question remains pivotal to thinking through the future implications and past iterations of both transnational *and* intersectional frames: "What kinds of racialized, gendered selves get produced at the conjuncture of the transnational and the neo-colonial?" (2001, 496). As Obioma Nnaemeka points out:

> Theorizing in a cross-cultural context is fraught with intellec-tual, political, and ethical questions: the question of provenance (where is the theory coming from?); the question of subjectivity (who authorizes?); the question of positionality (which specific locations and standing [social, political, and intellectual] does it legitimize?). The imperial nature of theory formation must be interrogated. (2003, 362)

I am calling, then, for a continued focus on intersectionality, but not because intersectionality should become *the* global theory; however, its insights and analyses need not be elided in work that seeks to account more fully for the politics of nation, global flows of power and knowl-edge, and questions of the neocolonial. At its best, transnational femi-nist work and intersectional analyses account for multiply constituted subjects and interacting systems of power and inequality, globally and locally. Transnational feminist theorizing and alliance building will only be strengthened by deep engagement with intersectionality and vice versa. However, to engage with intersectional and transnational analyses simultaneously and adequately, the field must contend with the ways in which each of these political and theoretical turns is too often undertheorized or even resisted outright in much of the work done in the name of Women's and Gender Studies.

Notes

1. Guy-Sheftall traces the historical trajectory of intersectional black feminist thought as an approach and analytical framework even though the term "intersectionality" was not necessarily in use.
2. Connections between liberation politics and the politics of location are explored in several pivotal works, including: Anzaldúa 1990; Cade 1970; Hull, Scott, and B. Smith 1982; Mohanty, Russo, and Torres 1991; and Moraga and Anzaldúa 1983.
3. See May 2007 and 2009.
4. Ringrose (2007) focuses on how structures of power are intangible for those systemically advantaged by such systems. Since discourses of choice and agency cloud students' ability to analyze systemic and simultaneous privilege and oppression in their own lives and in the larger social world, a focus on intentionality and choice is inadequate without examining how structural determinants bear upon people's lives.
5. My analysis is informed by Patricia Williams' essay, "The Death of the Profane," which examines "color-blind" legal writing and ostensibly color-blind policies and practices, including the use of buzzers in New York boutiques. Williams argues: "the repeated public urgings that blacks understand the buzzer system by putting themselves in shoes of white storeowners" works on an economy of violence and "exclusionary hatred" because it requires that "blacks look into the mirror of frightened white faces for the reality of their undesirability" (1991, 46).
6. See Maparyan's essay on "Feminism," in this volume, for more discussion on feminism's variability.
7. Ringrose contends that intersectionality is "being used in feminist educational spaces in ways that water down the approach and that relativize, individualize, and liberalize issues of oppression and power" (2007, 265), paradoxically favoring meritocracy. Her analysis offers insight with regard to how research designs aimed at employing intersectionality can, analogously, fall short.
8. See Morgensen, in this volume, for more on the ways in which Women's and Gender Studies has failed to follow through on the theorizing of women of color feminisms.

9. See Anzaldúa 1999; Christian 1990; Collins 1990; Crenshaw 2000; Combahee 1983; Guy-Sheftall 1995b.

10. See Anzaldúa 1999; Zinn and Dill 1996, 328; Lugones 2006, 76–78; Sandoval 2000, 86.

11. See Anzaldúa 1990b, 145 and 1990e, 378; Henderson 1989, 117; Phoenix and Pattynama 2006, 187; Sandoval 2000, 88; Yuval-Davis 2007.

12. See Bowleg 2008, 316–18; Hancock 2007, 66; Harnois 2005, 813; Jordan-Zachery 2007, 261.

13. See Beale 1970, 92–93; Collins 2008, 72 and 2004, 95–96; Jordan-Zachery 2007, 259; King 1988; Lemons 2001, 87; Lorde 1984, 140; B. Smith 1983, xxxii–xxviii; Zinn and Dill 1996, 237.

14. See Alarcón 1990, 366; Lemons 2001, 87; B. Smith 1983, xliii.

15. See Alarcón 1990, 356; Bowleg 2008, 312; Crenshaw 2000, 223; A. Davis 1984; DuCille 2001, 254; Henderson 1989, 117; Jordan-Zachery 2007, 254; Ringrose 2007, 267; Sandoval 2000, 75–76.

16. See Anzaldúa 1990d, xix; and Minh-ha 1990, 375.

17. See Crenshaw 2000, 209–13; Lorde 1984, 67, 132; Cole 2008, 446; Lemons 2001, 86–87; Marable 2001, 124; Neal 1995.

18. See Alarcón 1990; Anzaldúa 1990d and 1990e; McCall 2005; Murray 1995; Nnaemeka 2003.

10
Identity (Politics)

Scott Lauria Morgensen

As a key category of analysis in Women's and Gender Studies (WGS), the term "identity" has also invoked or been tied to the term "politics"—often by making identity work into a politics for the field. Critics of WGS, both antifeminist and feminist, have at times framed the field as an anti-intellectual site for policing the politics of identity. Yet these historical struggles over identity have also inspired critical theories that now lead work in WGS and beyond. I examine these new theories as effects of the destabilizations of "identity (politics)" that followed critical interventions in the field by women of color feminism, interventions sustained today by critical race, Indigenous, and transnational feminisms. These projects continue to remake WGS (by the variety of names it is called), as potentially crucial sites for theorizing identities and politics within the power relations of a colonial and globalized world.

From its earliest days, debates over the identity of "women" became an avowed or disavowed centerpiece of WGS. In the United States and Canada, the activist efforts of the "second wave" worked to define the field around women as a site of political consciousness (Aikau 2007, hooks 2000). Antifeminists responded by critiquing WGS as no more than political diatribe masquerading as intellectual work.[1] But reading the field as mired in the politics of identity also shaped feminist accounts. Amid the feminist sex debates, or the rise of queer and trans politics, many recalled struggles over policing admittance to the categories "women" and "feminist." In "Thinking Sex," Gayle Rubin critiqued radical feminism by arguing that sexuality studies could not get a fair hearing in WGS at the time and must locate elsewhere (1992 [1984]). In a later, yet linked moment, Wendy Brown, in "The Impossibility of Women's Studies," answered calls that all people once excluded should rejoin the field by asking if their diversity so shattered any premise of shared experience as to make the project of "women's" studies impossible (2008 [1997]). I address those legacies by recounting how the problematics of identity politics were explained by the theories and practices of women of color feminism. Women of color feminism differed from other critiques of identity politics in WGS as essentialist or anti-essentialist, political or apolitical, by marking that, in any form, they remained *racialized* within the *national* field of a white settler society. By centering the intersectionality of race, nation, and global location in any claim about gender, feminists of color defined "women" and "feminism" as internally diverse and globally multiple, and WGS as a relational space across differences that questioned Western feminist desires for unity. Yet, at the same time, close engagement of feminists of color with the politics of identity precisely constituted a theoretical and activist contribution which continues to educate WGS in how to explain those politics today.

My chapter develops two major arguments. The conflictual formation of WGS by way of identity politics potentially makes the field a crucial site for studying identities and their politicization, albeit not by investing in them (e.g., to identify with and as them) but by critically historicizing them. Yet I arrive at this argument via another: the potential for WGS to be a site to study identities and their politicization will manifest only once WGS answers the living legacies of women of color feminism, which long ago confronted the field with its limits and opened both "identity" and "politics" to question. Both my personal narrative and my account of the field reflect my deep commitment to this argument. Read together, they suggest that women of color feminism will remain more important to feminism than to WGS unless the field owns up to its burden of responsibility to women of color feminism and radically transforms. More often, though, WGS responds ambivalently to women of color feminism, which I read as an effect of whiteness, settler colonialism, and imperialism leading white people in settler states and imperial metropoles to engage only those topics that do not displace their centrality in a still-colonial world. Such a move lets them propose a unitary category, "women," and its possessive form to center the field in the first place. In contrast, feminists of color (have) consistently theorized "women" and "women's" not by eliminating these terms but by complicating what either term may mean. They invite reinterpreting identities and their politics by centering what Cathy Cohen calls the "cross-cutting" power relations marked by theory of intersectionality[2] and, as I discuss, the destabilization of modernist identities and social movements that follow from the theory and practice of feminist of color alliances (Cohen 1999). I indicate this potential by referencing work on the global politics of HIV/AIDS, an area where my current work contributes to WGS. Here, and in many other cases, we see that the problems and possibilities of identity and politics in a colonial and globalized world demand engagement with women of color feminist thought. To the extent that WGS does so, it will responsibly and accurately engage the conditions of the world in which we live while advancing knowledge of subjects and power for both the field specifically and social theory more broadly.

Critical Journeys with Women of Color Feminisms

The antiracist and anticolonial work of feminists of color produced me as an accountable contributor to feminism. After more than two decades, as a professor in departments identified historically as "Women's Studies," my work remains responsible to women of color feminist solidarities, which I engage as a white queer cisgender man doing research in accountable relationships to antiracist, anticolonial and transnational feminist, queer, and HIV/AIDS movements.

My ties to WGS arose after I came to university as a first-generation and working student. Newly gay-identified, I sought analyses of homophobia and sexism that would support my new sense of self. A scholarship brought me first to a wealthy private U.S. university polarized by its conservative white faculty/student majority living in a poor and politically radical African American and Latina/o neighborhood. Here, in the mid-1980s, I encountered feminist pedagogy among white women faculty who taught radical and cultural feminisms as if they were multiracial and universal theories of women's oppression and liberation. During my own mixed-class upbringing in white rural and urban spaces, I had aligned with women as elders and peers who modeled women's leadership and respect for differences within white social circles. When I first arrived at university I sought out similar spaces, and the white women's spaces of WGS courses felt familiar, including when they defended women's diversity. When I presented myself as a potential learner in this space, I was asked as the only man to be a quiet observer. Here, women educated one another—and (tangentially) me—about heteropatriarchy in ways that matched my expectations. I learned that patriarchy was a cultural universal to which misogyny was fundamental; in contrast, ancient European matriarchies, Indigenous religions, and utopian communities of modern (read: non-Indigenous) women offered alternatives. While my silent learning affirmed women's leadership, it entailed my not being asked by others, nor asking myself, why I was there or how what I learned affected me. In turn, the radical and cultural feminisms that contextualized our studies framed masculinity as inherently problematic. I felt called to distance myself from my identity as a man, although hostility here towards trans women and queer male gender performance (both defined as misogynist) left me with little sense of other options. My role as a young man in WGS thus remained that of a passive witness, neither asked by others nor volunteering to act. Ultimately, my time in this space was brief, and while I left feeling educated, I had no sense that I could, or should, hold my life in ongoing engagement with feminism.

I learned the specificities of this space, and of my role within it, after I dropped my scholarship and transferred to work and pay my own way at mixed-class public universities. Here, at schools with large proportions of students of color and histories of antiracist activism, I met WGS programs with majorities of white women being called upon to make intersectional accounts of gender, sexuality, race, class and nation in a colonial and globalizing world the primary contexts of feminist work. Radical and cultural feminisms did appear here, but alongside other strands of feminism, all of whose formation by intersecting power relations had to be known to determine if they could account for all, or *any*, women. These critical interventions were led by networks of feminists self-identified as women of color who formed solidarity across their differences to oppose the racism, colonialism and imperialism that affected them, their often working-class communities, and WGS. If such networks existed at my old university—and today I believe that they did—they had gained no notice among my feminist mentors and myself; we invoked Indigenous and Third World women without engaging any *actual* Indigenous or Third World women, including the Latinas and African American women living nearby who did not attend our elite school.

My sense of self radically transformed at public universities once I encountered intersectional feminist accounts of my formation by multiple power relations and my responsibility to oppose them. I critically faced my own whiteness—as a white *man*, who inherited the economic, political and cultural legacies of white supremacy in the United States. As a result, I recognized masculinity and patriarchy for the first time as multiple. I no longer presumed that I had inherited a universal power as a man, but one particularly inimical and historically specific: the heteropatriarchal legacies of white supremacist settler colonialism and imperialism in the United States. I was called to theorize and challenge this specific hegemonic manhood on antiracist, anticolonial, and anti-imperial feminist grounds. My life changed by pursuing this work under the allied leadership of feminists of color. White women near me were also called—for their healing and for the possibility of feminist solidarity—to break their alignments with whiteness. Our respective locations remained distinct, and my actions remained accountable to them as women. But for the first time, I found that I and white women were being called to reflect on our potentially *shared* power to act as oppressors of women of color and, indeed, men of color, especially if racism, colonialism or global capitalism ever went unaddressed by us.[3] As one of the few white men in WGS where I lived, I did not meet a specific role model for my own learning process. But antiracist feminist critique clearly included men as contributors, in the tradition of women of color calling men of color to critique sexism within the racial justice movements that they shared. In this context, by trial and error, I learned to act responsibly as a white man challenged to change while accountably contributing to antiracist feminism. I now saw my prior relationship to WGS, in which I agreed with anything that feminist women said, as a complicity in violence that white feminist women used to protect their race privilege. In response, I aligned with white women who modeled their responsibility to pursue antiracist feminism under leadership by feminists of color. We met in WGS as a volatile space that demanded we place differences in conversation to do the feminist work modeled by women of color who themselves bridged *their own* national, religious, racial, and cultural differences to form contentious solidarities (Harris and Ordoña 1990). We learned that "women" was unimaginable as a uniform group and that "identity" as women was not guaranteed, while "politics" became the *work* of discovering whether feminist alliance could form at all. My history as a participant in WGS thus taught me what I also learned from literatures in women of color, Indigenous, Third World and transnational feminism: far from being reductive of identity or politics, these projects make multiplicity in conversation *the* ground for feminist work.

My writing here has invoked "women of color" in ways suggested by Gloria Anzaldúa, Chela Sandoval, and Chandra Mohanty, as a category that troubles essentialist notions of gender and race by theorizing them in relationship across differences presented for alliance (Anzaldúa 1990, Mohanty 1991, Sandoval 2000). In this way, "women of color feminism" names work that destabilizes belief in a shared feminist nature by emphasizing the work of solidarity across divergent experiences and power relations. As Mohanty argues, solidarity for "women of color" is neither natural nor inevitable, but inherently political (1991a, 7). Such a definition conflicts with modernist beliefs in identity or politics that would frame women as a class or "people" who share something more with one another than any share with men. Feminists of color situated women and all people in the power relations of a colonial and globalizing world and called them to pursue antiracist feminism in every space they entered. To some degree such insights are gained any time WGS shifts from the possessive formulation "women's" to emphasize instead the study of women, gender, or even sexuality, or to recenter the political term "feminist," if this move shifts WGS away from questions of entitlement and toward defining shared stakes in intellectual and political work.[4] But "women of color" feminism centered around a distinct leadership style that fostered antiracist feminist coalitions, in which white women were called to collaborate and men—even, white men—were held responsible to allied action. In order to further situate this idea, I now revisit how women of color feminist thought displaced whiteness, settler colonialism, and imperialism in Western feminism, which will lead me to propose how their legacies inspire new directions in WGS.

Identity (Politics) in Women's and Gender Studies: Troubling Modernist Commitments

Even as Women's and Gender Studies formed in the 1960s and 1970s in the United States and Canada, women of color challenged sexism, racism, and colonialism in their lives and in the field simultaneously. If at times they passed through white "women's" movements, their work arose within Third World, Indigenous, and people of color movements or by forming distinctive women of color movements (Gluck et al. 1997; Blackwell 2003). In activism and critical theory, feminists of color announced collective differences from Western feminist thought and movement. Their work might refuse feminist identity if this evokes white middle-class women's alignment with white settler society, or it might claim a feminist identity within a particular racial/ethnic or national constituency. In Chela Sandoval's terms, such efforts linked by acting *differentially* to academic WGS (2000); rather than demanding "inclusion" as minority members, women of color pursued distinctive work that engaged WGS at a distance even while displacing efforts to contain them.

In the United States, this work was achieved in black feminist thought by defining "identity politics" as a method to displace whiteness and colonialism in feminist theory and WGS. In 1977, members of the Combahee River Collective modeled a politics "committed to struggling against racial, sexual, heterosexual, and class oppression [...] based upon the fact that the major systems of oppression are interlocking" (1983, 264). Their declaration of the "simultaneity of oppressions" would inform later theories of intersectionality. Arguing for black women and all women of color, "that the only people who care enough about us to work consistently for our liberation are us," the Collective stated that, "focusing on our own oppression is embodied in the concept of identity politics" (267). This reflects the Collective's sense that, "all the political movements that have preceded us"—including black liberation, Marxism, and white feminism—effectively modeled "that anyone is more worthy of liberation than ourselves" (267). Thus, black feminism was defended on a principle that the "most radical politics come directly from our identity, as opposed to working to end some-one else's oppression" (267). Here, black women's identity is a location not contained by singular identities of race, class, gender, or nation. Its specificity is not as a people or class, but as a *position* that bridges and exceeds normatively-imagined identities and requires a distinctive account. As the Collective argues, the politics of "sex, race, and class" are "difficult to separate [...] because in our lives they are most often experienced simultaneously" (267). This formulation defends identity by fracturing definitions of it as singular or integral, or of its politics as liberating groups defined in such a way. Black feminism, as "identity politics," thus announces an epistemological break from definitions of "identity politics" in all surrounding projects, including white feminism and WGS. This distinction retains a relationship to race and nation that "gender" does not provide. As the Collective argues, "Our situation as Black people necessitates that we have solidarity around the fact of race, which white women of course do not need to have with white men, unless it is their negative solidarity as racial oppressors" (267).

Saying "we struggle together with Black men against racism, just as we struggle with Black men against sexism" (267), the Collective reminds us that black feminist identity politics does not fit any form of WGS that reduces to identity as "women," or, its possessive form. Neither will it be grounded in feminist spaces that white women form, because it will appear in mobilizations of people of color where white feminism and WGS did not originate. When arguing that "all the major systems of oppression are interlocking" (267), black feminists spoke as exiles from movements that would privilege one mode of oppression over others. Their theory of the "simultaneity of oppressions" questioned the ability of modernist identity politics to represent, include, or liberate women of color—notably, feminism defined in Western terms. Thus, before U.S. and Canadian feminists found the consensus to "include" women of color, feminists of color announced theories and methods that *could not be* "included" by already having displaced the logics and methods of Western feminism and WGS.

Along with questioning the terms of organizing, women of color feminist thought displaced modernist theories of women's and feminist subjectivity. Norma Alarcón theorized subjectivity for feminists of color by interpreting the voices gathered by Cherríe Moraga and Gloria Anzaldúa as "the theoretical subjects of *This Bridge Called My Back*" (1990). As Alarcón argued of this key text in U.S. women of color feminism:

> Consciousness as the site of multiple voicings is the theoretical subject, par excellence, of *Bridge*. Concomitantly, these voicings (or thematic threads) are not viewed as necessarily originating with the subject, but as discourses that transverse consciousness and which the subject must struggle with constantly. [...] The need to assign multiple registers of existence is an effect of the belief that knowledge of one's subjectivity cannot be arrived at through a single discursive "theme." Indeed, the multiple-voiced subjectivity is lived in resistance to competing notions for one's allegiance or self-identification. (1990, 412–13)

Alarcón's multiply-voiced subject echoes within conversations among feminists of color in the 1980s, notably in Gloria Anzaldúa's formulation of "mestiza consciousness" in *Borderlands/La Frontera* (1987). By figuring "multiple voicings" as "discourses" that condition the subject but do not originate with her, Alarcón argues that subjectivity is conditioned by language and power, and known through struggle. Her claim is conversant with poststructuralist and deconstructionist theories, and it contradicts essentialist definitions of subjectivity. But her claim centers the experiences of women of color facing "competing notions for one's allegiance" to "a single discursive 'theme'" (413). Opposing the same modes of delimiting women of color that Alarcón critiques, Chandra Mohanty references Alarcón, Sandoval, Moraga, Anzaldúa, Trinh T. Minh-ha, and bell hooks when she argues that

> a number of scholars in the U.S. have written about the inherently *political* definition of the term *women of color* (a term often used interchangeably with *third world women*, as I am doing

here). This is a term which designates a political constituency, not a biological or even sociological one. [...] What seems to constitute "women of color" or "third world women" as a viable oppositional alliance is a *common context of struggle* rather than color or racial identifications. (Mohanty 1991a, 7, original emphases)

Mohanty's framing of "women of color" as an "oppositional alliance" defines this identity as a politics, and one that is not reducible to an essence within the subject. Thus, as a politicized identity, "women of color" shatters modernist definitions of identity by correctly marking them as normative fictions. If allied women of color must contest such fictions, how much more is required of those who actually feel comfortable with normative definitions of identity? This lesson echoes the Combahee River Collective, in that the identity politics promoted by feminists of color aimed to undermine the normative logic and methods of identity and politics in the white supremacist and settler colonial societies in which they lived.

The destabilizing of modernist identities and politics within women of color feminism is elucidated by Chela Sandoval. From the time of her report on women of color organizing at the 1981 National Women's Studies Association conference "Women Respond to Racism," Sandoval engaged the theoretical legacies of women of color feminism as a basis for critiquing post-Enlightenment thought and its influence on feminism (Sandoval 1990). In *Methodology of the Oppressed* (2000), Sandoval adapts Fredric Jameson's reading of "postmodernism" as the economic and cultural conditions of late modern globalization to argue that feminists of color adeptly understood, negotiated, and challenged its power. Jameson complains that postmodernism opens to question all definitions of the subject and power, thereby displacing modern critiques such as Marxism that no longer seem capable of explaining or changing the world. Sandoval interprets postmodernism, and Jameson's reaction, as signs that global capitalism, anticolonial liberation struggles, and poststructuralism have made the "First World citizen-subject" lose its sense of place. Although this situation is "new" to Jameson, it merely echoes the displacements long experienced by colonized peoples. Sandoval applies her argument to respond to critics of feminists of color for failing to align with the major twentieth century social movements of feminism, anticapitalism, antiracism, and national liberation. Women of color were often branded as disloyal to a "true" identity or politics if they participated in multiple movements without committing to just one. Sandoval says that this theory of "oppositional consciousness" reflects modernist ideas that subjects and power relations are singular, and the movements to liberate subjects from power must be as well (42). She argues that it resembles Jameson's nostalgia for a stability prior to postmodernism—albeit, one that only existed if one was protected from the displacements postmodernism now brings to everyone. Sandoval's account portrays feminists of color as having responded to their multiple experiences of displacement by refusing the lie of a singular subjectivity and forming movements that, in their mobility and flexibility, effectively negotiate the changing conditions of postmodernity.

For Sandoval, the failure of feminists of color to be contained by modernist social movements *was* a critique of those movements' epistemological limits. In fact, this "failure" modeled a unique mode of oppositional consciousness: the "differential" mode, which acts by critically traversing all others (2000). In this light, the failure of modernist movements to engage women of color marked those movements' limits in comprehending postmodern power, just as the mobility of feminists of color across them demonstrated an understanding of that power and a capacity to navigate and challenge it. Sandoval argues further that the differential mode of oppositional consciousness can be engaged by all people resisting the power of global capitalism today. Differential work adapts participation in modernist, single-issue movements "into tactical weaponry for intervening in shifting currents of power" (Sandoval 2000, 57). Here, familiar forms of identity and politics remain important even if they are destabilized when their participants act differentially. This reminds us that destabilization is not synonymous with dismissal or erasure. Identities and politics can only be destabilized if they exist and exert a power that critics wish to challenge. A differential feminist practice thus acts, as Alarcón and Mohanty suggest, as a tactical mobility within and across multiple discourses. Those discourses' power—including a power to constrain identities or politics—does not end but it becomes more porous the more that it is critically and creatively engaged.

Given the sophistication of women of color feminist theories, such as Sandoval's, any description of them or their movements as excessively identitarian is a misreading. While it could seem to white women that distinctly theorizing women of color marginalizes white women in feminism, Maria Lugones wrote with Elizabeth Spelman in 1983 that only in recognizing their differences could they form relationships based in alliance (Lugones and Spelman 2005). Additionally, announcing a specific location for theory adapts theory of the feminist standpoint in the black feminist legacy of Patricia Hill Collins (Collins 1990). Against perceptions that feminists of color reduced antiracism or anticolonialism to a reductive identity politics, Mohanty argued that the term "women of color" defines an anti-essentialist alliance politics that opposes a *prior* racial, national, and global essentializing of "women" in Western feminism (Mohanty 1991b). By theorizing gender as a racial and national location, feminists of color made race and nation central to feminist thought, thus complicating claims about "women." Given that studying race, nation, and gender interprets women alongside men and people of all gender identities, women of color feminism also suggests that "women" may not remain the central category of Women's Studies. Thus, far from restricting discussion of identity, women of color feminism radically opens and transforms the theory of identity as a basis for work in WGS.

Revisiting legacies of women of color feminism becomes more crucial if WGS learns to embrace the destabilization of identities and politics in ways that reassert Western feminism. Genealogies of the field often cite the 1980s as a moment when white feminist scholars in North America and Europe questioned identity politics by citing poststructuralism—as in the work of Judith Butler in *Gender Trouble* (1990) and Denise Riley in *Am I That Name?* (1988). These texts by white feminists were developed concurrently with the major intellectual and political work of women of color feminism. But if WGS scholars trace the source of their critiques to "poststructuralism," they may reproduce whiteness, colonialism and imperialism by eliding how poststructuralism answered prior destabilizations of identity and politics by feminists of color. One helpful response would be to address women of color feminism whenever the effects of poststructuralism in WGS are addressed. For instance, Butler cites Anzaldúa's theory of mestiza consciousness and theories of coalition among feminists of color as key to her critique of feminist identity politics (1990, 18–22). While Pauline Moya calls Butler's citation of Anzaldúa appropriative, I am more interested in it as evidence that Butler recognized that her words addressed an ongoing moment of destabilization in feminism by women of color (Moya 1997). More importantly, all this occurred *before* Butler's popularization let other feminists—in support, or critique—make poststructuralism seem responsible for a shift that Butler herself traced to feminists of color. Thus, as Moya argues, both Butler's early work and its translation into hegemonic feminism show that work by women of color remained subsidiary whenever it was translated into a Western feminist canon. Butler addresses her elision of race in the second edition of *Gender Trouble*, where she names her stakes in critiquing racism and theorizing gender's racialization (Butler 1999). In the wake of such work, any history that positions *Gender Trouble* as key to destabilizing identity politics in WGS will repeat the text's original failure to frame women of color feminism as anything other than a sidestep towards a feminism whose racial and national locations remain unmarked. If this were to occur, disruptions of Western feminism by feminists of color would remain opaque *even* to accounts that embrace destabilization.

In place of such misreadings, WGS can recognize its formation at a distance from the critical insights of allied feminists of color, which long ago troubled its founding logics, and refocus its work in accountable engagement with their intellectual and activist leadership.[5] Doing so will disturb modernist commitments to identity and politics in WGS and its successor projects, while directing them to center the racial and national formation of gender and sexuality under ongoing conditions of colonization and globalization. Making the field accountable to women of color feminism in this way may empower it to study and destabilize the power-laden construction and politicization of identities as central to its work.

Women, HIV/AIDS, and Futures for the Field

In conclusion, I briefly consider what effects may follow once Women's and Gender Studies examines a contemporary world defined by late modern globalization and its colonial conditions. The myriad mobilizations of identities and their politics in this moment call out for investigation and destabilization with the insights of women of color feminism. Many examples exist of such work leading WGS and interdisciplinary theory: in readings of transnational feminist alliance by M. Jacqui Alexander and Chandra Mohanty (2010); in Andrea Smith's interpretation of Indigenous women pursuing (in Smith's terms) "unlikely alliances" while working for decolonization (2008); and in writing by women of color activists challenging the "NGO-ization" of social movements, as in the work of INCITE! (2007). I engage such themes alongside feminist scholars crossing the social sciences, humanities, natural sciences, and arts in our work to document and critically theorize the HIV/AIDS pandemic. In my case, engaging Indigenous AIDS activism made me accountable to Indigenous feminist, queer, and Two-Spirit activists who defend gender and sexual diversity by leading Indigenous nations in struggles to counter settler colonialism and pursue decolonization (Morgensen 2011). Indigenous AIDS activists taught me that the conditions of settler colonialism in a globalized world present key determinants of disease and health for Indigenous people, condition the pandemic's gendered and sexual contours, and require sustained critique in national and global AIDS activisms.

The global phenomenon of HIV/AIDS readily invites the explanatory power of women of color feminism and its ties to antiracist, Indigenous, and transnational feminist thought. We learn that power crosses disparate locations in ways that identities cannot contain or explain, as when women, men who have sex with men, sex workers, and IV drug users come to be linked by disease, stigmatization, public health management, and activism. We learn further that their potential solidarities are structured first by racism, capitalism, colonization, and globalization to grant vastly differing life chances, with women of color—trans and cisgender—being disproportionately vulnerable to HIV and becoming the predominant constituencies living with and affected by HIV/AIDS worldwide. Currently, global health programs are announcing "women" as the "new face" of AIDS by managing those marked as heterosexual, married women subordinated to male power—a formulation that, when referencing Indigenous women and women of color, reproduces colonial discourses of racialized women as in need of saving by Western civilization. Yet women's AIDS activisms in the Global South and North consistently refuse the status of abjected racialized objects of enlightened care, while centering members of their communities who are otherwise marginalized by sex work, drug use, or gender or sexual practices. In these ways, the AIDS pandemic and activist responses to it affirm Sandoval's insight that the power relations of late modern globalization multiplied the sites where identities are politicized, even while fracturing their ability to stabilize subjects and groups.

Comprehending this contemporary situation thus calls for intersectional, differential, and cross-cutting theories that mark and respond to the multiple power relations driving the pandemic and critical responses to it. Critical study of identities and politics is thus needed now more than ever, and legacies of women of color feminist thought offer key inspiration in such work. But if such work will lead to better accounts of HIV/AIDS, it will not fold into accounts of "women" or "Women's and Gender Studies" that leave whiteness, settler colonialism, and late capitalism uncritiqued. To the extent that WGS transforms, in kind, it can be a key site of such work. Effectively, the very histories of debate that seemed to put the field in jeopardy may spur its revitalization as a space for debating them under new conditions. This suggests a fresh response to dismissals of WGS as an anti-intellectual site of identity politics. Instead, pursuing critical theories of power and subjectivity in a globalizing world, the field can emerge in direct relationship to legacies of women of color, Indigenous, critical race, and transnational feminist thought.

While I close on this hopeful thought, such a result will follow only if practitioners in WGS focus on questioning disciplinary boundaries and fostering alliance politics within and beyond the academy. In the United States and Canada, white women (and men) who inherit the power of settler colonialism and global capitalism remain the majority of the field's leaders with the authority to set its agendas. White settler practitioners of Women's/Feminist/Gender Studies must commit to: challenging normative whiteness and settler colonialism; hiring, retaining, promoting, and seeking the leadership of faculty of color; and holding academia accountable to leadership beyond the academy by Indigenous women and women of color across the Global North and South. In the white settler and imperial academy, this is radical work. It will not proceed if white faculty in historically white WGS programs keep to

themselves the authority to decide how to teach women of color feminist thought, notably by "including" it in curricula that originated in
or remain aligned with other feminist stakes. Destabilizing modernist
commitments to identities and politics will transform normative course
design and pedagogy and will closely engage the field with stakeholders
both inside and outside the academy. Scholars and teachers keeping the
field accountable to women of color feminisms and Indigenous, critical race, and transnational feminist thought may redefine WGS and its
successor projects as inherently troubling of whiteness, settler colonialism, and imperialism. On this path, there will be no return to a WGS
that singularly commits to identity as a basis for intellectual or political
work. But, thinking with Sandoval, WGS may grow into a site where
interrogating identity forms a space of tactical politics that, even while
troubling itself, also troubles the power relations defining our contemporary world.

Notes

1. Of course, these are critiques that can and do gain traction if the downsiz-
   ing of public higher education promotes eliminating WGS.
2. See May in this volume for more on this term.
3. For texts antecedent to this era that address these implications for white
   women (including white Jewish women), see Bulkin et al. 1984, Zinn
   1990.
4. See, for example, University of California, Santa Cruz Department of
   Feminist Studies (name change 2005); University of Minnesota Department of Gender, Women, and Sexuality Studies (name change 2007);
   Queen's University Department of Gender Studies (name change 2009).
   Books discussing the turn from "women's" as a shift from restrictive models of feminist identity and politics include Kennedy and Beins 2005,
   Wiegman 2002b.
5. See May's chapter on "intersectionality" in this volume for a more detailed
   exploration of this long overlooking of the critiques raised by women of
   color feminisms about (white) WGS.

11

QUEER

Jennifer Purvis

Beyond Historical Injury: Rallying with the Deviants of Women's and Gender Studies

Queer = twisting, making strange: a noun, a verb, an adjective. Once a weapon in the arsenal of hate speech against so-called gender and sexual deviants, this term now serves as a powerful source of political energy. It signifies not only a range of variant genders and non-(hetero)normative sexualities but a posture of resistance, a questioning attitude, and a set of techniques or approaches.[1] It calls upon us to think beyond what may be known, seen, ascertained, pinned down, disciplined, institutionalized, and controlled. It positions us to move toward new horizons. But in spite of its formidable potency and broad range of meanings and effects, there is still some hesitation to deploy the term "queer," given its former status as an epithet, alongside the view that it poses potential threats to the successes of Women's and Gender Studies, including institutional acceptance. There is also concern that it undermines the coherence of identity categories, which function not simply as markers of historical injury but as "rallying points for political mobilization" that "appear to hold out the promise of unity, solidarity, universality" (Butler 1993, 188). Though WGS is committed to critiquing universalizing terms and categories, including "women," the destabilization of political units creates disappointment, feelings of loss, and, sometimes, rancor. However, despite such hesitations and concerns, I propose that we (re)centralize queer as the quintessential positionality of WGS and (re)embrace our queer cognizance, already intrinsically connected to the field's most effective scholarship and praxis. Because our most transformative possibilities are linked to this queerness, we must address a lack of awareness concerning queer matters, or simply a lack of commitment to queer recognition and inclusion, and any compromises effected by our desire for institutional success. A crucial starting point for this process is the acknowledgement that WGS is *always already queer.*

The need for a more queerly-aligned WGS is evidenced by many events and phenomena, but can be readily identified in certain key moments of the past forty years. Many readers are, no doubt, familiar with the oft-referenced event whereupon feminist scholars and activists gathered for the momentous conference at Barnard College, The Scholar and the Feminist IX: "Towards a Politics of Sexuality" in 1982.[2] Not only were conference participants forced to cross picket lines in order to attend the conference, but many were subjected to violent censure and suffered long-term consequences in their careers, including dismissal and denial of tenure.[3] Following this eruption in the early 1980s, many feminists were divided, into "pro-sex" and "anti-sex" camps, or categories of sex-positive and sex-negative feminists, misnomers that flatten sexuality into a false binary, as Merri Lisa Johnson explores further in this volume. These categories *both* sidestep the critical import of sexually liberatory practices, queer identifications, and politically radical dispositions *and* obscure valid arguments against violent, misogynistic pornography, and other forms or representations of nonconsensual violence. This encounter intensified what had been already embattled relationships among feminist groups and fuelled an ongoing rift among feminists and within WGS.

From this site of explosive political tension—and its bifurcation of the feminist movement and academic feminists alike—emerged Carol Vance's groundbreaking anthology, *Pleasure and Danger: Exploring Female Sexuality* (1984). Its contributors interrogate parochial attitudes towards the primary issues of butch-femme dynamics, BDSM, pornography, and sex work. These sex-radical authors challenge the notion that there is a correct feminist sexuality and outline a politics of sexuality beyond the confines of strict normative mandates. They urge us to critique sexual repression and violence towards women in a corrupt environment of male domination but, simultaneously, to move beyond an overemphasis on the dangers of sexuality—to say "yes" to pleasure while working towards gender justice, to refuse the choice to identify one's feminism with *either* pleasure *or* danger.

While this event and anthology have been taken, collectively, as *the* flashpoint of queer controversy within WGS, we may further trace the "fear of queer" and the need for a more vigilantly queer-minded WGS to another volatile and polarizing moment, from which emerged a familiar icon—the Lavender Menace. A literal and figural creature, a series of episodes and a stubborn spectre, the Lavender Menace has long threatened radical solidarity amongst feminists and WGS practitioners. In a sense, she is the embodiment of intrafeminist dissent concerning queer matters, but she also guides us towards queer outcomes. In fact, many within WGS are more familiar with the reclamation of the phrase than the original insult. Her emergence and subsequent transformation are linked to an event that occurred a decade prior to the confrontation at Barnard, where lesbian and Queer feminists, excluded by Betty Friedan from The Second Congress to Unite Women in 1969, were pejoratively branded "The Lavender Menace." They then formed a group by this name, thus reclaiming an epithet used against them as a point of solidarity from which they protested homophobia and the marginalization of lesbian theory in 70s feminism. Despite the coinage, Friedan was not alone in thinking that nonstraight and sex-radical feminists posed a threat to the success of *liberal feminists*[4] who, even today, seek parity within existing systems and identify with norms that idealize white, male, heterosexual standards.[5]

Due to critical concern precisely for those who have been neglected, devalued, silenced, marginalized, stigmatized, shamed, traumatized, and even annihilated, WGS has consistently challenged the normative centers of privilege and identity that gave rise to episodes like those at Barnard in the early 80s and generate spectacles such as the Lavender Menace. That is why such denials have proven such painful episodes. Nevertheless, these incidents, read critically, ultimately draw attention to the power of discursive regimes which define the ideal citizen, person, and sexual/gendered subject and operatively exclude certain "others." Likewise, they define the ideal feminist, lesbian, woman, activist, or

academic and perpetuate their own operative exclusions within politics and the academy, which we may also analyze and redress. Thus,
the figure of the Lavender Menace not only marks a particularly disap-
pointing and unsavory episode (or trend) in feminist "herstory," but she
names its path to resistance and serves as a warning to those who may
forsake "the abject multitude against whose experience we define our
own liberation" (Love 2007, 10). The Lavender Menace, or the spectre
of whatever hue we assign to queer, continues to haunt WGS and must
be confronted if the field is to retain or (re)claim its radical edge.

Recognizing the Essential Queerness of Women's and Gender Studies

There are three major categories of meaning associated with the concept,
"queer," ranging from the (1) *nonheterosexual*, or nonstraight (potentially homonormative and the most pernicious of the three because of
its prevalence as the *only* understanding of *queer* among many and its
reification of the straight/gay binary) to the (2) *nonheteronormative* (the
most intentionally political of the three) and the (3) *deviant and non-
normative*, either sexually or genderwise (which can be problematic, or
at the least politically incoherent—especially if included in this category
are practices like pedophilia alongside nonmarried sexual relationships
and an array of unconventional romantic arrangements). Certain figures
prominent in queer theory, such as Eve Kosofsky Sedgwick, maintain
queer's relationship to non-hetero-sexualities, or at least maintain its
primary affiliation as one tied to sexual identity and sexual practices
outside of heterosexuality—though in her later work Sedgwick remarks,
"Everyone knows there are some lesbians and gay men who could never
count as queer and other people who vibrate to the chord of queer without having much same-sex eroticism, or without routing their same-sex
eroticism through the identity labels lesbian or gay" (2003, 63). Other
figures—among them, Judith/Jack Halberstam—stretch the bounds of
queerness to include a range of so-called "deviant" non-normative sexualities or sexual practices, including those of sex workers and others who
stand outside of "repro time" (2005).[6]

Within this spectrum, the second category—that of non(hetero)
normative and/or gender nonconforming practices and persons—also

includes queer feminisms and queer feminists of all genders and sexual persuasions. This is the sense of queer most in concert with what I locate at the heart of Women's and Gender Studies' feminism: its always already queer identity, or its queer essence. It speaks through those of us who highlight the problems associated with dominant understandings of sex, sexuality, and gender and those of us who promote unsettling critical practices and textual strategies and a general awareness of the instability of categories, subjects, and ordering principles (even disciplines themselves). This articulation of queer overlaps with other critical perspectives, such as those that aim to dismantle dominant constructions of race, class, national identity, and ability, and represents the most politically effective resonance of *queer*. The idea of a queer "essence" may sound like a contradiction in terms, given that the field has long critiqued the naturalized scripts associated with conventional gender roles and hetero-dominant white male culture, dismissing claims of essence for both women and men. In fact, WGS has been questioning, for some time, the very binary systems that divide people into women and men, except where political interests necessitate this. This essential queerness, however, emanates from common purposes, and thus my use of "essence" is strategic. Fundamental objectives include: ending gendered oppression; eradicating phobic responses to minority sexualities and gender variance; exposing rigid patterns of sex and gender identification; and opposing unjust and punitive regimes of coherence that coerce and constrain us.

The most effective forms of WGS are committed to educating, informing, preparing, and empowering unruly women and other feminists, which entails dismantling the structures that support the reification of an "othered" category, women, and similar patterns of naturalized and congealed identity-construction. WGS at its best dissembles any and all interpenetrating orders of dominance that create categories of valued and privileged subjects who reign over despised and oppressed others: for example, targeting compulsory heterosexuality, which compels citizen-subjects to either conform to sex and gender norms or suffer the dire consequences of being unable or unwilling to replicate society's existing power relations. Through its queer strategies, WGS targets other interconnected relations of power that persist in attributing to women, Queers, people of color, persons exploited by capitalism, and those from developing nations the status of the inhuman, of property, or objects of exchange value or bare use. Under such conditions, these "others," about which WGS is profoundly concerned, are not recognized as ends in themselves, but as means to an end, or a set of ends. If left unquestioned, these ends, supported by patterns of thought and firmly entrenched hegemonic values (that maintain the superiority of white, privileged, able-bodied male subjects), will continue to circulate, ensuring that such dominance will continue to be actualized, systemically.

However, there are, as I have noted, moments of internal conflict that threaten the field from continuing on a path towards building a more effective, more queerly feminist future—not simply those episodes that have been chronicled, but a host of experiences, events, and "tendencies" that undermine the queerness of the field. One general tendency is the embrace of an identity politics that entails necessary us/them, inside/outside frameworks of inclusion and exclusion. Though provisional categories of coherence are necessary for making advances within existing structures, this type of identity politics often works against the interests of the most marginalized subjects: the abjected, the dismissed, the culturally unintelligible. Instead, I am arguing that we must adopt an identity for WGS based on the centering of difference, or *alterity* (irreducible difference), and of utmost importance, feminist and queer difference. This involves highlighting the existence as well as the efforts and insights of non-gender conforming women warriors, feminist trans subjects, the queer-minded/anti-heteronormative, gender variant or genderqueer allies, champions of women and other disenfranchised peoples, and a host of numerous others I have not named and who we cannot imagine at this juncture. There is a dire need to "get inside" and *also* shake things up, a "both/and" approach, highlighted by Cathy Cohen's call to queer politics:

> A reconceptualization of the politics of marginal groups allows us not only to privilege the specific lived experiences of distinct communities, but also to search for those interconnected sites of resistance from which we can wage broader political struggles.... Such a project is important because it provides a framework from which the difficult work of coalition politics can begin. And it is in these complicated and contradictory spaces

that the liberatory and left politics that so many of us work for
is located. (1997, 462)

But shaking things up means challenging the long-standing desire for
WGS to be a "home" for this kind of work.

Towards Queer Community: Resisting the Comforts of Home

Despite our status as a haven for students and coalitional colleagues and
our efforts to epitomize the "Safe Zone," Women's and Gender Studies
spaces are not always "queer-friendly," as my previous examples suggest. For instance, since my first National Women's Studies Association
Conference in 2001, I have noticed inconsistencies between espoused
commitments, such as the embrace of "feminist community," and the
lived reality of inhabiting WGS spaces. Many speak out about feeling
out of place, dismissed, misapprehended, or invisible: Queer femmes
assumed to be straight, straight women assumed to be heteronormative
and, therefore, uncritical, and others who are silenced, erased, or marginalized. During my inaugural NWSA experience, my companion, a
visible Queer hailed by insider nods throughout, quipped, "You know
what you are? You're a *homeless-sexual*!" Although I was actively rebel-
ling against strict notions of "what a proper feminist looks like" and
rejecting the obvious means by which a self-identifying Queer achieves
visibility, her humour did little to assuage my profound disappointment
in the apparent limits of the Women's Studies "community" as I experienced it.[7] However, in retrospect, the neologism takes on new resonance
and interrogatory power. Since then, I have also come to grasp how
firmly entrenched the prevailing patterns of feminist interrelationality
really are, and to discern how identificatory sites maintain dominant
kinship order and operate alongside and in concert with other frameworks that order rigid (e.g., straight/gay) identity politics.

Even as my subsequent faculty position as a feminist theorist in
what was then a Women's Studies department in the U.S. Deep South
meant that I was interpellated as Q/queer, and I came to understand
the political valences of queer's contestation and embraced it, personally and professionally, over a sexuality and a politics of "fluidity,"
Q/queer marginalization never feels quite "comfortable." Reflecting

on the affective elements of inhabiting queer spaces, Michael Snediker states, "My experience of feeling ontologically incoherent ... had none of the thrill of reading about being incoherent.... What I wanted for myself was the opposite of what I found intellectually most interesting and vital" (2009, 6). However, the feminist project of WGS is not—and should not be—directed towards feeling good or being part of a "happy feminist family." We can, and should, strive towards greater levels of inclusivity and actively reach out to the uninitiated and those with less institutional power, but it is also imperative that we interrogate the terms of inclusion and work to surpass the stubborn inability to comprehend anything outside of—and disruptive to—limited us/them, inside/outside, and hetero/homo binary constructs, within the field and beyond. To this end, it is vital that we: revisit our field's constitutive terms and conceptualize structuring mechanisms more queerly; realign paradigmatic attachments to support a multivalent vision of interrelationality; and promote ideas and language that convey intersubjective relations as well as textual and political ones as not only open to difference but *based on difference*. This is not for the sake of comfort, but in the service of a vision of WGS mobilized on behalf of those for whom structural change is most necessary.

Prevailing fantasies of familial unity and dominant metaphors of sisterhood and maternity not only perpetuate patterns of disjuncture that fuel disappointment; they delimit the field. Such fantasies reinscribe reprocentrism and preclude more queerly feminist possibilities within WGS. Feminist critics have long warned us of the dangers of taking up Freudian fictions, including the fantasy of the family romance.[8] In contrast, we must proceed more queerly: resist the family trope as a model for feminist interrelationality and dethrone kinship order, primary among the mechanisms that create and reinforce hegemonic heterosexuality. Shared goals, such as ending phobic responses to otherness, eradicating systemic oppressions based on divergence from an ideal, or normative, identity, interrogating and confronting the terms of compulsory heterosexuality, and liberating sexuality in keeping with the goals of gender justice and reproductive justice, cannot be sufficiently addressed without adequate attention to difference, without departing from or truly queering "the family" and developing more adequate models of feminist community based on affinity, rather than sameness. The ubiquity of heterodominant thinking—which entails the privilege of remaining unaware of one's privilege—allows for certain heterocentric frameworks and dominant voices to persist and continue to suppress our critical mettle.

Thus, my analysis raises another related issue, point of struggle, or moment of queer reckoning: the search for home, be it a personal, political, or academic one. More of an overarching theme than a historical moment or figure of controversy, the search for home, like the family romance, is seductive, yet illusory and problematic. In many queer narratives, home is the object, the telos. This makes sense, given the dislocated, uncomfortable state of existence lived by marginal subjects and the literal homelessness experienced by many cast-out Queer youth, or even the relationships of Q/queer adults to their families of origin. However, the drive towards home is not an effective political trajectory if home is constructed as a political, intellectual, or disciplinary space that is familiar, comfortable, and comforting—a place of stability or sameness. If home is viewed as a place of rest and comfort, we should seek its opposite. Nan Alamilla Boyd concurs: "I hope that as well-established women's studies programs continue to invite queer theory and critical race theory scholars onto their faculty, they will allow the most basic metaphors of home ... to be deconstructed and rebuilt on, perhaps, a less stable foundation" (2005, 106). Diminished stability does not mean that we lose hope or wander aimlessly. If we are open to queer possibilities, we may in fact be enlivened by the optimism of queer approaches and directed by more adequate queer values. Snediker states, "Queer optimism doesn't aspire toward happiness... in this sense, [it] can be considered a form of meta-optimism: it wants to *think* about feeling good, to make disparate aspects of feeling good thinkable" (2009, 3).

The invocation of queerness brings possibilities, though not always immediately realized, and inevitably expands discursive limits, which leads to a greater range of cultural intelligibility and, consequently, less "homelessness," in a manner of speaking. Yet in what ways can a certain sense of homelessness, or "homeless-sexuality," yield positive results? In her description of the relationship of migrant bodies to diasporic spaces, Sara Ahmed states, "The disorientation of the sense of home, as the 'out of place' or 'out of line' effect of unsettling arrivals, involves what we could call a migrant orientation" (2006b, 10). Becoming unmoored from the stable context in which we comfortably dwell—psychically and corporeally, intellectually, or politically—may be experienced as a kind of violence, but an invigorating, productive violence. The shifting ground of subjectivity/politics/feminisms brings new perspectives, which inspire new becomings and create new communities. As Lisa Duggan suggests, queer community is a collectivity unified by "shared dissent from the dominant organization of sex and gender," rather than sex/gender identifications (1992, 20). Likewise, the oft-cited words of Michael Warner indicate that queer defies the "minoritizing logic of toleration or simple political interest-representation in favor of a more thorough resistance to regimes of the normal" (1991, 16). The efforts of a queer community are directed against a "wide field of normalization, rather than simple intolerance, as the site of [unwelcome] violence. Its brilliance as a naming strategy lies in combining resistance on the broad social terrain of the normal with more specific resistance on the terrains of phobia and queer-bashing, on the one hand, or of pleasure on the other" (16). Queer community, politics, or approaches do not preclude minority-based les-bi-gay programs and agendas; these may act in concert. Yet there are far greater prospects on the queer/futural horizon.

Becoming-Queer: Disorientation and Women's and Gender Studies' Queer Futures

The arrival of queer marks a conceptual shift instrumental to effective Women's and Gender Studies politics, pedagogy, and scholarship. Emerging from the critical advances of poststructuralism, deconstruction, and postmodernism, *queer* provides, for many, a welcome alternative to inadequate instantiations of identity politics.[9] Undisciplined and resistant to institutionalization, *queer* offers a slippery alternative to the straight/gay and M/F choices that have constrained us, both in our lived realities and in our teaching and research agendas. Queer involves twisting, turning, complicating, intensifying. This is the power and passion of WGS: interdisciplinary, intersectional, creative, visionary, intergenerational, futural.[10] Yet there remains a persistent fear that this positionality results in conceptual sloppiness or meaningless pluralism. In part, this can be attributed to its constant motion, or state of "play." There is a marked resistance to stasis associated with queer because stasis so often leads to unfortunate outcomes; we are best served by active questioning. And there are indeed many instances where discussions of queer matters shift between people, groups of people, identity formations, politics, sexual acts, national and transnational entities, and constituencies across time. This may generate confusion. However, there is a definitive slippage between *Queers, queer(/-ing),* and *queer politics* precisely *because* there is an irrefutable link between a "deviant" population and the set of coordinates that allows for this population to be subjected to various forms of phobia and queer-bashing, between the practices of said deviants and resistant responses to these harms.

When we define queer politics as a response to the harms that emanate from "regimes of the normal" or legible constructions of identity, the agendas informed by queer politics entail advocacy on behalf of many marginalized people. Queer approaches target discursive regimes that perpetually and unjustly parcel out inclusion, privilege, legitimacy, and human value. This is why it is vital for those previously denied access to inclusion (and those allied with them) to question flattened categories, flawed constructions of normalcy, and corrupt visions of kinship and community, rather than purchase membership at the cost of others. As Love states, "Resisting the call of gay normalization means refusing to write off the most vulnerable, the least presentable, and all the dead" (2007, 30). Queer concerns, intentions, politics, strategies, and agendas ask not that minority subjects simply strive for inclusion *or* remain in the margins of the non-normative, but ask that we get inside *and* shake things up, that we look back at a legacy of oppressive regimes and their intrinsic harms, *and* also look ahead, to persistent regimes and their potential demise—to the queer horizon.

Identification or *orientation* are limited projects, whether in reference to feminist generations, or waves, or to binary systems of sexuality or gender, especially where such maneuvers entail uncritical alliances with corrupt, privileged, and exclusionary norms. Far from learning from the mistakes of the past—especially when we view the mistakes of the past as *residing only in the past*—WGS appears to be repeating missteps and shortcomings. By remaining attached to fictions of coherence, normalcy, and clear-cut "orientations," we allow corrupt visions and conceptual weaknesses to limit the breadth and effectiveness of our work. We are, by and large, aware of the negative effects of oppositional logic, which have resulted from an overreliance on binary pairs, such as: normal-abnormal, public-private, culture-nature, man-woman, and human-animal. Identifying with the dominant class or setting oneself apart from it by laying claim to its supposed "opposite" have proven deficient and dangerous. Thus, beyond *identification* with a dominant norm, or *counteridentification* with its (equal or superior) opposite—for example, hailing women's "special capacities" for childrearing/caretaking, nurturing the environment, or demonstrating compassion—a queer feminist/WGS positionality *disidentifies* from existing frameworks by rejecting the inherent paucity of either/or choices. In his work on queers of color, José Esteban Muñoz urges us to reject this binary logic of straight/gay and instead situates *disidentification* at the center of his project, a queer hermeneutic of racialized otherness (1999). Unlike identification and counteridentification, *disidentification* refuses available binary terms on the grounds that they are inadequate and compromising. This is the stance most in keeping with post-binary approaches to sex, sexuality, race, and gender. As an alternative to identification, *disidentification* asserts resistance to the normative terms of identification and allows for the consequent transformation of identificatory sites, strongly associated with hybridized positions (1999). The scrambling of codes ("recycling and rethinking coded meaning") serves to expose and critique the universalizing and exclusionary terms of dominant culture (1999, 31).

This positionality is profoundly relevant to WGS, for its refusal of verticality and the progressive telos of linearity corresponds to the refusal to "identify" or locate oneself or one's practices within traditional historiography or disciplinary boundaries. This term highlights the interdisciplinary, mobile, and rhizomatic character of WGS. Drawing upon Deleuze and Guattari's concept of the *rhizome*—which behaves like crabgrass, with its extensive underground root systems and its structure of spreading-outward, indicating no clear beginning or end—we may conceptualize WGS as an interconnected web of ideas and critical practices that take shape more or less on a plane. The concept of WGS as a *field* (in this sense of the word) thus places emphasis on the horizontality of our relations. Our field may be characterized as a rhizomatic landscape with multiple lines of flight and many becomings. This reflects our interconnected methods and agendas, porous disciplinary boundaries, and resistance to being "disciplined" along conventional lines. In contrast with the arborescent tree, the dominant symbol of knowledge, history, time, and narrative, with its distinct set of roots, its linear development, and its phallic posture, this notion of a rhizomatic system provides a nonhierarchical model more suited to our mobility, openness, and emphasis on change—in other words, the *becoming-queer* of WGS. Unlike trajectories that lead us to a comfortable home, *disidentification* may be an uneasy location, but it is the positionality from which the field will have its greatest effects. The embrace of *disorientation*, which brings *disidentification* to the impulse for orientation, intensifies and channels the inherently queer impulses of WGS.

Conclusion: Unleashing The Queer Menace Within

Mobile (or labile),[11] in constant movement, interdisciplinary, even transdisciplinary (in its strategies, topics, and scholarly conventions), multi-faceted, boundary-crossing, creative intersexional,[12] transnational—the anti-imperialism of Women's and Gender Studies is destined not for an "arrival place" but an unsettling space of contest and interrogation (not only of others and othering discourses but of ourselves), a realm of respectful dissonance, of welcome violence, where strangers are heard and, despite any potential discomfort, allowed to become part of the polyphonic voice (or chorus of voices) against injustice. It is the refusal to identify or to adopt an easy or clear-cut orientation that defines WGS as a field and determines its successes: on a plane, growing outward (not upward, or on the backs of others), against the tide of conformity (even in conservative academic climates increasingly hostile to that which *does not quite fit*). This maneuver brings the greatest number of allies to its fold. Though provisional truths are often necessary for change, the false comfort provided by stable and exclusionary categories is not an adequate resting place for this self-reflective, self-interrogating assemblage of scholars and practitioners. The cost of such security is too great and weighs too heavily on the collective conscience of the field, as evidenced by an abiding self-interrogation (in academic texts and forums) and our persistent return to unsettling events and phenomena, such as the notorious early-80s Barnard Conference, the Lavender Menace, and even our own personal moments of unease. Disorientation—a disidentificatory response to orientation—may be an uncomfortable state of existence or space to call our own, but when has WGS been anything less than dynamic, potent, and resilient?

Rigorous instantiations of feminism have always been actively engaged in questioning the integrity of the privileged hetero-center of normative subjectivity, raising objections to the nearly exclusive access of white, privileged, able-bodied, hetero-masculine XY-males to cultural intelligibility and, beyond this, exposing all manner of normative centers as not only exclusionary but supported by terms and constructs which are inherently corrupt. Likewise, WGS, as a field of critical inquiry and a sphere of political agency, has, from its beginnings, challenged norms and ideals of citizenship, personhood, embodied/gendered subjectivity, and sexuality—and the rights and privileges assigned thereto. To invoke a familiar adage, *feminism was queer before queer was queer.* Can we say the same of WGS? Are there insurmountable limitations installed by its inceptive frameworks? The long-standing goal of representational and political equality and the concomitant reliance upon the category, women, are two examples of elements that define yet delimit the field. To be sure, WGS has taken shape in response to a generalized sexed hierarchy, and, from this, the category, women, emerged. Yet this category is subject to interrogation and functions only as a term under erasure, strategically posited by savvy, antifundamentalist practitioners and scholars of WGS. And from this queering of *women* emanates critical concern for a range of marginalized groups and a sustained focus on the workings of numerous intersecting vectors of oppression. However, at this juncture, we may do well to challenge ourselves by asking: Do we sufficiently address queer issues? Do we effectively critique the coextensive workings of sexism and heterosexism? In what ways does the Lavender Menace still haunt WGS?

Though I was relentlessly teased as a child on the basis of my surname ("Pervert!"), I eventually came to recognize myself in that call amidst politically astute, queer-minded friends, colleagues, and graduate students, who, knowing my politics and theoretical attachments, playfully address me by variations on this theme, including Dr. Pervert. In a similar vein, I propose that we, as a field, reclaim that which has been cast out and unleash our inner queer menace, alive and well in many spheres of WGS. As Judith Butler suggests, "An ability to affirm what is contingent and incoherent in oneself may allow one to affirm others, who may or may not 'mirror' one's own constitution" (2005, 41). Queerness, whether manifested in the realm of sexuality, gender, or politics, inspires a revitalized sense of feminist community and models of interrelationality that challenge us not only to recognize and respect but centralize difference—where women, Q/queers, and other minoritarian subjects have status *as subjects* with the potential to disrupt existing economies of exchange. These very subjects demand that we engage in the effective collaborative, coalitional dialogue of queer community. This involves constant negotiation and a Derridean vision of hospitality, where we welcome the stranger, the queer stranger, or queerness itself, understood as that which unsettles and dismantles dominant ways of thinking—not only about sexuality and gendered/embodied subjectivity, but interrelationality and even desire. Only in our queerest configuration will we exceed the bounds of what we have imagined is possible.

I propose, therefore, an embrace of queer, even as we struggle against extinction—for the sake of all those not privileged by dominant white heteropatriarchy, or reigning hetero-norms, in order to have greater influence through solidarity and realize our most transformative effects. Like each of us, WGS is not identical to itself; its mirrored reflection is always inadequate to its scope. Therefore, it becomes even more necessary for each and every scholar-practitioner, at every level, from novice to founder, to engage in the difficult task of ongoing critical reflection: that is, to recognize our inconsistencies, to look back and remember, and yet look forward, towards the queer horizon. My specific call in this chapter is one directed at unchecked privilege—with its flawed visions of identity, community, kinship, and home—and unfulfilled WGS potential. It asks that we acknowledge our own internalized lavender-baiting, both as individuals and as a field, and that we resist the temptations of cozy comfort, "the family romance," or coming home. For when we confront the queer menace for who she is—*the stranger within*—the result is *disorientation*, a running away from everything we were ever taught to call home. This may create new levels of discomfort, a sense of homelessness, or the recognition of *homeless-sexuality*. However, *disorientation*, as a strategy, a positionality—as WGS' *political identity*—may entail the growing pains necessary not only to survive but to thrive in our most effective incarnation to date.

Notes

1. I distinguish *queer* as a broad field of meaning from *Queer* in reference to people, where capitalization affords this distinction. Where I summon both at once (as in the case of marginalization within academia) I employ Q/queer to retain the distinction between people and their position/approach (to emphasize the distinction between embodying queerness or living queerly, and taking on queerness in one's work/politics, which may be executed from a position of relative privilege or safety, such as heterosexuality or gender normativity).

2. See http://www.barnard.edu/sfonline/sfxxx/intro_02.htm for more on this touchstone event and the controversies it generated.

3. Those picketed by name included Gayle Rubin, Joan Nestle, Dorothy Allison, and Amber Hollibaugh, who stated: "Coming from a family that taught me never to cross a picket line, one of the worst times I ever had was crossing the only one I ever did: a feminist picket line of Women against Pornography at the Barnard conference. I thought to myself, 'This is really telling. I'm crossing a picket line, with women carrying signs with *my* name on them, saying that I'm perverted, that I don't belong in this movement'" (2000, 248).

4. Taking inspiration from the phrase, the Red Menace, Betty Friedan is said to have called Rita Mae Brown a Lavender Menace when Brown and others protested the marginalization of lesbians at the Second Congress to Unite Women (organized by NOW in November of 1969)—particularly, the omission of the New York chapter of the Daughters of Bilitis from the list of sponsors: "Lesbians, [Friedan] believed, would blight the reputation of the National Organization for Women if its members were labelled 'man-haters' and 'a bunch of dykes'" (Jay 1999, 137). These events inspired Brown to resign from NOW and help form the Lavender Menace. Later renamed the Radicalesbians, this group wrote the well-known position paper, "The Woman-Identified Woman" (1970; see Brownmiller 1999; Jay 1999; Gerhard 2001).

5. Love argues that the same desire for inclusion within a norm that demands denigrating the "queer fringe" is currently exerting pressure on the gay and lesbian population: "Given the new opportunities available to *some* gays and lesbians, the temptation to forget—to forget the outrages and humiliations of gay and lesbian history and to ignore the ongoing suffering of those not borne up by the rising tide of gay normalization—is stronger than ever" (2007, 10). "One may enter the mainstream on the condition that one breaks ties with all those who cannot make it—the nonwhite and the nonmonogamous, the poor and the gender deviant, the fat, the disabled, the unemployed, the infected, and a host of unmentionable others" (10; see also Hollibaugh 2000, 265–66).

6. A thread throughout Halberstam's book, "repro time" suggests, among other things, that time is "naturally" ordered by purported biological clocks, imagined children's needs, the rules of bourgeois respectability,

familial and national stability, and a clear delineation between youth and adulthood, where adults no longer participate in culture but stay at home and create environments believed to be optimal for child-rearing.

7. McCaughey, in this volume, offers a compelling challenge to common sense notions of "community" in WGS.
8. Jane Gallop, for instance, cautions feminists "to stop reading everything through the family romance" (1992, 239; see also Heller 1995).
9. Morgensen's chapter in this volume offers a more nuanced reading of identity (politics) in WGS. See also Carrillo Rowe for more on how the institutionalization of WGS is effected.
10. Although these terms are common within the field, other chapters in this volume problematize any easy usage or simple understanding of them. See Lichtenstein and May on interdisciplinarity and intersectionality, respectively.
11. Labile (from the Old French: apt to slip) is a resonant term within French and psychoanalytic feminisms. Used negatively in the past in reference to hysterics, it has itself been queered. It is an instability recast by feminists as positive: as in, highly adaptable, fluid, porous, and even surprising. It is a term that signifies that which is constantly changing (or open to change), unstable, or always in transition.
12. A permutation of intersectionality, designed to ensure the consideration of major vectors of oppression—not simply race, class, and gender but the vector of identity and oppression most often left out: that of sexuality.

EPISTEMOLOGIES RETHOUGHT

Points to Ponder

1. How would the core knowledges of WGS shift if "Intersectionality," "Identity (Politics)," or "Queer"—as outlined by their authors—operated as a central epistemological framework? What specific practices or intellectual assumptions would be challenged—and changed?
2. What are some of the ways to account for the paradox of nominal inclusion and frequent lack of impact on knowledge produced that the chapters on "Intersectionality" and "Identity (Politics)" identify? What do both chapters challenge about the assumed relationship between identities and knowledge in WGS?
3. How might WGS heed Purvis' call to embrace "homelessness" in pedagogical, administrative, and institutional contexts? What would a "homeless" WGS have to give up—and what would it gain?

PART 4
SILENCES AND DISAVOWALS

The four terms brought together in this section challenge Women's and Gender Studies (WGS) practitioners to continue to think about the absences and oversights in the field, this time focusing especially on underlying constructs that have not been, and perhaps cannot be or must not be, spoken of in WGS. Terms such as "Discipline," "History," "Secularity," and "Sexuality" bring to the forefront a series of unacknowledged assumptions that, their authors argue, WGS has alternatively denied, renounced, or failed to recognize as part of the field. Much as with the foundational assumptions or ubiquitous descriptions terms, the argument here is that these terms also structure the field: what is gained—as well as lost—by denying WGS' status as a discipline? How does an inattention to the complexity of the field's pasts limit the kinds of questions WGS practitioners raise in the present? In what ways does the field's assumed secularity work against its goals for inclusivity? What are alternative ways of talking about sexuality in the field that can account for the nuances and complexities of locations, and move beyond simple binaries of pleasure and danger?

Each of these terms in many ways intersects with other terms thus far in this book. "Discipline," for instance, obviously connects to "interdisciplinarity," but also to "feminism" and "activism" in that it asks why WGS has long claimed not to be a discipline yet acted as if all academic (and other) feminist work anywhere constitutes the field. "History" looks at the ways in which WGS has, and has not, rendered versions of a past in its structure and curriculum, clearly linking with discussions in "waves" and "pedagogy," and questioning the consequences when the present is reflected as more complex and nuanced than the past. The long unacknowledged presumption that WGS is "secular" has, its author contends, structured the field in its relationships to (only particular versions of) "feminism," with repercussions for the goals explicated in "intersectionality" and "identity (politics)." And while "sexuality" could clearly be inserted into many other sections in this book, its presence in this section highlights its author's argument that WGS has conceptualized this term in such narrow ways, often reverting to the simple binary between pleasure and danger and thereby rendering silent other possibilities, and other necessary narratives.

Taken together, these terms force us to challenge some of our most longstanding and unspoken assumptions in the field, and ask us to rethink what WGS would and could look like if we rethought these silenced structuring narratives. Their collective demand is that we never stop investigating how WGS, often and usually in spite of its stated desires, is complicit in producing knowledge that reproduces absences.

12

DISCIPLINE

Ann Braithwaite

Drawing Equivalences

1. "Is Women's Studies a discipline of its own, that place in the university where radical, women-centered scholarship grows, develops, and expands? Or shall feminist scholarship... be incorporated into the disciplines so that eventually Women's Studies as a separate entity will become obsolete?" (Bowles and Duelli Klein 1983, 1–2)

2. "Many contemporary feminist scholars currently have limited traffic with Women's Studies programs—they may cross list a course or two, or allow their names to be affiliated with the program, but remain peripheral to the curriculum and governance of the program." (Brown 2008, 34)

3. "In short, can and should Women's Studies exist as a separate body of knowledge and methodology, relatively autonomous....? Or does and should it exist only in sustained and interdependent dialogue with bodies of knowledge and methodologies in existing disciplines?" (Friedman 1998, 311)

I start this chapter about the function of the term "discipline" in Women's and Gender Studies (WGS) with these examples because they are emblematic of something that has both fascinated and troubled me over the past few years, as a scholar, teacher, and program administrator in this field. In all of these roles, I am repeatedly struck by the consistent drawing of an equivalence between academic "feminist" work in any field and WGS[1]—a belief marked most usually by an interchangeable use of the terms "feminist" and "WGS," by the expectation that one is the same as the other (and thus, as in Brown's case, worthy of remark if someone doing one isn't affiliated with the other), and by the assumption that if one is doing "feminist" work in any discipline, one is also doing WGS—as evidenced in such phrases as "doing WGS in X discipline." As the examples above illustrate, WGS is usually positioned as being composed of and equivalent to academic feminism in (all) other disciplines—as, effectively, the sum of these parts. This belief is so ubiquitous and so normative in WGS in its institutional arrangements, its intellectual premises, and its pedagogical practices that it remains largely unremarked on—and thus, also, unexamined as a foundational assumption in the field.

In the introduction to their anthology *Women's Studies for the Future,* Elizabeth Kennedy and Agatha Beins reference a 2004 brochure from Duke University's Women's Studies Program that offers one of the few dissident voices to challenge this collapse of the field with all academic feminisms across the university by asking: "what are the knowledge traditions, critical vocabularies and methodological presumptions that attach to Women's Studies and differentiate it from feminist scholarship in the disciplines?" (2005, 23). On one level, this question resonates with the long-standing "autonomy or integration" debates about the field, articulated so powerfully in Gloria Bowles and Renate Duelli Klein's 1983 anthology *Theories of Women's Studies,* where contributors explored whether what they called Women's Studies should exist as a separate field in the university, or whether its aim was to disseminate academic feminism throughout the existing disciplines. But the question in this brochure goes even further—since the contributors to that autonomy vs. integration debate largely shared the premise that Women's Studies did in fact equal academic feminist scholarly work, and were more concerned with whether there was a necessity for an institutional site for that work than they were about what in fact constituted the field.[2] The challenge issued in this brochure, though, is to rethink that long-standing premise, and to ask what else now constitutes the field of WGS, beyond equating it to the totality of all academic feminisms brought together. I highlight this brochure question here precisely because it hasn't been widely taken up in any sustained or articulated way, reflecting both that taken-for-granted assumption that academic feminisms equal WGS, and a larger refusal to think about the question of the field's identity/ies in a more systematic way that could explore its similarities to *and* its differences from those other academic feminisms. And to not address this question is to leave WGS facing a number of consequences that delimit both its present practices and its future possibilities. Although often differently important for thinking about institutional claims than it is for intellectual or pedagogical ones, the issue of WGS-specific intellectual identity/ies is central to my focus here. Because ultimately, I find myself wondering in the face of this assumed equivalence: is WGS really strengthened by seeking to represent as many other disciplines as possible (to say nothing of "feminism" outside of academia) in its structures and practices? Or has the time come to delimit WGS? And if so, is it time to face, head on, the difficult, anxiety-provoking question: "delimit it to what?"

Rethinking "Discipline"

As I contemplate the ubiquity of this equivalence between Women's and Gender Studies and academic feminisms, I find myself increasingly thinking that as much as this conflation reflects the oft claimed "interdisciplinarity" of the field (replete with its own difficult, conflicted, and multiple meanings, which Lichtenstein explores in such great detail in this volume), it is also symptomatic of a long-standing refusal to claim WGS as a "discipline." Although both terms are central structuring claims in the field's formation, they operate in different ways and with different consequences for the field. My focus here is on the more silent term, to begin to explore both the function of, and "what's at stake" in, this refusal of the term "discipline"—because, as Biddy Martin so persuasively argues, "In the process of engaging what has been disavowed, refused, or ignored, we might unsettle what have become routine and, thus, impoverished practices" (2008, 187). In engaging with the disavowal of "discipline," then, my aim in this chapter is twofold: (1) to think more carefully about what is meant by this term and question why WGS has so often resisted using the term to describe itself; and (2) to explore the consequences both *for* the field and for *thinking about* the field of this central (albeit often unspoken) refusal, by exploring more closely that conflation of WGS and/as academic feminisms.

As many theorists and historians of "disciplines" have observed, there is nothing inevitable about the distinctions that are commonly made between different academic subject areas.[3] And certainly outside of the university context and its emphasis on disciplines as the basis of its academic organization, knowledge is not separated into disciplines: i.e., "WGS" is not a term used to describe anything outside of the university—where "feminism" usually does that work instead. Areas of knowledge commonly recognized in a university setting as disciplines are more creations of historical moments and institutional and locational necessity than reflections of any naturally occurring or necessary divisions between types of knowledge; thus, as Messer-Davidow, Shumway, and Sylvan argue, to explore disciplines and the differentiations between them is to ask questions about discipline-ness or "disciplinarity" (as they term it), to examine how and in what ways, at particular times and places, those apparent differentiations of knowledge are brought about: "Disciplinarity is about the coherence of a set of otherwise disparate elements: objects of study, methods of analysis, scholars, students, journals, and grants ... we could say that disciplinarity is the means by which *ensembles of diverse parts* are brought into particular types of knowledge relations with each other" (1993, 3, emphasis added). To study disciplinarity is thus to defamiliarize a discipline, to see it as the product of a variety of different factors—of time and place, but also of purpose and function. Klein furthers this point about disciplines being constructed by noting that, "If there is an undisputed truth about disciplinarity, it is that disciplines change.... disciplines have not been static because they do not live in isolation. They are constantly influenced by points of view and methods of related disciplines" (1993, 186).[4] If disciplines have long been recognized and lauded as ways to differentiate both a set of practices and a set of practitioners from each other, for these authors, those borders always demand exploring which "diverse parts" have been brought together, and how and why they are made to relate to each other.

One of the most powerful perceptions—and myths—about disciplines in the modern university is that they are unified bodies of knowledges, methods, approaches, and practitioners that make them different from each other: indeed, as Coyner notes, "from the outside, they seem more uniform, more structured, more methodical, more 'disciplined' than areas closer at hand" (1983, 47). Klein points out the implications of this idea, arguing that, "unidisciplinary competence is a myth, because the degree of specialization and the volume of information that fall within the boundaries of a named academic discipline are larger than any single individual can master.... Broad disciplinary labels confer a false unity on discipline" (1993, 188–90). Disciplinary labels can only confer that false unity by overlooking other features central to them, such as: (1) the differences between subdisciplines in any field; (2) connections between subspecialties across different fields; and (3) the frequency of cross disciplinary influences in the modern university.

Let me use an example from another field in order to further illustrate Klein's point. At the university where I work, the Department of Psychology consists of ten full time faculty members, who range from a person who does neuroscientific research to a person whose research explores historical and critical approaches to psychology and psychoanalysis. Holding that these ten people, with their varied research projects, intellectual premises, and teaching focuses, constitute a unified field of inquiry and knowledge production necessitates overlooking: (1) the immense differences between the range of specialties in the discipline, with different approaches, methodologies, theoretical languages, etc.; (2) that those specialties often find commonality outside of their own disciplinary homes (i.e., that the neurological researcher does most of her work with anatomists from the vet school); and (3) that in all universities, other disciplines also have numerous points of intersection with some parts of this field (i.e., Sociology or Philosophy). Clearly, in this example (which is hardly unique), Psychology is not a unified and distinct field, in spite of its institutional positioning as such. Nor does this "disciplinary" grouping of practices and practitioners necessarily denote a shared mastery of, or clearly delineated parameters around, a field[5]—although, institutionally, this is the more usual perception of any discipline.

As the above quick look at the fluidity of disciplines demonstrates, disciplines and disciplinarity must always be thought about both historically (as they are defined and change over time), and contextually (how they might be differently conceptualized and practiced in a variety

of contexts or settings). Disciplines get named and renamed, their differences get defined and redefined, all suggesting that the designation
"discipline" is never the static naming of a field, but always a product
of constant negotiation and struggle that redraws boundaries and redis-
tributes areas of investigation—and all in a process that largely remains
unnoticed and unacknowledged.[6]

Thus, although much ink has been spilt on arguments for identifying WGS as either a "discipline" or "interdiscipline" (or even a trans-
or multi-discipline), such attempts inevitably run into an irresolvable
morass of conflicting ideas about all these terms. And indeed, as with
many fields in academia today, practitioners in WGS no doubt use both
of these (and other) terms to describe this field, depending on institutional location, audience (i.e., students, colleagues, administrators,
funders), desired outcomes, etc. Furthermore, there is no doubt that
much of what I have just described as constituting a "discipline" seems
to also describe how "interdisciplinary" is largely understood—as being
about overlaps, intersections, blurred boundaries, and new and shifting configurations of knowledge. Rather than getting bogged down in
this debate here, then, I want to move beyond the usual "discipline or
interdisciplinary field" talk and think instead about *what's at stake* in
refusing "discipline" to describe WGS. Looking more closely at the disavowal of this term exposes how that disavowal has shaped and framed
the field, institutionally and intellectually. It reveals something about
investments in particular kinds of definitions and ways of thinking over
others, it allows us to see what is included and what is excluded in those
definitions, and it points us to different or alternative ways of thinking
about what we do and how we do it and why we do it—that is, to different ways of thinking about our involvements in the production of
knowledge in and under the name "WGS."

Whither "Discipline" in Women's and Gender Studies?

Given the above argument about the multiple possibilities, tensions and
contradictions, and overlaps and intersections involved in the term "discipline," I find myself wondering why Women's and Gender Studies has
so often, and vehemently, not only refused that term to describe itself, but
also refused to question its own static understanding of what that term

means. With all of its theoretically sophisticated critical approaches and challenges to status quo knowledge and knowledge production in the university (and elsewhere), why hasn't WGS also been at the forefront of examining the concept of discipline itself? Why is it that the breadth and scope of work that rethinks this concept is not dominated by people coming out of one of the institutional and intellectual sites supposedly the most committed to rethinking knowledge production—WGS? And if, as so many commentators on disciplines have noted, the definition and arrangement of a discipline is more a political and ideological question than anything else—well, isn't WGS all about exploring political and ideological questions, challenging rather than accepting status quo assumptions about the organization of the world, including, one would expect, its own? Both the silence and the absence here are thus striking for what they suggest about what else WGS is absolved of—or absolves itself of—having to (re)think through this disavowal.

The repeated resistance to the label discipline—in spite of the fluidity and instability of this term to describe any knowledge project—I want to argue, points to a number of other questions and debates about both the field's foundational assumptions and normative (knowledge-making) practices that too often aren't acknowledged. For example, what kinds of identity and identification possibilities has the refusal of this term constructed for the field, and for those who practice in it? The absence of engagement with what the above outlined thinking about discipline might open up for contemplation is, I would argue, a refusal precisely to ask that question of "diverse parts" mentioned above—that is, to ask what is counting as WGS, and how, in particular contexts; it is the sidestepping of asking how WGS might be related to, but not completely equivalent to, all academic feminisms more broadly. Overall, then, the disavowal of this term has also too often been the refusal to be accountable for (or at least self-reflexive about) how the field is constructed or what its structuring assumptions are, and has left it ill-equipped to articulate an intellectual, institutional, and pedagogical project that isn't simply that sum of all scholarly feminist work. Thinking about how WGS has (not) engaged with this term and concept thus calls attention to those unspoken and unexamined assumptions about the field's subject, about its borders and parameters, and about its relation to other fields of inquiry (or disciplines)—all central and contentious issues it currently faces (and which many of the essays in this book take up in some detail). At the very least, forcing those questions to the fore-front impels those of us who practice under and identify with the name "WGS" to face why that question is so difficult—and to acknowledge the anxieties and ambivalences raised by even open-ended and contin-gent definitions of the field. To ask—to demand—that WGS engage with discipline is not to look for one stable definition in its difference from other fields, but is instead to insist that central to the field is a focus not just on producing knowledges, but on accounting for the *process* of knowledge production itself, and especially in the university context that constantly demands (and rewards) differentiation between knowl-edges, or disciplines. It is thus to ask, to return to my key example here, why—and which—"academic feminisms" are brought together as the "diverse parts" that make up or equal WGS, and what other "parts" are either not defined as scholarly feminisms or not included in/as WGS. It is to insist that WGS embark on the project of articulating what makes it *not* simply the same as academic feminisms, and to suggest the pos-sibility that this continued refusal, forty years into this field's formation, can no longer (if it ever could) serve either its epistemological or social justice impetuses. It is, ultimately, to state that it is time for WGS to be "on its own" and to face whatever that position raises.[7]

Women's and Gender Studies' Identity Issues

Practices

In order to explore this refusal and some of its consequences further, I want to draw on two (of many possible) examples and offer some brief reflections on how their set of assumptions about academic feminisms and/as Women's and Gender Studies forestalls engagement with the term discipline in the ways outlined above—and in doing so also closes off challenging their own knowledge production. In her now (in)famous essay (originally published in 1997), "The Impossibility of Women's Studies," Wendy Brown starts her ruminations on WGS by outlin-ing the issues brought up for her program at UC Santa Cruz during a curriculum review process. In thinking about their collection of core and elective courses, she notes, they "found [themselves] completely stumped over the question of what a Women's Studies curriculum should contain" (2008, 19), and at a loss to articulate "what a well-educated student in Women's Studies ought to know and with what tools she ought to craft her thinking" (2008, 19–20). And this difficulty was only exacerbated when they tried to contemplate a graduate program: "we have struggled repeatedly to conjure the intellectual basis for a Ph.D. program in Women's Studies" (2008, 22). Ultimately, by the end of her essay, she comes down on the side of dismantling their program in favour of "mainstreaming" its discussions into the other disciplines. In this "solution," for her, WGS would no longer exist institutionally, but students would still be able to get that education, because those knowledges would be disseminated more broadly across the curriculum (a solution that sounds much like earlier rationales for "integration" rather than "autonomy").

What strikes me in this quandary faced by her department, though, is how symptomatic it is of precisely the kind of refusal to think about WGS through the lenses of discipline in the ways outlined above. Brown's (and her colleagues') worry that the more they looked at their curriculum and faculty specializations, the more they could "find no there there ... [or that] the question of what constituted the fundamentals of knowledge in Women's Studies [was] so elusive to us" (2008, 20), characterizes precisely the not engaging with this term that concerns me here—with the result that they could/did not then think more systematically about what WGS does with and through all of those courses. Ironically, while Brown asks a number of questions about "what constitutes a Women's Studies course" (is it, she briefly ponders, about topic? perspective? the person teaching? something else?)—questions that seem to suggest there really is a "there there"—neither she nor her program can find their way to answering them, nor to at least making those questions part of their WGS curriculum. Brown's ultimate "solution" of dismantling WGS, then, can only make sense because, in the end, she really doesn't see it as doing anything intellectually different from academic feminisms more broadly: hence why she and her colleagues couldn't come up with even a short list of what they thought they did in their program.[8] Indeed, and more tellingly, she doesn't see WGS—under that name—as an intellectual project at all; rather, her view of the field, and the reason she comes to believe that its time is past, is that it is "organized by social identity rather than by genre of inquiry" (2008, 23), and thus is (and has to be) too conservative to fully include all academic feminisms or feminist scholars—and it certainly doesn't do anything beyond that work.

Given my argument thus far about the need to get more detailed about the intellectual project of WGS specifically, it is clear that Brown's definition of the field as ultimately an identity-driven project is quite different than mine (and many other people's who have responded to her; i.e., Wiegman 2005 or Zimmerman 2005). But what particularly interests me here is her program's lack of contemplating WGS' particularities in relation to all that other scholarship, even through all the years preceding that curriculum review. Thus, even while Brown acknowledges that all disciplines "wobble, their identities mutate, their rules and regulations appear contingent and contestable" (2008, 23), she cannot engage with the question of WGS as different or more than the sum of its other academic parts, since WGS, for her, has to stay as an essentially stable project precisely because it is organized around a social identity—women—and, thus, remain fundamentally indefinable as an intellectual project on its own. Indeed, Brown argues that WGS cannot be the place of "sustaining gender as a critical, self-reflexive category" (2008, 24), because that challenge to the "coherence or boundedness of its object of study" (2008, 24) runs counter to its organization around the identity category "women." And, thus, because it must constantly resist challenges to the stability of its circumscribed object, women, WGS can never ask the question of what "diverse parts" are brought together and can certainly never be accountable to that process, even though it is precisely this assumption that many would argue needs the most questioning in her rendition of this field. The collapse of all academic feminisms into/as WGS for Brown becomes both necessary and impossible to challenge/change, because WGS is not a separate intellectual project, but simply a no-longer-necessary institutional site.

While Brown's essay has sparked a number of responses in the years since its publication, I want to turn instead to Sandra Coyner who, writing fourteen years before Brown, in 1983, offers a succinct counterpoint (that has not been widely taken up) to the kind of thinking about the field's parameters, particularities, and identities exemplified by Brown. In arguing that "Women's Studies should abandon our fierce adherence to 'interdisciplinarity' and become more like an academic discipline" (1983, 46), Coyner's essay reverses the usual terms of the relationship between WGS and academic feminisms, and argues for seeing the field as doing something very specific and different than other feminist scholarly work. Although some of her argument reflects a very different understanding of the subject of WGS (i.e., she is largely writing about "Women's Studies" prior to its renaming, its imbrication with poststructuralist approaches to its putative subject "woman," or its reach into questions of broader identity categories),[9] she nonetheless offers a compelling challenge to the understanding mobilized by Brown. The refusal to think about the particularities of the field, she argues, actually "*underestimates* the importance of Women's Studies" (1983, 54), because "beyond changing the disciplines, our central goal should be to build our own new knowledge" (1983, 56). Even more, she argues, "we need to be aware of how the disciplines can contribute to Women's Studies, not just the other way around" (1983, 56)—or, in other words, WGS needs to be seen as a separate site where its work doesn't simply shore up those other disciplines.

What I find especially provocative about her focus on WGS as being about reflecting on the production of knowledge through those other disciplines, though, is that it posits it as more than the sum of all of those other feminist scholarly activities. Rather than the more usual perception of feminist scholarship as only occurring in other disciplines and then counting as WGS, she argues instead for a mutually informing relationship between them, where each does its own intellectual work. Although not fully articulated, Coyner's view nonetheless sees WGS as being both engaged with *and* separate from other disciplines, and recognizes that that distinction makes a difference; as she compellingly asks, "are we sociologists, historians, and artists who happen to be interested in women—or are we Women's Studies people who happen to be particularly interested in social roles, history, and art?" (1983, 59). Without pinning down borders and boundaries for the field, Coyner's essay is an early—and rare—example of engaging with the kinds of questions raised by discipline outlined above in a way that Brown's, written many years later, isn't. Coyner concludes: "it clearly will not do to imagine Women's Studies as the sum of other disciplines ..." (1983, 61). WGS, in her formulation, is *both* academic feminisms *and* the (intellectual and institutional) place where the terms of that inclusion or incorporation are questioned. Coyner's understanding does what Brown's cannot—it insists on the need for WGS to think with rather than against discipline, intellectually and institutionally; this insistence on a WGS "on its own" (long before Wiegman's invocation of that phrase) can begin to both think/rethink ubiquitous practices of the field and attend to what "diverse parts" are and aren't brought together to constitute the field.

Practitioners

As much as the refusal to think about disciplines as open-ended and fluid has repercussions for assumptions about the field's subject (and hence its borders with other areas), even more unacknowledged are the effects that this refusal has on practitioners of and in Women's and Gender Studies. Coyner's 1983 essay is prescient here for its early recognition that the issue of discipline also raises the question of intellectual identity and identification for its practitioners—because the structuring belief of the field that "we are not a discipline" also structures the ways we (can) identify with and invest in this field. In reflecting on what claiming disciplinary status would mean, Coyner notes, "I suspect that we have attracted to our ranks many faculty who are more interested in teaching than in research" (1983, 54). Coyner's observation here names (in 1983) what has also become a central issue for many subsequent commentators on the field, who likewise note that while many people see WGS as a site of teaching—with which they identify, fewer identify with it as an intellectual "home" for their scholarly work; as Allen and Kitch comment, "Women's Studies becomes a site for teaching or support but not a permanent residence or a professional proving ground" (1998, 290). Echoing much the same observation, Wiegman comments on "how powerfully the disciplines—cast here in the language of 'home'—serve as the knowledge formations under which feminist intellectual subjects continue to be formed" (2001, 517), while Allen and Kitch further observe what they call "'disciplinary drift,' the tendency for Women's Studies scholarship to revert back to disciplinary frameworks" (1998, 286). And many others have noted the same phenomena: from Brown in the quote at the beginning of this essay that points out that many feminist scholars don't identify with WGS intellectually (or affiliate with it institutionally), to Coyner again, who early on asked, "what is the significance of the choice made by so many women faculty to call themselves 'feminist scholars' within their disciplines rather than making firmer ties to Women's Studies as a discipline and as an institutional entity?" (1991, 353), to Vivian May, who more recently notes how many job advertisements for WGS positions "ask for interdisciplinary *teaching* experience, but implicitly favour disciplinary *scholarship* or *degrees*" (2005, 190; emphasis in original).[10] The equivalence of WGS and academic feminisms, though, makes it an "easy" place to hang one's teaching hat—since in this conflation all academic feminist work is (or is part of) WGS pedagogically; one's scholarly work, however, belongs to "the disciplines." Thus, to use only one possible example, a "feminist psychologist" may teach WGS, but identifies her/his scholarly work with a "discipline"—which WGS apparently isn't. What are the consequences, though, when we do not identify ourselves in and as WGS's scholarly workers/producers, or when our practices make that identification impossible? As Allen and Kitch maintain, "disciplinary feminist work is not and does not claim to be interdisciplinary Women's Studies research.... Stopping with discipline-focused research may ultimately call into question the very need for a field called Women's Studies ..." (1998, 281)—a potential consequence at both the institutional and the intellectual level. Clearly, the ways in which WGS is understood as an identifiable intellectual field "on its own" has consequences for its identity, its practitioners' identities, and thus also, its intellectual and institutional future(s).

Discipline, then, matters—not just for institutional identities, but for how and with what practitioners in the academy identify themselves intellectually, and thus also, for what can be undertaken in the name of the field. Even if disciplines can never pin down a definition, even if there is no disciplinary essentialism and unidisciplinarity is a myth, questions of identity cannot be left entirely open, since WGS, as with any field, also means something to those of us who practice it and practice in it—intellectually, institutionally, pedagogically, professionally, and even emotionally. Discipline is how we recognize each other and how we construct and sustain intellectual community—a process that must always be in flux and accountable, that can never be an easy resting place, but that also can't be overlooked for what it makes possible

either.[11] I do not want to romanticize some kind of disciplinary longing here, or to be nostalgic for a disciplinary "home." And there is no
doubt that WGS is not an easy or comfortable home for many of its
practitioners—for reasons having to do with precisely how accountable
it is or isn't to those questions of its subjects, borders, and identities;
indeed, there is a long history of the inhospitableness of the field (as
Noble, Carrillo Rowe, and Purvis all explore so compellingly in their
chapters here). But to refuse to become settled in the places we inhabit
both intellectually and institutionally, to ask multiple questions about
the narratives that construct those places, cannot be the same as refusing to explore the particularities of knowledge production in different settings and the ways in which we have particular investments in
those—although it must also be to refuse to let those become settled
and sedimented in turn.

Conclusion—"Discipline's" Futures

On one level of course, I could worry about the implications of my own
argument throughout this chapter. As someone who is resolutely against
fixing identity, with absolutely no desire to define Women's and Gender
Studies in any kind of static or definitive way—and then have to gate-
keep that definition, and as someone who wants many possibilities in
and for the field, perhaps I shouldn't even worry about the equivalences
made between WGS and academic feminisms more broadly. And as
someone who teaches at a small institution, where I am the only person
appointed in WGS, and where as coordinator I'm also tasked with looking for more courses to crosslist, I certainly could be seen to be modeling institutionally precisely the collapsing of academic feminisms with
WGS that this chapter is challenging intellectually.

And yet, in spite of (or because of?) the above, I also worry about
that endless proliferation of courses that "count" as or come to equal
WGS—or more precisely, I worry about the terms under which that
endless proliferation occurs. Because if I am not necessarily arguing
against the breadth and variability of this field, I am arguing that such
proliferation has to occur along with an engagement with the concept
of discipline—and a constant accountability for the "diverse parts" it

brings together. I'm certainly not interested in insisting that WGS is or isn't a discipline in the more usual ways in which this discussion has been taken up, nor in demarcating ways in which it is ostensibly inter-disciplinary rather than disciplinary—and I don't much believe that this kind of distinction accurately describes intellectual work in the contemporary university. But if the designation discipline is always about raising identity questions and looking at how knowledge areas are defined, about examining borders and their differentiations, about keeping open possibilities and fluidity, about being aware of the multiple conditions of knowledge production, then I do want to call WGS a discipline—precisely because of what that term can now open up for our shared (re) thinking.

Of course, claiming discipline, no matter how open-ended and fluid, is also anxiety-provoking. Even as I argue that WGS cannot be everywhere, that it must "settle" (contingently and never for long), I worry also about having to "settle"—in all the meanings of that word. In saying that WGS cannot be everywhere, that it has to be "on its own" (intellectually and institutionally), I also hesitate, worried that I'll be called on to now define and differentiate it, to draw its parameters in relation (to return to my example here) to all that other academic feminist work. In this anxiety, I am, I suspect, not alone; if Coyner's 1983 call to think about WGS as a discipline hasn't been taken up in any widely accepted way, perhaps this is precisely because of the anxiety and ambivalence about "settling" anywhere. But, I also remind myself in the face of—and facing—this anxiety, all disciplines demand fluidity and accountability, demand recognizing and learning to live with mul-tiplicities—and "settling" is never the same as "settling for" or "settling in." Instead, discipline makes the questioning of the field and its invest-ments part of the intellectual project of that field. And, as this kind of discipline, WGS does what I've been trying to do here; in holding up practices and assumptions of the field to ask both "why these" and "what do they accomplish," it insists on an accountability for the diverse parts it brings together. It may challenge easy intellectual or academic iden-tity politics, but it doesn't foreclose the issue of identification, instead seeing it as always in process, never set. And that's the only "discipline" of WGS I will "settle" for.

Notes

1. There is also a long history in WGS of equivalences being made between feminist social movements outside academia and WGS. See Maparyan and Orr in this volume for more on these assumptions. See also Braithwaite (2004). And what comes to count as scholarly "feminism" is an equally nebulous and fraught question.
2. Sandra Coyner's (1983) essay, "Women's Studies as an Academic Discipline: Why and How to Do It," offers a different interpretation of this relationship, which I take up in more detail later in this chapter.
3. See, for example: Moran (2002); Klein (1993, 1996); Hark (2005, 2007); and Messer-Davidow, Shumway, and Sylvan (1993).
4. See also Hark (2005, 2007) on this idea.
5. For more on this notion of mastery in WGS, see May (2005) on the "messiness" or "problem of excess" –which returns especially around debates over the Ph.D. in WGS, and Friedman (1998), who labels this the problem of the "too much-ness" of WGS.
6. Hark argues that "discipline" is currently being questioned all over academia (not just in WGS), often in favour of other terms such as inter/multi/trans-disciplinary; indeed, she notes that increasingly, discipline is seen as a "sign of the university's immobility" (2005, 1), or that which marks it as not current and up-to-date.
7. "Women's Studies on its own" is, of course, a reference to Robyn Wiegman's 2002 edited collection by that name–a framing whose consequences this chapter attempts to explore. For more on the need to rethink WGS in relation to "discipline," see Boxer (2000), Martin (2008), Bowles and Duelli Klein (1983), and Yee (1997).
8. See Zimmerman (2005) for a pointed response to Brown and the issue of "what constitutes WGS." Even NWSA (the National Women's Studies Association in the U.S.) lists a series of common (albeit no doubt neither all inclusive nor completely agreed upon) learning outcomes in WGS; see also Amy Levin's report, "Questions for a New Century: WGS and Integrative Learning" (2007).
9. Although Coyner is clearly using the terminology "Women's Studies," and is writing long before the current renaming of the field as WGS, I will use WGS in my discussion of her work when referring to the field generally, to keep consistency throughout this chapter.
10. Coyner also notes that we have no term to describe ourselves as the field's practitioners in the same kind of language that people describe themselves as, for example, historians or sociologists; "the words 'Women's Studies' rarely specify an identity. If it is a discipline, its name does not extend to practitioners, as psychology names psychologists and philosophy names philosophers" (1991, 349).
11. See Caughie's article entitled "Professional Identity Politics" (2003b) for one especially trenchant exploration of the power and necessity of intellectual identifications.

13
HISTORY

Wendy Kolmar

My thinking about the subject of this chapter began in the mid-1990s during a conversation with my colleagues about naming our new Masters program in Women's Studies/Gender Studies/Women's and Gender Studies.[1] For every name that was suggested, someone would say: "that's so essentialist," "so 80s," "so second wave," "so ...'"; each comment was a dismissal of some past version of the field with which the speaker would not wish to associate our program and favored some preferred present version which was implicitly current, a better reflection of the "now" of the field. Those comments set me thinking about the implications of such supersessionist dismissals, which are hardly exclusive to my campus, and wondering what they bring to light about the relationship that the field of Women's and Gender Studies (WGS) has to both its past and to "pastness" in general.

From my feminist theory students, particularly in a course on the history of feminist thought, I hear echoes of these comments. When assigned a reading from an earlier period, whether from the nineteenth century or the 1970s, students often come to class feeling incensed with and superior to the writer who "just doesn't understand intersectionality" or who is "so heteronormative" or who "thinks 'woman' is a fixed category." While I am grateful that my students have retained arguments they learned in other classes and are using them critically in mine, I am struck by the presentism of their thinking, by their demands that earlier texts conform to current theoretical paradigms. Instead, I want them to understand the historical contingency of their own terms and to see how the earlier pieces they read open spaces in discourse and politics for them to think the things they now take as "truths" of feminist thought.

In this chapter, I want to think through (in dialogue with the work of other feminist scholars) the questions raised for me by my students and colleagues about our relationships to history, whether of continuity or discontinuity, in the field of WGS. So this chapter is about the term "history,"[2] and the place or status of historicizing, of thinking with, through and about history, within the field of WGS, both in the content we teach and in the stories we tell about the field. It worries about our presentism and a certain myopia or nostalgia that sets in when we look backwards; it resists a fixed teleology in which certain pasts lead inevitably to us and our successors (or fail to do so); and it hopes for some ways to think more complexly about both pasts and futures. I come to this not as an historian but as a feminist scholar of Victorian Literature who regularly teaches courses on the history of feminist thought and contemporary feminist theory. But, most important for me, I come to this chapter as a teacher worrying about what ideas of and from history we are (or are not) teaching the students in our field and in the process reaffirming for ourselves. So, let me be up front about where I am both coming from and going: I do not believe that we, or our students, can do without a past, or pasts. Too much is lost if we choose to be a field that lives and thinks only in the present tense (with a tentative or worried future subjunctive here and there), a field that is interested in the past only as it mirrors our present concerns. Rather, we need usable pasts and sophisticated analytical and critical tools for thinking about them.

This chapter concerns itself with history in two senses suggested by my opening examples: (1) history *in* the field of WGS—the content of our courses, curricula, and scholarship; and (2) the history *of* the field of WGS—the recent rather vexed arguments among feminist scholars about the story of our field and whether we can tell it. No doubt, those two histories inform each other; how we feel about those histories inflects our relationship to history and the past more broadly and affects our choices about what we teach and how we teach it. I will come later to the implications of the stories we tell about our field, but I want to begin with some questions about the content of the field itself. What do we teach in the WGS curriculum? Is there anything about the way we have constructed the field, about knowledge production in the field, about the questions we ask and the ways we go about engaging them, that have determined our ways of teaching the past? Do we have (or have we had) methods and questions that require historical thinking? Have those methods and questions been marginalized in the field as we presently teach and imagine it? Have we chosen certain theoretical or disciplinary paradigms that occlude history and set aside others that might bring the historical more to light?

The Evidence of the Curriculum

A brief survey of the major textbooks used in introductory Women's and Gender Studies courses, examined in tandem with comments from faculty teaching feminist theory courses, can give us some summary evidence of the status of history in this curriculum in the United States today. Looking at five major introductory texts,[3] each of which is a reader with multiple selections, I found that none of them contained more than five percent material from before 1960. The best contained five readings from this period; most contained one or two. Readings from "the second wave"—roughly 1960–1980—represented less than ten percent of the readings in each book. The largest number of second wave readings was thirteen—eight percent of the readings in that particular book. Most common among the early readings was the Seneca Falls declaration followed by excerpts from work by Mary Wollstonecraft, Margaret Sanger, and Emma Goldman; among the second wave readings, Audre Lorde was most common with Adrienne Rich, Betty Freidan, and Gloria Steinem also frequently included. What is most striking to me, beyond the generally small number of historical readings of any kind, is the fact that in each instance these readings stand alone. Readings from more contemporary periods seem to have been selected with the objective of highlighting debates, controversies, and complexity, so multiple readings on a single issue or topic are included; in no case is a similar strategy employed to highlight controversies in an earlier period. The result of such choices is that the complexity of debates about women and gender in the past is flattened; the readings that are chosen are generally selected to point to and ground contemporary debates, with the result that the past is represented only as prelude to our own moment and continuous with it, but without the present's intensity of conflict and debate. Striking to me is the absence in all of these readers of a single work by a woman of color before 1960. The picture that emerges from these choices, then, is of a feminist history that was totally white before the 1970s, involving no women of color in its early work. Women of color, most often Audre Lorde, are included at that particular moment, in the late 1970s and early 1980s, when "white Women's Studies" is said to have listened to the voices of women of color and changed.[4] Their inclusion at this point means that the texts reproduce a story told from the perspective of white women; they fail to develop the many other stories that might be told.

My evidence for the content of the feminist theory curriculum comes from the comments my co-editor, Fran Bartkowski, and I received as we worked on the third edition of *Feminist Theory: A Reader* (2001). In reviewing responses of about 50 faculty users of the second edition, I was struck by three commonalities among their comments: (1) no faculty member suggested adding a text from any period before 1985; (2) the readings people used least were the readings from the earlier periods: 1789–1920 and 1920–1963; (3) the period from which faculty were most willing to drop virtually everything was the period from 1920–1963. The most commonly used early readings were, not unsurprisingly, the Seneca Falls Declaration, Mary Wollstonecraft, John Stuart Mill, Sojourner Truth, Margaret Sanger, and Virginia Woolf. Less commonly known readings, particularly from the period between 1920 and 1963—Joan Riviere, Ruth Herschberger, Mary Beard, Stella Browne— were most often recommended for omission, because they were seldom or never assigned. Thus, where we had, in our first two editions, consciously tried to make visible the conversations that were going on in that period that falls between the so-called first and second waves, the faculty using our book had, for the most part, opted for the dominant narrative that says that nothing happened in feminism in that period in spite of the counter-evidence provided by the essays in front of them. What troubles me then, is that syllabi based on these choices, which ultimately forced us to make cuts in the reader, reproduce for students a debunked[5] but clearly still powerful narrative about the period between 1920 and 1963 as the "doldrums" of the modern feminist movement—

rather than offering students evidence that counters that narrative. Based on these two rather idiosyncratic samples of the content of introductory and theory courses, I would say that the WGS core curriculum in the United States generally lacks a strong attention to the past and largely fails to include historical materials in a way that represents the past complexly. So, what is it about the field that has produced such a curriculum?

Structure of Knowledge: Concepts and Questions

Can we identify something about the intellectual structure of our field, its founding assumptions or its theoretical development, that would explain these seemingly presentist choices? Is it the influences of disciplines and their methodologies? The dialogue with and appropriation of various theoretical paradigms? We insist on the interdisciplinarity of the field, but, if, as Diane Lichtenstein suggests elsewhere in this collection, our interdisciplinarity is a little more amorphous and ill-defined than we would like to think, perhaps certain disciplinary influences have come to predominate, particularly those of the largely presentist social sciences,[6] influencing our choices about and relationships with the past. Some feminist scholars in the social sciences have begun to worry about their disciplines' inattention to history. For example, in introducing her argument about the need for political and social science to attend to temporality, Valerie Bryson asserts that "much contemporary sociological and political thought is concerned with obtaining a 'timeless snapshot' of how societies and political systems function, with political choices often isolated from their historical context,... and time itself treated as noteworthy only when discussing the rare moments of sudden change" (2007, 10). The institutional and curricular locations that Women's and Gender Studies occupies also suggest the significant influence of the social sciences on the field. Many institutions count WGS courses to fulfill a social sciences requirement, and many WGS programs are housed within institutional units defined primarily as social science.[7] Do these institutional requirements and locations push the field to be more like the social sciences in its curricular choices, its formation of knowledge, and its methods?[8] If the social sciences, as Colin Hay suggests, largely offers "an analysis from which all temporal traces have been removed" (in Bryson 2007, 10), have their methods and approaches pushed WGS curricula and course content in a more presentist and ahistorical direction?

It's not as though all WGS concepts and questions are/have been presentist. But it may be that the historicity or temporality of key questions or concepts gets obscured, whether by disciplinary paradigms or by the fact that familiarity with a term or debate means that we no longer think about its grounding assumptions. For example, an historical assumption is foundational to the essentialism/social constructionism debate. Essentialism is in part seen as flawed because of its inherently ahistorical and transhistorical claims. Social constructionism counters essentialism with an historical and temporal claim: that gender has been made in social and historical processes and can therefore be undone through the same processes; it was made in time and can be unmade in time. Judith Butler makes this point in *Bodies that Matter*, "Construction not only takes place *in* time, but is itself a temporal process which operates through the reiteration of norms; sex is both produced and destabilized in the course of this reiteration" (1993, 10). Feminist scholarly thinking relies on the implicit historicity of such concepts, but we often don't make visible, and therefore forget, the historical claim embedded in a term like social construction.

On the other hand, many of the central questions that shaped the field in its early days were inherently historical. "Where are the women?," the founding question that propelled feminist scholarship in many disciplines (and brought us Women's History Month, "Women who Dare" calendars, etc.), is an archaeological question demanding that we excavate the pasts of disciplines, cultures, and societies to find the thought, work, creative production, and action of women. Though recent theory that has problematized the category of woman[9] has made us aware of the limitations of this question, the work done by scholars asking that question reshaped canons in literature, art history, and music and produced detailed accounts of the cultural, social, political, and lived experience of many different women who were invisible to us fifty years ago. This question also initiated the inclusive curriculum work of the 1980s and 90s, which has significantly altered what is taught in many disciplines within the contemporary university.[10]

The other question that motivated much early scholarship in the field—"what is the origin of women's oppression?"—is a fundamentally historical question (except when biology is the answer); it demands origin stories and historical narratives in response, meant to excavate the past and to ground action for change in the present. Stories of the origins of women's oppression are as various as the theoretical and conceptual approaches in the field, but the fundamental question each asks is: where is the past that can explain our present and direct our future? For example, Gayle Rubin's "The Traffic in Women" (1975), Sheri Ortner's "Is Female to Male as Nature is to Culture" (1974), and Gerda Lerner's *The Creation of Patriarchy* (1974), are three classic origins arguments that look to anthropological evidence for explanations of a system of oppression that crosses times and cultures and can make sense of our current gender arrangements. Lerner's project, like those of most scholars who start from this question, is "to give the system of male dominance historicity" (1986, 36).

Of course, "where are ...?" and "what's the origin ...?" seem to us now slightly old-fashioned questions or perhaps not the right questions at all. We see them as naïve, excessively empiricist, too invested in single-causes and a coherent subject, too unaware of the contingency and political commitments of such stories. Katie King rightly suggests, writing about origin stories from the women's movement, that all such stories are "interested stories" which "construct the present moment, and a political position in it, by invoking a point in time out of which that present moment unfolds—if not inevitably, then at least with a certain coherence" (1994, 124). But, when we critique or reject those questions, are we too participating in a kind of feminist storytelling that is erasing a particular past in the service of a more current version? That storytelling may not leave us space to consider whether there is anything useful for the production of knowledge in WGS about continuing to ask some version of those questions.

In her 2005 essay about knowledge production in the field from the 1970s to the 1990s, Claire Hemmings explores two competing narratives that characterize this kind of storytelling. One narrative is "a story of progress beyond falsely boundaried categories and identities" which traces the shift from "the naïve, essentialist seventies, through the black feminist critiques and 'sex wars' of the eighties, and into the 'difference' nineties" (2005a 116); the other is a story "of loss of commitment to social and political change" (116) which mourns the unity of the early women's movement destroyed by individual careerism and intellectual and political fragmentation. Each of these stories, despite their different valences, traces "a process of imagined linear displacement" (131), defining a teleology in which, for better or for worse, some feminist present replaces and erases the pasts of the movement and the field. Like Hemmings, I want to attend to such displacements of prior knowledge and questions and to the ways in which those displacements continue to be enacted in the field.

In telling the story of the postmodern erasure of earlier totalizing and essentialist feminisms, Hemmings lumps socialist feminism in with other 1970s feminisms, but I wonder if another theoretical perspective that brings history into the argument is being displaced there. When WGS scholars set aside socialist/Marxist/materialist feminism as another totalizing, patriarchal discourse, the field also loses the methodology of historical materialism and the modes of thinking that go with it (and incidentally also an approach to thinking that was attentive to class—a term that has largely dropped out of our contemporary feminist thought).

Feminist historical materialism taught us to understand patriarchy, sex, gender, class, and race as historically specific, produced from the material conditions of a particular time and place and therefore continually changing as these conditions change. We now take this insight—that inequalities based on these dimensions of identity have been made in history and can be similarly unmade—almost for granted. The historicism of Marxist/socialist/materialist feminist theory of the 1970s and early 1980s countered the deep ahistoricism of radical cultural feminism because, as Heidi Hartman suggests in her essay, "Feminist Analysis By Itself Is Inadequate," "it has been blind to history and insufficiently materialist," failing to provide us with the necessary understanding of "patriarchy as a social and historical structure" (1979, 1–2). More recently, Rosemary Hennessey and Chris Ingraham see these theoretical perspectives sidelined by the ahistoricism of postmodernism: "Marxist feminism sees in much postmodern theory," they write, "a refusal to acknowledge the historical dimension of postmodernism and a limited and partial notion of the social—in Marx's words, an effort to fight phrases only with phrases" (1997, 9).

So, did the arrival of postmodern theories and approaches move the field in deeply ahistoricist directions? Many feminist scholars consider this moment, as Linda Alcoff does, a "crisis" in feminist theory (1988). They worry that postmodern approaches left feminism no ground to stand on, making politics impossible as neither its object of concern nor the subjectivity of its actors could be any longer understood as stable and knowable. "[J]ust at the moment when so many of us who have been silenced begin to demand the right to name ourselves, to act as subjects rather than objects of history," writes Nancy Hartsock in her essay in *Feminism/Postmodernism*, "just then the concept of subjecthood becomes problematic" (1990, 157–75).

The work of Michel Foucault has had a particularly complicated place in the feminist scholarly debates about postmodernism and history within feminist theory. Foucault comes in for a good chunk of the blame and is often lumped in with other posmodernists, because his arguments seem, as Hartsock suggests, to destabilize the individual subject of feminism in any moment, making both politics and history impossible (1990). But Foucault's work—most particularly *Discipline and Punish* (1977) and *The History of Sexuality* (1988)—has also offered many feminists a way to think about gender and sexuality through time without some of the traps of an empiricist and totalizing history (which omitted women's lives). The very practice of genealogy that is foundational for the essays in this volume comes, as our editors indicate in their introduction, from the work of Foucault. Some feminist scholars see Foucault's notion that the individual is "totally imprinted by history," as Linda Alcoff puts it, "eras[ing] any room for maneuver by the individual within a social discourse or set of institutions" (1988, 407). But for others, Irene Diamond and Lee Quimby, for example, Foucault can still be a resource for feminist historical work. They argue that: "Foucault's own labors in explicating how disciplinary power molds through localized mechanisms of enticement, regulation, surveillance, and classification are invaluable for demonstrating how specific historical and cultural practices constitute distinct forms of selfhood" (1988, xiii–xiv).

The question for this essay is whether, as some have claimed, postmodernism has made thinking about history within Women's and

Gender Studies impossible. I would argue that feminist scholars' engagements with Foucault and other post-modern theorists have led to some of the most productive speculations about how to produce feminist knowledge that locates gender, race, and sexuality in time and history without reproducing the essentialism and exclusionary practices to which those early questions brought us. Donna Haraway, in "Situated Knowledges," defines one version of such an approach. She argues that we need "simultaneously an account of radical historical contingency for all knowledge claims and knowing subjects, a critical practice for recognizing our own 'semiotic technologies' for making meanings *and* a no-nonsense commitment to faithful accounts of a 'real' world" (1988, 579). Her essay is an argument for "situated and embodied knowledges and against various forms of unlocatable, and so irresponsible, knowledge claims" (583). What her argument makes clear, and what is important for my argument here, is that situated knowledges are by definition responsible to history, even a history of ruptures and discontinuity, and to the particularities of the lives and experiences of knowers differently located *in time* as well as in contemporary social and global spaces.

Stories of the Field: Waves, Generations, Loss, and Betrayal

If disciplinary and theoretical influences on the field of Women's and Gender Studies have shaped the choices we make about what goes into the curriculum and the ways we interact with the history of thought and movement, so have the metaphors we have created; dominant among them are the metaphors of waves and generations. I would argue, as others have, that these metaphors constrain our ability to think complexly about the past because of the ways in which they flatten that history and make us attend to certain aspects of the past while failing to see others.

The metaphor of waves is perhaps our most taken for granted model for a history of feminism. It has become a convenient shorthand for describing the nineteenth through twenty-first century history, at least of activism on behalf of women's equality. As ubiquitous as it is heavily critiqued, it persists in textbooks, book titles, and our common parlance. Though we may problematize it with quotation marks, pun about it in our titles,[11] and critique the oversights and exclusions it promotes, it is always ready to hand when we talk about the feminist past. I would guess that many students could produce it as a narrative of the past more readily than any other. In her chapter in this volume, Astrid Henry carefully dissects this metaphor and the ways in which it occludes historical, generational, and conceptual complexities and "reduces the present and the future to a series of familial squabbles and Manichean conflicts." In the interest of space here, I refer readers to Henry's essay for a fuller discussion of the waves metaphor. But a couple of questions linger for me: if we choose to problematize and dismiss waves as a usable metaphor, are we jettisoning the only story we tell about our past as a story of activism? Have so many "third wave" anthologies chosen to reclaim or revise the waves metaphor because they are looking for a history of action as well as thought? Many of us in this field (students and faculty) are hungry for models of action, stories of successes, failures and internal struggles, rifts and disuptions, of issues that never went anywhere as well as the ones we have singled out as successes. This is not an argument to save what I view as a limited and problematic metaphor, but simply a suggestion that we understand what may be one thing that has contributed to its persistence and take account of it in inventing alternative metaphors for telling feminist histories.

The metaphor of generations has been closely linked to waves, as Henry argues, and seems almost as ubiquitous and problematic. It has many of the same limitations as wave metaphors, with the added problematic of a familial frame of reference which names us all mothers and/ or daughters and invests us in a model of time shaped by cycles of reproduction. That desire for linear narrative and for foremothers who justify the thought and action of their feminist daughters, who then seem to reproduce them as part of the natural flow of feminist history, makes us look back to prior periods and select only what seems to justify present thought and action. Whatever might challenge, disrupt or counteract those generational stories, we set aside. Whichever the metaphor we choose, most have the problem Jane O. Newman articulates in her essay on presentism: they "fail ...to challenge both students and ourselves to theorize alterity as an issue of change over time as well as of geographical distance, ethnic difference, and sexual choice...." When we use them, "we repress ... the 'thickness' of historical difference itself" (2002, 144–45).

In February 1989, *The Women's Review of Books* published a special section on "Women's Studies at Twenty."[12] In bold face at the top of the first page is the following statement: "Born from the Women's Movement at the end of the sixties, Women's Studies now has a past as well as a future." With a confident sense of causation and chronology, this statement seems to declare that the field has arrived; it is old enough to have a history "as well as a future." Just a decade later, the field was in a far less certain and much more questioning mood, as our editors' introduction describes this moment in their discussion of reflexivity in the field. While that moment is certainly generative in all the ways they describe, that process of self-examination—of rethinking where the field has been and where it's going—also produced multiple uneasy narratives and some very conflicted emotions, reflected in the pervasive language of post-ness and afterlives, of disappointment, impossibility, and failure. In this moment, WGS' relationship with its past is characterized either by nostalgia or by a sense of anger and betrayal. "Academic feminism's apocalyptic narrative," Robyn Wiegman observes, "speaks then in two different modalities of affective longing—one looks retrospectively at a past that contained a vision of a whole and transformed future; the other looks at the future and registers loss and betrayal as feminism's present is found to be disturbingly 'otherwise'" (2000, 833). In that moment, many feminist academics wondered, as Bonnie Zimmerman does in her article on the National Women's Studies Association, if "Women's Studies as an educational and social movement had been so severely compromised that it was no longer worth working within it" (2002, viii). Have we opted not to find ways back into our pasts because we simply cannot deal with all of this anger, betrayal, and shame? I wonder if our troubled relationship with our institutional history as a field has made us reluctant to do history at all. Can we only be haunted by our history, or can we find some productive ways to use and engage it?

Imagining Alternatives: Changing Times

Some Women's and Gender Studies scholars[13] have tried to imagine alternatives to our temporal dilemmas. One of the most interesting of these is Victoria Hesford in her essay "Feminism and its Ghosts: The Spectre of the Feminist-as-Lesbian" (2005). Hesford takes the metaphor of a feminism haunted by its uneasy pasts and, borrowing a methodology from Avery Gordon which she calls "looking for ghosts,"[14] transforms it to define a new relationship with the past:

> ... haunting produces a defamilarizing relationship to the past that simultaneously opens up the present to the possibility of a different future. For feminists in particular, to have a haunted relationship with the feminist past is to be able to bear witness to the possibilities, often unrealized, of that past and to actively resist the policing and defensiveness that have marked much of feminisms relationship to its diverse history in recent years. (2005, 230)

Like Newman's proposal that we must allow the past its alterity, Hesford's "defamiliarizing" relationship with the past opens for us a range of possible ways of doing and understanding history.

To pay no attention to history in our work, to omit history from the curriculum, or to settle for too easy, familiar, or obfuscating metaphors and narratives of history is to deny us all usable pasts. How can we learn how change happens—how feminists rethink flawed positions or concepts—when we either never see the past or we see so little or so simplified a version (or one colored with nostalgia, ambivalence, or anger) that we are at a loss to make connections? Maybe the pasts that students understand or construct to make sense for themselves of who they are and where they are going and what they need to fight for will bear no resemblance to my version, and maybe I won't even recognize those pasts, but that is okay with me.

Hesford's haunting, and similar approaches proposed by other scholars, may show us some ways toward a WGS worth fighting for. Such a WGS would make space for—would in fact insist on—histories of multiple locations, of multiple voices speaking, histories as complex, messy, and undecided as the present. Some of these histories would be continuous with our present, laying the groundwork for what we think, know, struggle for, and teach now. Some would be utterly discontinuous, truly sites of difference and "defamiliarization." They would not lead in a straight line to us. Some may be sites of shame where women working in some way "for women" actively impeded the success of other struggles or took positions we would now repudiate, or they might be sites where we were deeply wrong about our thinking or our practices/ activism. All of these pasts belong to us. We simply have to ask questions about those pasts—questions as challenging, edgy, and subtle as the questions we try to ask about the present and the future—and we have to grapple with the complexities and difficulties those questions reveal about what we teach and how we understand the temporality of our field. Sometimes we may have difficulty living with these pasts but, finally, I would contend, we cannot live without them.

Notes

1. My thanks to all the people who have helped me think through this contents of this chapter over the years I've pondered it—my Drew colleagues Sharon Sundue, Peggy Samuels, Debra Liebowitz as well as Gail Cohee, Judy Gerson, and the editors of this volume as well as a number of its other contributors.
2. This chapter does not claim to think about the field of women's/gender/ feminist history as it has developed within, in dialogue with and critique of the discipline of history. Women's history, as it has emerged over the past thirty to forty years, is a complex and nuanced field with its own methodologies and methodological and theoretical debates.
3. Balliet 2007; Grewal and Kaplan 2006; Kesselman, McNair, and Schniedewind 2008; Shaw and Lee 2009; Taylor, Rupp, and Whittier 2009.
4. This moment is marked by the publication of such volumes as Hull, Bell Scott, and Smith, 1982; Moraga and Anzaldúa 1983; Lorde 1984.
5. See, for example, Rupp and Taylor 1987; Tarrant 2006.
6. The claim that most social sciences disciplines, perhaps with the exceptions of anthropology and archaeology, are largely presentist is, in some ways, a broad generalization while in other ways almost a truism. Valerie Bryson, herself a social scientist, sees these fields as lacking attention to the past. For some further summative evidence: Looking at the references and discussion in a 2000 issue of Annals of the Social and Political Science focused on "Feminist Views of Social Science," only nine sources of the 447 cited in the ten essays, just over two percent, were published before 1970. Six of the ten articles cite no sources from before 1970.
7. I noticed this particularly at a recent PAD meeting at NWSA during a conversation about the place of WGS in general education.
8. Of the scholars who edit the introductory texts I examined above, the majority also do come from social science disciplines.
9. The use of the term "woman" as signifying a coherent category has been challenged by the work of post-modern and French feminist scholars, feminist scholars of color, and by gay, lesbian, and queer scholars among

others. For example: Marks and de Courtivron 1981—which made available in English the work of French feminists, Hélène Cixous, Luce Irigaray, Monique Wittig and Julia Kristeva; Riley 1988; de Lauretis 1986; much of Judith Butler's work, but especially "Against Proper Objects" 1994; Lorde 1984; hooks 1981.

10. See, for example, Schuster and van Dyne 1985; Sherman and Torten Beck 1980; Farnham 1987; Minnich 1990.

11. Dicker and Peipmeier 2003; Reger 2005; Berger 2006.

12. One of many special issues, reports, and volumes celebrating WGS at twenty or twenty-five issued around this time. Other examples: Guy-Sheftall 1995c; *Signs* 2000; *NWSA Journal* Summer 2000; *Feminist Studies* 1998.

13. Among the many scholars who propose new approaches to negotiating with the past are Roof 1997, Gubar 2006, and the editors and many of the authors of this collection.

14. See, Gordon 1996.

14
SECULARITY

Karlyn Crowley

I do some informal polling at a Women's and Gender Studies (WGS) conference. My question: "where are spirituality and religion in Women's and Gender Studies?" It is a simple question, but one that provoked puzzlement, and I consistently got the same response: a blank, stumped look, followed by the nervous question, "the Goddess?" Faculty were surprised I had even asked. Many did not see how the topic was relevant. Or perhaps it is just hard to pose questions that academics do not have lengthy responses to. Several faculty members thought I was asking a question about Religious Studies; others thought I wondered about personal spiritual practices. In other words, responses were either disciplinary based—religion is out there in another field—or personal. I could have asked nearly any other question about subject formation—race, gender, class, sexuality—and nothing would have stumped scholars or felt as irrelevant to WGS as this one. My question is about the absence of conversations about spirituality and religion in WGS; that is, why do we not talk about spirituality and religion, and what happens when we don't?

This chapter historicizes, contextualizes, and questions the unacknowledged "secularity" of WGS; it attempts to make manifest what have so far been invisible spaces in WGS, spirituality and religion, and also to make explicit how absenting those topics affects the field. Specifically, this chapter investigates how the fact that secularism is rarely overtly discussed privileges certain narratives and muffles others. My question is not a question about the field of Religious Studies, and I am not a Religious Studies scholar. My question is about the absence of conversations about spirituality and religion in WGS by scholars who are not affiliated with Religious Studies, but are nevertheless interested in answering the urgent questions of our field. I ask: is it possible that the efforts to make the field interdisciplinary and global can ever be realized without the incorporation of spirituality and religion? Is it possible that the field can ever be truly multiracial and anti-white supremacist without, at the minimum, recognizing spiritual and religious discourse? Is it possible that we are unwittingly creating an impoverished discipline by not explicitly addressing these discourses? Ultimately, this chapter asks about the field of Women's and Gender Studies: to what are we devoted?

Secularity in Women's and Gender Studies: Two Nodal Points

It began at an ashram. Ashrams turn out to be the most affordable vacation a graduate student can have, and I needed a place to clean out and perk up. Across the table from me at dinner were two women talking about their "Native American rituals" weekend. Sigh. I was back in it. My first response was exhaustion at the never ending opportunities for whites to exploit other traditions of color (of course, the irony of me, a white woman, being at a yoga ashram was not lost on me). But I wanted to keep eating, and so I kept listening. While they both made suspect and romantic comments about Native practices, they also specifically kept talking about gender. One woman wanted to read stories of "powerful old Native women," to which her friend replied, "Don't you just feel the need to be eldered?" As I watched them emphatically nod their heads "yes" that they needed to be "eldered" or mentored by an older, wiser woman, I realized with both surprise and reservation that this nearly all-female weekend might have less to do with Native identity than it had to do with gender. I make this provocative statement in the context of assumed intersectionality, where race and gender are mutually constitutive. However, what I came to discover, and what led me to write an entire project on gender and New Age culture, is that because white racial appropriation was so abhorrent to scholars, the complexity of that appropriation was not investigated but dismissed outright. New Age culture has largely been written off by academic scholars, particularly those in Women's and Gender Studies, as racist, colonialist, essentialist, and, well, generally retrograde. While most of these accusations are true, I want to ask: but what exactly are the spiritual satisfactions of these practices? If we agree, as our starting point, that many New Age practices are racially problematic, what then do they actually say about not just race, but gender? And why are they so popular, popular enough for several decades that the New Age bookstore in almost every town has taken out the feminist one? What I encountered in my research, especially in examining the work of WGS scholars on New Age culture, the little that there was of it, was disdain and dismissal. When I discussed these issues with scholars, I witnessed the eyeball rolling and wave of the hand. Those responses only made me more curious. What is it about the New Age that gets WGS scholars upset enough that rational forms of scholarly inquiry are thrown out the window? Where was (and is) the intellectual curiosity among WGS scholars? This was my first nodal point.

At Harvard University in the Fall of 2002, I sat in a room with several hundred others for two days listening to the most important founders of "Women's Studies in Religion" answer two questions in an attempt to capture the field's oral history: (1) why are you a feminist? and (2) how does this relate to your work on religion? This unusual conference structure turned out to be effective: every speaker shared her personal and intellectual autobiography and indicated how it fed the early body of work known as Feminist Theology. The speakers roster was stunning: Carol P. Christ, Mary Daly, Riffat Hassan, Ada Maria Isasi-Diaz, Virginia Mollenkott, Judith Plaskow, Letty Cottin Pogrebin, Rosemary Radford Ruether, Elisabeth Schüssler Fiorenza, Margaret Toscano, and Addie Wyatt, to name a few. In particular, I was moved by Azizah al-Hibri, author of *Women and Islam*, who stressed the importance of speaking to Muslim women on their own terms. While this nonimperialist approach should be the assumed position for WGS scholars, after 9/11 it frequently was not. Both lay and academic feminist thinkers often spoke from a secular paradigm when talking about the oppressed state of Muslim women, a paradigm that al-Hibri identified: "in the Muslim world, if you come to the problem from a faith-based approach, Muslims are more likely to listen to you than if you come to them saying 'You still believe in religion? Why don't you modernize and become secular?' That goes nowhere" (2004, 53). al-Hibri explained further that when she presented feminist theological interpretations of the Qur'an, Western feminists were disdainful to the point that she felt her "Muslim sisters needed to be helped from the onslaught of my western feminist sisters" (52). Even after founding Karamah, a Muslim Women Lawyers for Human Rights organization, al-Hibri noted that it "was not appreciated by secular feminists in the United States" (53). al-Hibri's words flattened me. I didn't want to be one of *those* Western feminists. The idea of "secular" as a negative (rather than positive) modifier for "feminist" had never occurred to me. Why? This was my second nodal point.

The "Progressive-Secular Imaginary" in Women's and Gender Studies: Everywhere and Nowhere

These two nodal points, seemingly unrelated though parallel, illuminate secular impulses at work in the field of Women's and Gender Studies. Both theoretical responses—the disavowal of the gendered valances of New Age culture and the disbelief in complex Islamic feminist futures—rest on argumentative warrants of foundational secularism. Saba Mahmood notes the limiting function of certain left, secular suppositions when discussing the multidimensionality of gender identity in Islamic revival movements:

> The reason progressive leftists like myself have such difficulty recognizing these aspects of Islamic revival movements, I think, owes in part to our profound dis-ease with the appearance of religion outside the private space of individualized belief. For those with well-honed secular-liberal and progressive sensibilities, the slightest eruption of religion into the public domain is frequently experienced as a dangerous affront, one that threatens to subject us to a normative morality dictated by mullahs and priests. This fear is accompanied by a deep self-assurance about the truth of the *progressive-secular imaginary*, one that

assumes that the life forms it offers are the best way out for
these unenlightened souls.... (2005, xi, emphasis added)

In WGS, the "progressive-secular imaginary" has been inextricably
linked to female emancipation. The text of New Age abhorrence says,
"Why would women participate in such backward, marginal, private
practices that dupe them rather than in a public feminist protest that
would liberate them?" The subtext skeptical of Islamic piety implies,
"Why would women participate in such historically patriarchal practices that enslave them rather than in a Western, feminist politics that
would liberate them?" Both versions imagine gender liberation through
the secular while eviscerating other permutations of gender identity.

Few WGS scholars state their secular paradigms outright. They are
assumed. This supposition operates in a discipline that thinks of itself
as the most self-conscious and self-reflexive. A hallmark of WGS is its
ability to theorize a problem while already having developed a meta-
critique of that theorizing.[1] We claim to be a discipline self-aware of
identity categories, stand points, and positions; we grapple with our history to not play out old colonialist, racist scripts. Yet the "politics of location" that fosters this meta-critique breaks down when it comes to the
secular. The secular is our discipline's "view from nowhere" (Haraway
1988, 191). It is the place we never claim, yet it is the position that is
everywhere. So what exactly is secularism? And what are the costs of
neglecting it?

Defining the Stakes of Secularity

Secularity is generally known as that which is *not* religious. It is defined
as "of or pertaining to the world" and "used as a negative term, with
the meaning non-ecclesiastical, non-religious, or non-sacred" (OED).
While denotatively secularism is defined by its opposite, or what it is
not—the spiritual and religious—connotatively, secularism has trig-
gered everything from the "positive" (modernization, the rise of a democratic nation-state, the separation of church and state) to the "negative"
(the decline of civilization, the erosion of morality, the death of God).
In *Secularisms*, editors Janet Jakobsen and Ann Pellegrini interrogate
the binary assumptions that link secularism with a "promise of univer-

sality and reasonableness" and spirituality/religion with "the narrowness and fanaticism of religion" (2008, 3). They cite how secularism has historically been associated with at least seven qualities: "1) Rationalization; 2) Enlightenment; 3) Social-Structural Differentiation; 4) Freedom; 5) Privatization; 6) Universalism; and 7) Modernization and Progress" (2008, 5). That is, secularism is assumed to be what reasonable, modern people aspire to, while spirituality/religion is a collection of hoary superstitions. Not only is spirituality/religion seen as atavistic and uninformed, it has also been critiqued as another site of patriarchal power. Secularism can be seen as a rebellion against this gendered power structure—when Mary Daly staged a walkout of the Harvard Memorial church in 1971 and never went back, it was a literal and figurative act for many feminist theorists.[2]

When we use the words spiritual and religious—secularity's opposite—what do we mean exactly? The "spiritual" is generally defined as both concomitant with the religious and also in reaction to it. An interesting development of the last few decades is the desire of some to declare, "I am spiritual, but not religious." Robert Fuller suggests that while the words "spiritual" and "religious" used to be synonyms, connoting "belief in a Higher Power of some kind," increasingly the "spiritual" became associated with the "private realm" while the "religious" was associated with the "public realm of membership in religious institutions, participation in formal rituals, and adherence to official denominational doctrines" (2001, 5). The etymological distinctions and similarities are useful in relation to WGS where "religion" is often linked with the patriarchal while the "spiritual" appears sometimes to float above oppressive systems. Thus WGS scholars who discuss spirituality and religion tend to use the term "spiritual" as a potential liberatory force, perhaps partly because it has seemed to be free from its denotative androcentrism.

When the terms "spiritual" and "religious" do theoretical work, they are often used in certain secular patterns. Tracy Fessenden tracks how these terms operate in the disciplines of Religious Studies and Literature. In Religious Studies, Fessenden quotes Robert Orsi who says the discipline is: "organized 'around the (usually hidden and unacknowledged) poles of good religion/bad religion.' 'Good' religion is good in the measure that it tends toward invisibility or unobtrusiveness: 'rational, word-centered, nonritualistic, middle class, unemotional, compatible with democracy and the liberal state'" (2007, 1–2). Orsi discusses how Religious Studies has marked everything "not good" as "'cults, sects, primitives, and so on'" (2). The result of this bifurcation is that the "good" religions are seen as distinctly American because they are linked with democratic progress. Fessenden then argues that while this classification has gone on in Religious Studies, a discipline supposedly self-conscious about its religious categorizing, in American Literary Studies, the study of "religion" has been almost entirely absent as a social formation (in contrast to other social configurations like gender, race, sexuality) and that secularism "flourishes as an operative rubric" (2).

For many readers, the above may seem unproblematically true: religion *is* a holdover from a distant time, and one that we can easily dispense with in progress forward; this narrative rapidly becomes more complicated when we look at other communities—most noticeably communities of color and non-Western communities—where spirituality/religion powerfully informs gendered identity. Kathleen Sands makes the case that because "second-wave feminism in the mainstream defined itself around … valorizing the secular and devaluing religion in public life ('in direct opposition to the generic religious appeal of the first wave')" and because "at its inception, the second wave typically cast religion as solidly antifeminist" (2008, 316, 317) there were several costs, one of them being racialized awareness. Sands continues, "The ideological secularism of second-wave feminism certainly added to its difficulty spreading roots beyond the white middle class since religious adherence often is higher outside this demographic, for example, among African American and immigrant women" (317). These raced effects are not just demographic in number, but epistemological; that is, the cost of secularity to the field of WGS is about its inability to imagine certain racial futures.

An assumed secularism also works in the service of conservative impulses, perhaps to the horror of supposedly progressive, liberal—read secular—thinkers. Fessenden states:

> An avowedly secular United States is broadly accommodating of mainstream and evangelical Protestantism, minimally less so of Catholicism, unevenly of Judaism, much less so of

Islam, perhaps still less so of Native American religious practices that fall outside the bounds of the acceptably decorative or "spiritual"—then religion comes to be defined as "Christian" by default, and an implicit association between "American" and "Christian" is upheld even by those who have, one imagines, very little invested in its maintenance. (2007, 3)

Thus, to neglect religion as a "social formation," to evacuate the category, is to make it defacto Protestant. It is an understatement to say that uncovering "defacto Protestantism" as unconscious gender theorizing is a rude awakening for WGS. As Jakobsen and Pellegrini describe, "Our argument is not that this secularism is really (essentially) religion in disguise, but rather that in its dominant, market-based incarnation it constitutes a specifically Protestant form of secularism" (2008, 3). In other words, "secularism remains tied to a particular religion, just as the secular calendar remains tied to Christianity" (3). To imagine secularism as neutral is not only false, but in WGS it means to impose a form of Protestantism that is particularly friendly with ideas of the neoliberal, market-driven state. While the standpoint of assumed secularity ostensibly frees gendered subjects from a coercive state apparatus, it complies with dominant ideologies of acceptable subjecthood within a democracy.

The seemingly progressive politics of WGS also enacts the two narratives that Fessenden parses: first, equally subdividing into "good" and "bad" religions; and second, rather than studying the "good" religions as in Religious Studies, the "good" is largely critiqued for its apparent sexist impulses, but left alone—untheorized or critiqued as anti-secular and thus anti-woman. Critics associate "modernity," "progress," and "secularism" with the improvement of the lot of women. Vincent Pecora, in his *Secularization and Cultural Criticism: Religion, Nation, and Modernity*, notes we are living at a historical moment in which the narrative that "modernization … requires secularization to succeed" may not be true even when it comes to the "socio-cultural," where Pecora's example is "the treatment of women" as the sign of progress (2006, 16). But is it? Recently (in the past few years) on the Women's Studies email list (WMST-L), the feminist journalist Katha Pollitt (2009) said, "The more religious the country, the worse it is for women." Is this true?

Or is it just a secular fantasy? Is it an accident when the *Toronto Star* declares the "Ten Worst Countries for Women" that not a single one is a secular (or mostly European) nation, but that secular nations naturally occupy the top five best with (1) Iceland, (2) Norway, (3) Australia, and (4) Canada—all white-majority populations, unlike all ten countries at the bottom? This is not to sneer at elaborate, systematic state structures that benefit women, but to highlight the degree to which an assumed secularism dictates what is "best for women" and what is "best" seems distinctly secular.

By not interrogating these categories of the good and the bad religions, the secular and the religious, and the racial, cultural, and colonialist impulses at work, WGS often succumbs to two main secular narratives: (1) spirituality/religion is seemingly absent or neglected while signifying certain normative assumptions; (2) spirituality/religion is placed into easy binarisms and dismissed. The function of embracing secularism in an unacknowledged way infiltrates WGS theorizing from the miniscule to the grand. For example, Sands notes that second-wave feminism's secularity "rendered invisible the religious feminisms of both centuries [nineteenth and twentieth]" (2008, 317). Rendering certain histories invisible is one manifestation of unacknowledged secularism. Because secularism and religion are "complicated" (Jakobsen and Pellegrini 2008, 3), I want to explore several sites that indicate just what is at stake in our field's secularity. I begin by returning to "the Goddess" as a WGS text which has occupied the space of the spiritual, but begrudgingly because it falls into the "bad" category of religion and seems racially suspect. By staging this debate which seems to be about the problem of the Goddess, I argue that it is more about secular privilege and fantasies of white liberal correction or how whites take other whites to task more harshly to shore up their own racial and secular self-righteousness. I begin with the easily abjected and move to the unconscious abject or the way race, spirituality, and religion are bound up together in such powerful ways as to create nearly a "second field," one that embraces the spiritual and religious, one coexisting alongside WGS. In both cases, I argue that the secularity of the discipline means that it cannot theorize its dreamed of anti-white supremacist future.

Goddess Trouble

With the rise of second-wave feminism in the 1970s, many women separated themselves from what they perceived as "patriarchal"—the state, the family, education, religion—in order to create distinct feminist spheres of influence. In the religious sphere, women developed gynocentric spiritual practices to counter alienating androcentric ones. Goddess worship presumes that roughly 10,000 years ago, women ruled the earth peacefully, and that in a future time, women will rule again.[3] In the 1980s and 90s, the proliferation of Goddess articles, books, websites, and groups indicated that the "Goddess Movement" had grown to such a degree that even conservative scholar Philip Davis called it "one of the most striking religious success stories of the late twentieth century" (1998, 4).

However, though Goddess worshippers themselves believe that this history is indisputable, recent Women's and Gender Studies scholars are more skeptical and say that their evidence is deeply flawed. Many feminist academics argue that it is impossible to prove that a matriarchal past ever existed. Feminist archaeologists such as Margaret Conkey and Ruth Tringham assert that Goddess historians lack scientific proof and exhibit an "indifference to—and rejection of—historical specificity" (1995, 209). They argue that Marija Gimbutas, the most famous Goddess historian, relies on outdated and reductive methodologies that are no longer valid to prove her points (Meskell 1995, 83). These critics claim that Goddess worshippers construct a "gynocentric" past by reducing numerous possible interpretations of objects and paintings to a single "essentialist" one. For instance, the large-breasted, heavy-hipped figurines that Goddess worshippers claim are representations of the Goddess could be read in a number of ways—as sexual fantasy objects for men, for example. Protuberant breasts and pronounced hips do not a matriarchy make. Micaela di Leonardo voices her frustration with Goddess worshippers who insist on their one reading when she criticizes a spiritual seeker whose essentialist impulses are "a potted combination of woman the gatherer, lunar cycles and goddess worship," and laments that "even feminists with no interest in specious evolutionary reasoning have fallen victim to the vision of an innately nurturant, maternal womankind" (1998, 27). Instead, feminist archaeologists say that Goddess worshippers should accept "ambiguity" when interpreting prehistory and its gender roles because no claims can be made with certainty (Conkey and Tringham 1995, 231).

Ultimately, WGS scholars have been disappointed by the Goddess Movement, which they see as "a seemingly feminist social movement within popular culture [which] conflicts with many of the goals and hopes of ... an explicitly feminist, engendered archaeology" (Conkey and Tringham 1995, 205).[4] Even Cynthia Eller, who has written the most thorough and even-handed account of the construction of the matriarchal prehistory thesis, suggests that while this myth may serve a "feminist function" by inspiring women in a way that political activism might not, in the end, the matriarchal myth harms contemporary feminism by living in an apolitical past, instead of a political present (2000, 18). This fight over a matriarchal past provokes such strong arguments from feminist academics and Goddess worshippers that the dispute has reached a stalemate where "neither side speaks to the other" (Goodison and Morris 1998, 6).

While I believe that this stalemate exists for a variety of reasons, for the purposes of thinking about "secularism," I argue that Goddess worshippers are an easy target because they seem racially retrograde and outside the bounds of "acceptable" secularism—they represent a bad religion. It is as if the field of WGS is embarrassed by Goddess worship, and shields its eyes from the horror. Judith Butler in "Sexual Politics, Torture, and Secular Time," argues that "The link between freedom and temporal progress is often what is being indexed when pundits and public policy representatives refer to concepts like modernity or, indeed, secularism" (2008, 3). Goddess worshippers are distinctly pre-modern and thus violate secularism and the forward march of women's progress. White women worship black goddesses, collapse history, revive essentialism, and enact ritual hysteria—all unacceptable. Again, this is not about understanding Goddess worship itself (which I think has deep intellectual flaws but also a somewhat understandable emotional appeal), but about the WGS response to white female spirituality/religion as an acceptable location of critique. Taking religion seriously— with its affective cathections, its fuzzy histories, its fundamental laws, and its deep rituals—is almost unthinkable. Thus anything deemed a "bad religion" is dismissed rather than explored, rejected rather than interrogated, buried rather than excavated. Manifestations of popular gender expressions and practices that appeal to wide numbers of women, in particular, are not legitimate objects of study. In this way, WGS, as a field, cuts off entire areas of exploration because some objects are properly gendered while others are not.

Secular Privilege and the Persistent Whiteness of Women's and Gender Studies

One of the fundamental collections in Women's and Gender Studies, *This Bridge Called My Back* (Moraga and Anzaldúa 1983), is so frequently taught and cited that it is known as a founding text of the field. As one of the most important contributions by women of color, tributes and subsequent volumes to the original abound. What many readers willfully ignore is that the collection also prominently features discussions of spirituality and religion. For instance, Gloria Anzaldúa has an exchange with Luisah Teish, self-described ritual priestess and author, and asks her such things as "What do you see as your task in this life and how did you find that out?" (1983, 221) and "What part does feminist spirituality have in taking back our own power?" (223). To look at the scholarship on this text, it would seem that this exchange never happened. In spite of the centrality of Anzaldúa's text to many, the discussions of spirituality/religion are neatly elided. Why is this? Does the discussion of the spiritual make everyone that uncomfortable? Is it that this exchange veers into a spiritual category ("New Age" even) that makes theorists squeamish? While the idea of the spiritual reappears in subsequent "Bridge" volumes, it is rarely discussed in academic appraisals of the text. This gap says more about what critics want to remember about "Bridge"—the political, the intersectional, the affective. But where and how is the term "spiritual" used for feminist theorists of color, in particular? How does it change the text? And why is it not common (i.e., circulating) knowledge in the wider WGS field?

AnaLouise Keating has named an evasion toward the spiritual in Gloria Anzaldúa's work as "spirit-phobia" (2008, 55). Keating is one of the few who has insisted that "scholars avoid Anzaldúa's politics of spirit," and has noted the neglect of Anzaldúa's notion of "spiritual activism" (54); those who do so are "condemned as essentialist, escapist, naive, or in other ways apolitical" (55). Keating also points out that scholars who acknowledge the spiritual may hurt their careers or have their scholarship dismissed as "New Age." Finally, she states how with Anzaldúa specifically, scholars may be "suspicious of Anzaldúa's references to spirits and souls, question her discussions of precolonial traditions, and discredit her theoretical and philosophical achievements" (55). Even as Keating describes succinctly all of the reasons why this element of Anzalúda's work is ignored, she maintains that Anzalúda's concept of "spiritual activism" is crucial to a future, inclusive WGS project. Keating claims:

> Unlike "New Age" versions of spirituality, which focus almost exclusively on the personal (so that the goals become acquiring increased wealth, a "good life," or other solipsistic materialistic terms), spiritual activism begins with the personal yet moves outward, acknowledging our radical interconnectedness. This is spirituality for social change, spirituality that recognizes the many differences among us yet insists on our commonalities and uses these commonalities as catalysts for transformation. What a contrast: while identity politics requires holding onto specific categories of identity, spiritual activism demands that we let them go. (18)

Anzaldúa's "spiritual activism" is now a term taken up by other feminist scholars of color to mark new theorizing postidentity politics that draw on a different theoretical tradition altogether.

While Robyn Wiegman has observed that for the field of WGS the "identitarian rubric has failed" (2002, 129), a number of feminists of color are destabilizing identity politics through concepts of the spiritual rather than poststructuralist concepts of the fractured subject and queer iterations of identity. Layli Phillips names "spiritualized" as one of the five most important qualities defining womanism in *The Womanist Reader* and suggests that "womanism openly acknowledges a spiritual/transcendental realm with which human life, livingkind, and the material world are all intertwined" (2006, xxvi). Notably, Phillips distinguishes these qualities from poststructuralism, which is not a part of womanism, according to her. In creating a definitional framework for the term womanism, Phillips urges that "feminism and womanism cannot be conflated, nor can it be said that womanism is a 'version' of feminism" (2006, xxi). In other words, womanism is something that she calls "sisters" with black feminism, but has its own, separate identity (2006, xxxiv).

Obviously, it is critical that a major theoretical concept in the field of WGS—womanism—has a spiritual dimension, *and* that the quality of that dimension changes the very nature of the term. For Phillips, the epistemology of womanism is wholly distinct. This example is just one that indicates the extent to which the inclusion of spirituality and religion does not just alter the field, indeed, it would redefine it. Can scholars even imagine what such a field might look like? For example, Jacqui Alexander redefines WGS core terms *entirely* through the sacred: experience becomes "sacred experience," the personal becomes "the personal as spiritual," work becomes "spiritual work," and so on. Labor, consciousness, and subjectivity are all made sacred. The body, as she says, "is not an encasement for the Soul, but also a medium of Spirit" (2005, 298):

> Experience is a category of great epistemic import to feminism. But we have understood it primarily as secularized, as if it were absent Spirit and thus antithetical, albeit indirectly, to the Sacred. In shifting the ground of experience from secular to the Sacred, we can better position, as Lata Mani has proposed, the personal as spiritual. (2005, 295)

So while WGS has moved from a focus on identity to one on difference, this particular difference—the spiritual—has remained nearly invisible. Meanwhile, some scholars, and scholars of color in particular, are repositioning the field by it.

Andrea Smith, for example, discusses how unacknowledged secularity prompts a breakdown in disciplinary theorizing. This is not minor discourse failure, but one that ignores revolutionary alliances potentially at work. In her prescient work, *Native Americans and the Christian Right: The Gendered Politics of Unlikely Alliances*, Smith notes:

As someone rooted in both Native Rights activism and evangelical Christianity, I have found that neither academic nor activist
understandings of religion and politics have been able to account
for the variety of social justice activisms that I have participated
in. As I read the scholarly and activist accounts of evangelicalism, which tend to depict evangelicalism as monolithically conservative, I see virtually no mention of the many people within
these churches, including myself, who do not follow the Repub-
lican Party line. Similarly, scholarship on Native activism tends
to either ignore contradictions and tensions within Native organizations or to dismiss it as unimportant. (2008, x)

Smith's work attempts to deflate romantic notions of Native spirituality while interrogating false ideas of evangelicalism to see where these
seeming divergent communities actually employ not so disparate discourses to powerful effect. While Smith illuminates the erasure of feminisms in both evangelical and Native communities, she is particularly
interested in the coalitional aspects of feminist organizing in both communities. Because of Smith's ability to foreground secular absences, she
puts into conversation new discourses and alliances that open the field,
ones that undoubtedly present a real challenge to most WGS scholars
who have an understandable deep distrust of evangelicalism.

Again, the few who have taken up the critique of the secularity of
WGS are feminists of color: Gloria Anzaldúa, Jacqui Alexander, Leela
Fernandes, Analouise Keating, Saba Mahmood, and Andrea Smith.
This is not an accident. Linda Woodhead notes in her article in which
she uses the useful term "secular privilege" that:

If religion is particularly important to the disprivileged, it is
often the disprivileged within the disprivileged groups, or the
"minorities within minorities" (Bader: 2007) for whom it is
most essential. This is the opposite observation to the feminist
and enlightened liberal observation that it is minorities within
minorities who are most in need of the protection of state-
backed human rights legislation. (2009, 2)

If secularism in WGS is not a blank, but de facto Protestantism, then it represents an articulation of liberal feminism and an extension of the state, in particular. And in this context, a "transnational critical consciousness" for WGS is impossible (Wiegman 2002, 7). The very critiques that encourage us to be anti-imperialist encourage a sloppy relativism that misunderstands religious and spiritual commitment—at the disservice of feminist theorists of color, in particular.

I argue that it is time for an "anthropology of secularism," as Talal Asad has described it, for WGS (2003, 17). What would that mean? Part of what that will mean is that WGS scholars can no longer simply turn religion into "culture" when it is convenient. I observe often that white WGS scholars, out of a seeming respect for religious differences of color, turn religion into culture when it is "of color."[5] In short, when religion is abhorrent, it is discussed in the field as religion, but when it must be understood as acceptable—when the context demands a kind of tolerance and understanding lest a white woman appear racist—religion is often turned into culture to make it palatable. I observe white feminists allowing for discussions of religion from women of color, discussions that go uninterrogated, because religion is translated as culturally important and necessary rather than accepted on its own terms as belief. These approaches—immediate dismissal and unwitting transmutation—display an unconscious discomfort with the spiritual and religious; neither is honest.

An "anthropology of secularism" in WGS will mean that notions of freedom and agency, ones so central to the foundations of Western feminism, will be interrogated at their secular roots. Mahmood suggests that "To the degree that feminism is a politically prescriptive project, it requires the remaking of sensibilities and commitments of women whose lives contrast with feminism's emancipatory visions" (2005, 197). In the West, these "emancipatory visions" have been secular. It will mean that ideas of time, the State, identity, alliance-building, histories—all of our most central terms—must be theorized anew in the light of their secular "neutrality." Postidentity politics may have a new language. Various iterations of activism like "spiritual activism" will need new paradigms. Bodies—people—on the margins of our discipline, those who are spiritual and religious, suddenly come into view.

In their article, "Whither Black Women's Studies: An Interview, 1997–2004," Beverly Guy-Sheftall and Evelynn M. Hammonds discuss what they "most worry about in terms of the future of Women's Studies" (2005, 69). Guy-Sheftall responds:

> I continue to worry about the inability of Women's Studies to deal—in appropriate ways—with issues of race and difference, particularly difference in a cross-cultural context. I don't think Women's Studies does a good job of addressing women's issues outside the West. Those issues are not always related to race. It could be religion ... (69)

I not only agree with Guy-Sheftall that it *could* be religion—a site of future disciplinary theorizing—I argue that it *must* be. It is my contention that WGS will never recover from white supremacy without taking spirituality and religion seriously, without examining its secularity. When I ask to what is Women's and Gender Studies devoted, currently I argue it is to a Western progress narrative that, while supposedly liberating, continues imperialist practices in the very place that no one suspects—faithful secularism.[6]

Notes

1. I want to thank Catherine Orr for emphasizing this critical point about the discipline's history.
2. Mary Daly gave an "anti-sermon" at the Harvard Memorial Church in 1971 and organized a walkout on religious patriarchy. See Daly 1994.
3. Cynthia Eller notes helpfully that the "rough consensus" that a matriarchy existed for goddess worshippers was formed under "the pressure of three key developments: 1) the steadfast rejection of matriarchal myth by most feminist anthropologists; 2) a burgeoning feminist spirituality movement intent on placing goddess worship in prehistory; and 3) the pioneering archaeological work of Marija Gimbutas" (34).
4. I am not interested in or capable of contradicting specific archaeological claims that others do elsewhere in an excellent manner, e.g., Tringham 1991. Furthermore, as many archaeologists recognized the contingent nature of their prehistorical knowledge claims, reconstructing prehistory became best understood as a "simulacrum" or an "identical copy for which no original has ever existed" (Conkey and Williams 1991, 116). Since the past is not an "original," but a fabrication, most archaeologists make claims hesitantly about what can and cannot be known about prehistoric

life. For instance, archaeologist Margaret Conkey suggests that in prehistory, "subsistence and economics are 'fairly easy' to know, whereas social organization and religious and spiritual life are close to impossible to know" (Conkey and Williams 1991, 110).

5. I want to thank T.L. Cowan for an illuminating conversation on this tension.

6. Portions of this chapter have been reprinted by permission from *Feminism's New Age: Gender, Appropriation, and the Afterlife of Essentialism* edited by Karlyn Crowley, the State University of New York Press ©2011, State University of New York. All Rights Reserved.

15
SEXUALITY

Merri Lisa Johnson

[I]n landscape architecture the term desire lines is used to describe unofficial paths, those marks left on the ground that show everyday comings and goings, where people deviate from the paths they are supposed to follow. Deviation leaves its own marks on the ground, which can even help generate alternative lines, which cross the ground in unexpected ways.

(Ahmed 2006a, 570)

In the discipline of Women's and Gender Studies (WGS) as it manifests in the small towns of the U.S. Southeast, the discourse of sexuality is TMI—too much information—by definition. It is impolite. It is beside the point. It is *warning* and *panic* and *gutter* and *butterflies* when the dean calls the program director in for a meeting on an unspecified topic.

It is the dream where all your teeth fall out.

It is a steady stream of nervous laughter and eyes that are always looking elsewhere, toward some imagined place where jobs are safe and women can speak freely about bodies, desires, orientations, and the walls that can be taken down between who you were raised to be and who you have become.

The summer I moved to Spartanburg, all the penis-shaped vibrators had just been confiscated from Priscilla's, the sex toy store between my house and the campus. A billboard for Truth Ministries loomed above

Reidville Road, a high traffic street connecting downtown Spartanburg to one of its many access points to I-26 and I-85. It posed the traffic-stopping Jerry-Springer-esque question, *Are you gay and don't want to be?* The climate for gays and lesbians in the Upstate of South Carolina is not good, as the website of the South Carolina Equality Coalition pronounced in response to a fatal gay bashing in Greenville in the spring of 2007. The norms of sexuality that characterize my geographical and institutional location—a branch campus of a state university in a region known for its history of repressive sexual regulations for female and feminized bodies—could easily silence me on matters of sexuality, and sometimes they do. But more often, the pressure of this context has resulted, paradoxically, in a proliferation of events and courses on the subject.

In brief, my approach to sexuality as a WGS issue has been to *foreground it* and to *reverse the usual marginalizations* of "minority" voices (sexual or racial) to make up for the cultural omissions, misinformation, and stigmas surrounding the topic in mainstream U.S. discourses. When speaking among friends, I have called this programming ethos a "love the sin" administrative philosophy driven by a commitment to intersexional analysis, a coinage that places sexuality at the center of WGS analysis rather than leaving it off or placing it at the end of a sequence (race, class, gender, sexuality). My approach is shaped (sometimes limited, sometimes enhanced) by my embodiment as a white southern middle-class low-femme lesbian who is "out at work," as the sticker on my file cabinet informs my visitors. The most prominent and well-attended events sponsored by my program have featured scholars and performance artists speaking from the intersexion of queerness and blackness.

Yet this margin-as-a-space-of-radical-openness is not where I was expected to go as a WGS administrator in the rural Southeast. I learned this lesson before the leaves turned orange in my first semester on campus. There was a phone call. There was a sleepless night. There was a dream where I opened my mouth to speak but what came out instead of words were bits of enamel, soft as overcooked noodles. I cupped my hand below my chin to catch them.

The Centrality of Sexuality to Women's and Gender Studies

Barely two weeks into my first semester teaching a course on Queer Theory, a very quick and unsatisfying cultural debate took place about the validity of sexuality as a classroom topic in public universities in my home state of Georgia.[1] The story spread like wildfire and commanded the attention of Atlanta's newspaper of record, the *Atlanta Journal and Constitution*:

> An expected showdown over sex experts at Georgia State University failed to materialize Tuesday after the school's professors wowed the House Higher Education Committee and a leading legislative critic backed off. The minor controversy had flared last week after Rep. Calvin Hill (R-Canton) e-mailed supporters lambasting the University System of Georgia for offering classes in oral sex, male prostitution and "queer theory," which is a field of gender studies ... (Sheinin 2009)

Several professors from GSU testified before the House Higher Education Committee, defending their fields of specialization in heroic tones and adopting postures of moral indignation:

> Kirk Elifson is listed as an expert in male prostitution...."We've done some cutting-edge research in HIV," he said. "I'm proud of the work I've done."... Mindy Stombler, another Sociology instructor, is listed as an expert in oral sex. She said her research is aimed at studying attitudes of teens toward sex, who, she said, are increasingly having oral sex and see it as "casual and socially acceptable" (Sheinin 2009)

This defense mobilized a conservative social script to justify sexuality as a legitimate arena for faculty research and course content:

We study sex in order to stop the spread of disease.
We study sex in order to save adolescent girls from the disgrace of the blowjob.
We study sex in order to control it.

A spokesperson for the National Sexuality Resource Center, Christopher White, rallied support for sexuality from the other end of the defensive spectrum, euphorically overstating the subject's importance and then downshifting to a neutral position that the study of sexuality should be protected under the auspices of academic freedom: "While we could spend hours arguing with [legislators] about sexuality studies and related work and its importance, we are better off defending the pursuit of knowledge and scholarly inquiry—the purpose of which is to have a better understanding of humanity and our world in order to work for change for the betterment of humankind ..." (White 2009).

The debate in Georgia soon revealed itself as a tempest in a teapot, and legislators did in fact back down. For those of us teaching WGS courses addressing sexuality in this uneasy moment of economic shortfalls and budget cuts, the speedy resolution was a relief on the immediate practical level.

On the ideological level, however, something was left wanting.

Something failed to materialize.

In her analysis of a similar conflict in Arizona, Miranda Joseph asserted that the academic freedom defense can come across as a weak response from administrators who may share conservative views of sexuality studies as "reprehensible" (Joseph 2002, 285). This may not be true in all cases—in fact, the invocation of academic freedom has been called "the most powerful and convincing way to defend women's studies" (McCaughey 2008)—but "academic freedom" operates as a circumlocution around the unspoken center of a potentially more transformative response from feminists and queer theorists in WGS.

These two arguments—the danger narrative and the academic freedom narrative—come quickly to the tips of our tongues because they are useful in the short-term. They defuse moral panic and identify academia as a safe zone for intellectual inquiry. The problem with both rhetorical strategies lies in their failure to explain sexuality as a positive dimension of human experience and to resist the stigmatization of female sexual pleasure, queer heterosexualities, nonconforming gender expression, and gay, lesbian, queer, or same-gender-loving sexual orientations. The residual shame professors may feel (that I, *entre nous*, sometimes feel) about teaching and studying sexuality results in part from this incomplete defense, a problem that calls to mind a description by Gayle Rubin of sex as uniquely freighted with political meaning:

> Sex is presumed guilty until proven innocent. Virtually all erotic behavior is considered bad unless a specific reason to exempt it has been established. The most acceptable excuses are marriage, reproduction, and love. Sometimes scientific curiosity, aesthetic experience, or a long-term intimate relationship may serve. But the exercise of erotic capacity, intelligence, or creativity all require pretexts that are unnecessary for other pleasures, such as the enjoyment of food, fiction, or astronomy. (1992, 278)

The demand to justify or rationalize pleasure, reiterated by the most recent sex panic in Georgia, is a patriarchal and heterosexist harassment with a very long history that requires inventive conceptual moves from WGS practitioners. Given the fact that sexuality is "a source of vulnerability" for the field because "conservative attacks on the academy, and especially on public education, find their entry point through an attack on feminist and sexuality studies" (Joseph 2002, 284–85), the work of compiling a critical genealogy of pathbreaking, polyvocal, restorative, even honey-mad discourses of sexuality in WGS is urgent, necessary, and delightful. I offer the following four proposals as a starting place for this reclamation project.

Proposal #1: Stop Saying "Sex Wars"

Some of the field's most compelling, revolutionary, and dynamic ideas revolve around sexuality, unveiling the culturally mystified topics of asymmetrical gender roles, compulsory heterosexuality, and, on bold days, the emancipatory potential of pornography, sex work, sadomasochism, adultery, polyamory, and butch-femme role play. But ever since the infamous Barnard conference in 1982, a painful conflict wherein some feminist participants picketed panels on sex work and sadomasochism, and other feminists crossed picket lines to present their work under these signs of stigma and condemnation, this rich discussion has been reduced to a hopeless divide between irreconcilable positions—pro-sex versus anti-sex, pleasure versus danger—and characterized as the feminist "sex wars." Over the past decade, the term has been marked with skepticism as scholars preface it with the words "so-called" (as in, "so-called sex wars"). Building on this momentum, I propose that we move beyond this skepticism to a rejection of the term in order to reclaim the full picture of the debate, which is not so much a war as a philosophical inquiry into a spectrum of feminist sexual ethics.

In one particularly detailed sketch of this spectrum, Wendy Chapkis breaks the binary poles of "anti-sex" and "pro-sex" feminisms into their composite parts. First, she distinguishes between two forms of *radical* or *danger-sensitive* feminism: pro-positive-sex feminists like Gloria Steinem and Robin Morgan, women "engaged in the recuperative project of attempting to uncover an eros free of the distortions of patriarchy" (1997, 13), and "anti-sex feminists," a misnomer for radical feminist theorists such as Catharine MacKinnon and Andrea Dworkin who see sexual intercourse as not merely contaminated but "constituted by male domination" (1997, 17) and who argue that "sex resists resignification" (1997, 19) but do not oppose sex in a comprehensive way. Chapkis further distinguishes between two forms of *sex radical* or *pleasure-sensitive* feminism: libertarian feminists like Camille Paglia who see sex as a source of women's power over men, and sex radical feminists like Rubin, Pat Califia, Carol Queen, Carole Vance, Lisa Duggan, and Nan Hunter who assert that women's power can be exercised by subverting the meanings of sexuality in "the existing sexual order" (1997, 30).

Through such remappings of sexuality apart from the "sex wars," the shortcomings of each position can be acknowledged without negating their contributions to public discourse on sexuality. Chris Cuomo is exemplary in this tact, as she points out the failure of "libertarian feminists" to explain "*why* certain freedoms and pleasures matter," along with the failure of "moralizing feminists" to concede the "resistant potential" of "contradictory pleasures" (2003, 65), even as she argues that this "perennial feminist controversy ... may not be as intractable as it appears" (2003, 58). Indeed, from the very beginning of the "sex war," theorists such as Carole Vance and Ann Ferguson have pointed out the feminist moral imperative to address sexuality simultaneously as a site of pleasure and danger. Experienced by many Women's and Gender Studies practitioners as a "bitter opposition" (Ferguson 1984, 107) or "feud-like impasse" (Cuomo 2003, 65), these disagreements actually hinge on "differences in relative emphasis" among "reconcilable" positions (Chancer 1998, 17). The militant trope of the "sex wars" obscures the nuances of these debates and undermines the integrity of feminist intellectual history on sexuality.

Having stipulated that it was not a "war," however, I still find myself wanting to say that the various ideas grouped under the umbrella of danger-sensitive theories of sexuality get more traction in WGS than those grouped under the umbrella of pleasure-sensitive theories, a concern I have expressed at length elsewhere (Johnson 2002, 2007). To be clear, my argument is not that the danger narrative about sexuality is unfounded or unimportant but rather that the pleasure narrative is an underutilized structure of feeling in the struggle to unloose sexuality from its patriarchal, heterosexist, racist, imperialist, and classist ideological frame. It is not the case that WGS has failed to develop positive-value arguments about sexuality, but those arguments have not become part of the general public's common sense about sexuality in the southeastern region of the United States, a belief system still structured in large part by shame, stigma, and the specter of eternal damnation. The most visible pleasure narratives that resulted from the infamous Barnard conference, however, may not be the best place to direct the attention of students and community members. Feminist pornography, for instance, may be a less effective classroom topic for validating female sexual pleasure than feminist theology.

Proposal #2: Resist Disavowals of Spirituality, Silence, and Strategic Assimilation

At the inaugural gay pride march and festival in Spartanburg, South Carolina on June 20, 2009, approximately 100 protestors attended and held signs above their heads about sodomy, abominations, and the gay lifestyle as a highway to hell as 700 LGBTQQI folks and their allies paraded by with signs calling for marriage equality, identifying love as a family value, exclaiming that "God don't make no junk," and urging the audience along the way not to feed the protesters. In this cultural context of belated, polite, and normative gay civil rights campaigns—a place where *gay? fine by me* t-shirts are considered edgy content for campus events and courageous choices by the untenured junior faculty who organize them—it is crucial to know one's audience and to appeal to them on their own terms, to a degree. Developing sensitivity to regional ideologies and institutional demographics has led me to reconsider Women's and Gender Studies truisms about coming to voice (*Your silence will not protect you*) and questioning the authority of the church (*Eve was framed*). Specifically, I have sought a pedagogy of sexuality that respects the raced, classed, and regionally located negotiations of power and knowledge being undertaken by students at USC Upstate when they enroll in a WGS course on sexuality.

Our mission statement as a metropolitan university notwithstanding, this campus is a rural setting located in the heart of the Bible Belt that draws many students from rural South Carolina (from the abandoned mill towns of the Upstate down to the coastal swamps of the Low Country). The rurality of the institution is visible, among other places, in the students' parochial views of sexuality. In a student population comprised of southern working class first-generation college students, with a significant representation of African Americans (35%), many of whom—white and black—have been raised in families and communities that place a high value on religious doctrine that is often explicitly anti-erotic and homophobic, the positive-value and pleasure-sensitive discourses of sexuality that accompany gay pride marches and other assertions of "the erotic as power" (Lorde 1984, 51) can be introduced with less friction through nonsecular feminist paradigms.[2] Although I gravitate toward theoretical articles about leatherdyke boys and their daddies (Hale 1997), critical feminist memoirs of lesbian sadomasochism (Allison 1996), the queerness of suicide bombers (Puar 2007), and other topics that stretch the limits of my understanding, I feature a different set of texts for this audience. Interspersed among the sex radical voices that drew me to WGS, students are assigned readings on pro-pleasure theologies from a variety of religious faiths, including Catholic feminist inquiries into "good sex" (Jung and Coray 2001; Jung and Hunt 2009), a Lutheran feminist argument for the female orgasm as a moral imperative (Pellauer 1993), and a womanist call for a "sexual discourse of resistance" to be generated by and disseminated in the black church (Douglas 1989). Framing sexual pleasure, sexual diversity, and female sexual autonomy in terms that acknowledge the formative influence of religious discourse and cultural Christianity—without the push-pull

dynamic of arguing point-by-point against a biblically motivated punitive view—is one way to avoid triggering defensive reactions in students
who bear strong convictions that the road to hell is paved with "plea-
sure-without-penalties" (Phillips 2000). Although Audre Lorde's essay,
"Uses of the Erotic: The Erotic as Power," is not a piece of theology, her
language leans toward the spiritual, and I think of feminist and womanist theologies of sexuality as forming part of a Lordian intellectual
tradition in their commitment to recuperating the erotic as a place to
find meaning and identity (1984).

The southern historian Darlene Clark Hines offers a historical portrait of racialized sexualities in the United States that illuminates why
reading assignments on the erotic might make for uneven classroom
discussion among African American students, especially in the presence of a white professor and/or white students. Hines argues that the
repercussions of slavery as a system that used black women's bodies in
ruthless and corrupt ways continue to shape black female sexual subjectivity, as black women have refused the dominant culture's hypersexual-
ized images of them by cultivating a "culture of dissemblance," defined
as "the behavior and attitudes of Black women that created an appearance of openness and disclosure but actually shielded the truth of their
inner lives and selves from their oppressors" (1989, 912). This creative
response permitted black women to "accrue the psychic space and har-
ness the resources needed to hold their own in the often one-sided and
mismatched resistance struggle" (1989, 915). Recognizing the defensive
uses of silence for black women complicates the goals and methodology of the WGS classroom in circulating various critical, oppositional,
transformative, and euphoric discourses of sexuality. Pushing on the
silences of black women can easily fall out of alignment with feminist
and antiracist values. In the same way that queer ethnographers have
noted that certain sexual discourses, such as the coming out story or
transgender identity, do not "travel" across boundaries of ethnicity and
nationality (Manalansan 2003, 19, 27), the usual WGS encourage-
ments to speak out about sexual desire, sexual orientation, and other
components of the erotic can be felt as unfriendly commands to make
oneself vulnerable and therefore might also be limited in their range of
application.

Proposal #3: Abandon the Logic of Transgression

Turning the question around, queer black feminism positions Women's and Gender Studies as that which needs to come to voice about sexuality in new and different ways. In an autobiographical-theoretical performance, "Queer Black Feminism: The Pleasure Principle," Laura Alexandra Harris proposes "that queer black feminism can rupture the silences contained in the words and practices of [feminist, black feminist, and queer theory]" (1996, 3). Describing her methodology as "a greedy and attentive cartography" (1996, 8), Harris moves provocatively in the direction of examining "alternative forms of power queer black female sexuality creates" with the playful if dispiriting caveat that she "relinquish[es] all commonly held notions of success in the pursuit of this venture" (1996, 7). Harris acknowledges the alienation from discussions of sexuality in WGS that some of her black heterosexual women and fem lesbian friends have expressed as they laugh at or dismiss altogether the feminist "sex wars": "They were the high-heeled, painted, cleavaged, and perfumed images of women feminism wanted to wash off and liberate. And when these women refused a liberation that appeared to them as just another brand of repression—feminism rejected them. Maybe what feminists did not know is that these women made fun of them" (1996, 13). A feminist theory that could not apprehend "getting fucked as one of the few moments of power and pleasure [working-class black women] could engage in" (1996, 15) was not a theory worth having, from their perspective. Her intervention in "sex wars" discourse is motivated in part by the question ("a problem, not a solution" [1996, 4]) of a race-cognizant, pleasure-centric discourse of sexuality. "This is perhaps one of the most important concerns for a queer black feminist practice," she predicts, "to make the terrain of feminist sexual politics a discourse on race" (1996, 11), while also recognizing the reclamation of pleasure by her black female friends and her white working class mother as a kind of class protest against a system that typically links pleasure with privileges restricted to the leisure class (1996, 23). Harris thus insists on pleasure even though it defies the gravity of her own historical and cultural context. She leans into the inadequate perforated support of a colon, and she says the whole time she knows it will not hold.

She leaps into pleasure anyway.

There is something here to be admired.

There is something here to be held out to other people.

Harris' work departs significantly from that of bell hooks, whose popularity among students and scholars alike is unsurpassed. In one of her many essays on the commodification of black female sexuality in popular culture, hooks calls for "black females [to] assert sexual agency in ways that liberate us from the confines of colonized desire, of racist/sexist imagery and practice" by defining a decolonized black female sexuality as "a rich sensual erotic energy that is not directed outward" and "is not there to allure or entrap" but rather to find "pleasure and delight in themselves;" and, she concludes, "we must make the oppositional space where our sexuality can be named and represented, where we are sexual subjects—no longer bound and trapped" (1992, 75–77). Harris, though, works in a different register from hooks, one that is transformative but not oppositional, critical but not prescriptive; she chooses not to experience queer black feminist sexuality in feminist exclusions of queer black women as challenge, burden, bindings, or trap—presaging recent queer theories of critical utopianism (Munoz 2009) and queer freedom (Winnubst 2006). Harris does something more lighthearted. She laughs, and she remembers other women laughing.

In reworking the meanings of these personal memories, Harris devises a queer black feminist discourse of sexuality that includes the experience of black lesbian and straight working-class white women "as more than an object of reform" (1996, 26) without locking the queer black feminist subject into a tiresome and endless oppositionality. Beyond extending the WGS map of sexuality in more accurate, complete, and useful directions, we might instead follow the example of Harris in simply stepping off the map and abandoning the logic of transgression. The map we have—of good and bad, proper and improper, obedience and transgression—is the problem. The map we want cannot be formed in oppositional reaction to the existing map. As Shannon Winnubst argues, "transgressions against the map's demands will only reassert the centralizing power of the map itself. To act 'otherwise' will involve acts that are not thinkable on the map" (2006, 187). Winnubst advocates a noninstrumentalist discourse of sexuality, a philosophical position that sheds a different kind of light on the anecdote about the "standoff" between Georgia legislators and WGS professors of sexuality studies. In addition to adding a positive-value, pleasure-sensitive discourse of sexuality to the more common defenses (the danger narrative of sexuality and academic freedom), a fourth possibility emerges here: Don't invoke a use-value defense at all. Don't respond. Don't let *their* questions become *our* questions.

Don't feed the protestors.
Deviation leaves it own marks on the ground.

Proposal #4: Tell the Truth about Your Own Negotiations of Sexuality

> *The queer in all of us clamors for pleasure and change, will not be tamed or regulated, wants a say in the creation of a new reality.*

> (Queen 2003, 14)

In my youngest published feminist voice, I spoke in uneven tones that mixed bravado and dare and defiance like dark paints edged with hesitation, desperate longings for approval, and blank spots of silence. I grappled with my emergent feminist consciousness as it appeared to conflict with or restrict or reduce my personal life to false consciousness, male-identification, and overall naïveté in my pursuit of normative relationship goals, inarticulate requests for more equitable and pleasurable sexual experiences with my boyfriend, and erotic fantasies featuring myself as a perpetrator of nonconsensual sex acts. I struggled for a discourse of sexuality that could assist me in a more nuanced way with the work of making meaning and choices and changes and pleasures and new templates for a nonpatriarchal sexual ethic. I did not take courses in Women's and Gender Studies proper, but a wide range of graduate courses on feminist pedagogy, literature by women, feminist cultural and media studies, transcolonial figurations, and contemporary trans-Atlantic literature exposed me to discourses of sexuality that worked to decolonize minds through an unremitting focus on sexual danger: female genital mutilation, marital and acquaintance rape, Shakespeare's sister looking for artistic growth and getting pregnant and killing herself instead, the false consciousness of blonde highlights and tight skirts and high heels and skin care products, the eroticization of violence, women's lust for self-annihilation. I understood the discourse of sexuality in WGS—like the closely related discourses of desire and pleasure—to be fully conveyed in the strict simplicity of *no means no*.

> I thought this discipline said sexuality was a ruse of patriarchy.
> I believed the urban legends about the field.
> Burned bras, hairy legs, sex-is-rape, straight women sleeping with
> the enemy.

I read less and less feminism and more and more queer theory, and over time the queer theory led me on a roundabout path back to feminism. Sexuality looked different there this time. I was different. The moment was different. The feminists—who were also often queers—looked and sounded different. The pleasure-centric discourse of sexuality is available in abundance for those who want to find it. Perhaps the discipline of WGS engages in its own culture of dissemblance—writing of loopholes and black (w)holes and categories that will not hold—even as it clamors for pleasure and change. From my current standpoint, I experience the discourse of sexuality not as restriction, guilt, blame, and frustration, but as mobility, flexibility, fluidity, and psychological integration because I experience it as (a) queer.

Ironically, my queer southern standpoint parallels the conflicts between the social history of African American women and the utopian imagination of queer black feminism. There are regional, historical, and personal limits to what I can say or know about sexuality, and it can be difficult to sort one kind of limit from another. While I am philosophically inclined to support queer feminist models of sexual fluidity and the epistemological challenges presented by bisexuality, polyamory, sex worker feminism, sex radical feminism, and queer theory, in my everyday life the look and feel of sexuality are tame in comparison. I live in a place where just being a lesbian—as opposed to being genderqueer or trans or leather or poly—is marked as wild and excessive. Even though I find sexual fluidity completely persuasive as the "truth" of desire—that individuals can and do change their sexual orientation, that these changes are sometimes undertaken deliberately and therefore bear significantly on debates about choice and immutable traits, that categories are artificial and constructed and absolutely queer—I still sometimes feel the need for a reassuring fiction of sexual identity.

In fact, I experience a significant degree of psychological and social freedom as a result of adopting the label of "lesbian." This freedom is most legible when situated in the details of my own particular history, an autobiographical narrative that has been limited more than it seems possible by the force of compulsory heterosexuality. Despite my unremitting and life-long desire for women, I remained stuck in unsatisfying heterosexual relationships for many years, punctuated by brief confused erotic encounters with other "straight" women, until finally undergoing a painfully belated period of "coming out" as lesbian in my early thirties. I am still, at thirty-eight, a late-blooming adolescent lesbian, and I cling tenaciously to my hard-won status outside the parameters of proper heterosexual adult womanhood. Seventeen years after my first flawed gestures of adulthood, a hetero marriage at age nineteen, followed by a divorce at age twenty, I flew to Northampton, Massachusetts to marry my dyke-butch-daddy-boi lover and codified my lesbian authenticity in a celebration rejected by queer feminists as homonormative.

We registered at Pottery Barn.

My euphoric invocation of the label, the word, the orientation, the standpoint, and the identity of lesbian feels very much "like a whole world [got] opened up," to borrow Sara Ahmed's words for a queer phenomenology of sexual orientation (2006a, 564), and this state of amazement feels, once again, at odds with my queer feminist philosophies of sexual fluidity. This internal tension is less irksome to me than it once was, as I have let the goal of feminist perfectionism in my sexual politics go, giving myself credit for the changes I have made instead of berating myself for those still hidden over the next horizon. Ahmed acknowledges the labor of "mov[ing] one's sexual orientation from straight to lesbian" as a big undertaking that "requires reinhabiting one's body" (2006a, 563). Now that I have claimed a lesbian identity and an object towards which to direct my lesbian desire, I find I want to linger over this wildness. I am dynamically compelled and energized by this new labor.

But the space accorded to my lesbian body is not all free and wild.

Let me be honest about something.

I did not go to the inaugural Spartanburg pride parade. I was LGBTQ Caucus Chair of the Southeastern Women's Studies Association at the time, but in Spartanburg that and a quarter will get me a cup of coffee. Rumors circulated that queers might get shot on sight. I didn't want to die. I just got married. I still had a chapter on sexuality to write. My point is this: If I prefer the frank, the explicit, the non-repro-centric, the nonutilitarian, if I long to meander and muse on pleasure instead of worrying myself sick over sexual dangers, if I borrow a bit of defiance from queer theorists, if I return to feminist arguments for free love and the vindication not only of women but of whores, or if I revisit my own protofeminist adolescent consciousness as I chanted along with Salt 'n Pepa, "if she wanna be a freak and sell it on the weekends it's none of your business," it is not in service of a bad-girl-for-effect rhetoric. It is not a decision to stop worrying and enjoy my symptoms. It is not because I am here and queer and free.

> Behind the story I tell is the story I don't.
> Behind the story you hear is the one I wish I could make you hear.
> Behind my carefully buttoned collar is my nakedness ... (Allison 1996, 39)

The fact of living in a hetero-supremacist eroto-phobic repro-centric culture underscores the seriousness of my longing for WGS to speak sexuality in the tone of *more joy, less shame*, to theorize sexual orientation as fluid, desire as mobile, pleasure as life-affirming and life-threatening, depending on the context. I speak sexuality as a spilling over of pleasure as I select speakers and construct my courses, not because I have achieved the elusive climactic goal of shameless pleasures or fearless fluidities or the autoerotic irreverence of two lips that are not one. I speak sexuality in this way because I am still afraid to show up at the parade. I speak sexuality in this way because—like so many people I know—I still long for something better.

> We can begin in another spot.... We can say that our sexuality is more complex than the things that have been done to us ... We can dare to create outrageous visions. (Hollibaugh 1984, 407)

I step off the map and wait for a new picture to materialize.

Notes

1. These political arguments have been staged in a number of other states over the preceding fifteen or so years, including University of Arizona in 1994 (Joseph 2002), Virginia Tech in 1996 (McCaughey 2008), and SUNY New Paltz in 1997 (Duggan 2004), not to mention the more targeted protests attempting to ban *The Vagina Monologues* from all seventeen campuses in the North Carolina state university system for being anti-male and anti-heterosexual and for presenting women as perpetual victims (McCaughey 2011, personal correspondence).

2. Crowley, in this volume, explores in detail the presumption that WGS (and perhaps all academia) is always considered secular, arguing that the secularity of the field prevents WGS from reaching its goals of being "truly multi-racial and anti-white supremacist." My call for a racially cognizant and regionally located pedagogy of sexuality underscores the importance of recognizing discourses of sexuality that are non-secular and liberatory.

SILENCES AND DISAVOWALS

Points to Ponder

1. In what ways can we "read" silences in WGS disciplinary contexts? Does every silence need to be spoken of and remedied? Can all silences ever be broken, and what they reveal be included in WGS?
2. How might the refusal of WGS to call itself a discipline perpetuate the endless deferral of difficult questions such as those posed by "History," "Secularity," and "Sexuality?" How do these chapters use core assumptions of WGS to expose these silences and demand their redress as necessary to the future(s) of the field?
3. Does an academic discipline need a history? How does a past "matter"; that is, what impact do alternate views of WGS "pasts" have on the field?

PART 5
ESTABLISHMENT CHALLENGES

This last section brings together "Trans-," "Institutionalization," and "Transnational," terms that demand that we (re)consider the institutional arrangements that structure the ways in which we practice Women's and Gender Studies (WGS) in the academy. They each start with an observation about how WGS is practiced in university contexts and draw attention to the field's various forms of "complicity" in its institutional demands—pedagogically, administratively, and intellectually. In doing this, though, they also lay bare some of the consequences for the field, noting especially the exclusions reflected and questions never asked by way of these arrangements. How, for example, has WGS fomented a form of gender panic in the midst of its own revolutionary questions about gendered identities? How has the oft-told tale of the field's institutionalization in the academy and its subsequent loss of political effectiveness actually kept us from telling another story of institutionalization, one that emphasizes the racialized scripts in play between white women, women of color, and white men in that structure? What has the trend to "internationalize" WGS meant for its abilities to maintain its critical edge within the contexts of the increasingly globalized university that rewards capital's demand for flexible subjectivities?

As with all the terms thus far, the three here could easily be combined with others from this book, highlighting other conversations and overlaps. Here, though, they work together to challenge a variety of practices in the field, from assumptions about "(in)appropriate" bodies and identities, to intellectual and pedagogical practices that all belie the stated aims of WGS. In some ways bouncing off of other ubiquitous descriptions of the field, such as "activism," "besiegement," or "community," these terms also refuse easy binaries of inside/outside academe but instead explore how WGS operates institutionally in complex and even paradoxical ways. Each offers a challenge to WGS' institutional arrangements, and asks: how else could we "do" WGS? What would the field look like intellectually and institutionally if arranged around another set of questions, narratives, and mandates? What happens when particular bodies, ideas, and practices seem too far (for some people) from WGS? Or too close (for some people) to the university? WGS, these authors argue, cannot escape accounting for its own positioning in contemporary institutions of higher education as well as for what has had to be shunted aside in its current arrangements in those contexts.

16

TRANS-

Bobby Noble

Preliminaries

I begin with an ending. After extended deliberation, I have left my current institutional (dis)location in a "School of Women's Studies."[1] This reallocation can never fully be detailed in one book chapter, but there are reckonings and arguments to be reflected upon, which will constitute the bulk of what I do here. Two concurrent axioms structure this chapter. First, I came into this discipline as a female-to-male transsexual, knowing much more about feminism and the discipline of Women's Studies (as it was known then) than either knew about me, and even though I am *of* both, I am no longer reducible to their privileged subject. Such relations of not knowing are, I argue, the stuff of a willful ignorance that will be the downfall of this as an institutional discipline if it continues to remain unchanged by what some of us live, ironically enough, as its unanticipated successes.[2] As I argued in *Sons of the Movement: FtMs Risking Incoherence in a Post-Queer Cultural Landscape*, the existence of transmen and other feminist sons *qua* feminists, as well as trans scholarship more broadly, marks not "feminism and Women and Gender Studies (WGS) under siege from the enemy within," but feminism's victories in producing (albeit in directions neither fully owned nor celebrated and often aggressively refused) choice about bodies and about politicized, critical masculinity as *feminism* (2006). Second, to accomplish what feminism and WGS claims it wants to, this discipline must both cultivate a political, epistemological, and pedagogical practice vehemently in excess of itself, while simultaneously resisting the imperative to contain such excesses; otherwise, it risks a loss of credibility, inflicting serious harm in the name of "social justice." Ultimately, my *transing out* is a-locational—that is, about both location and dislocation—and marks the ironic failure of the latter (privileging of excess) and the violent success of the former (the disavowal of what must not be known).

Field Notes: *Trans-ing* as Method

While not merely "trans" (if by this we mean a minoritized reduction to identity-based practices of transsexual and transgender), such a-locationality certainly is *trans-ing*, if we rethink the term in a more complex sense as an excess of personhood as constructed within binarized truth regimes. The constructions of "trans-ness" advocated in this chapter are not reducible to identity-based practices of transsexual and transgender or transnational, that is, "trans" (without a hyphen) as referencing a minoritized group of individuals for whom embodiment in place or sex are somehow incoherent. While such trans-ed embodiments are most certainly vital to my argument, I am also mapping a universalized practice of "trans-" (with a hyphen) for how it indexes discursive and intersectional formations of complex embodiment and personhood that must transcend their hegemonic formation, a formation impossible to live. In such a configuration, trans- induces both critical crossings and mobilities of categorically fixed territories (be they bodies or nations), *and* how they are imagined and materialized. The degree to which Women's and Gender Studies can go even this far depends upon our commitment to an intersectional method. So many scholars, including Vivian May and Scott Morgensen in this volume, for example, have elaborated intersectional frameworks reminding us that "gender" categories do not exist in isolation. Gender categories are always articulated through other axes of subject formation, especially when those do not seem immediately obvious. As such, then, trans- cannot be understood in relation to gender or nation alone, but must be rethought *through and as always–already* intersectional; this would allow us to track categorical crossings, leakages, and slippages in, around, and through multiple and simultaneous configurations of bodily and conceptual being (those always already nationalized AND gendered) that might allow for their reassembly. It is both intersectional deconstruction and critical reassembly that this chapter tracks. While it is true that "T" (trans) is often lumped together in the colloquial "LGBTQ," there are many reasons why such a lumping makes little sense. At its best, queer theory has often advocated quite vehemently against stable identity claims. Trans activisms, on the other hand, focus on and advocate around the opposite—that is, the right to make the very claims about identifications and corporeal materializations that queer theory claims to disavow. But Susan Stryker, Paisley Currah, and Lisa Jean Moore elaborate many of these while also delinking trans- from a limited identity politics organized only around gender, seeking rather to burst "transgender wide open, and link [...] the questions of space and movement that the term implies to other critical crossings of categorical territories" (2008, 12). Part of the intellectual and conceptual work done by such a-locationality is thus akin to writing the body in a "locative tense"—not in a queer tense. A locative tense or case in Latin or in Indo-European languages is one that performatively expresses noun referentiality; such location is signaled by the writing of the final vowel in the stem, communicating something like the "place where" the action of the sentence is set or takes place, a location inferred by the precision of the verb tense. Such a capacity does not exist in the English language. But if we are theorizing location as a form of discursive grammar, the *trans-ing* I live, enable, and theorize here functions close to the locative case. It throws assumed referential grammars into crisis, so that the ease of situating referential bodies, identities, and fields of study becomes incoherent and quite unstable. Such conceptual, discursive, and ideological *trans-ing* methodologies (have to) recalibrate and dislocate the truth regime of binarized sexes stabilizing the field of what has passed as Women's Studies.

It is evident that such truth regimes build themselves quite unevenly and are circumnavigated by *trans-entities* inside the context of WGS in complex ways. I am using the term trans-entities here for a couple of reasons. I borrow it from two queer-identified trans people of colour—Wil and Papì—who are the subjects of one of the most interesting docu-porn films of late, *Trans Entities: The Nasty Love of Papì and Wil*, produced by Morty Diamond (2007). Wil and Papì coin the term "trans entities" as a way to describe themselves, noting the need for such descriptions given the often binarized options made available through such language as female-to-male, male-to-female, transsexual, and so forth. Arguing that such binarized options are themselves the products of clinically regulated medical diagnostic technologies, Wil and Papì—both of whom, at the time of filming *Trans Entities* were non-operative—carefully index the way that such languages and their clinical grammars are also inherently racist, colonizing the space of trans- as too often white. Their use of the term "entities" instead of "gender" or "sexual," then, signals one response to alienation lived on a day-to-day basis as a result of clinical and binarized language systems that create little possibility for practices that reflect their multiply situated identities. For example, they remind us of what poststructuralism has already taught us: that language itself is a practice of alienation, all the more so for those aggressively subject to the violences of white supremacy, poverty, empire, clinical regulation, pathologization, and coercive normalizations. As such, it isn't possible to detail one kind of alienation without contextualizing alienation as both a condition of capital and a precondition of the kinds of cultural capital accruing differently to different bodies positioned inside the educational corporate complex. Judith Butler has noted the way that harm and risk both have disproportionate impact depending upon structural levels of precariousness in the first place (2004b). It goes without saying that such unevenness is a result of privilege both across capacities outside of and inside of the educational-corporate complex but also inside the discipline of WGS as well. Given that the discipline has had, as its *raison d'être*, the demarcation and remediation of such precariousness, its failures become all the more potent—and problematic. If WGS programs develop uniquely across specific institutional sites as well as in relation to each other, then dominant narratives of crisis—both in the field of WGS and in the imaginations of its faculty and students—posed by trans-entities as subjects not reducible to the privileged subject of the discipline must be calibrated by the work these trans-entities accomplish—or not—across those same institutional territories. While there has been much debate over the last twenty-five years about transsexual and/or transgender bodies in feminist spaces, including in WGS programs, conferences, and scholarship, current debates about such trans- entities—as well as the future possibilities signaled by those incoherent bodies—have been articulated through an elaboration of contradiction, excess, terror, and conceptual intransigence—all earmarks of fundamentalism. Paradoxically enough, the case that necessitates trans-entities in these locations, of course, must be subject to the same failures as a coherent project in order for its critical potentialities to do their work: in other words, the success of a trans- critique must be in its ability to dislocate (rather than capitulate to) a mapping which has as its own project the stabilization of that which must be undone by trans- bodies. In particular, the FtM trans- body reminds the discipline—and its practitioners—that the body politic does not have a symmetrical relationship to the body institutional, nor do these bodies share the same temporalities. To frame this with more precision: feminist and queer communities outside of the university have been (with varying degrees of success) dealing with the presence of trans- bodies for a substantial period of time. Why have institutional practices within the academy lagged so far behind?

Dislocating Women's and Gender Studies: Feminist Fundamentalisms

While a rhetoric of openness, inclusivity and interdisciplinarity appear to be saturating Women's and Gender Studies at an institutional level, the opposite is true at an administrative and collegial level, where some of the discipline's scholars and practitioners remain trans-illiterate—passionately ignorant and deeply intransigent of what real integration of such entities will necessitate. "Integration" of trans- bodies necessitates structural and conceptual disintegration and re-construction of the sexed and gendered ground of the WGS project. Instead of this reconstruction, though, hegemonic practices of a trans-illiteracy fold that trans-entity into a noncritical binarized sex system, one in which that body can only make sense as *either* a male or female body, as if these are the only two choices, or as if a body cannot be more than one gender—indeed, be more than gendered—in the first place. For that body to access the institutionalized program *qua trans* would mean that the conceptual ground of gender in Women's Studies would need to be radically troubled (and so it should be). Such gender trouble, though, is too often answered in the form of a gender-panicked tearful plea over "what's happening to the women of *Women*'s Studies"—a self-generated, performative statement of innocence and victimhood, where the plea functions to reorient unproblematically back to the lives of "every day and real" women, and where what is mandated here is that "women" be understood to mean biologically-born white women. A trans-feminist logic, though, necessitates a profound challenge to the ease with which that universal "woman" is exchanged as knowledge commodity and posited as an essential truth of so-called sound, respectable, demonstrable, empirical social science method. Critical trans- perspectives should be making it much harder to make truth claims about the universalizability of "women"—experientially or otherwise—without at least using it with much more precision to identify a relation to "woman" that is no longer reducible to the female body or to white women's universalized experiences standing in for all women's experiences, unless those are otherwise minoritized by qualifications.

If trans- as "critical crossings of categorical territories" (again, not to be reduced to the clinical transsexual body) accomplishes its work, especially in WGS, then the universality and territorialization of the term "woman" should be problematized somehow, beyond the additive and tokenistic practice of writing "women and trans people" (desirable but sparse in appearance) which makes no conceptual, curricular, epistemological, or nomenclature modifications in day-to-day practice (such as in memos that use exclusively female pronouns to refer to faculty and students). The gender-panicked imperative of *"remember the women"* marks what I call an unequivocal gender fundamentalism, which (not unlike that of nationalism, military-state, white supremacist, Christian, to name only a few) functions to ground both a feminist imaginary and its methodology of social, moral, and biological coercive normalization. In using the term "fundamentalist methodology," I am borrowing from Carol Schick, JoAnn Jaffee, and Ailsa Watkinson's *Contesting Fundamentalism*, in which the authors state that the "fundamentalist methodology involves re-imagining the past and invoking an authentic community with deterministic social characteristics. In doing so, it produces a paradox—the fundamentalist simultaneously engages in nostalgia for the past while displaying historical amnesia about a system of living that never existed" (2004, 9). Trans-entities have always been present inside feminist spaces; to make a claim to the contrary is to fly in the face of at least thirty years of writing and debate about the presence of trans bodies "on the front line." The degree to which those bodies remain *located within* or *dislocated from* stories about actively re-imagined pasts as well as academic and disciplinary communities and their nomenclatures is precisely the stake to be won or lost (Hall, 1981).

Trans-ing Feminist Gender Studies: Re-Assemblages

Such stories about Women's and Gender Studies are often told by doubling back teleologically over a presentist version of a past, accomplishing the work of reifying self-generating questions about the field. The strangely imperializing temporalities of WGS and the stories it tells about itself have been the subject of many edited and usually American collections published in and about the field. One Canadian collection is worth lingering over: Canadian WGS scholars Ann Braithwaite, Susan Heald, Susanne Luhmann, and Sharon Rosenberg and their important 2004 collection, *Troubling Women's Studies: Pasts, Presents and Possibilities*. This strong assembly of important voices details the impact of disciplinary self-critiques with sophisticated, nuanced, and precisioned analysis. All four of its authors are WGS practitioners in varying capacities, geographical locations, and institutional security, and each foregrounds problematics emerging self-reflexively in—perhaps even *as*—the field of WGS: narratives about origins and history; ambivalence about institutionality; generational metaphors and the kinds of work they accomplish; and the material and textual forms many of these problematics take, including memorializations, autobiographical writing, and memoirs. Contained in this thoughtful collection is a sharp critique of (much of the) story-telling about the discipline. Despite the differences inside the papers by Braithwaite, Rosenberg, Luhmann, and Heald, all trouble the singularity of stories told and meanings established in order to attend to "how a multiplicity of identities and positionalities continually redefin[ing] this project called Women's Studies is one of the strengths of the field" (29). At the same time, while *Troubling Women's Studies* formulates a critique of emerging master narratives of this discipline/interdiscipline, it still falls short of what it itself espouses—that is, it does not develop a complex enough elaboration of the confluence of discourses and positionalities supposedly constituting this field.

There are a number of key moments in *Troubling Women's Studies* where its authors flirt with the cautionary tale I tell here about the productive hauntings of the field by trans-entities—but none commit to a serious engagement with the implications and indeed, losses, of such ghosts. Nor does the collection theorize such intransigent disciplinary failures as evidence of feminist fundamentalism or of what Robyn Wiegman names "normatively literal domains of sexual difference." Wiegman states:

> The sudden shift from sexuality to gender that marks the transition between Women's Studies and gender studies demonstrates the end of gender's critical mobility to signify outside and beyond the domain of specific identities, becoming instead the collaborative term for new identities that need to be given representational visibility. It is at just such a moment that *women* takes on a most patriarchal signification, becoming the referent for the particular in a dynamic that reduces it to the normatively literal domain of sexual difference. Why feminism would want to author such a reduction of women is perhaps not immediately clear.... (2002c, 131)

Wiegman's nomenclature, "patriarchal signification," is telling, and somewhat akin to what I am arguing functions as "fundamentalism." Wiegman does not make an overly simplistic claim to *substitute* gender for women, nor to add Others onto Women, but neither does she advocate against such shifts. Instead, she is *trans-ing* one categorical territoriality against, across, and through the other to produce the "space of connection and circulation between the macro- and the micro-political registers through which the lives of bodies become enmeshed in the lives of nations, states, and capital-formations" (Stryker, Currah, and Moore 2008, 14). Wiegman seeks an intervention, but she is not calling for a new "wave," as such a construction would remain fully compatible with currently existing feminist presentist, linear narratives.[3] But she is also extremely careful to insist that how we conceive of feminist knowledge production is a work-in-progress; feminism has not yet completed its institutional work. What she calls for instead, then, without fully articulating it as such, is a deterritorialization of the temporal sequencing of feminist self-narrations and a reconciling of those critical territories with the imperatives of intersectionality. In other words, Wiegman seeks a critical trans-formation, and what is this if *not* a turn to the paradoxical temporal crossings induced by the term/concept trans-?

Wiegman's *trans-ing* of time across, within, and over feminism's praxis does to feminist historical narratives what "gender transition" does to sexed bodies and their attendant subjectivities. There is, at the very least, a doubling of consciousness as profoundly complex relative to time. Where gender reassignment procedures must be, as Butler notes, enabled by "individual choice … dependent from the start on conditions that none of us author at will" (2004a, 101), so too is feminism's institutional materialization a practice none of us author at will. Wiegman argues that critical interventions in academic feminist locations have "*come too early* in part because we are *not late enough* in our thinking about how to avoid dyadic rubrics and build critical vocabularies that make possible the intersectional imperative that we believe we believe in" (2002c, 133, emphasis added). As such, she identifies these modernist operations of history as the process which has produced feminism in its academic locations—but which is also the process which now constrains it. Such circumlocutions of time against its own linearity is a reconfiguration of time as trans- and also works quite perversely against the generational and anxious metaphors frequently passing as the debate between "second wave feminism" and "third wave feminism" (where "third" is often synonymous with "not getting it right"). As Astrid Henry points out in this volume, the wave metaphor is always already a problematic construction of history, since both time and temporality productively work against such seamless narratives of progress. At the same time, such circumventions are also part of what Heywood and Drake identify as the lived messiness of consciousness—of what I am calling *trans-ing* temporalities: "This is a contradiction that feminism's third wave has to face: an often conscious knowledge of the ways in which we are compelled and constructed by the very things that undermine us" (1997, 11).

Caveats about wave metaphors notwithstanding, Heywood and Drake make the astute observation that such dislocative knowingness is "often conscious" for its subjects (although perhaps not for those with no taste for self-reflexivity) as much as it is vital for discerning the imperative to undo the current ghosts of modernity and their subjectivities. Hence, the argument I make here about the possibility of theorizing trans-: not just as a conceptual mechanism but also as an imperative in the (dis) locative case—a formulation coming, paradoxically of course, too early but not yet late enough as Wiegman indicates. In the first instance, the need to undo feminism with such an intervention is itself the measure and sign of the very instabilities within the category "woman" that are either self-evident as a politic, or not. In this case, such a working of trans- has come far too early, especially when erroneously hailed as the downfall or end of feminism or of WGS or both (*"remember the women"*). But in the second instance, coming not late enough, trans- continues to be the central pillar around which critiques of hegemonic American/Canadian and white feminism have been organized since, at the very least, *This Bridge Called My Back* (Moraga and Anzaldúa 1983) began to performatively and theoretically codify the transnational theories and practices that have always constituted feminism, despite white feminism's dismissals of such trans-entities as particularized or minoritized. Both the latter (race-panic) and former (gender-panic) are telling of the grammars of feminism as it has been institutionalized in the academy, something detailed in a profoundly significant body of antiracist, postcolonial, decolonizing feminist work. However, if we could remove the panic, these transformations of feminist theory and knowledge production have been significant and successful. What difference, if any, might it make to forge a strategic convergence between these two materializations of trans-feminisms? What kinds of labor (for white trans subjectivities) and/or utility (for troubling the hegemonically fundamental/fundamentalist female nation) might be extracted from such *trans-ing* diasporic dislocatives?

I am not unaware that the question I am attempting to ask here is one deeply embedded within the matter of its own ghostly histories. As I have detailed elsewhere, I have a long feminist history as a white butch, and now, as a white man, where I understand the coherence between these two seemingly diametrically opposed subject positions being established through my whiteness (2006). That is to say, even though I have (in equal parts voluntarily and involuntarily) relinquished my claim on all things *lesbian*, I have not given up a thirty year feminist history which has seen me as both man and butch, each *trans-ing* back over, across, and within each other and the same body, coming later in time, here and now (that is, post-transition) than it came before, there and then (that is, pre-transition). (To frame this within the clinical grammers of the alibi of essence necessary to access sex-reassignment procedures: if before, I was a man trapped in a butch's body, am I now, given that thirty year history and its very potent lessons, a butch trapped in a man's body?) While it remains true that enacting *trans-(ly)* is not reducible to *being* a "man"—though, what is also true is that being a *white passing trans-man* is absolutely reducible to being written a *"white man"*—insofar as it is whiteness modifying gender. In this writing, it is race that emerges as the calibrator of privilege, not the "fact" of being gendered or sexed. And certainly, as trans-folk slowly transit into institutionalized feminist spaces, even more so as tenure-stream faculty members, several questions emerge that might lead to WGS being able to tell entirely different kinds of stories about itself.

For example, to what degree is white privilege at work as trans-entities find their way into institutionalized feminist spaces? The inclusion of some trans-entities and not "Others" into such spaces might well be happening as a result of a skewed perception of pre-transition sex-based identity politics and a skewed perception of an ongoing relation to "woman"; that is to say, only one trans woman that I am aware of has been hired in a Canadian "Women's Studies" program. White trans-men teaching in WGS are faring better although not without a great deal of difficulty achieving recognition *qua* trans- in some cases; compare this, for example, with the fact that only one man of colour— and certainly no straight men of colour—have been hired or transferred into WGS in a Canadian university (that I can discern) despite the fact that feminist research *"on women"* has been done by scholars of many genders and racialized subject positions for a substantial period of time. Of course, these are extremely tentative speculations, and I offer them as such, but they remain telling of the question I am seeking to articulate here: to what extent has the institutionalized practice of WGS enforced the categorical coherence of "woman"—functioning both as

racialized and as sex-binarized? Again, it is important to note that these
are not the same thing; nor am I attempting to superimpose them onto
each other. But if these speculations are at all tenable, then thinking
feminism through a trans- modality might bear productive fruit but
also, more importantly, potent interventions. For instance: What would
it take to theorize productive, anti-empire and anti-white supremacist
conceptual feminist linkages between the *trans-ing* of transnational and
the *trans* of trans-gender? Is there potent conceptual feminist kin here?
I'm certainly very much aware of the pernicious and complex ways that
white subjectivity can play ethnicity cards, sexuality cards, class cards,
queer cards, age cards, transsexual cards as ways of declaring imagined
clemency from white supremacy and its privileging of white skinned
bodies. Still, as I read collection after collection of feminist theory, I
see work that stops abruptly short of a full elaboration of what it might
mean to circumvent the language of sexed embodiment as a foundation
of critiques of white supremacy. Such truncations, located inside institutions and as institutional narratives, memories, and practices, have now
permanently found their place, inscribing their beginnings, middles,
and for my own narrative, ends onto the structures in which they are
quite comfortably housed.

And so, as this collection goes to press, my time in WGS as a full
time faculty member has come to an end. It would be an understatement to say that this was a complicated decision, made as a response to
impossible circumstances deeply embedded within the framework and
questions raised in this chapter. My time as a full time faculty member
(2004–2009) overlapped with my gender transition. I've detailed much
about this transition in *Sons of the Movement*, but another way of telling
this story is this: I came out as a lesbian in 1978, transitioned (which
for me meant hormones and top surgery) beginning in 2001, and just
transitioned again professionally and institutionally from WGS back to
English as an accommodation to what I have detailed in this chapter
as a complicated series of failures in this discipline to manage what is
trans-ing through such a sentence with complexity. My first request to
my Dean was for a 100 percent reallocation; in consultation with some
of my colleagues, I changed this request to a 60/40 appointment in part
to ensure a commitment to a *trans-ing* presence in a discipline to date

unyielding to the transformations that feminism itself set into locomotion, the power to move from one place to another.

There is by now a great deal of trans- scholarship detailing the fact that, despite fundamentalist-feminist gender panics, "feminism" and "trans" are not oxymoronic. As Toronto-based frontline trans-service provider Kyle Scanlon (2006) suggests, saying "trans- and feminism" should instead be considered a redundancy. The fact that they are not is a discursively produced hegemony, one that requires constant and active, as well as defensive, production. Detailing the reasons why they might be considered as antagonists would necessitate a long review of so-called feminist classics and their vile, panicked transphobia; instead I leave it to Scanlon's insightful wit to flag the issues: "My recommendation? Feminist scholars could play a tremendous role in drawing attention to the real-life experiences, needs, and issues of trans people if only they could turn their attention away from their own idealized concepts of what fun it must be to explore masculinity" (2006, 94). Scanlon is also careful to detail what feminist academic literature imagines it owns—that is, the practice of intersectionality—something we believe we believe in, but something that, as May points out so compellingly in this volume, fails dismally as an institutional praxis more often than not. "Now it's feminists themselves who need to get real about the kinds of gender privileges they take for granted. I refer to the privilege of being a person whose assigned sex at birth matches their gender identity throughout their lives .... I call [this] biocentrism ... in a world of binary gender systems" (Scanlon 2006, 93–94).

My original draw to the modalities of feminist poststructuralist theory as well as to the potentialities of *trans-ing* feminism as an antidisciplinary methodology is in part autobiographical and set into motion by my own personal and disciplinary incoherence as a response to fundamentalist biocentrisms. In the urgency to stabilize women, "men"—whether trans- or not—is equally stabilized and othered, seemingly by necessity in the same gesture, and functioning all too often as a repository for all things non-female and so, suspect. Holding the possibility that the bodies of trans-entities can fold these diametrically opposed categories through each other seems a sheer (and very dangerous) impossibility, one with violent consequences for those who need them to be diametrically opposed. Pronouns are a case in point. In the best of all possible worlds, the day-to-day language and practice of pronouns—in my case, *he*—certainly offers a form of recognition which, in the best-case scenario, initiates a form of respect in its iteration. At other times, the *he* is a response of violence to the conceptual terror induced by the presence of a body both *he* and *she* at the same moment, neither one nor the other enough to stop the incoherence from traumatizing foundations. The *he* then becomes a reductionist, fundamentalist response to the certainties it troubles, a performative shove out the door. Like any trauma, though, it persists and returns in the inescapability of its belated impact; as Rosenberg vitally points out, the task might be to contemplate rupture and to live with the unbearable (2004, 219). Of course, Rosenberg is calibrating the traumas of death and of violence, in particular, of the Montreal massacre; but her words signal a process of attempting to respond to what seems like an unbearable interruption of business as usual in and for the field, as in the ruptures and tears to the everyday essentialist assumptions about the shared locative equation of female = woman = women's experience = "Women's Studies" (and WGS) that a trans- body induces. And, in return, such calibrations figure the responses done in return back to the trans- body; how do I bring to bear on my every day world something in excess of the visible post-transition, that is, a thirty year lesbian history, an entire upbringing and socialization as a young woman, eldest daughter in a single-parent family on social assistance and living in poverty, many, many experiences in a "female" body, experiences around which WGS imagines itself to be organized—but experiences of femaleness now carried in a male body and so within the locations/locutions of the discipline so fully unintelligible and disavowed? This is trans- rupture, interruption of the body and *as* body, as incoherent discontinuity for which there are few mechanisms of comprehension.

Such attempts at dealing with the trauma induced by a *trans-ing* body seem like the repeated and persistent attempts to pop a severely dislocated shoulder back into place; under some conditions, it might seem like the right thing to do, but more often than not, it ends up creating far more damage than correction. But what is also true is that my thinking about a *trans-ing* practice also wants to calibrate dislocative ways of conceptualizing and, indeed, practicing whiteness in a similarly trans- disruption of white supremacy. By way of thinking hard, then, about day-to-day realities, what exercises of conceptual maneouverings and what kinds of daily institutional *trans-ing* practices are necessary inside of WGS to ensure that traumatizing ruptures both do and do not "succeed?" Cathy Caruth, of course, phrases this much more eloquently when she writes: "… in trauma, the greatest confrontation with reality may also occur as an absolute numbing to it … trauma precludes its registration" (1996, 6). In part, I am suggesting here that the mere presence of trans- bodies holding such impossibilities create traumas which are answered by aggression far before those traumas are even registered by those most undone by their presence. The foundationalist, panicked, and fundamentalist plea "remember the women" is itself a trace of what otherwise might be productive traumas; but fundamentalisms *are* what fundamentalisms *do*. Gender panic—like race panic—restores whiteness and women as the proper universalizable object with so much force that to imagine otherwise is to be imagined as so fundamentally Other that such articulations are demarcated as impossible before they can even be asserted. This is indeed one of the most precarious tests of *trans-ing* as I am conceptualizing it here—asking it to transition across the "homes" fundamentalist WGS has carved into and as colonial spaces of nation, spaces violently traumatizing to its persistent ghosts. At the very least, might this reconceptualization itself address a crisis of coherence and in practice? Or will WGS develop as further symptomologies of the failure of those new ways? The dislocative methodology of an answer has already been signaled—but institutionally ignored—by Rosenberg's conclusion: that perhaps what is necessary is a "marker in which to become lost rather than a category of knowledge presumed secure" (2004, 226).

In the end, on the eve of my departure from it—that is, from WGS—I'm left with entirely more questions about this practice now than ever before. I remain curious as well about the kinds of stories that will be told about not only my own departure but also those of some of my colleagues. What happens when two 100 percent faculty members transit out of one of the largest programs in Canada in the same year, taking up the opportunity to reallocate 60 percent of their bodies to other departments in order to continue to do trans-feminist, antiracist work? If we write this in the way I am suggesting, is the voluntary and quite literal

splitting of two trans-entities out of WGS a measure of the entrench-
ment *in* feminist fundamentalist foundationalisms? What kinds of
lost-ness might *these* losses induce? Are these untenable losses fundamentalist products of an anxious and melancholic self-reflexivity secur-
ing a field around its insecurities, or relocations of a neoliberal white
feminist discipline correcting itself? And if we answer yes to both, is it
time, again, to declare this precise institutionalization of the project an
impossibility and move on?

Notes

1. The School of Women's Studies at York University, Toronto, Canada.
2. Many chapters in this anthology point out the ways in which WGS has
   not taken up the promises espoused by its apparent adoption of particular
   viewpoints; see, for example, the chapters by Morgensen, Purvis, and May.
3. See Henry here for much more on this idea of "waves" in feminisms and
   WGS, and the shortfalls of this metaphor for the narratives we construct
   and tell about this field.

17

INSTITUTIONALIZATION

Aimee Carrillo Rowe

Although many Women's and Gender Studies (WGS) practitioners have expressed an interest in the institutionalization of the field,[1] their responses to the field's emerging legitimization and "professionalization" have ranged from hand-wringing, to nostalgia, to "breast-beating," from critical and deconstructive assessments to struggles over essentialism, to the formation of new estrangements and alliances. But how do our social locations differently position us in relation to this debate? When I encountered U.S. Third World Feminism, I felt as if I had found myself in ways I didn't even know I had lost. I was in graduate school—a young, burgeoning queer, mixed-race Chicana, questioning the bounds of compulsory whiteness and heterosexuality in which I had been raised. I started to see power everywhere, and I was keen to find ways of usurping, sharing, and redirecting its force. I always seemed to find myself in the middle—a bridge between white women and women of color, who were often in conflict. So my path into struggles over institutional power, alliances, and racial difference was personal, and these forces were always intertwined and inseparable. But there was one thing I didn't understand: if I was raised white and heterosexual, but could *become* a queer woman of color, why couldn't anyone, *everyone*, be remade? I realized that my, and any, "remaking" had to do with the alliances (multiracial and other) we build. White women, or mixed women (like me), who have close ties with women of color learn through these relationships to identify with women of color because we *see* the force of racial difference; white women of privilege who build connections exclusively with other whites invest heavily in *not* seeing it.

This chapter draws on the research my in-between social location has inspired on the intersection of race, heterosexuality, and gender as forces that shape the institutionalization of WGS. I draw on the research from my larger book project—life interviews with twenty-eight academic feminists (ten women of color and eighteen white women)[2]—to analyze how race and heterosexuality shape this process. White women and women of color become unevenly empowered within the academy by virtue of their differentiated capacity, or desire, to register as "woman" in their alliances with white men. I focus on the *relations* through which subjects are constituted—not as static identities, but as ongoing affective investments that become sedimented *as* identities. Calling this framework a *politics of relation*, I argue that the process of WGS institutionalization has been structured through white and "heterosocial" modes of belonging. The following section reviews the account of the institutionalization of WGS as a story of pure (activist) origins that have been corrupted by the lure of institutional power. The next section unpacks this idea to instead theorize this process as a *relational* project: "women" come to inhabit academia through white and heterosocial belongings. Finally, I consider what WGS as a field might look like from an "outsider-within"[3] vantage and ask what more radical critiques of the institutionalization of WGS that vantage makes available.

The Institutionalization of Women's and Gender Studies

For Women's and Gender Studies practitioners the story of the institutionalization of the field is often vexed by fundamental contradictions in relation to power. Robyn Wiegman assesses the paradoxes of power and resistance in her introduction to the edited volume, *Women's Studies On Its Own*, noting: "the inaugurating critique of institutional power that founded feminism's academic intervention now exists in contradiction with the contemporary production of both academic feminists and their proliferating objects of study" (2002b, 2). As Alison Piepmeier argues in this volume, the increasingly institutionalized forms of WGS have compelled many of its practitioners to grapple with the discipline's newfound power.[4] "If feminists have achieved positions of power, and if feminist arguments have achieved a certain cultural weight," Diane Elam asks, "how is feminism to deal with this phenomenon?" (1997, 56). Elam's question reverberates across contemporary feminist discourse as WGS' knowledge forms and sites of production gain cultural currency within the academy. The emergence of autonomous programs and, more recently, departments and Ph.D. programs, has provided an institutional home in which academic feminists may work in unprecedented spatial and institutional proximity to each other and mentor a still growing undergraduate and graduate student body. The rise in WGS majors and the formation of doctoral programs provide the conditions for (some) academic feminists to secure not only shelter, but institutional power as well.

An enterprise that was dubbed by those on its inside as the "theoretical arm of the feminist movement"[5] encounters its limits at a series of disjunctures: over the coherence of its object of study and "women's" relation to "gender,"[6] how to address its own power[7] and remain true to its activist roots[8] and, perhaps most crucially, how to come to adequate terms with its racist and (trans)nationalist exclusions.[9] Special issues and edited collections deploy a series of metaphors that seek to capture the precarious relationship between WGS and its institutional location: it is characterized a project on the "edge" (Scott 2008), and "on its own" (Wiegman 2002b), even as an "impossibility" (Brown 2008); as a discipline, an interdiscipline, a field, and a "(non)field" (Lee 2000).

While this "success" would seem, at first glance, to provide a fruitful setting for progressive feminist work to get done, how to manage and productively deploy power is no straightforward task. The debate tends to circulate around questions of the field's ambiguous insider/outsider status, often eliding questions of racial difference and power imbalances among feminists.[10] While the latter questions have been raised by women of color, they have not been integrated into the debate over the institutionalization of WGS.[11] This disconnect is due to its contradictory relationship to power and the destabilization of its object of study.[12] Wendy Brown argues that the poststructuralist and third world feminist destabilizations of the category, "woman," render WGS as a field "impossible" (2008). This raises questions over how the category "woman" emerges, yet fails to examine racial difference as a constitutive force in its production. Alternately, Rachel Lee underscores the insight that white women and women of color are not only "different" from one another, but those differences are unevenly "*ranked*" (2000, 91). As Bobby Noble's chapter incisively demonstrates from a trans perspective, the struggle over the category "woman" is an ongoing problem for WGS. Race critiques waged by women of color and white allies are often dismissed as capitulating to a cycle of "guilt and blame" or silencing and "censoring" white women.[13] As WGS gains cultural currency across various registers of higher education, the relationships among feminist thought, the category "woman," and the women's movement become tenuous at best, generating an "increasing uneasiness, among many feminist scholars, sometimes overt despair, over the future of academic feminism" (Wiegman 2002a, 18). Questions over WGS' future are inextricably bound to often quite different perceptions of its present and past. Efforts to define the field's roots in social movement history signal the ambivalence that arises at a series of (inter)disciplinary disjunctures: between efforts to reinvigorate the leftist politics constitutive of the field's formation and a nostalgia for an imagined pure space of radical feminist inquiry; between feminist of color critiques over white feminism's exclusions and white feminism's investments in its own gender-based marginality; between oppression and privilege, silence and voice, accountability and innocence.

While these extensive debates signal a lively and potentially productive struggle among WGS practitioners, the function of alliances—those intimate ties that also circulate institutional power—has yet to receive adequate attention. Attending to the relational conditions under which WGS has gained this "insider" status exposes its institutionalization as being produced through the universalization of *particular* women (and, by extension, knowledge forms) over and against "others." In the following section, I argue that the formation of the ostensibly universal category "woman" around the identities and experiences only of particular women has served as the often-overlooked foundation for WGS' institutionalizing process. The discourse that naturalizes WGS' institutionalized status as an accomplishment ignores its formation through ongoing relational practices. For example, Beverly Guy-Sheftall questions this "success" story by foregrounding the "institutionally fragile" nature of "black women's studies," which she notes, "probably has

almost no institutional strength" (2008, 161). Her observation reveals
the multiple manifestations the discipline takes and exposes its uneven
institutional terrain. Whose or which articulation of the field may be
said to have secured power? How has this process of institutionalization
emerged vis-à-vis the production of "woman" as a category of analysis?
And how has this production unevenly empowered differently positioned women who might differently animate both this category and
the project of "feminism" as the subjects and objects of its inquiry?

The ambivalent affect that animates the discourse of the institutionalization of WGS signals its vexed relationship to race politics as
questions of difference arise forcefully, if all too infrequently, within
this conversation. While it would seem that attention to the immediate
and lived nature of power relations depicted within the feminist slogan
"the personal is political" would lend itself to a comprehensive view of
the politics of difference, feminists of color have consistently pointed
out that feminism too often operates through a gender-exclusive logic:
power is equated with marginality, which is equated with (white) gender oppression. This view erases power as complex and as constituting subjects through simultaneous and competing relations of privilege/
supremacy *and* marginality. Feminists of color have underscored the
limits of white feminism's capacity to speak for all women, to adequately
theorize oppression, and to build epistemologies that would enable tran-
sracial feminist alliances. As I argue more fully in *Power Lines* (2008),
this problem of white women speaking for all women permeates the
problem of knowledge production in the field of WGS.

The bodies of women of color and third world feminist epistemologies
materialize as specters, haunting the WGS project by rendering palpa-
ble its limits, contradictions, and vulnerabilities. While these critiques
constitute a major contribution to feminist thought, it is postmodernism
and professionalism that are most frequently referenced[14] as the sources
of crisis for WGS. Certainly postmodern incursions into the field have
contributed to this object crisis, even as the professionalization of the
project also potentially generates competition among academic feminists and an academically-driven imperative that frames the conditions
of our labor. But racialized difference functions as a subtext to all of
these debates, troubling the academic feminist project, and demanding
an accounting with power that few privileged feminists are willing to

undertake. Feminists of color are positioned to respond to, as opposed to wield, power, as they make such demands of white feminists.

A Family Affair: Whiteness, Heterosociality, and "Women on the Inside"

This section considers how white women discuss the production of their subjectivities within a post-civil rights context in which an institutional imperative arose. Turning to the stories shared by white women interviewees, we see how these larger political forces shape the life stories and academic experiences of white women and women of color. Affirmative action generated difference-based programs and thus the "need" for "women" to increasingly take positions of authority: as one interviewee explained, "they needed a woman." Women's and Gender Studies would not be hu/manned by men, but by women. This context produced the institutional "need" as a political struggle within the academy. The institutional intimacies through which "woman" emerges are conditioned by white and what I call heterosocial modes of belonging as white women build familial ties with white men in power. This intimacy is figured through the trope of the white family, a narrative of belonging that provides real and imagined relations through which possessive investments in whiteness[15] are executed. The legal structures that organize family building, such as marriage and inheritance, enable whites to accumulate and exchange property within the intimate site of the family. This family structure extends beyond the white domestic sphere to mediate workplace intimacies, particularly as women and men became coworkers in new and unprecedented ways. White women's stories suggest that the trope of the family served as an organizing principle for building cross-gender, white on white intimacies in academia.

To learn how they negotiated institutional access in the academy, I asked my interviewees a series of questions about their careers and the relative challenges that "career advancement" posed for them.[16] While many white women described barriers that they faced as women and as feminists, several intimated having an "easier time" *because* they are women. Carol, for example, described her career advancement as "pretty smooth" because "[the white male administrators] needed a woman" to build WGS. While any number of women could potentially fill this category, women like Carol, who built familial ties with white men, came to animate the category "woman." Carol described her close tie with her dean, "[He was] just the best man. He was brilliant ... and I adored him, and he really adored me and we just, you know, he's like a father figure and he really helped me a lot. And so I think I was chosen for a number of reasons that weren't purely academic." Carol is the daughter in relation to the dean's "father figure" status, a family tie that provides an intimate channel through which power is transmitted. Carol surmised that she "was chosen for a number of reasons that weren't purely academic." Her remark underscores the flow of power enabled by the inherited structure of white family building: *within* racial lines and *across* gender lines. Carol's particular social location becomes both universalized (as "woman") and institutionally empowered to stand in for the category that would serve as the basis for the WGS program she would go on to build.

This power transmission marks the intersection between white and heterosexual modes of belonging.[17] The exigency for gender equity generated by the women's movement reconfigures how power flows, compelling white men to share power with "women." The homosocial transmission of power "between men"—in which women serve the symbolic function of "cementing the bonds of men with men" (Sedgwick 1985, 26)—may be rethought to account for the politics of relation that defined this historical juncture. Carol's familial model marks an intimate route to channel power through a *cultural imaginary* of "woman," sutured to white masculinity through the affective charge felt and imaged as familial intimacies. Carol describes her subject position through the figure of "woman"—bound to, and simultaneously subordinated by "white man"—as she positions herself as daughter. The bond between them is cemented through the traffic in women, configured as an idealized trope, (white) "woman," which gives her positionality meaning, value, and intelligibility. While homosociality exposes how power functions through male same-gender desire, heterosociality reveals how gender subordination and white/heterosexual privilege intertwine. Carol's account marks this double-gesture: the transmission of power (her "smooth" career advancement) is bound to her subordinate family status. Her dean is a "choosing" subject, and Carol is the object of his action; her dean is a "father figure," and Carol is a subordinate daughter.

Another interviewee, Nancy, like Carol, had "successfully" navigated academia in spite of her class differences (Nancy described her background as working class, while Carol has always been "upper-middle class"). Nancy felt she was selected as a "woman" to service the institutional need of the formation of the field of WGS:

> Well, probably [my success is] because I'm a woman and connected to Women's Studies. It was really my avenue into administrative things … I think that gave me access to the academy in ways that I wouldn't have had, if I hadn't had that connection … If I weren't a woman, that wouldn't have happened.[18]

Nancy casts her subjectivity as "a woman" within the institutional context in which that "connect[ion] to Women's Studies" provides her with an "avenue to administrative things." The institutional need for "a woman" to build "Women's Studies" produces her subjectivity through the lines of institutional access—both personal and field foundational—this need makes available and through the grids of intelligibility through which she is rendered "woman" and by which, in turn, the discipline is founded. Thus the women whose subjectivities arise at this heterosocial juncture secure power, trafficking in the figure of "woman" whose idealized femininity they approximate, as they are recruited to the project of institution building. These relations provide an alternate account for the story that early "Women's Studies" was to function as the "theoretical arm of the women's movement." Just as the women's movement was vexed with its own exclusions, the institutionalization of WGS was founded through fundamental exclusions and subordinations that span the intimate/institutional bonds between white women and white men.

Unlike Carol, who saw her dean as a father figure, Nancy did not identify a particular familial figure. "This is not how I think they perceive all white women," Nancy begins, "but I think they often perceive me as kind of a contradiction." This contradictory reading is the relational quality that inscribes her white femininity over and against the gendered/racialized performances of other (potential) "women":

They know I'm a very strong feminist, but I'm also very femi-
nine. I mean, I remember once when I was at [a university], I
hadn't been there very long, and I had very long nails, and nail
polish. And someone made a comment to me that they saw me
in a meeting and here I had, you know, blonde hair and nails
and a very coordinated outfit and so they didn't expect much
to come out of my mouth. And then when I talked, [laughs] I
guess I made some sense.

The detail with which she specifies tropes of white femininity, which
held an appeal to the men with whom she worked, signals both the
content of the "successful" performance of the category, and also the
self-consciousness with which she accomplishes it. These tropes of white
femininity (long nails, nail polish, blonde hair) as performed through
her particular body (fair-skinned, tall, willowy) universalize and idealize white female corporeality. Not only are signifiers of whiteness (skin
tone, facial features, hair texture and length) necessary to this production, but also those which differentiate among white women's signifying
practices (bodily size, movement, ability, dress, mode of interaction).

Nancy's femininity emerges over and against that of other women
whose gendered, racialized, and heterosexed performances serve as the
backdrop against which her performance of white woman succeeds.
Heterosociality, then, is a mode of belonging unevenly available to white
women, conditioned by their capacity to traffic in the idealized figure
of (white) woman to cement their ties to white men. "Do you think
that they maybe have any specific expectations around white femininity
within that context?" I ask Nancy, who replies:

N: I don't know about expectations, but I think there's just a continual
level of comfort.

A: That white men might be more comfortable with white women than
women of color?

N: Mmm-hmm [nodding]. Because it's more of what you're used to, at
home.

A: Right. There is something, it seems, about the proximity in terms
of white women and white men are supposed to be part of a heterosexual union.

N: Right, we're already used to inhabiting the same world.

Nancy's response reveals the importance of white male "comfort" in the production of the category, white woman. This comfort arises through relational practices marked by their proximity, where heterosociality gains traction through shared social space: white men and women "inhabit the same world." The "home" functions as the metaphoric space through which her intelligibility as woman is rendered, gesturing to the trope of idealized woman (figured through the comfort of "home") in which the heterosocial exchange traffics. Nancy's account underscores her investment in maintaining white men's "continual level of comfort," even as it displaces and universalizes the internalized white male gaze, cast through the "you" who is "used to" white woman's presence within the domestic sphere.

The nexus of white and heterosocial relations through which power is transmitted in these stories invites white women to invest in their paradoxically intertwined privilege and marginality. The power they gain within these exchanges is *contingent* upon their remaining complicit with their secondary status. This paradoxical investment continues to vex the institutionalization of WGS. The founding of the discipline, which becomes possible through this social contract, is thus circumscribed by the familial order, which conditions these alliances and the flow of institutional power they enable. But the affect with which these women convey their accounts suggests not that they experience these power dynamics as damaging but rather as a source of comfort or pleasure that is inseparable from their affective investment in power. Carol "adores" her "father figure" dean, and Nancy dwells on the details of her "contradictory" positionality as simultaneously soft and strong. Their capacity to resist containment privileges a possessive investment in white femininity.

This is not to downplay or disregard the struggles white women face in academia. Rather, white heterosociality provides a relational account for the crisis over the institutionalization of (white) WGS within a context that remains largely hostile toward the presence of (white) feminists. Feminist theory and criticism continues to document (white) women's positioning in subordinate and supportive roles in their personal and academic lives. Further, "antifeminism" is so commonplace in the academy that feminists are organizing to document "antifeminist harassment" as a "new form of mistreatment that is related to, though different from, sexual harassment" (Clark et al. 1996, ix). How do we square WGS' institutionalization with these ongoing struggles? White heterosociality accounts for these tensions by providing a relational view of the formation of the category "woman" and the institutionalization of the field, which are both structured through a power/subordination paradox. The "supportive roles" women take up and the sexual harassment to which they are subjected reveal the limits of white heterosociality—not as anomaly, but as built into the very fabric of academia. White heterosociality emerges at the interface between the intimate and the institutional to provide a set of relational practices and expectations which serve a pedagogical function—teaching, in a sense, white men and women how to interact within an institutional frame. Its familial structure organizes a set of rituals and signifying practices, institutional benefits and compromises, which frame the relational conditions under which white women emerge as institutional(ized) subjects and through which they are authorized to represent "feminism" within the academy.

Re-Versing Rejection:[19] Racialized Femininities and Heterosociality

Alternately women of color often express an ambivalent relationship to academia, which requires them to engage in what I call *differential belongings*[20] within and across relational sites. One interviewee, Rita, is an assistant professor who identifies as an African American lesbian from a working-class background. Rita expressed a great deal of ambivalence for academia: she considers leaving academia, struggles as a graduate student and single parent, holds multiple jobs at a series of institutions, and endures "intense racism." The academy materializes as a fraught site in which her subjectivity is enduring, resourceful, and in these ways, powerful. In response to my question about how (hetero) sexuality shapes her relationships with white men, Rita responded, "I think that's with white women. I think black figures get viewed differently [pause]. That's jungle fever rather." Rita's account equates heterosociality with the normative positionality of white women, while "black figures get viewed *differently*"—through the metaphor of "jungle fever rather," which suggests unstable or fitful expressions of desire inspired by the excess of the "jungle" as a primitive site that resides on the edge of signification. Unlike white heterosociality, such desires are unrestrained by the rituals and emotional entanglements associated with white men's relations with white women.

The slippage within her account between "woman" and "figures" also underscores her framing of black femininity as a social *construction*—as a "figure" as opposed to a person. Moving the conversation from her own experience to "black figures" self-consciously frames her positionality as a black woman as a trope (black woman = black figure = jungle fever)—as distinct from "white women" who can leverage white male desire for their own benefit. Her theorization of "black figures" as gaining meaning within a savage register resonates with black feminist thought, such as bell hooks' analysis of the cultural production of black femininity: "sexually available and licentious … the black female body gains attention only when it is synonymous with accessibility, availability, when it is sexually deviant" (hooks 1992, 65–66). Rita provides an outsider-within critique of power relations, the production of the category "women," and ultimately the formation of Women's and Gender Studies—even as she writes her own agency within and against the violent social text in which her "figure" is rendered intelligible.

Rita goes on to explain what she meant by "jungle fever" as she narrated a situation in which she unwittingly "gains [the] attention" of her white male colleague. "I've never seen it as sexual. Well," she continued, "I was going to tell you about an incident involving a man." Her disavowal of the "sexual" nature of the incident retains the distinction between the relational formation of "white women" and "black figures" as she strives to retain her "feminist principles" within a "compromising" situation:

> So we're walking down the hall and I thanked him for creating my schedule in this odd way I had asked him to do and I was really happy. I'd been asking for it for a while and he has generally been ignoring it, I guess, or not paying enough attention … He put his hand on my arm and didn't take it away and I couldn't tell if it was a platonic touch or not … He used his body to dominate my body. I felt very slimy. I compromised my

feminist principles. I didn't say anything. I just smiled and tried
to get away.

Rita's framing of the "incident" as "not sexual" reinscribes my question to her about heterosexual relations with white men in terms which
underscore the "domination" which ensues not as mutuality, pleasure,
or desire, but rather as a show of bodily force. Rita characterizes theirs
as an ambivalent relationship, one which vacillates between collegiality
and rejection. The relational placement into which she is inserted within
this rubric of violence and desire is contingent upon her subalternity,
which leaves her without recourse within the moment of the encounter:
"I felt very slimy. I compromised my feminist principles I didn't say
anything. I just smiled and tried to get away."[21] Rita rejects the white
heterosocial framing imposed by my question through her differential
movement between voice and silence, belonging and rejection.

As women of color navigate various histories of colonial control and
the normativity of white femininity, they re-verse the rejections that
would potentially silence them. This assertion of agency empowers
them to engage differential belongings to move in and out of sites of
alliance, rejection, and ambivalence. Rita's positioning is slotted within
sexualized and racialized histories of dominance in which her body
becomes intelligible to this white man not as potential family member
but as a site of corporeal subjection. Another interviewee, Andrea, likewise shared a story in which a white male administrator positioned her
as a sex worker. A Chicana from a working-class background, Andrea
described a career criss-crossed with institutional relocations; she is now
a full professor who worked for a time in administration. In our conversation about her relations with white men in power, she described a
situation at her first job. She was at a reception for new faculty where she
was "trying to avoid the guy taking the photographs because they had
hired two black, one Chicana (me) and one Asian American woman,"
when she:

> turned around and found myself with the president of the uni-
> versity and he started this stupid conversation about how the
> first time that he'd ever met a Mexican woman was a prostitute
> in Tijuana. I'm looking at this guy like, 'what the hell am I

supposed to respond to this?' This is my first job ... and he's the president of the university, and so I just changed the subject. So it wasn't like any specific thing, it was just like these totally inappropriate things that would come out of their mouths that would make it perfectly clear what they were thinking or whatever.

Andrea re-verses this rejection through a series of verbal and nonverbal gestures: the irony with which she weaves the story, the poise with which she casts her own character over and against the "inappropriate[ness]" of the white man/men in her story, her discursive re-versal of the institutional power dynamics.

Andrea is the protagonist who gains power through her capacity to maintain her composure in the midst of a colonial encounter in which the white male subject becomes undone by her presence. The epistemic and sexual violence at stake in her telling are simultaneously pervasive and sidelined as she subtextually delegitimizes his stereotype as tactless. Thus her framing re-verses the power dynamics in the story through her rendition of the president's "inappropriate" actions and her face-saving gesture ("I just changed the subject"). Her critique of the university's efforts to appropriate her brown body is underscored through her understated reclamation of civility. At this reception in which she would be awkwardly positioned before the camera in the slot of performing monkey, her story renders the white male administrators as out of place—failing to accommodate the terms of civilized belonging. While she narrates her rejection, in which woman of color emerges as sexual labor in relation to "white man," her inscription re-verses this script to reveal the absurdity upon which it is based. The discrepancy between spatial and affective proximity, which characterize this encounter in which "Mexican woman" meets "white man" on relatively equal terms, provides an account for the president's "inappropriate" behavior. Unable to reconcile these competing relational forces, the president draws upon the trope of Mexican woman as "prostitute" to decode her presence. Andrea's ironic telling reveals the incisive critique of the outsider-within position that marks the limit point of the liberal academy's color blind logic.

Conclusion: "Women" on the Inside, the Outsider-Within, and the Institutionalization of Feminism

This chapter reveals the relational contours through which variously located academic feminists navigate the interface between the intimate and the institutional in their alliances with white men in positions of power. I provide a sketch of the racialized and heterosexed relational conditions under which Women's and Gender Studies becomes institutionalized as white women and women of color become unevenly empowered within the academy by virtue of their differentiated capacity to, or desire to, register as "woman" in relation to white men. Those white women who connect with white men through familial tropes become intelligible as "women" through their capacity to traffic in the figure of "woman." That figure is reified within the white family structure, which provides a set of relational practices through which white men and these white women can engage within a reliable social text. These women were inaugurated as "women" at the founding moment of "Women's Studies" to serve the institution's "need"—incorporated to build these programs. The white heterosexuality through which their identities as "women" were institutionalized signals a foundational contradiction at the heart of WGS—a fundamental compromise Lorde describes as a feminist "pitfall."

While women of color are largely cut off from lines of institutional power that are more often made available to their white female counterparts, they actively cultivate another form of power that is based in a critical reading of power relations. Positioned as outsiders-within, their capacity to be located within, but not quite of, the white familial structure of academic social relations provides them with an antiracist feminist critique of power that tends to be obscured within the white women's narratives. These re-versals in which women of color offer critiques and stage their own agency aim to rewrite the conditions of their subalternity that arise from their status as outsiders-within. The institutionalization of WGS must be read within the context of its relational production. Juxtaposing these accounts suggests that white men, in many ways, may be understood as the unacknowledged architects of this process. The salience of the white male gaze and the investment in white men's comfort vis-à-vis the emergence of "woman" within the project of WGS must be interrogated. This chapter points to a lacuna within the relational production of contemporary hegemonic WGS in the academy: white women's stories suggest that subordination serves as the condition of possibility for their production as women on the inside. Such stories also suggest that relational conditions productive of the insider status achieved by particular white women may be antithetical not only to the empowerment of women of color, but to white (identi-fied) women as well.

The critiques available to women of color, who occupy outsider-within positionalities in the academy, resist and provide a potentially radical rewriting of this relational social text. Yet for the private transcripts of women of color to become legitimate public transcripts within WGS, we need to excavate the entanglement between white and heterosexual supremacy and the liberal humanist logic of these projects would have to be excavated. The subordinated status of third world feminist cri-tiques within WGS, then, is an ironic posture as it is this very status that marks its potential. The subaltern status of the re-versals of these women of color shares a series of strategies for resistance, retelling, and differential belonging that—if centered within WGS and alliance praxis—would require a renegotiation of power relations and compel white women to unravel the paradox of privilege/marginality that struc-tures white heterosociality's condition of possibility.

Notes

1. In spite of women of color critiques, the debate has often been defined around feminism's ambiguous insider/outsider status in the U.S. academy, eliding questions of racial difference and power imbalances.
2. This chapter draws on my book, *Power Lines: On the Subject of Feminist Alliances* 2008.
3. See Collins 1990.
4. See, for example, Aisenberg and Harrington 1988; Guy-Sheftall 2008; Wiegman 2002b.
5. See Graul et al. 1972. And for a productive critique of the "nostalgia" that permeates such origin stories, see Braithwaite 2004.
6. For these debates see Auslander 1997; Brown 2008; and Wiegman 2002c.
7. See Elam 1997.
8. See Zimmerman 2002.

9. For a more extensive critique, see feminist of color theorizations, such as Bannerji et al. 1992; Moraga and Anzaldúa 1981; Alexander and Mohanty 1997; Lee 2000; Yee 1997.

10. For women of color critiques of the exclusionary forces of WGS see Chilly Collective 1995; and Turner, Viernes, and Meyers 2000.

11. For discussions of the institutionalization of WGS and the stakes of what might be lost, see Crowley 1990; de Lauretis 1986; Looser and Kaplan 1997; Stanton and Stewart 1998; The Social Justice Group at the Center for Advanced Feminist Studies 2000.

12. A number of edited volumes and special issues of feminist journals mark and provide commentary on this crisis, including: Scott 2008; a special issue of *Feminist Studies* (1998); Clark et al. 1996; Looser and Kaplan 1997; and Bhavnani 2001.

13. See Gubar 1998.

14. See Anzaldúa 2002; Collins 1990; hooks 1984; Hull, Scott, and Smith 1982; Hurtado 1996; and Mabokela 2001.

15. See Lipsitz 1998.

16. For white women the question was, "Would you compare your career advancement as relatively smooth, or was it more difficult, compared to what you know of the experiences of white men?" then "compared with women of color?" I asked women of color the same question with regard to white men, and then in comparison to white women.

17. While white women have been the primary beneficiaries of affirmative action, the practice registers through the category of racial difference (seen as "racial preference") (see "Is Sisterhood Conditional?" Wise 2001).

18. The following citations from Carol, Nancy, Rita, and Andrea are taken from interviews I conducted for *PowerLines* (2008).

19. Hurtado (1996) argues that the difference between white women and women of color can be understood through their relations to white men: white women are subordinated through seduction, women of color are subordinated through rejection. "Re-versing rejection" enables women of color to narrate their encounters with white men in empowering terms.

20. This concept builds on Chela Sandoval's "differential consciousness" (2000) to consider how this women of color consciousness is formed through shifting belongings—and to invite differently located subjects to consider how they might move across lines of difference.

21. Hammonds provides a productive lens for reading the contradictions and silences in Rita's story. If black academic feminists are "engaged in a process of fighting to reclaim the body," and that body is "still being used by others to discredit them as producers of knowledge and as speaking subjects" then at the moment when Rita is "dominated," she momentarily loses this battle to the white man who controls and determines her schedule and thereby "dominates her body" (Hammonds 1997, 177–78). She draws on a legacy of black feminist thought to re-verse his rejection in her self-staging as actively choosing to move in and out of the relationship.

18
TRANSNATIONAL

Laura Parisi

When is the transnational a normativizing gesture—and when does it perform a radical, decolonizing function?

(Alexander and Mohanty 2010, 24)

I consider myself a survivor of three curriculum transformations in three different Women's and Gender Studies (WGS) departments (two in the United States, and one at my current institution in Canada). What these curriculum overhauls have in common is that they all took place in the late 1990s and the early-mid 2000s, and they all had the goal of incorporating the ever-growing and more prominent field of transnational feminist theory, as well as the methodological shift towards intersectional approaches. The conversations around the who, what, when, why, and especially how, to transnationalize were fraught with difficulty. At my current institution, our faculty decided that even though we all came from different disciplinary backgrounds, we wanted our introductory course, which serves as the foundational course for the rest of our curriculum, to reflect transnational feminist and intersectional approaches (although, as someone trained in feminist international relations who was already teaching courses utilizing these approaches, I was probably the most comfortable with this decision). Now that I have had ample time to reflect, I am increasingly concerned about the implications of the adoption of this theoretical perspective for our WGS undergraduate curriculum.

What is at stake in adopting feminist transnational frameworks in our curricula? As universities and WGS programs/departments increasingly move towards some form of "internationalizing the curriculum," the discourse informing the process has become confusing and ambiguous. The terms "internationalize," "globalize," and "transnationalize" are often used interchangeably, with little regard to either the implications of adopting any of these terms, or one over the others. To someone trained in international relations (such as myself), the term "international" has a very specific meaning: it refers to the particular historical, cultural, political, and socio-economic locations and practices of states, and how these factors shape relations and the interactions between states. In these approaches, the state is the crucial site of analysis. Internationalizing the curriculum thus keeps states and state power very much in place, and multiculturalism and diversity—rather than interrogations of state power—become the focus. Transnational, on the other hand, points to an emphasis on flows across borders (of capital, people, environmental processes, etc.) and the differential impact of these processes. I think that the narrative that we implicitly tell ourselves about our use of transnational perspectives in WGS is that they challenge this understanding of "internationalization" in critical and important ways, but as someone who has been deeply influenced by transnational feminist scholars in terms of my own scholarship and teaching, it is this narrative that I want to explore and critique here.

Many universities in Canada and the United States are deploying internationalization agendas as a way to help students develop "cross-cultural" competencies and as a means to claiming a form of global citizenship. I want to ask, though, whether the emphasis in WGS on transnationalizing the curriculum is unintentionally complicit with broader university agendas of internationalization in ways that we are reluctant to acknowledge. Is the university's emphasis on global citizenship merely a marketing ploy to prey on a (Western) desire for otherness and the consumption of knowledge? And are we in WGS then simply reproducing and supporting hegemonic and imperialist notions of Western citizenship through the internationalization of our own curriculum?

As feminist scholars, we must critically engage with questions about the relationships among feminism, globalization, and the production and organization of knowledge because they challenge us to consider the extent to which transnational feminist frameworks present viable alternatives to the status quo in our curriculum development and related pedagogical practices. As the above questions indicate, though, we need to be clear in and reflexive about our objectives for what it means to impart ideas about transnational feminism in our WGS courses. In this chapter, then, I want to reflect on the ways WGS departments and programs both collude with and contest the move to internationalize the university curriculum through their deployment of transnational feminist perspectives. I will unpack some of the often unintentional confusions in and consequences of the slippages between international and transnational approaches that are adopted in many of our programs, and consider, in conjunction with the concerns that Vivian May raises at the end of her chapter in this volume, if the emphasis on "the transnational" might be a new "add and stir"[1] moment in WGS.

Why Transnational Feminism? A Brief Genealogy

Why have so many Women's and Gender Studies departments felt the need to make the shift to either internationalizing or transnationalizing their curricula (or perhaps some combination of the two)? What were the incentives and motivations? I suggest that there were two (but not only two) major contributing and intersecting factors: (1) the overall trend in Canadian and U.S. universities of adopting the language of internationalization and prioritizing its implementation through top-down, strategic planning mandates from administrators; and (2) the development of "global feminism" which sparked a flurry of responses from transnational feminist theorists.

The trend of internationalizing the university, which began in the 1980s, is an ongoing one, as universities have not been immune to the effects of deepening economic, political, cultural, and technological globalization. The underlying rationale for internationalizing the university is often centered around notions of "student preparedness." This theme crops up repeatedly; for example, my academic institution's Strategic Plan states that "all of our students are expected to engage as global citizens" because "global communications, economic and social interdependence, and international co-operation and tensions have made our engagement at the international level both a responsibility and a prerequisite for our success" (University of Victoria 2007, 10). As such, my university has put a great deal of emphasis on the internationalization of the curriculum and civic engagement as a way to prepare students to be more competitive as workers in the global labor market. This focus perpetuates the current global configuration of economic and political power, since countries in the global North, such as Canada and the United States, have a deeply vested interest in maintaining such structures. As Minoo Moallem argues, the "mainstream assumption about internationalization is that it is the spread of knowledge that is produced in the West and consumed in various parts of the world" (2006, 332).

WGS departments have responded to these types of institutional mandates in a variety of ways. In reviewing feminist work for the purposes of this chapter, I discovered that the volume of scholarship discussing "internationalizing" and/or "globalizing" the WGS curriculum[2] greatly exceeds that of scholarship focusing on "transnationalizing" the curriculum.[3] This is not to say that transnationalism is not discussed, but it is not always explicitly referred to as such. I suggest that this blurring of terms and perspectives is a function of the fact that the scholarship surrounding internationalizing this curriculum begins at the end of the Cold War and parallels the deepening and spread of "global" or "international" feminism during the United Nations Decade on Women (1975–85) and neoliberalism in the 1990s; therefore, it has tended to adopt the terminology and perhaps the hegemonic viewpoint of the time, despite the many challenges to it, such as the seminal publication of Chandra Talpade Mohanty's 1986 article, "Under Western Eyes: Feminist Scholarship and Colonial Discourses." The parallel discourse around global feminism was further solidified by the publication of Robin Morgan's *Sisterhood is Global* in 1984, an anthology that celebrates the rise and development of the "global feminist movement." Although Morgan's work has been subject to numerous critiques[4] which I will not delve into here, I nevertheless locate her text as one that helped bring the idea of a "global feminist movement" into the vernacular, and that has influenced current manifestations of global or international feminism as well as subsequent critiques by transnational feminists. The idea of global sisterhood, as elucidated by Morgan, has undergirded the project of global feminism, which is fostered through the claim that women comprise a "sisterhood" due to our shared "common condition" of oppression under universal patriarchy, even though we may experience it in different degrees (1996, 4). Central to the global/international feminist discourse is the focus on the commonalities of women's oppression (e.g., sexual rights and violence against women) rather than on the differences among them.

The struggles and tensions between feminists in the global North and South during this period both illustrated the limits of an internationalist or global feminism and invoked a spirited response from both postcolonial and transnational feminist scholars and activists. Mohanty, for instance, challenged the global feminist assumption of "women as an oppressed group" by elucidating several problems with this framing (1991b). At the most basic level, to identify all women as oppressed results in a binary understanding of power (powerful/powerless), which renders women as always powerless and without agency. Mohanty refined this argument by situating the assumption of "women as an oppressed group" in the context of Western global/international feminist writing about Third World[5] women.

Heeding Mohanty's call, by the 1990s transnational feminist scholarship[6] invoked an integrative theoretical framework of feminism, poststructuralism, and Marxism[7] and highlighted the gendered, racialized, classed, and sexualized dynamics of the permeability of borders through analyses of border flows—i.e., ideas, culture, capital, people, environmental processes, etc.—that moved away from "local, regional, and national culture to relations and processes across cultures" (Alexander and Mohanty 1997, xix). This allowed for an analysis of local practices in relation to cross-national processes. Guiding this work were the principles that distinguish the "transnational" from the "international." According to Alexander and Mohanty, a transnational feminist analysis includes the following:

1. A way of thinking about women in similar contexts across the world, in *different* geographic spaces, rather than as *all* women across the world (emphasis in the original);

2. An understanding of a set of unequal relationships among and between peoples, rather than a set of traits embodied in all non-U.S. citizens;

3. A consideration of the term "international" in relation to an analysis of economic, political, and ideological processes which foreground the operations of race and capitalism.[8] (1997, xix)

I highlight the links among feminist organizing, movements, and the academy as a way to foreground how these theoretical debates have influenced the dialogue in WGS about how best to position our work and our institutional programs/departments in universities which are embracing internationalization agendas. This dialogue is explored in special issues on the internationalization of that curriculum in journals such as *Women's Studies International Forum* (1991) and *Women's Studies Quarterly* (1998), and in books such as *Encompassing Gender: Integrating International Studies and Women's Studies* (Lay, Monk, and Rosenfelt 2002).

Yet even in these special issues and anthologies, there is inconsistency about terminology (that mirrors inconsistency about meanings and strategies). For example, in the introduction to a special issue of *Women's Studies International Forum* on "Global Feminism in the Curriculum," Monk, Betteridge, and Newhall make several important claims that move the emphasis away from "globalizing" or "internationalizing" towards a notion of "transnationalizing," even though they do not explicitly identify it as such (1991). Although the language of global sisterhood is still occasionally invoked in this chapter, the authors note that all women are affected by the contours of the global economy, environmental degradation, and the global military industrial complex in different and uneven ways—a framing that is consistent with some features of transnational feminism, as outlined above. They also acknowledge the lack of *an* international perspective, the importance of avoiding homogenizing traps by considering diversity within nations, and the necessity of highlighting colonial discourses and practices in creating and maintaining the "other." Despite these admissions, the authors shy away from declaring a full commitment to transnational feminist practices and frameworks in the curriculum.

In contrast, as far as I have been able to determine, there have been no similarly devoted special issues to transnationalizing the WGS curriculum, despite the proliferation of transnational feminist scholarship, including Inderpal Grewal and Caren Kaplan's introductory textbook, *An Introduction to Women's Studies: Gender in a Transnational World*, now in its second edition—a book which indicates that some programs must be transnationalizing their curricula, or at the very least, emphasizing the transnational in their introductory courses. In their introduction, Grewal and Kaplan very explicitly position the text as a corrective against global feminism, signaling their desire to move away from past models of feminist analysis that relied either on the "common world of women" approach or the "women in development" approach (an approach that supports the First World/Third World binary in which women of the Third World are positioned as needing to "catch up" with the First World) (2006, xvii). The latter approach completely ignores structural inequalities produced by systems of global capitalism, militarization, etc. Grewal and Kaplan reject earlier feminist definitions of internationalization, arguing that "to think more internationally means that we learn to make connections between the lives and cultures of women in diverse places without reducing all women's experiences into a 'common culture'" (xxi). Thus, Grewal and Kaplan offer up their text as a new way to "internationalize" the WGS curriculum: positioning transnational feminist approaches to understand the differential and gendered, racialized, sexualized, and classed impact of globalization flows in all of its forms (technological, economic, cultural, political, environmental, ideological, etc.).

As feminist scholars and teachers, we need also to understand our work in the context of the university as an institution of global capital, which disciplines and locates both knowledge and bodies in particular ways (Hong 2008). Given this, transnational feminist approaches in our curricula seem like a natural frame through which to challenge the university's capitalist logic, and transnational feminist practices can engage in tracing the impacts of the uneven circuits of capitalism and culture that universities produce, thus highlighting, contesting, and subverting these practices that sustain hegemonic relations both within and outside the academy. Dawn Rae Davis suggests that along with intersectional frameworks, transnational feminism serves to "displace white, middle-class, and First World-centered subjectivities within the epistemological desires of the classroom, as well as more broadly across feminist knowledge production" (2010, 137). WGS as a discipline uses a similar argument in its narrative about its challenges to the dominant power relations that are produced in universities, which often mirror states' interests.

Yet, it is important, as Grewal and Kaplan argue, to remember that the model of transnational feminism advocated for here is not necessarily a "cleaned-up" version of international feminism—since "transnational feminism is not to be celebrated as free" from oppressive conditions—and that all feminisms embody power hierarchies (2002, 73). As Vivian May (this volume) observes, domestic politics of race and gender can also be displaced through the adoption of transnational feminist approaches, arguing that there is a need for more intersectional analyses in Canada and the United States, too. Sandra K. Soto explains that the experiences and identities of U.S. women of color are cast as being in contradistinction to transnational feminism, which perhaps unwittingly collapses and homogenizes women of color in the United States in much the same way as global feminism homogenizes Third World women. Soto contends that the study of women of color ought to be seen as a complement to transnational feminism because it "helps us understand the varied and unequivalent processes that generate racial difference, that gender subjects, and that encourage self-identification as women of color in a transnational world" (2005, 119). In this rendering, it may also be useful to understand transnationalism as diasporic, though it is certainly not unproblematic. For example, when thinking about Indigenous peoples in Canada and the United States, since in this context, disaporic linkages of racialized women may also constitute them as settlers. Indeed, as Alexander and Mohanty observe: "We were not born women of color, but became women of color here" (1997, xiv). But perhaps this is precisely the point that Soto is trying to make— that the category of and relations among women of color needs to be more fully accounted for in transnational feminism, not only *within* the contested category of the "West" but also through an examination of South-South solidarity, which is differently global (Chowdhury 2009).

Ultimately, however, what sets transnational feminism apart is its *practices,* which "involve forms of alliance, subversion, and complicity within which asymmetries and inequalities can be critiqued" (Grewal and Kaplan 2002, 73). Transnational feminist practices reject systems based on inequality and exploitation by tracing the uneven circuits of culture and capital which produce them, rather than accepting the power inequalities as a given, as the international frameworks tend to do. As such, this perspective gives us the tools to be self-reflective in our practices and in our responses to internationalization discourses on multiple levels.

Institutional Challenges

As the opening quote of this chapter asks, "when does transnational feminism perform a radical decolonizing function and when does it perform a normativizing one?" (Alexander and Mohanty 2010, 24). I want to suggest that transnational feminism can and does perform both functions, sometimes simultaneously, primarily through the slippage between the usage of "internationalizing" and "transnationalizing." As more and more universities are adopting the internationalization model, it may be that *appearing* to adopt an internationalist perspective in the mainstream sense is tantamount to our survival, while at the same time maintaining an internal critique of the institutionalization of this discourse in our classrooms and in our research through the adoption of a transnational feminist lens is equally, if not more, important. Below I briefly note three strategies that Women's and Gender Studies scholars have deployed to this end:

1. Building strategic cross-campus alliances: Moghadam (2001) suggests that WGS programs bear a special responsibility to ensure that gender concerns are represented in other departments' internationalized curricula. She details a number of collaborative efforts on her part, highlighting, for example, her success in persuading the Agriculture department at her university to offer a *Women in Development* course, which serves the agenda of entrenching the WGS program in the university, and an even larger agenda of the university's overall internationalization emphasis. Though difficult to execute given "our current fragmentation of knowledge into disciplines and departments,"

the university curricula must be radically reconstructed both to contest the control and "the shape of knowledge, teaching, and research" and it must be done through the building of inter/cross/multidisciplinary alliances (Kolodny 2000, 136). The types of moves that Moghadam and Kolodny argue for would not only forge connections with departments that may not actively embrace feminist scholarship, they would also allow us to work more productively with feminist scholars in departments other than WGS. In this sense, feminism can maintain its radical place in the academy.[9]

2. Production of transnational, not global, citizens: Both graduate and undergraduate student job placement has become an important indicator of how both the university and WGS assess our "value" and success. As the term "transnationalism" can also connote the NGOization of social movements that are engaged in anticapitalist and anti-imperial struggles (Grewal and Kaplan 2001), it is not surprising that many of us find ourselves preparing students for just this kind of work. Transnational feminist scholarship, though, has been simultaneously open to the possibilities of such developments and critical of them. For while "globalization from below" has exciting possibilities, we must also be attentive to how in some instances NGOization reformulates transnational feminist practices into a newly constituted version of global/international feminism and/or serves to reify state boundaries and interests (Alvarez 1999). And as far as most universities are concerned, WGS students engaged in international or local NGO work are precisely the kinds of "global citizens" desired by the "internationalized" university. Thus even when we maintain that we are engaged in something quite different with our students, i.e., questioning the assumptions of global citizenship, and especially the assumption that students in the West/North need to be prepared to rescue and save the rest of the world, the university has little interest in whether or not a transnational or international perspective is adopted by said WGS students, as long as it can "tick off" the global citizenship box on its checklist.

3. Pursuit of external and internal funding opportunities: Many funding opportunities are linked to internationalization projects. Saparinah Sadli and Marilyn Porter describe a Canadian International Development Agency funded project, between Memorial University in Canada and the University of Indonesia, to establish a WGS program at the latter institution (1999). Despite potential problems in accepting this type of funding, these projects give high visibility to WGS departments as well as the university at large. They can be counted as "successes" in terms of internationalization and marketed effectively to students and the public at large. Increasingly, internal funding and opportunities also exist for internationalizing curricula, and no department wants to be left behind in claiming a share of increasingly scarce resources.

The above discussion points to the complex ways that WGS is rendered vulnerable in the academy in the current phase of neoliberalism and highlights the need for multiple strategies around internationalization to prove the "value" of the field at many universities. Yet, as I discuss below, there are also pitfalls in adopting these strategies in terms of curriculum reform and pedagogical practices.

Adopting Transnational Feminist Frameworks: What is at Stake?

Given the conceptual and institutional challenges outlined above, how do we go about transnationalizing Women's and Gender Studies curricula? As well suited as transnational feminist frameworks and methods may be for challenging the neoliberal state-centered approach that is usually embodied in the term "international," in practice they are very difficult to implement in the classroom, both in terms of pedagogy and in terms of designing curricula.

How do we actually transnationalize the curriculum? Despite the proliferation of transnational feminist scholarship during the past two decades, this was still a dominant topic of discussion at several recent National Women's Studies Association meetings. As Grewal and Kaplan suggest, "the question becomes how to link diverse feminisms without requiring either equivalence or a master theory" (1994, 14). In some sense, the internationalization process is easier given its emphasis on states—it lends itself nicely to comparative methodology, although it cannot delve into the question of differential power and effects across borders. And the organization of curriculum as demanded by the university and by course syllabi makes it difficult to circumvent the state and comparative models all together. In a certain sense, transnational processes have to be located somewhere in order to illustrate the concept of "directionality of flows."

Most often, though, what seems to take place in the curriculum is an unacknowledged placing of the United States as the center and diffuser of these problematic flows (Gunew 2002). This is perhaps understandable given the disproportionate amount of power that the United States currently holds, but at the same time this emphasis actually reifies the importance of the United States as a sovereign entity. Capital, cultural, environmental, etc., flows from other countries are rarely placed at the center of analysis, including other countries from the Global North, the former Second World countries, as well as South-South relations. In teaching Grewal and Kaplan's introductory text in Canada, my students often comment on how the United States is positioned as the jumping off point in the book; even though this is not necessarily Grewal and Kaplan's intention, the perception my students have says something about how transnational feminist scholarship is being produced, recognized/perceived, and organized. Even when analyses of transnational flows by feminists in the Global South are included in our curriculum, Marnia Lazreg argues that it tends to be the same authors representing "the Third World voice" on the transnational continuum over and over again, due to an uneven access to the translation and publication of their works for Western or Canadian and U.S. audiences (2000, 35–36).

In a certain sense, the emphasis on North-South transnational flows in the WGS curriculum maintains an implicit understanding of borders and nations even as it seeks to challenge them. Flows are often conceptualized to cross state borders rather than the borders of nations, such as Indigenous nations in both the North and South or nations which traverse multiple state borders (i.e., Kurds who live in Turkey and Iraq). Thus, there tends to be a different understanding of the state in this version of transnationalism in the curriculum. This is not to imply that transnational feminist scholars haven't grappled with these issues. For example, Grewal and Kaplan reject what they see as outdated feminist analyses of center-periphery models in favor of feminist mappings or "scattered hegemonies" of power which produce multiple centers and peripheries and move us away from state based analysis (1994). The question, though, becomes how do we reflect this in our curriculum? One possible response to thinking about the limits of the First World-Third world dichotomy (center-periphery) is offered by Mohanty, who discusses why perhaps a One-Third World/Two-Thirds World may be better suited for transnational feminist endeavors. She suggests that these categories highlight the quality of life in both the North and the South based on social minorities and social majorities and lend themselves to analysis of the fluidity and power of global forces which shape these communities and the connections between them. Yet, Mohanty also notes that the problem with these concepts is that they don't have the same discursive power in drawing attention to colonization as does the North/South or First World/ Third World binary (2003, 226–27). Despite our best intentions, the retaining of this dichotomy can influence curriculum development in particular ways, such as reinforcing state boundaries (i.e., women in the United States, women in India) and an "us-versus-them" discourse that skews it towards the mainstream and feminist internationalist model.

However, Davis argues that this problem is not insurmountable, and that in fact comparative frameworks can be useful in setting the groundwork for intersectional and transnational perspectives in the classroom as a way to interrogate the problems of reifying and homogenizing categories (2010, 142). One problem that many transnational and postcolonial feminists have consistently identified in both international feminism and mainstream internationalism is the way that the so-called "West" and "Third World" are positioned in "cross-cultural dialogues." The West is often assumed to embody a space of equality, freedom, and democracy (Russo 2006, 573), whereas the Third World is rendered as a space that needs to be saved, or rescued (Grewal 2005). Davis contends we can use comparative frameworks as a way to break down these binaries rather than reinforce them by challenging students to locate themselves within specific cultural constructs and to think critically about "difference as a relational effect" that is "both discursively and materially produced" (2010, 142–43). Davis's point about using comparative frameworks to explore relationality instead of employing and reifying boundaries strikes me as an important contribution to the discussion of transnationalizing the curriculum, both in terms of how we choose material, and how we present it. Her discussion also reminds us that transnationalizing the curriculum is a process of sorts—the students may be unable to grasp the uneven effects of transnational flows unless they are able to understand how they themselves are materially and discursively produced by hegemonic systems to begin with. Given my own experiences in the classroom, I think that this is a valuable way to disrupt Western-ness as a way to take on the complicated issues of diaspora, migration, and ongoing colonial practices.[10]

Expertise

However, even if the above pedagogical approaches are useful, can we all employ them? Or do we run into the issue of our own lack of knowledge in elucidating this kind of complexity? There are several narratives about expertise that are worth exploring here. First, Clare Hemmings grapples with the idea of "internationalizing" the curriculum and attendant pedagogies that require the inclusion of more and different perspectives beyond the scope of her expertise, and she worries that "adding more" does not do much in the way of transforming curriculum (2005b). Hemmings cautions us to think about ethics and responsibility in transnationalizing the curriculum in terms of our accountability. For example, she discusses how including a reading on gender and sexuality in China just to make her course more international feels irresponsible to her as a curricular and pedagogical practice, since these topics are outside her area of expertise. I suspect many of us feel tripped up by this type of issue when trying to map global circuits of power while at the same time trying to avoid what Mohanty identifies as either "feminist-as-tourist" (or consumer) model, in which "other" women outside of North America are "consumed" in the pursuit of knowledge, or "feminist-as-explorer" model in which both the local and the global are "defined as non-Euro-American" (2003, 240).

While I understand, take seriously, and have myself felt the dilemmas about expertise raised by Hemmings and Mohanty, I also think that we can find ways around those by returning to and highlighting

Alexander and Mohanty's (1997) guidelines for transnational feminist analysis, discussed above, for thinking about how to frame course topics in a transnational way. Rather than believe that I have to know everything (or even much) about gender and sexuality arrangements in China in order to discuss labor practices in that country, for instance, I focus instead on how the transnational construction of labor is discursively and materially produced as feminized, racialized, and classed through global capital, and how these tropes then link Chinese factory workers to Canadian and U.S. retail workers and consumers in very complex ways. I start by showing the documentary *China Blue*, which details the lives of young women from rural China who migrate to an urban area to work for a blue jeans factory (2005). The closing shot of the film depicts a young white woman arranging the jeans on a sale rack in an English-speaking country. In conjunction with the film, I also give a lecture on the interrelationship between the gendered and racialized global division of labor, export processing zones, and the role of Wal-Mart as an employer in China, the United States, and Canada. Though this example does not entirely get around the problem of expertise about any of the countries involved in this global chain of production and consumption, it does allow for an analysis of the ways in which the effects of globalization are uneven and connected, without employing the "feminist-as-tourist" and "feminist-as-explorer" models.

Piya Chatterjee relates a different problem surrounding the notion of expertise and ethics in the classroom (2002). She notes that through her training as an anthropologist she is expected to have a certain "knowledge" about cultural practices, etc., and that her location in the academy provides her with a level of authority and privilege denied to most other Third World women. Yet, at the same time, she is a producer of knowledge about Third World Women, and by making their experiences visible, she is also rendering them as objects of study; indeed, she implies that she herself becomes an object of study for her students based on whatever preconceived notions they hold about the world before they even step foot into her classroom. Chatterjee reflects on what response her "post/colonial, immigrant, South Asian, bourgeois, female body" (2002, 105) elicits in the classroom, as a reminder of the paradox that transnationalizing curriculum and pedagogy can present.

Reflecting on Chatterjee's story, what does it mean, then, for a white feminist scholar, such as myself, to engage in transnational feminist approaches in my classroom? Am I, as May (in this volume) cautions, contributing to the idealization of white womanhood? Elora Halim Chowdhury argues that "women of color and transnational feminists can speak to only certain issues narrowly conceptualized by hegemonic feminism as 'special tracks' whereas white women, specializing in 'feminist theory' … are free to position themselves everywhere" (2009, 58). Chowdhury also contends that the term "transnational" is often "code for hiring non-US women of color who are considered by academic establishments less threatening, not as political, and more compliant" (2009, 56). Might not our students also read their professors in this way? In what ways does this render some of us more vulnerable than others when employing transnational feminist pedagogy in our classrooms? Who is understood as having "expertise"?

Chatterjee and Chowdhury raise important points about who is accorded expertise status with regards to transnational feminism both within the classroom and within departments themselves, and why it is important that Women's and Gender Studies departments and programs not treat transnational feminism as a "special track" and assign it as the responsibility of one professor in the department, who, as Chowdhury notes, is most likely a racialized and perhaps non-Western woman (2009). If transnational feminist approaches become the shared responsibility of all departmental members though an integrated curriculum, there is opportunity to dismantle, displace, and decenter both mainstream and feminist internationalist approaches—even though it may seem safer to cling to feminist internationalist approaches that have a better fit with many universities' agendas of producing global citizens for the marketplace, especially since international feminism can present itself as unproblematically transnational in its perceived ability to be "cosmopolitan, generous, [and] antiracist" (Barlow 2000, 1103).

Some Final Thoughts

May (in this volume) exhorts us to grapple with the theoretical limits of transnational frameworks as well as the resistance to these perspectives in Women's and Gender Studies. This chapter serves as a partial response to that challenge by examining the ways in which the conceptual slippage between the use of the terms "international" and "transnational" has shaped the position of WGS in the academy, and how we might think about where to go from here if we are to move out of an "add and stir" (or normativizing) moment to a more radical, decolonizing one, as called for by Alexander and Mohanty (2010).

In light of recent world events, such as the financial crisis and the demands for democracy in various parts of the world, the need for transnational feminist analyses is more crucial than ever. However, we need to be more attentive to potential slippages, disavowals, and silences when employing feminist transnational perspectives in order to more effectively navigate our increasingly globalized world. In particular, this means deepening the intersectional analysis within transnational feminist approaches. Although Moallem cautions that the danger in transnational feminist perspectives is that they privilege a "modernist framework that relies on the notion of an 'avant-garde' subject/discourse who leads the way toward liberation from all oppressive structures, relying on a utopian vision of society" (2006, 334), they can also allow for strategic and subversive interventions in the use of the international in our curricula, our universities, and our societies. Transnational feminist frameworks—and their implementation in WGS—provide important tools to reflect on and challenge the disciplining of knowledge and bodies in the service of the university and global capital.

Notes

1. This metaphor was often used in WGS in the 1980s to address a quite different phenomenon in the mainstream university curriculum in which adding books about women to courses was equated to achieving gender equality or erroneously understood as making the course feminist. See Moallem (2006) for her critique of internationalization as an "add and stir" moment in WGS.
2. See, for example, Lesink 1991, Monk, Betteridge, and Newhall 1991, *Women's Studies Quarterly* 1998, Cohn 1999, Sadli and Porter 1999, Moghadam 2001, and Lay, Monk, and Rosenfelt 2002.
3. See, for example, Grewal and Kaplan 2002 and Lazreg 2000.
4. See, for example, Mohanty 2003, Chapter 4.
5. In later work, Mohanty 2003 (Chapter 9) addresses the problems of the First World/Third World dichotomy. I am using the terminology here since this is what she used in the original essay.

6. See, for example, Grewal and Kaplan 1994, Basu 1995, Alexander and Mohanty 1997, and Shohat 1998.
7. See Grewal and Kaplan 1994.
8. See Grewal and Kaplan 2001 for five ways the term "transnational" circulates in the academy.
9. Maparyan, in this volume, provocatively suggests that WGS is the location not for feminism per se so much as for a kind of coalition building among disparate and seemingly unrelated interests, disciplines, groups, etc., all invested in broader social justice goals.
10. See Mohanty 2003 for a fuller description of anti-globalization pedagogy that extends some of the points introduced in this discussion.

ESTABLISHMENT CHALLENGES

Points to Ponder

1. In what ways do "Trans-," "Institutionalization," and "Transnational" speak to WGS' difficulties in resisting "the colonizing function" of the institutions of which it is a part? How do they complicate simple notions of complicity with or resistance to dominant structures and discourses?
2. How do "Trans-" and "Institutionalization" challenge the focus on "women" in WGS? What do their arguments suggest about the field's identity, and its possible future(s)?
3. How does "Trans-" as a method help us rethink the nationalist discourses that, as "Transnational" argues, ironically undergird the university's contemporary mission to "internationalize?"

CONCLUSION
CONTINUING THE CONVERSATION

Catherine M. Orr, Ann Braithwaite,
and Diane Lichtenstein

Individually and collectively, the eighteen preceding chapters have challenged Women's and Gender Studies (WGS) to rethink many of its most basic assumptions and stock narratives. Through critical examinations of many of the field's key terms, the authors have pointed out the unspoken, the unacknowledged, and even the unseen in the common intellectual claims and routine practices of WGS. Some of these observations have no doubt been startling and jarring, to say nothing of humbling and eye-opening. But we hope they've also been invigorating, exciting, and helpful in pushing the reader to think about this field in new and compelling ways. Our intention was to provoke all of us to rethink how we "do" WGS and to imagine alternatives.

One of the things that intrigued us the most through the process of writing this book was that even in the earliest drafts of its chapters, we noted authors making overlapping arguments about the consequences of these terms for WGS. While they hadn't yet read each others' contributions, many of their perceptions—both about the versions of WGS the key terms produced and the costs associated with those versions— were often strikingly similar. We were repeatedly taken with their collective argument that WGS has too often not followed through on its own promises, has disavowed what it struggled to set in motion, and, in turn, has not realized its own possibilities. What now strikes us about these chapters is how much they are in conversation with each other; they don't always agree—in fact they sometimes disagree a fair bit with each other, but they all embody careful thinking about and engagement with a similar set of concerns.

In the spirit of "continuing the conversation," what follows is not a conclusion in the more typical sense of a wrapping up of the book's argument(s) and making a quick exit. Rather, we want to highlight this idea of conversation by staging a number of possible encounters among the chapters over the book's entirety (as opposed to just within sections). These questions evoke only some of the possible dialogues and discussions that could potentially evolve from these chapters or from these terms. But they are our way both to "finish" this book and to begin new conversations with new participants.

- What are some of the ways in which Lichtenstein's "Interdisciplinarity" intersects with its obvious corollary term, "Discipline," to explore claims made about the intellectual work of the field?
- How do the chapters in "Foundational Assumptions" explore the ways in which WGS has set itself up as different from other disciplines in the university? Drawing on Side's "Methods" chapter, how important is it to have a unique piece of intellectual territory to defend in higher education contexts?
- How do the chapters on "Waves" or "Sexuality" or "Activism" (which WGS could also claim as foundational to differentiating it from other disciplines) help us think through the costs associated with the desire to be different? What paradoxes of disciplinarity does this desire for difference point to?
- How does the anxiety documented in "Methods" contribute to other stories we tell in WGS both about "Community" as well as "Besiegement?"
- How much do WGS' pedagogical desires for social transformation rest on particular assumptions about the field as an embodiment of "Activism" in the academy (as discussed in Orr's chapter)? How does a pedagogical practice that sees identification (with the professor or as a feminist) as success perpetuate dominant narratives about the field's ideal subject? How do arguments about the field's racialized and gendered subjectiv-

ity, as outlined in "Institutionalization" and "Trans-," challenge this perception of "Pedagogy?"

- How are the dominant narratives detailed in "Community" and "Besiegement" exposed more fully as racialized scripts when considered through Carrillo Rowe's chapter on "Institutionalization?"

- Because all of the terms in the section on "Ubiquitous Descriptions" explore, in part at least, the question of how WGS produces, organizes, or overlooks particular identities—performatively, generationally, or institutionally—how might other chapters that take up arguments about identities in WGS—"Queer" or "Identity (Politics)" or "Trans-"—respond to this section's terms?

- The chapters on "Activism," "Waves," "History," and "Secularity" identify silences and demonstrate the need to tell alternate stories of both the field's pasts and presents. What do these silences have in common? How exactly should the field implement the different approaches that each chapter offers for addressing the silences?

- How can following the "critical practices" outlined in May's "Intersectionality" chapter help to achieve the outcomes advocated in Orr's "Activism," Kolmar's "History," and Johnson's "Sexuality" chapters?

- How might the approaches to theorizing in the section on "Epistemologies Rethought" address the "everything and nothing" paradox that Side observes in her chapter on "Methods," or the "no there there" characterization of WGS that Braithwaite cites in "Discipline?" For example, how do they push perceptions about the boundaries of the field and thereby locate definitions of (or identities for) WGS?

- How might the metaphors of homelessness in "Queer" and the emphasis on migration and flows in "Transnational" mutually inform WGS as a decolonizing knowledge project? What are the arguments for giving up on "home" for the sake of this new kind of decolonizing intellectual work? What other chapters also take up this argument for the benefits of ceding home and its apparent comforts?

- How does Crowley's "Secularity" chapter bolster Maparyan's argument about the need to rethink feminism as the organizing concept for WGS?
- In the same way that Johnson exposes the impact of socially conservative discourses (i.e., of conservative Christianity) about sexuality in WGS, might we also think of the same kinds of discourses at the institutional and/or societal level playing a key role in conversations about "Interdisciplinarity," "Transnational," and "Besiegement?"
- How might the "anger, betrayal, and shame" that Kolmar argues "haunts" WGS' pasts have affected (and still affect) the field's claims of "Besiegement?" What other ways might WGS deal with this haunting, besides the kinds of disavowals articulated in these chapters?
- Parisi's "Transnational" chapter documents a number of conceptual shortcomings in that term's ability to help WGS achieve its inclusive goals. What various levels of scepticism or enthusiasm do other chapters (e.g., "Feminism," "Pedagogy," "Queer," "Trans-") exhibit about their term's ability to achieve those inclusive goals? What might these differences tell us about theorizing about and through key terms?
- Even though chapters in the section on "Establishment Challenges," (as well as "Queer" and "Identity (Politics)") would at one level seem to be about integrating previously excluded bodies and identities into WGS, the authors of "Trans-," "Institutionalization," and "Transnational" make clear that the challenges posed by these terms are much more than another "add and stir" gesture. How do these chapters variously take up the ways in which the boundaries of WGS are inevitably contested through re-investigating these terms?
- Many chapters throughout this book document a kind of institutionally sanctioned white privilege operating in university contexts, including in WGS programs and departments. How might the theoretical frameworks advanced in chapters such as "Trans-," "Institutionalization," "Intersectionality," and "Identity (Politics)" help WGS practitioners develop effective interventions into practices of white privilege at the institutional level?

WEB RESOURCES

The following resources are divided into four sections: (1) Women's and Gender Studies: General Resources; (2) Women's and Gender Studies: Resources Exploring Key Terms and Issues; (3) Sexuality, Genderqueer, Trans Resources; and (4) Antiracist, Transnational, Women of Color Resources.

Readers should note that websites do change or disappear. We have endeavoured here to include sites that have a fair amount of longevity. We have also included a few blogs, recognizing that blogs sometimes have quite tenuous life spans. And, of course, this list is only a very partial reflection of the immense number of resources available.

1. Women's and Gender Studies: General Resources

National Women's Studies Association (NWSA)
Website for the national organization in the United States
http://www.nwsa.org

Canadian Women's Studies Association/L'association canadienne des études sur les femmes
Website for the national organization in Canada
http://www.yorku.ca/cwsaacef

Southeastern Women's Studies Association (SEWSA)
Regional NWSA organziation
http://sewsa.nwsa.org/

Women's Studies/Women's Issues Resource Sites – University of Maryland
Selective and annotated list of web sites containing resources and information about Women's and Gender Studies/women's issues
http://userpages.umbc.edu/~korenman/wmst/links_actv.html

Women's and Gender Studies Programs, Departments, and Research Centers
List of more than 900 links to programs, departments, and research centers with
web sites
http://userpages.umbc.edu/~korenman/wmst/programs.html

Athena Project
Explorations of issues central to Women's and Gender Studies' definition and
practice across Europe
http://www.rosadoc.be/athena/

2. Women's and Gender Studies: Resources Exploring Key Terms and Issues

Gender and Women's Studies and the Question of Activism
Discussion of WGS and activism among professors at Villanova University
http://www.youtube.com/watch?v=B1lc0uVyoPw

Blog of the Society of Friends of the Texts: Monthly Discussion Post December 2010
Discussion post focused on John Mowitt's concept of antidisciplinarity as explicated in his book *Text*
http://www.friendsofthetext.org/?p=318

New Majorities II Conference
Report on conference about the state of Gender and Sexuality Studies in the
Academy hosted by New York University
http://www.csgsnyu.org/2011/05/review-new-majorities-ii-a-cross-coun-
    try-duet-on-the-state-of-gender-and-sexuality-studies-in-the-academy/

Herizons magazine—"Women's Studies" article by Renee Bondy
An article from the Canadian feminist magazine *Herizons* that explores debates
around name changes in the discipline
http://www.herizons.ca/node/439

Questions for a New Century: Women's Studies and Integrative Learning
Report prepared for the National Women's Studies Association in 2007 that
explores common outcomes and assessments of WGS
http://www.nwsa.org/downloads/WS_Integrative_Learning_Levine.pdf

Women's and Gender Studies Core Books List
Website maintained by the University of Wisconsin library system—very broad
definition of "Women's and Gender Studies" as all academic feminist references
http://uwdc.library.wisc.edu/collections/ACRLWSS

Women's Studies and Religion Program: Harvard Divinity School
Site includes a searchable bibliography and links to other sites on women and religion
http://www.hds.harvard.edu/wsrp/

Association for Integrative Studies
Academic professional association devoted to Interdisciplinary Studies; valuable for comparison of definitions of interdisciplinarity
http://www.units.muohio.edu/aisorg/

Center for the Study of Interdisciplinarity at University of North Texas
Provides resources, promotes experiments, identifies institutional barriers, establishes indicators for success of projects, and develops best practices for thinking about what constitutes interdisciplinarity
http://www.csid.unt.edu/

Interdisciplines
Group of French philosophers, artists, social scientists, and digital designers which runs online conferences and promotes intelligent use of new technologies across and between disciplines
http://interdisciplines.org/index.php

The Supressed Histories Archives: Real Women, Global Vision
Goddess/women's history archive, compiled by Max Dashu, documents female images through history, especially spiritual ones
http://www.suppressedhistories.net/

Interviews conducted by Patrick Brindle, Research Methods Publisher at SAGE
Dr. Sharlene Nagy Hesse-Biber talks about feminist research methods in this two-part interview
http://www.youtube.com/watch?v=xGtF_C_r1HE

Third Wave Foundation
A feminist, activist foundation that works to support young women and transgender youth working towards gender, racial, economic, and social justice
www.thirdwavefoundation.org

National Women's History Project
Organizes and sponsors activities that promote women as influential forces in society and provides information about the unfolding roles of women in American history
http://www.nwhp.org/

3. Sexuality, Genderqueer, Trans Resources

Queertheory.com
Resources for all things related to queer culture, queer studies, gender studies, queer theory, and related fields
http://www.queertheory.com/

Queer Theory Links
Multiple links to online resources about queer theory
http://www.queerbychoice.com/qtheorylinks.html

Lambda Legal
National organization committed to achieving full recognition of the civil rights of lesbians, gay men, bisexuals, transgender people, and those with HIV through impact litigation, education and public policy work
http://www.lambdalegal.org/

Trans@MIT Allies Toolkit
Useful terminology provided as part of MIT trans resources website
http://web.mit.edu/trans/TGterminology.pdf

National Sexuality Resource Center
NSRC is committed to advancing sexual literacy through science, sexuality education, and social policy formation
http://nsrc.sfsu.edu/

Parents and Friends of Lesbians and Gays (PFLAG) – Trans Support
Support, research, and outreach for people who are transgendered
http://www.pflagcanada.ca/en/helpframe-e.asp?helpframe=links-e.asp?audience=transsexual

A Gender Variance Who's Who
Listing of key historical and contemporary trans theorists
http://zagria.blogspot.com/

T-Vox on Transfeminism
Site that articulates trans-feminisms in theory and practice
http://www.t-vox.org/index.php?title=Transfeminism_

Queer Black Feminist
San Francisco State University sociologist blogs about queer black feminism
http://queerblackfeminist.blogspot.com/

4. Antiracist, Transnational, Women of Color Resources

Agenda
African feminist journal that seeks to empower women for gender equity
http://www.tandf.co.uk/journals/RAGN

Black Feminism LIVES!
Blog site by black feminist (Alexis Pauline Gumbs) with womanist sensibilities
http://blackfeminismlives.tumblr.com/

Interview with Layli Maparyan
About Maparyan's work helping to establish Gender Studies at University of Liberia
http://ceasefireliberia.com/2010/07/interview-wlayli-maparyan/

Voices from the Gaps
Academic database of works by women writers and activists of color
http://voices.cla.umn.edu/

Incite: Women of Color Against Violence
Extensive network of activist women of color
http://www.incite-national.org/

Women of Color United: End Violence Against Women and HIV & AIDS
U.S.-based organization founded to advocate around the intersection of violence agains women and HIV/AIDS globally
http://www.womenofcolorunited.org/women-of-color-united-platform/

African American Policy Forum
Think tank advocating racial justice, gender equality, and human rights with an "intersectionality primer"
http://aapf.org/learn_the_issues/intersectionality/

Association for Women in Development
Guide for implementing intersectionality in advocacy, policy, and development work
http://www.awid.org/Library/Intersectionality-A-Tool-for-Gender-and-Economic-Justice2

Central American Women's Network
Examples of implementing intersectionality in work on violence against women and girls
http://www.cawn.org/11/index.htm

Womanist Musings
Blog by womanist which also features activist, antiracist guest bloggers
http://www.womanist-musings.com/

Antiracism.com
Targeted at youth antiracist activism and education; offers tools and dialogue about racism to promote social justice
http://www.antiracism.com/

The Critical Multicultural Pavillion
Resources for antiracist education, such as workshops and training opportunities
http://www.edchange.org/multicultural/index.html

The Antiracist Alliance
Resources and information about antiracist movement building
http://www.antiracistalliance.com/

Internationalization of Higher Education: Global Trends Regional Perspectives
Summary of survey about global education as well as links to popular press articles about the survey
http://www.iau-aiu.net/content/latest-activity

UN Women: United Nations Entity for Gender Equality and the Empowerment of Women
Hub for global and transnational feminism; information about networks, women's world conferences, etc.
http://www.unwomen.org/

WomenStats Project and Database
Database on women's status with 310 indicators of women's status in 174 countries, with maps
http://www.womanstats.org/

REFERENCES

Aaron, Jane, and Sylvia Walby. 1991. *Out of the Margins: Women's Studies in the Nineties*. London: Falmer Press.

Ahmed, Sara. 2006a. "Orientations: Toward a Queer Phenomenology." *GLQ: A Journal of Lesbian and Gay Studies* 12 (4): 543–74.

———. 2006b. *Queer Phenomenology: Orientations, Objects, Others*. Durham, NC: Duke University Press.

Aikau, Hokulani K. 2007. "Between Wind and Water: Thinking about the Third Wave as Metaphor and Materiality." In *Feminist Waves, Feminist Generations*, edited by Hokulani K. Aikau, Karla A. Erickson, and Jennifer L. Pierce, 232–49. Minneapolis: University of Minnesota Press.

Aisenberg, Nadya, and Mona Harrington. 1988. *Women of Academe: Outsiders in the Sacred Grove*. Amherst: University of Massachusetts.

al-Hibri, Azizah. 2004. "Azizah al-Hibri." In *Transforming the Faiths of Our Fathers: Women Who Changed American Religion*, edited by Ann Braude, 47–54. New York: Palgrave.

Alarcón, Norma. 1990. "The Theoretical Subject(s) of This Bridge Called My Back and Anglo American Feminism." In *Making Face, Making Soul* Haciendo Caras: *Creative and Critical Perspectives by Feminists of Color*, edited by Gloria E. Anzaldúa, 356–69. San Francisco: Aunt Lute Books.

Alcoff, Linda. 1988. "Cultural Feminism versus Post-Structuralism: The Identity Crisis in Feminist Theory." *Signs: Journal of Women in Culture and Society* 13 (3): 405–36.

Alexander, M. Jacqui. 2005. *Pedagogies of Crossing: Meditations on Feminism, Sexual Politics, Memory, and the Sacred*. Durham, NC: Duke University Press.

Alexander, M. Jacqui, and Chandra Talpade Mohanty, eds. 1997. *Feminist Genealogies, Colonial Legacies, Democratic Futures*. New York: Routledge.

———. 2001. "Genealogies, Legacies, Movements." In *Feminism and 'Race,'* edited by Kum-Kum Bhavnani, 492–515. Oxford: Oxford University Press.

———. 2010. "Cartographies of Knowledge and Power: Transnational Feminism as Radical Praxis." In *Critical Transnational Feminist Praxis*, edited by Amanda Lock Swarr and Richa Nagar, 23–45. Albany: SUNY Press.

Allen, Judith A., and Sally L. Kitch. 1998. "Disciplined by Disciplines? The Need for an *Interdisciplinary* Research Mission in Women's Studies." *Feminist Studies* 24 (2): 275–99.

Allison, Dorothy. 1996. *Two or Three Things I Know for Sure*. New York: Penguin.

Altman, Meryl. 2003. "Beyond Trashiness: The Sexual Language of 1970s Feminist Fiction." *Journal of International Women's Studies* 4 (2): 7–19.

Alvarez, Sonia E. 1999. "Advocating Feminism: The Latin American Feminist NGO 'Boom'." *International Feminist Journal of Politics* 1 (2): 181–209.

Anzaldúa, Gloria. 1983. "O.K. Momma, Who the Hell Am I?: An Interview with Luisah Teish." In *This Bridge Called My Back: Writings by Radical Women of Color*, 221–31, edited by Cherríe Moraga and Gloria Anzaldúa. New York: Kitchen Table, Women of Color Press.

———. ed. 1990a. *Making Face, Making Soul* Haciendo Caras: *Creative and Critical Perspectives by Feminists of Color*. San Francisco: Aunt Lute Books.

———. 1990b. *"En rapport*, In Opposition: *Cobrando cuentas a las nuestras."* In *Making Face, Making Soul* Haciendo Caras: *Creative and Critical Perspectives by Feminists of Color*, edited by Gloria E. Anzaldúa, 142–48. San Francisco: Aunt Lute Books.

———. 1990c. *"Hablando cara a cara*/Speaking Face to Face." In *Making Face, Making Soul* Haciendo Caras: *Creative and Critical Perspectives by Feminists of Color*, edited by Gloria E. Anzaldúa, 46–54. San Francisco: Aunt Lute Books.

——— 1990d. *"Haciendo caras, una entrada."* In *Making Face, Making Soul* Haciendo Caras: *Creative and Critical Perspectives by Feminists of Color*, edited by Gloria E. Anzaldúa, xv–xxviii. San Francisco: Aunt Lute Books.

———. 1990e. *"La conciencia de la mestiza*: Towards a New Consciousness." In *Making Face, Making Soul* Haciendo Caras: *Creative and Critical Perspectives by Feminists of Color*, edited by Gloria E. Anzaldúa, 377–89. San Francisco: Aunt Lute Books.

———. 1990f. "Bridge, Drawbridge, Sandbar, Island: Lesbians of Color Hacienda Alianzas." In *Bridges of Power*, edited by L. Albrecht, and R. Brewer, 216–31. Philadelphia: New Society.

———. 1999. *Borderlands*/La frontera: *The New Mestiza*. San Francisco: Aunt Lute Books. First published 1987.

———. 2002. "Preface: (Un)natural Bridges, (Un)safe Spaces." In *This Bridge We Call Home*, edited by Gloria Anzaldúa and AnaLouise Keating. New York: Routledge.

Arenal, Electra. 2000. "What Women Writers?" In *The Politics of Women's Studies: Testimony from 30 Founding Mothers*, edited by Florence Howe, 183–93. New York: Feminist Press.

Asad, Talal. 2003. *Formations of the Secular: Christianity, Islam, Modernity*. Stanford, CA: Stanford University Press.

"Association for Integrative Studies." http://www.units.muohio.edu/aisorg.

Auslander, Leora. 1997. "Do Women's + Feminist + Men's + Lesbian and Gay + Queer Studies = Gender Studies?" *differences: A Journal of Feminist Cultural Studies* 9 (3): 1.

Babbitt, Susan E. 2001. "Objectivity and the Role of Bias." In *Engendering Rationalities*, edited by Nancy Tuana, and Sandra Morgen, 297–314. Albany: SUNY Press.

Bailey, Alison. 1998. "Privilege: Expanding on Marilyn Frye's 'Oppression'." *Journal of Social Philosophy* 29 (3): 104–19.

Baker, Russell. 1981. "There Is No There Here." *New York Times*, May 2: 23.

Balliet, Barbara J., ed. 2007. *Women, Culture, and Society: A Reader.* Dubuque: Kendall Hunt.

Bannerji, Himani, Linda Carty, Kari Delhi, Susan Heald, and Kate McKenna. 1992. *Unsettling Relations: The University as a Site of Feminist Struggles.* Boston: South End Press.

Barlow, Tani. 2000. "International Feminism of the Future." *Signs: Journal of Women in Culture and Society* 25 (4): 1099–1105.

Basu, Amrita, ed. 1995. *The Challenge of Local Feminisms: Women's Movements in Global Perspective.* Boulder: Westview Press.

Baxandall, Rosalyn. 2001. "Re-visioning the Women's Liberation Movement's Narrative: Early Second Wave African American Feminists." *Feminist Studies* 27(1): 225–45.

Beale, Frances. 1970. "Double Jeopardy: To Be Black and Female." In *The Black Woman*, edited by Toni Cade, 90–100. New York: Mentor.

Bedi, Kiran. 2002. *It's Always Possible: One Woman's Transformation of India's Prison System.* Honesdale, PA: Himalayan Institute Press.

Begley, Sharon. 2002. "A Crucial Test for Feminism." *Newsweek* 136 (18): 70.

Belenky, Mary Field, Blythe McVicker Clinchy, Nancy Rule Goldberger, and Jill Mattuck Tarule. 1986. *Women's Ways of Knowing: The Development of Self, Voice, and Mind.* New York: Basic Books.

Bell, Catherine. 1992. *Ritual Theory, Ritual Practice.* New York: Oxford University Press.

Berger, Melody. 2006. *We Don't Need Another Wave: Dispatches from the Next Generation of Feminists.* Berkeley CA: Seal Press.

Bhavnani, Kum-Kum, ed. 2001. *Feminism and 'Race.'* New York: Oxford University Press.

Binkley, Sam. 2007. *Getting Loose: Lifestyle Consumption in the 1970s.* Durham, NC: Duke University Press.

Bird, Elizabeth. 2001. "Disciplining the Interdisciplinary: Radicalism and the Academic Curriculum." *British Journal of Sociology of Education* 22 (4): 463–78.

Blackwell, Maylei. 2003. "Contested Histories: Las Hijas De Cuauhtémoc, Chicana Feminisms and Print Culture in the Chicano Movement, 1968–1973." In *Chicana Feminisms: A Critical Reader*, edited by Gabriella Arredondo, Aida Hurtado, Norma Klahn, Olga Nájera-Ramirez, and Patricia Zavella, 59–89. Durham, NC: Duke University Press.

Blee, Kathleen. 2002. "Contending with Disciplinarity." In *Women's Studies on Its Own*, edited by Robyn Wiegman, 177–82. Durham, NC: Duke University Press.

Bordo, Susan. 1999. "Feminist Skepticism and the 'Maleness' of Philosophy." In

Feminist Approaches to Theory and Methodology: An Interdisciplinary Reader, edited by Sharlene Hesse-Biber, Christina Gilmartin, and Robin Lydenberg, 29–44. New York: Oxford University Press.

Bowleg, Lisa. 2008. "When Black + Lesbian + Woman ≠ Black Lesbian Woman: The Methodological Challenges of Qualitative and Quantitative Intersectionality Research." *Sex Roles* 59 (5-6): 312–25.

Bowles, Gloria, and Renate Duelli Klein, eds. 1983. *Theories of Women's Studies*. London: Routledge and Kegan Paul.

Boxer, Marilyn Jacoby. 1988. "For and About Women: The Theory and Practice of Women's Studies in the United States." In *Reconstructing the Academy: Women's Education and Women's Studies*, edited by Elizabeth Minnich, Jean O'Barr, and Rachel Rosenfeld, 69–103. Chicago: University of Chicago Press. First published 1982.

———. 1998a. "Remapping the University: The Promise of the Women's Studies Ph.D." *Feminist Studies* 24 (2): 387–402.

———. 1998b. *When Women Ask the Questions: Creating Women's Studies in America*. Baltimore: The Johns Hopkins University Press.

———. 2000. "Unruly Knowledge: Women's Studies and the Problem of Disciplinarity." *NWSA Journal* 12 (2): 119–29.

Boyd, Nan Alamilla. 2005. "What Does Queer Studies Offer Women's Studies? The Problem and Promise of Instability." In *Women's Studies for the Future: Foundations, Interrogations, Politics*, edited by Elizabeth Lapovsky Kennedy, and Agatha Beins, 97–108. New Brunswick: Rutgers.

Braithwaite, Ann. 2004. "'Where We've Been' and 'Where We're Going': Reflecting on Reflections of Women's Studies and 'The Women's Movement'." In *Troubling Women's Studies: Pasts, Presents and Possibilities*, 91–146. Toronto: Sumach Press.

Braithwaite, Ann, Susan Heald, Susanne Luhmann, and Sharon Rosenberg. 2004. *Troubling Women's Studies: Pasts, Presents and Possibilities*. Toronto: Sumach Press.

———. 2004. "'Passing on' Women's Studies." In *Troubling Women's Studies: Pasts, Presents and Possibilities*, 9–41. Toronto: Sumach Press.

Briskin, Linda. 1990. *Feminist Pedagogy: Teaching and Learning Liberation*. Ottawa: Canadian Research Institute for the Advancement of Women.

Britzman, Deborah P. 1998. *Lost Subjects, Contested Objects: Toward a Psychoanalytic Inquiry of Learning*. Albany: SUNY Press.

Brown, Wendy. 2008. "The Impossibility of Women's Studies." *Women's Studies on the Edge*, edited by Joan Wallach Scott, 17–38. Durham, NC: Duke University Press. First published 1997.

Brownmiller, Susan. 1999. *In Our Time: A Memoir of a Revolution*. New York: Dial Press.

Bryson, Valerie. 2007. *Gender and the Politics of Time: Feminist Theory and Contemporary Debates*. Bristol: Policy Press. First published in 2002.

Buhle, Mari Jo. 2000. "Introduction." In *The Politics of Women's Studies: Testimony from 30 Founding Mothers*, edited by Florence Howe, xv–xxvi. New York: Feminist Press.

Buker, Eloise. 2003. "Is Women's Studies a Disciplinary or an Interdisciplinary Field of Inquiry?" *NWSA Journal* 15 (1): 73–93.

Bulkin, Elly, Minnie Bruce Pratt, and Barbara Smith. 1984. *Yours In Struggle: Three Feminists Perspectives on Anti-Semitism and Racism.* Ann Arbor, MI: Firebrand Books.

Butler, Judith. 1982. "Lesbian S & M: The Politics of Dis-illusion." In *Against Sadomasochism: A Radical Feminist Analysis,* edited by Robin Ruth Linden, Darlene R. Pagano, Diana E.H. Russell, and Susan Leigh Star, 169–82. San Francisco: Frog in the Well.

———. 1993. *Bodies that Matter: On the Discursive Limits of "Sex".* New York: Routledge.

———. 1994. "Against Proper Objects." *differences: A Journal of Feminist Cultural Studies* 6 (2–3): 1–27.

———. 1999. *Gender Trouble: Feminism and the Subversion of Identity, 2nd Edition.* New York: Routledge. First published in 1990.

———. 2004a. *Undoing Gender.* New York: Routledge.

———. 2004b. *Precarious Life: The Powers of Mourning and Violence.* London: Verso.

———. 2005. *Giving an Account of Oneself.* New York: Fordham University Press.

———. 2008. "Sexual Politics, Torture, and Secular Time." *British Journal of Sociology* 59 (1): 1–23.

Cade, Toni. 1970. *The Black Woman: An Anthology.* New York: Mentor.

Cao, Ngoc Phuong (Sister Chan Khong). 2007. *Learning True Love: Practicing Buddhism in a Time of War.* Berkeley: Parallax Press.

Carbado, Devon W. 1999. *Black Men on Race, Gender, and Sexuality.* New York: New York University Press.

Carrillo Rowe, Aimee. 2008. *Power Lines: On the Subject of Feminist Alliances.* Durham, NC: Duke University Press.

Caruth, Cathy. 1996. *Unclaimed Experience: Trauma, Narrative, and History.* Baltimore: Johns Hopkins Press.

Caughie, Pamela. 2003a. "Graduate Education in Women's Studies: Paradoxes and Challenges." *Feminist Studies* 29 (2): 405–08.

———. 2003b. "Professional Identity Politics." *Feminist Studies* 29 (2): 422–34.

Caughie, Pamela, and Jennifer Parks. 2009. "Disciplined or Punished? The Future of Graduate Education in Women's Studies." *Atlantis: A Women's Studies Journal* 33 (2): 32–41.

Chancer, Lynn. 1998. *Reconcilable Differences: Confronting Beauty, Pornography, and the Future of Feminism.* Berkeley: University of California Press.

Chapkis, Wendy. 1997. *Live Sex Acts: Women Performing Erotic Labor.* New York: Routledge.

Chatterjee, Piya. 2002. "Encountering 'Third World Women': Rac(e)ing the Global in a U.S. Classroom." *Pedagogy: Critical Approaches to Teaching Literature, Language, Composition, and Culture* 2 (1): 79–108.

Chilly Collective, eds. 1995. *Breaking Anonymity: The Chilly Climate for Women Faculty.* Waterloo: Wilfred Laurier Press.

China Blue. 2005. [Film] Directed by Micha X. Peled. San Francisco: Teddy Bear Films.

Christian, Barbara. 1990a. "The Race for Theory." In *Making Face, Making Soul Haciendo Caras: Creative and Critical Perspectives by Feminists of Color,* edited by Gloria E. Anzaldúa, 335–45. San Francisco: Aunt Lute Books.

———. 1990b. "Conference Call." *differences: A Journal of Feminist Cultural Studies* 2 (3): 52–108.

Christiansen-Ruffman, Linda. 2007. "Women, Knowledge and Change: Gender is Not Enough." *Resources for Feminist Research* 32 (1-2): 114–38.

Chowdhury, Elora Halim. 2009. "Locating Global Feminisms Elsewhere: Braiding U.S. Women of Color and Transnational Feminisms." *Cultural Dynamics* 21 (1): 51–78.

Clark, VéVé, Shirley Nelson Garner, Margaret Hignnot, and Ketru H. Katrak, eds. 1996. *Antifeminism in the Academy.* New York: Routledge.

Coates, Jacky, Michelle Dodds, and Jodi Jensen. 1998. "Isn't Just Being Here Political Enough? Feminist Action-Oriented Research as a Challenge to Graduate Women's Studies." *Feminist Studies* 24 (2): 333–47.

Cohen, Cathy. 1997. "Punks, Bulldaggers, and Welfare Queens: The Radical Potential of Queer Politics." *GLQ: A Journal of Lesbian and Gay Studies* 3: 437–65.

———. 1999. *The Boundaries of Blackness: AIDS and the Breakdown of Black Politics.* Chicago: University of Chicago Press.

Cohn, Carol. 1999. "Globalizing Women's Studies: Pitfalls and Possibilities." *International Feminist Journal of Politics* 1 (2): 257–83.

Cole, Elizabeth R. 2008. "Coalitions as a Model for Intersectionality: From Practice to Theory." *Sex Roles* 59 (5-6): 443–53.

Collins, Patricia Hill. 1990. *Black Feminist Thought: Knowledge, Consciousness, and the Politics of Empowerment.* Boston: Unwin Hyman.

———. 1998. *Fighting Words: Black Women and the Search for Justice.* Minneapolis: University of Minnesota.

———. 2004. *Black Sexual Politics: African Americans, Gender, and the New Racism.* New York: Routledge.

———. 2008. "Reply to Commentaries: *Black Sexual Politics* Revisited." *Studies in Gender and Sexuality* 9: 68–85.

Combahee River Collective. 1983. "The Combahee River Collective Statement." In *Home Girls: A Black Feminist Anthology,* edited by Barbara Smith, 272–82. New York: Kitchen Table Press. First Published 1977.

Conkey, Margaret W., and Ruth E. Tringham. 1995. "Archaeology and the Goddess: Exploring the Contours of Feminist Archaeology." In *Feminisms in the Academy,* edited by Domna C. Stanton, and Abigail J. Stewart, 199–247. Ann Arbor: University of Michigan Press.

Conkey, Margaret W., and Sarah H. Williams. 1991. "Original Narratives: The Political Economy of Gender in Archaeology." In *Gender at the Crossroads of Knowledge: Feminist Anthropology in the Postmodern Era,* edited by Micaela di Leonardo, 102–39. Berkeley: University of California Press.

Cooper, Anna Julia. 1988. *A Voice from the South by a Black Woman of the South.* New York: Oxford University Press. First Published 1892.

———. 1925. *L'Attitude de la France à l'égard de l'esclavage pendant la Révolution.* Paris: impr. de la cour d'appel, L. Maretheux.

Coyner, Sandra. 1983. "Women's Studies as an Academic Discipline: Why and How to Do It." In *Theories of Women's Studies,* edited by Gloria Bowles, and Renate Duelli Klein, 44–71. London: Routledge and Kegan Paul.

Coyner, Sandra. 1991. "Women's Studies." *NWSA Journal* 3 (3): 349–54.

Creet, Julia. 1991. "Daughters of the Movement: The Psychodynamics of Lesbian S/M Fantasy." *differences: A Journal of Feminist Cultural Studies* 3(2): 135–59.

Crenshaw, Kimberlé. 2000. "Demarginalizing the Intersection of Race and Sex: A Black Feminist Critique of Antidiscrimination Doctrine, Feminist Theory, and Antiracist Politics." In *The Black Feminist Reader,* edited by Joy James, and T. Denean Sharpley-Whiting, 208–38. Malden: Blackwell.

Crowley, Helen. 1990. "Women's Studies: Between a Rock and a Hard Place or Just Another Cell in the Beehive?" *Feminist Review* 61 (Spring): 131–50.

Cuomo, Chris. 2003. *The Philosopher Queen: Feminist Essays on War, Love, and Knowledge.* Lanham, MD: Rowman and Littlefield.

Davis, Angela Y. 1984. *Women, Race and Class.* New York: Vintage.

Davis, Dawn Rae. 2010. "Unmirroring Pedagogies: Teaching with Intersectional and Transnational Methods in the Women and Gender Studies Classroom." *Feminist Formations* 22 (1): 136–62.

Davis, Flora. 1991. *Moving the Mountain: The Women's Movement in America since 1960.* New York: Simon & Schuster.

Davis, Kathy. 2008. "Intersectionality as Buzzword: A Sociology of Science Perspective on What Makes a Feminist Theory Successful." *Feminist Theory* 9 (1): 67–85.

Davis, Philip G. 1998. *Goddess Unmasked: The Rise of Neopagan Feminist Spirituality.* Dallas: Spence Publishing Inc.

De la Tierra, Tatiana. 2002. "Aliens and Others in Search of the Tribe in Academe." In *This Bridge We Call Home: Radical Visions for Transformation,* edited by Gloria Anzaldúa, and AnaLouise Keating, 358–68. New York: Routledge.

De Lauretis, Teresa. 1986. "Feminist Studies/Critical Studies: Issues, Terms, and Contexts." In *Feminist Studies/Critical Studies,* edited by Teresa de Lauretis, 1–19. Bloomington: Indiana University Press.

Di Leonardo, Micaela. 1998. *Exotics at Home Anthropologies, Others, American Modernity.* Chicago: University of Chicago Press.

Diamond, Elin. 1992. "The Violence of 'We': Politicizing Identification." In *Critical Theory and Performance,* edited by Janelle G. Reinelt and Joseph R. Rosch, 390–98. Ann Arbor: University of Michigan Press.

Diamond, Irene, and Lee Quimby. 1988. *Feminism and Foucault: Reflections on Resistance.* Boston: Northeastern University Press.

Dicker, Rory, and Alison Piepmeier, eds. 2003. *Catching a Wave: Reclaiming Feminism for the 21st Century.* Boston: Northeastern University Press.

Dinnerstein, Myra. 2000. "A Political Education." In *The Politics of Women's Studies: Testimony from 30 Founding Mothers,* edited by Florence Howe, 291–305. New York: The Feminist Press.

Dolling, Irene, and Sabine Hark. 2000. "She Who Speaks Shadow Speaks Truth: Transdisciplinarity in Women's and Gender Studies." *Signs: Journal of Women in Culture and Society* 25 (4): 1195–98.

Donovan, Josephine. 2000. "A Cause of Our Own." In *The Politics of Women's Studies: Testimony from 30 Founding Mothers,* edited by Florence Howe, 93–103. New York: The Feminist Press.

Douglas, Kelly Brown. 1989. *Sexuality and the Black Church: A Womanist Perspective.* Maryknoll, NY: Orbis.

DuCille, Anne. 2001. "The Occult of True Black Womanhood: Critical Demeanor and Black Feminist Studies." In *Feminism & 'Race,'* edited by Kum-Kum Bhavnani, 233–60. New York: Oxford University Press.

Duelli-Klein, Renate, 1991. "Passion and Politics in Women's Studies in the Nineties." *Women's Studies International Forum,* 14 (3): 125–34.

Duggan, Lisa. 1992. "Making It Perfectly Queer." *Socialist Review* 22: 11–31.

———. 2004. *The Twilight of Equality: Neoliberalism, Cultural Politics, and the Attack on Democracy.* Boston: Beacon Press.

Elam, Diane. 1997. "Sisters are Doing It to Themselves." In *Generations: Academic Feminists in Dialogue,* edited by Devoney Looser and E. Ann Kaplan, 55–68. Minneapolis: University of Minnesota Press.

———. 2002. "Taking Account of Women's Studies." In *Women's Studies on Its Own,* edited by Robyn Wiegman, 218–23. Durham, NC: Duke University Press.

Eller, Cynthia. 2000. *The Myth of Matriarchal Prehistory: Why an Invented Past Won't Give Women a Future.* Boston: Beacon Press.

Ellsworth, Elizabeth. 1992. "Why Doesn't This Feel Empowering: Working Through the Repressive Myths of Critical Pedagogy." In *Feminisms and Critical Pedagogy,* edited by Carmen Luke and Jennifer Gore. 90–119. New York: Routledge. First published in 1989.

———. 1997. *Teaching Positions: Difference, Pedagogy, and the Power of Address.* New York: Teachers College Press.

Erickson, Karla A. 2007 "On Taking Feminism for Granted: Reflections of a Third Generation Feminist." In *Feminist Waves, Feminist Generations,* edited by Hokulani K. Aikau, Karla A. Erickson, and Jennifer L. Pierce, 318–47. Minneapolis: University of Minnesota Press.

Eudey, Betsy. 2007. "The Role of Women's and Gender Studies in Advancing Gender Equity." In *Handbook for Achieving Gender Equity Through Education,* edited by Susan S. Klein, 445–564. Mahwah, NJ: Erlbaum.

Farley, Tucker Pamella. 2000. "Changing Signs." In *The Politics of Women's Studies: Testimony from 30 Founding Mothers,* edited by Florence Howe, 264–75. New York: Feminist Press.

Farnham, Christie. 1987. *The Impact of Feminist Research in the Academy.* Bloomington: Indiana University Press.

Felman, Shoshana. 1987. *Jacques Lacan and the Adventure of Insight: Psychoanalysis in Contemporary Culture.* Cambridge: Harvard University Press.

Ferguson, Ann. 1984. "Sex War: The Debate between Radical and Libertarian Feminists." *Signs: A Journal of Women in Culture and Society* 10 (1): 106–12.

Fessenden, Tracy. 2007. *Culture and Redemption: Religion, the Secular, and American Literature*. Princeton: Princeton University Press.

Findlen, Barbara, ed. 1995. *Listen Up: Voices from the Next Feminist Generation*. Seattle, WA: Seal Press.

Finke, Laurie. 1993. "Knowledge as Bait: Feminism, Voice, and the Pedagogical Unconscious." *College English* 55 (1): 7–27.

Fonow, Mary Margaret, and Judith Cook. 2005. "Feminist Methodology: New Applications in the Academy and Public Policy." *Signs: A Journal of Women in Culture and Society* 30 (4): 2211–36.

Foucault, Michel. 1977. *Discipline and Punish*. Translated by Alan Sheridan. New York: Pantheon. First published in French in 1975.

———. 1988–90. *History of Sexuality*, 3 volumes: *Introduction, The Uses of Pleasure*, and *Care of the Self*. Translated by Robert Hurley. New York: Vintage Books. First published in French in 1976–1984.

Frazer, Nancy, and Nicola Lacey. 1993. *The Politics of Community: A Feminist Critique of the Liberal-Communitarian Debate*. Toronto: University of Toronto Press.

Freire, Paulo. 1970. *Pedagogy of the Oppressed*. New York: Continuum.

Friedman, Susan Stanford. 1998. "(Inter)Disciplinarity and the Question of the Women's Studies Ph.D." *Feminist Studies* 24 (2): 301–25.

———. 2001. "Academic Feminism and Interdisciplinarity." *Feminist Studies* 27 (2): 504–9.

———. 2002. "What Should Every Women's Studies Major Know? Reflections on the Capstone Seminar." In *Women's Studies On Its Own*, edited by Robyn Wiegman, 416–37. Durham, NC: Duke University Press.

Frye, Marilyn. 1983. "Oppression." In *The Politics of Reality: Essays in Feminist Theory*, 1–16. Trumansburg: Crossing Press.

Fuller, Robert. 2001. *Spiritual But Not Religious: Understanding Unchurched America*. New York: Oxford University Press.

Fuss, Diana. 1995. *The Identification Papers*. New York: Routledge.

"The Future of Women's Studies." January 2009. WMST-L archives. https://listserv.umd.ed/cgi-bin/wa?A1=ind0901e&L=wmst-1. Accessed May 2011.

Gallop, Jane. 1982. *The Daughter's Seduction: Feminism and Psychoanalysis*. Ithaca, NY: Cornell University Press.

———. 1988. *Thinking through the Body*. New York: Columbia University Press.

———. 1992. *Around 1981: Academic Feminist Literary Theory*. New York: Routledge.

———, ed. 1995. *Pedagogy: The Question of Impersonation*. Bloomington: Indiana University Press.

Garber, Marjorie. 2000. *Academic Instincts*. Princeton, NJ: Princeton University Press.

Garrison, Ednie Kaeh. 2005. "Are We On a Wavelength Yet? On Feminist Oceanography, Radios, and Third Wave Feminism." In *Different Wavelengths: Studies of the Contemporary Women's Movement*, edited by Jo Reger, 237–56. New York: Routledge.

———. 2000. "U.S. Feminism-Grrrl Style! Youth (Sub)Cultures and the Tech-nologics of the Third Wave." *Feminist Studies* 26 (1): 141–70.

Gerhard, Jane. 2001. *Desiring Revolution: Second-Wave Feminism and the Rewriting of American Sexual Thought, 1920–1982*. New York: Columbia University Press.

Giddings, Paula J. 2006. "Editor's Introduction." *Meridians* 7 (1): v–vii.

Gillis, Stacy, and Rebecca Munford. 2003. "Harvesting Our Strengths: Third Wave Feminism and Women's Studies." *Journal of International Women's Studies* 4 (2): 1–6.

Gluck, Sherna Berger, Maylei Blackwell, Sharon Cotrell, and Karen S. Harper. 1997. "Whose Feminism, Whose History?: Reflections on Excavating the History of (the) U.S. Women's Movement(s)." In *Community Activism and Feminist Politics: Organizing across Race, Class, and Gender*, edited by Nancy Naples, 31–56. New York: Routledge.

Goldsack, Laura. 1999. "A Haven in a Heartless World? Women and Domestic Violence." In *Ideal Homes? Social Change and Domestic Life*, edited by Tony Chapman and Jenny Hockey, 121–32. New York: Taylor & Francis.

Goodison, Lucy, and Christine Morris, eds. 1998. *Ancient Goddesses: The Myths and the Evidence*. London: British Museum Press.

Gordon, Avery. 1996. *Ghostly Matters: Haunting and the Sociological Imagination*. Minnesota: University of Minnesota Press.

Gordon, Linda. 1975. "A Socialist View of Women's Studies: A Reply to the Editorial, Volume 1, Number 1." *Signs: A Journal of Women in Culture and Society* 1 (2): 559–66.

Gore, Jennifer. 1992. *The Struggle for Pedagogies: Critical and Feminist Discourses as Regimes of Truth*. New York and London: Routledge.

Gorham, Deborah. 1996. "In Defense of Discipline Based Scholarship." In *Graduate Women's Studies: Visions and Realities*, edited by Ann Shteir, 59–68. Toronto: Inanna.

Govender, Pregs. 2007. *Love and Courage: A Story of Insubordination*. Auckland Park: Jacana Media (Pty) Ltd.

Grace, Nancy. 1996. "An Exploration of the Interdisciplinary Character of Women's Studies." *Issues in Integrative Studies* 14: 59–86.

Graff, Agnieszka. 2003. "Lost between the Waves?: The Paradoxes of Feminist Chronology and Activism in Contemporary Poland." *Journal of International Women's Studies* 4 (2): 100–16.

Graul, Christine, Elizabeth Kennedy, Lissian Robinson, and Bonnie Zimmer-man. 1972. "Women's Studies: A Case in Point." *Feminist Studies* 1 (2): 109–20.

Grewal, Inderpal. 2005. *Transnational America: Feminism, Diasporas, Neoliberal-isms*. Durham, NC: Duke University Press.

Grewal, Inderpal, and Caren Kaplan, eds. 1994. *Scattered Hegemonies: Postmo-dernity and Transnational Feminist Practices*. Minneapolis: University of Minnesota Press.

———. 2001. "Global Identities: Theorizing Transnational Studies of Sexual-ity." *Gay and Lesbian Quarterly* 7 (4): 663–79.

———. 2002. "Transnational Practices and Interdisciplinary Scholarship:

Refiguring Women's and Gender Studies." In *Women's Studies on Its Own*, edited by Robyn Wiegman, 66–81. Durham, NC: Duke University Press.

———, eds. 2006. *An Introduction to Women's Studies: Gender in a Transnational World*. 2nd ed. New York: McGraw-Hill.

Grosz, Elizabeth. 2000. "Histories of a Feminist Future." In *Feminisms at a Millennium*, edited by Judith A. Howard and Carolyn Allen, 28–32. Chicago: University of Chicago Press.

Gubar, Susan. 1998. "What Ails Feminist Criticism?" *Critical Inquiry* 24 (4): 878–902.

———. 2006. *Rooms of Our Own*. Illinois: University of Illinois Press.

Gumport, Patricia. 2002. *Academic Pathfinders: Knowledge Creation and Feminist Scholarship*. Westport, CT: Greenwood.

Gunew, Sneja. 2002. "Feminist Cultural Literacy: Translating Differences, Cannibal Options." In *Women's Studies on Its Own*, edited by Robyn Wiegman, 47–65. Durham, NC: Duke University Press.

Guy-Sheftall, Beverly, ed. 1995a. *Words of Fire: An Anthology of African-American Feminist Thought*. New York: New Press.

———. 1995b. "The Evolution of Feminist Consciousness Among African American Women." In *Words of Fire*, 1–22. New York: New Press.

———. 1995c. *Women's Studies, A Retrospective: A Report for the Ford Foundation*. New York: Ford Foundation.

Guy-Sheftall, Beverly, and Evelynn M. Hammonds. 2005. "Whither Black Women's Studies: An Interview, 1997–2004." In *Women's Studies for the Future: Foundations, Interrogations, Politics*, edited by Elizabeth Lapovsky Kennedy, and Agatha Beins, 61–72. New Brunswick, NJ: Rutgers University Press.

———. 2008. "Whither Black Women's Studies: An Interview." In *Women's Studies on the Edge*, edited by Joan Wallach Scott, 155–67. Durham, NC: Duke University Press. First published 1997.

Halberstam, Judith. 2005. *In a Queer Time and Place: Transgender Bodies, Subcultural Lives*. New York: New York University Press.

Hale, C. Jacob. 1997. "Leatherdyke Boys and Their Daddies: How to Have Sex without Women or Men." *Social Text* 52 (52): 223–36.

Hall, Stuart. 1981. "Notes on Deconstructing 'The Popular'." In *People's History and Socialist Theory*, edited by Raphael Samuel, 227–40. London: Routledge and Kegan Paul, Ltd.

Hammonds, Evelynn M. 1997. "Toward a Genealogy of Black Female Sexuality." In *Feminist Genealogies, Colonial Legacies, Democratic Futures*, edited by M. Jacqui Alexander and Chandra Talpade Mohanty, 170–82. New York: Routledge.

Hancock, Ange-Marie. 2007. "When Multiplication Doesn't Equal Quick Addition: Examining Intersectionality as a Research Paradigm." *Perspectives on Politics* 5 (1): 63–79.

Haraway, Donna. 1988. "Situated Knowledges: The Science Question in Feminism and the Privilege of Partial Perspective." *Feminist Studies* (14) 3: 575–99.

———. 1991 *Simians Cyborgs, and Women*. New York: Routledge.

Harding, Sandra. 1987. "Introduction: Is There a Feminist Method?" In *Feminism and Methodology*, edited by Sandra Harding, 1–14. Bloomington: Indiana University Press.

Hark, Sabine. 2005. "Blurring Boundaries, Crossing Borders, Traversing Frontiers: Inter- and Transdisciplinarity Revisited." The Workshop of the EU-funded research project, *Disciplinary Barriers between the Social Sciences and the Humanities*. Finland. Unpublished conference presentation.

———. 2007. "Magical Sign: On the Politics of Inter- and Transdisciplinarity." *GJSS—Graduate Journal of Social Science* 4 (2). http://www.gjss.nl/vol04/nr02/a02.

Harnois, Catherine. 2005. "Different Paths to Different Feminisms? Bridging Multiracial Feminist Theory and Quantitative Sociological Gender Research." *Gender & Society* 19 (6): 809–28.

Harris, Laura Alexandra. 1996. "Queer Black Feminism: The Pleasure Principle." *Feminist Review* 54: 3–30.

Harris, Virginia R., and Trinity A. Ordoña. 1990. "Developing Unity among Women of Color: Crossing the Barriers of Internalized Racism and Cross-Racial Hostility." In *Making Face, Making Soul* Haciendo Caras: *Creative and Critical Perspectives by Feminists of Color*, edited by Gloria E. Anzaldúa. San Francisco: Aunt Lute Books.

Hartmann, Heidi. 1979. "The Unhappy Marriage of Marxism and Feminism: Toward a More Progressive Union." *Capital and Class*. 3 (2): 1–33.

Hartsock, Nancy. 1990. "Foucault on Power: A Theory for Women?" In *Feminism/Postmodernism*, editied by Linda Nicholson, 157–75. New York: Routledge.

Hawken, Paul. 2007. *Blessed Unrest: How the Largest Movement In the World Came Into Being and Why No One Saw it Coming*. New York: Viking.

Heller, Dana. 1995. *Family Plots: The De-Oedipalization of Popular Culture*. Philadelphia: University of Pennsylvania Press.

Hemmings, Clare. 2005a. "Telling Feminist Stories." *Feminist Theory* 6 (2): 115–39.

———. 2005b. "Gender, Institutionalisation, and the Feminist Curriculum, or, What is at Stake in the Development of Critical Feminist Pedagogy?" In *TravellingConcepts.net*, edited by Clare Hemmings and Ann Kaloski. York: Raw Nerve Books. Accessed October 2, 2009. http://www.travellingconcepts.net/hemmings1.html.

———. 2011. *Why Stories Matter: The Political Grammar of Feminist Theory*. Durham, NC: Duke University Press.

Hemphill, Essex, ed. 1991. *Brother to Brother: New Writings by Black Gay Men*. Boston: Alyson.

Henderson, Mae Gwendolyn. 1989. "Speaking in Tongues: Dialogism and the Black Woman Writer's Literary Tradition." In *Changing Our Own Words: Essays on Criticism, Theory, and Writing by Black Women*, edited by Cheryl A. Wall, 16–37. New Brunswick, NJ: Rutgers University Press.

Henderson, Katharine Rhodes. 2006. *God's Troublemakers: How Women of Faith Are Changing the World*. New York: Continuum.

Hennessey, Rosemary and Chris Ingraham. 1997. "Introduction: Reclaiming Anticapitalist Feminism." In *Materialist Feminism: A Reader in Class, Difference and Women's Lives*, edited by Rosemary Hennessey and Chris Ingraham, 1–14. New York: Routledge.

Henry, Astrid. 2004. *Not My Mother's Sister: Generational Conflict and Third-Wave Feminism*. Bloomington: Indiana University Press.

Hesford, Victoria. 2005. "Feminism and its Ghosts: the Spectre of the Feminist as Lesbian." *Feminist Theory* 6 (3): 227–50.

Heywood, Leslie, and Jennifer Drake, eds. 1997. *Third Wave Agenda: Being Feminist, Doing Feminism*. Minneapolis: University of Minnesota Press.

Hines, Darlene Clark. 1989. "Rape and the Inner Lives of Black Women in the Middle West." *Signs: Journal of Women in Culture and Society* 14 (4): 912–20.

"History of Mount Holyoke College." https://www.mtholyoke.edu/inauguration/history_mhc.html. Accessed February 9, 2011.

Hogeland, Lisa Marie. 2001. "Against Generational Thinking, Or, Some Things that 'Third Wave' Feminism Isn't." *Women's Studies in Communication* 24 (1): 107–21.

Hollibaugh, Amber. 1992. "Desire for the Future: Radical Hope in Passion and Pleasure." In *Pleasure and Danger: Exploring Female Sexuality*, edited by Carol Vance, 401–10. London: Pandora Press. First Published 1984.

———. 2000. *My Dangerous Desires: A Queer Girl Dreaming Her Way Home* Durham, NC: Duke University Press.

Holloway, Karla F. C. 2006. "'Cruel Enough to Stop the Blood': Global Feminisms and the U.S. Body Politic, Or: 'They Done Taken My Blues and Gone'." *Meridians: Feminism, Race, Transnationalism* 7 (1): 1–18.

Hong, Grace Kyungwon. 2008. "'The Future of Our Worlds': Black Feminism and the Politics of Knowledge in the University under Globalization." *Meridians: Feminism, Race, Transnationalism* 8 (2): 95–115.

hooks, bell. 1981. *Ain't I A Woman? Black Women and Feminism*. Boston: South End Press.

———. 1984. *Feminist Theory from Margin to Center*. Boston: South End Press.

———. 1990. *Yearning: Race, Gender, and Cultural Politics*. Boston: South End Press.

———. 1992. *Black Looks: Race and Representation*. Boston: South End Press.

———. 1995. *Teaching to Transgress*. New York: Routledge.

———. 2000. *Feminism Is for Everybody*. Boston: South End Press.

Horowitz, David and Jacob Laksin. 2009. *One Party Classroom: How Radical Professors at American's Top Colleges Indoctrinate Students and Undermine Our Democracy*. New York: Crown Forum.

Howe, Florence, ed. 2000. *The Politics of Women's Studies: Testimony from 30 Founding Mothers*. New York: Feminist Press.

———. 2002. "Still Changing Academe After All These Years." *Women's Studies Quarterly* 30 (3/4): 27–32.

Howe, Florence and Carol Ahlum. 1973. "Women's Studies and Social Change." In *Academic Women on the Move*, edited by Alice Rossi and Ann Calderwood, 393–423. New York: Russell Sage Foundation.

Hull, Gloria, Patricia Bell Scott, and Barbara Smith, eds. 1982. *All the Women are White, All the Blacks Are Men, But Some of Us Are Brave: Black Women's Studies.* Old Westbury, NY: Feminist Press.

Hurdis, Rebecca. 2002. "Heartbroken: Women of Color Feminism and the Third Wave." In *Colonize This! Young Women of Color on Today's Feminism*, edited by Daisy Hernández and Bushra Rehman, 279–92. Seattle, WA: Seal Press.

Hurtado, Aida. 1996. *The Color of Privilege: Three Blasphemies on Race and Feminism.* Ann Arbor: University of Michigan.

Ilibagiza, Immaculée. 2006. *Left to Tell: Discovering God Amidst the Rwandan Holocaust.* Carlsbad, CA: Hay House.

INCITE! Women of Color Against Violence, eds. 2009. *The Revolution Will Not Be Funded: Beyond the Non-Profit Industrial Complex.* Boston: South End Press.

Jakobsen, Janet R., and Ann Pellegrini, eds. 2008. *Secularisms.* Durham, NC: Duke University Press.

Jaggar, Alison, ed. 2008. *Just Methods: An Interdisciplinary Feminist Reader.* Boulder, CO: Paradigm.

Jaggar, Allison M., and Paula S. Rothenberg, eds. 1978/1984/1993. *Feminist Frameworks: Alternative Theoretical Accounts of the Relations between Women and Men* (1st–3rd editions). New York: McGraw-Hill.

Jay, Karla. 1999. *Tales of the Lavender Menace: A Memoir of Liberation.* New York: Basic Books.

Jayarantre, Toby Epstein, and Abigail Stewart. 1991. "Qualitative and Quantitative Methods in the Social Sciences: Current Feminist Issues and Practical Solutions." In *Beyond Methodology: Feminist Scholarship as Lived Research*, edited by Mary Margaret Fonow and Judith Cook, 85–106. Bloomington: Indiana University Press.

Johnson, Merri Lisa, ed. 2002. *Jane Sexes It Up: True Confessions of Feminist Desire.* New York: Four Walls Eight Windows.

———, ed. 2007. *Third Wave Feminism and Television: Jane Puts It In a Box.* London: I.B. Tauris.

Jordan-Zachery, Julia. 2007. "Am I a Black Woman or a Woman Who Is Black? A Few Thoughts on the Meaning of Intersectionality." *Politics & Gender* 3 (2): 254–63.

Joseph, Miranda. 2002. "Analogy and Complicity: Women's Studies, Lesbian/Gay Studies, and Capitalism." In *Women's Studies On Its Own*, edited by Robyn Wiegman, 267–92. Durham, NC: Duke University Press.

Jung, Patricia Beattie, and Joseph A. Coray, eds. 2001. *Sexual Diversity and Catholicism: Toward the Development of Moral Theology.* Collegeville, MN: Liturgical Press.

Jung, Patricia Beattie, and Mary E. Hunt. 2009. "'Good Sex' and Religion: A Feminist Overview." *Journal of Sex Research* 46 (2-3): 156–67.

Katz, Cindi. 2001. "Disciplining Interdisciplinarity." *Feminist Studies* 27 (2): 519–25.

Katz, Cindi, and Nancy Miller. 2007. "Editors' Note." *Women's Studies Quarterly* 35 (3/4): 10–13.

Keating, AnaLouise, ed. 2000. *Gloria E. Anzaldúa: Interviews/Entrevistas*. New York: Routledge.

———, ed. 2005. *EntreMundos: Between Worlds: New Perspectives on Gloria Anzaldúa*. New York: Palgrave Macmillan.

———. 2008. "'I'm a Citizen of the Universe': Gloria Anzaldúa's Spiritual Activism as Catalyst for Social Change." *Feminist Studies* 34 (1/2): 53–69.

Kegan Gardiner, Judith. 2002. "Rethinking Collectivity: Chicago Feminism, Athenian Democracy, and the Consumer University." In *Women's Studies on Its Own*, edited by Robyn Wiegman, 191–201. Durham, NC: Duke University Press.

———. 2003. "Paradoxes of Empowerment: Interdisciplinary Graduate Pedagogy in Women's Studies." *Feminist Studies* 29 (2): 409–21.

Kennedy, Elizabeth L., and Agatha Beins, eds. 2005. *Women's Studies for the Future: Foundations, Interrogations, Politics*. New Brunswick, NJ: Rutgers University Press.

Kesselman, Amy, Lily D McNair, and Nancy Schniedewind, eds. 2008. *Women: Images and Realities, A Multicultural Anthology*. Columbus OH: McGraw-Hill.

King, Deborah K. 1988. "Multiple Jeopardy, Multiple Consciousness: The Context of a Black Feminist Ideology." *Signs: Journal of Women in Culture and Society* 14 (1): 42–72.

King, Katie. 1994. *Theory in its Feminist Travels: Conversations in U.S. Women's Movements*. Bloomington: Indiana University Press.

Kinser, Amber E. 2004. "Negotiating Spaces for/through Third-Wave Feminism." *NWSA Journal* 16 (3): 124–53.

Kirby, Sandra, Lorraine Greaves, and Colleen Reid. 2006. *Experience, Research, Social Change: Methods Beyond the Mainstream*. Toronto: Broadview Press.

Kitch, Sally. 2002. "Claiming Success: From Adversity to Responsibility in Women's Studies." *NWSA Journal* 14 (1): 160–81.

Klein, Julie Thompson. 1990. *Interdisciplinarity: History, Theory, and Practice*. Detroit: Wayne State University Press.

———. 1993. "Blurring, Cracking, and Crossing: Permeation and the Fracturing of Discipline." In *Knowledges: Historical and Critical Studies in Disciplinarity*, edited by Ellen Messer-Davidow, David R. Shumway, and David Sylvan, 185–211. Charlottesville: The University of Virginia Press.

———. 1996. *Crossing Boundaries: Knowledge, Disciplinarities, and Interdisciplinarities*. Charlottesville and London: The University Press of Virginia.

———. 2005. *Humanities, Culture, and Interdisicplinarity: The Changing Academy*. Albany: SUNY Press.

Klein, Julie Thompson, and William Newell. 1998. "Advancing Interdisciplinary Studies" In *Interdisciplinarity: Essays from the Literature*, edited by William Newell, 3–22. New York: College Entrance Examination Board. First published 1996.

Klein, Naomi. 2000. *No Logo*. New York: Picador.

Kolmar, Wendy, and Frances Bartkowski, eds. 2001. *Feminist Theory: A Reader*. New York: McGraw Hill.

Kolodny, Annette. 1998. *Failing the Future: A Dean Looks at Higher Education in the Twenty-first Century*. Durham, NC: Duke University Press.

———. 2000. "Women and Higher Education in the Twenty-first Century: Some Feminist and Global Perspectives." *NWSA Journal* 12 (2): 130–47.

Lather, Patti. 1991. *Getting Smart: Feminist Research and Pedagogy with/in the Postmodern*. New York: Routledge.

Lattuca, Lisa. 2001. *Creating Interdisciplinarity: Interdisciplinary Research and Teaching among College and University Faculty*. Nashville, TN: Vanderbilt University Press.

Laughlin, Kathleen A., Julie Gallagher, Dorothy Sue Cobble, Eileen Boris, Premilla Nadasen, Stephanie Gilmore, and Leandra Zarnow. 2010. "Is It Time to Jump Ship? Historians Rethink the Waves Metaphor." *Feminist Formations* 22 (1): 76–135.

Lay, Mary M., Janice Monk, and Deborah S. Rosenfelt, eds. 2002. *Encompassing Gender: Integrating International Studies and Women's Studies*. New York: Feminist Press.

Lazreg, Marnia. 2000. "The Triumphant Discourse of Global Feminism: Should Other Women be Known?" In *Going Global: The Transnational Reception of Third World Women Writers*, edited by Mal Amireh and Lisa Suhair Majaj, 29–38. New York: Garland.

Lear, Marsha W. 1968. "The Second Feminist Wave." *New York Times Magazine*, March 10.

Lee, Rachel. 2000. "Notes from the (Non)Field: Teaching and Theorizing Women of Color." *Meridians: Feminism, Race, Transnationalism* 1 (1): 85–109.

Lemons, Gary L. 2001. "'When and Where [We] Enter': In Search of a Feminist Forefather—Reclaiming the Womanist Legacy of W.E.B. DuBois." In *Traps: African American Men on Gender and Sexuality*, edited by Rudolph P. Byrd, and Beverly Guy-Sheftall, 71–89. Bloomington: Indiana University Press.

———. 2008. *Black Male Outsider: Teaching as a Pro-feminist Man, A Memoir*. Albany: State University of New York Press.

Lensink, Judy Nolte. 1991. "Strategies for Integrating International Material into the Introductory Women's Studies Course." *Women's Studies International Forum* 14 (4): 277–83.

Lerner, Gerda. 1986. *The Creation of Patriarchy*. Oxford: Oxford University Press. First published in 1974.

Letter to the *Post and Courier*. 2009. January 5. http://www.charleston.net/news/2009/jan/05/letters_editor67231/.

Levin, Amy. 2007. "Questions for a New Century: Women's Studies and Integrative Learning." College Park, MD: National Women's Studies Association. http://www.nwsa.org/downloads/WS_Integrative_Learning_Levine.pdf. Accessed October 2010.

Levine, Helen. 2008. "Fanning Fires: Women's Studies in a School of Social Work." In *Minds of Our Own: Inventing Feminist Scholarship and Women's Studies in Canada and Québec, 1966–1976*, edited by Wendy Robbins, Meg

Luxton, Margrit Eichler, and Francine Descarries, 54–60. Waterloo: Wilfrid Laurier Press.

Lipsitz, George. 1998. *Possessive Investments in Whiteness: How White People Benefit from Identity Politics*. Philadelphia: Temple University Press.

Little, Adrian. 2002. *The Politics of Community: Theory and Practice*. Edinburgh: Edinburgh University Press.

Looser, Devoney. 1997. "Introduction 2: Gen X Feminists? Youthism, Careerism, and the Third Wave." In *Generations: Academic Feminists in Dialogue,* edited by Devoney Looser, and E. Ann Kaplan, 31–54. Minneapolis: University of Minnesota Press.

———. 2002. "Battle Weary Feminists and Supercharged Grrls: Generational Differences and Outsider Status on Women's Studies Administration." In *Women's Studies on Its Own*, edited by Robyn Wiegman, 211–17. Durham, NC: Duke University Press.

Looser, Devoney, and E. Ann Kaplan, eds. 1997. *Generations: Academic Feminists in Dialogue*. Minneapolis: University of Minnesota Press.

Lorde, Audre. 1984. *Sister Outsider: Essays and Speeches by Audre Lorde*. Berkeley: The Crossing Press.

Love, Heather. 2007. *Feeling Backward: Loss and the Politics of Queer History*. Cambridge: Harvard University Press.

Lugones, María. 1990. "Playfulness, 'World'-Traveling and Loving Perception." In *Making Face, Making Soul* Haciendo Caras: *Creative and Critical Perspectives by Feminists of Color*, edited by Gloria E. Anzaldúa, 390–402. San Francisco: Aunt Lute Books.

———. 2006. "On Complex Communication." *Hypatia* 21 (3): 75–85.

Lugones, María and Joshua Price. 2003. "The Inseparability of Race, Class, and Gender." *Latino Studies Journal* 1 (2): 329–32.

Lugones, María, and Elizabeth Spelman. 2005. "Have We Got a Theory for You!: Feminist Theory, Cultural Imperialism and the Demand For 'The Woman's Voice'." In *Feminist Theory: A Reader*, edited by Wendy Kolmar and Frances Bartkowski. New York: McGraw Hill.

Luhmann, Susanne. 2004. "Trying Times for Women's Studies: Lost Pasts, Ambivalent Presents, and Predetermined Futures." In *Troubling Women's Studies: Pasts, Presents and Possibilities*, 149–94. Toronto: Sumach Press.

Lykke, Nina. 2007. "Response to Sabine Hark." *GJSS—Graduate Journal of Social Science* 4 (2). http://www.gjss.nl/vol04/nr02/a03.

Maathai, Wangari. 2007. *Unbowed: A Memoir*. New York: Anchor.

Mabokela, Reitumetse Obakeng. 2001. "Introduction: Soaring Beyond Boundaries." In *Sisters of the Academy: Emergent Black Women Scholars in Higher Education*, edited by Reitumetse Obakeng Mabokela and Ann L. Green, xiii–xx. Sterling, VA: Stylus Press.

Mahmood, Saba. 2005. *Politics of Piety: The Islamic Revival and the Feminist Subject*. Princeton: Princeton University Press.

Manalansan, Martin IV. 2003. *Global Divas: Filipino Gay Men in the Diaspora*. Durham, NC: Duke University Press.

Manicom, Ann. 1992. "Feminist Pedagogy: Transformations, Standpoints, and Politics." *Canadian Journal of Education* 17 (3): 365–89.

Maparyan, Layli. 2012. *The Womanist Idea*. New York: Routledge.

Marable, Manning. 2001. "Groundings with My Sisters: Patriarchy and the Exploitation of Black Women." In *Traps: African American Men on Gender and Sexuality*, edited by Rudolph P. Byrd and Beverley Guy-Sheftall, 119–52. Bloomington: Indiana University Press.

Marks, Elaine, and Isabelle de Courtivron, eds. 1980. *New French Feminisms*. Amherst: University of Massachusetts Press.

Martin, Biddy. 2008. "Success and Its Failures." In *Women's Studies on the Edge*, edited by Joan Wallach Scott, 169–97. Durham, NC: Duke University Press. First published 1997.

Martindale, Kathleen. 1992. "Theorizing Autobiography and Materialist Feminist Pedagogy." *Canadian Journal of Education* 17 (3): 321–40.

May, Vivian M. 2002. "Disciplinary Desires and Undisciplined Daughers: Negotiating the Politics of a Women's Studies Doctoral Education." *NWSA Journal* 14 (1): 134–59.

———. 2005. "Disciplining Feminist Futures?: 'Undisciplined' Reflections about the Women's Studies Ph.D." In *Women's Studies for the Future: Foundations, Interrogations, Politics*, edited by Elizabeth Lapovsky Kennedy, and Agatha Beins, 185–206. New Brunswick: Rutgers University Press.

———. 2007. *Anna Julia Cooper, Visionary Black Feminist: A Critical Introduction*. New York and London: Routledge.

———. 2009. "Writing the Self into Being: Anna Julia Cooper's Textual Politics." *African American Review* 43 (1): 17–34.

McCall, Leslie. 2005. "The Complexity of Intersectionality." *Signs: Journal of Women in Culture and Society* 30 (3): 1771–1800.

McCaughey, Martha. 2008. "Academic Freedom? The Right-Wing Campaign Against Women's Studies Turns a Treasured Ideal on its Head," *Ms. Magazine*. http://www.msmagazine.com/Summer2008/womensstudies.asp. Accessed June 2011.

McCaughey, Martha, and Cat Warren. 2006. "Right-Wing Attacks on Women's Studies." In *Handbook for Women's Studies Program Administrators*, edited by Martha McCaughey, 43–47. College Park, MD: National Women's Studies Association.

McIntosh, Peggy, and Elizabeth Kamarck Minnich. 1984. "Varieties of Women's Studies." *Women's Studies International Forum* 7 (3): 139–48.

Meskell, Lynn. 1995. "Goddeses, Gimbutas and New Age Archaeology." *Antiquit* 69 (262): 74–86.

Messer-Davidow, Ellen. 2002. *Disciplining Feminism: From Social Activism to Academic Discourse*. Durham, NC: Duke University Press.

Messer-Davidow, Ellen, David R. Shumway, and David J. Sylvan. 1993. "Introduction: Disciplinary Ways of Knowing." In *Knowledges: Historical and Critical Studies in Disciplinarity*, edited by Ellen Messer-Davidow, David R. Shumway, and David J. Sylvan. Charlottesville: University of Virginia Press.

Michael, John. 2000. *Anxious Intellects: Academic Professionals, Public Intellectuals, and Enlightenment Values*. Durham, NC: Duke University Press.

Minh-ha, Trinh T. 1990. "Not You/Like You: Post-Colonial Women and the Interlocking Questions of Identity and Difference." In *Making Face, Making Soul* Haciendo Caras: *Creative and Critical Perspectives by Feminists of Color*, edited by Gloria E. Anzaldúa, 371–75. San Francisco: Aunt Lute Books.

Minnich, Elizabeth. 1990. *Transforming Knowledge*. Philadelphia: Temple University Press.

Moallem, Minoo. 2006. "Feminist Scholarship and the Internationalization of Women's Studies." *Feminist Studies* 32 (2): 332–51.

Moghadam, Valentine M. 2001. "Institutionalizing and Globalizing Women's Studies at Illinois State University." *Gender Issues* 19 (2): 5–15.

Mohanty, Chandra Talpade. 1987. "Feminist Encounters: Locating the Politics of Experience." *Copyright* 1 (30): 30–44.

———. 1991a. "Cartographies of Struggle: Third World Women and the Politics of Feminism." In *Third World Women and the Politics of Feminism*, edited by Chandra Mohanty, Ann Russo, and Lourdes Torres, 1–52. Bloomington: Indiana University Press.

———. 1991b. "Under Western Eyes: Feminist Scholarship and Colonial Discourses." In *Third World Women and the Politics of Feminism*, edited by Chandra Mohanty, Ann Russo, and Lourdes Torres, 51–80. Bloomington: Indiana University Press. First published 1986.

———. 2003. *Feminism without Borders: Decolonizing Theory, Practicing Solidarity*. Durham, NC: Duke University Press.

Mohanty, Chandra Talpade, Ann Russo, and Lourdes Torres, eds. 1991. *Third World Women and the Politics of Feminism*. Bloomington: Indiana University Press.

Monk, Janice, Anne Betteridge, and Amy Newhall. 1991. "Introduction: Reaching for Global Feminism in the Curriculum." *Women's Studies International Forum* 14 (4): 239–47.

Moraga, Cherríe, and Gloria Anzaldúa. 1983. *This Bridge Called My Back: Writings by Radical Women of Color*. New York: Kitchen Table, Women of Color Press. First published in 1981.

Moran, Joe. 2002. *Interdisciplinarity*. London and New York: Routledge.

Morgan, Joan. 2000. *When Chicken-Heads Come Home to Roost: A Hip-Hop Feminist Breaks it Down*. New York: Touchstone.

Morgan, Kathryn Pauly. 1987. "The Perils and Paradoxes of Feminist Pedagogy." *Resources for Feminist Research* 16 (3): 49–52.

Morgan, Robin, ed. 1996. *Sisterhood Is Global: The International Women's Movement Anthology*. New York: The Feminist Press. First published 1984.

Morgensen, Scott Lauria. 2011. *Spaces between Us: Queer Settler Colonialism and Indigenous Decolonization*. Minneapolis: University of Minnesota Press.

Mowitt, John. 1992. *Text: The Genealogy of an Antidisciplinary Object*. Durham, NC: Duke University Press.

Moya, Paula. 1997. "Postmodernism, 'Realism,' And the Politics of Identity:

Cherríe Moraga and Chicana Feminism." In *Feminist Genealogies, Colonial Legacies, Democratic Futures,* edited by M. Jacqui Alexander, and Chandra Talpade Mohanty, 125–50. New York: Routledge.

———. 2002. *Learning from Experience: Minority Identities, Multicultural Struggles.* Berkeley: University of California Press.

Muñoz, José Esteban. 1999. *Disidentifications: Queers of Color and the Performance of Politics.* Minneapolis: University of Minnesota Press.

———. 2009. *Cruising Utopia: The Then and There of Queer Futurity.* New York: New York University Press.

Murray, Pauli. 1995. "The Liberation of Black Women." In *Words of Fire: An Anthology of African-American Feminist Thought,* edited by Beverly Guy-Sheftall, 186–97. New York: New Press.

Nash, Jennifer. 2008. "Re-Thinking Intersectionality." *Feminist Review* 89 (1): 1–15.

National Women's Studies Assocation. 2002. "Preamble to the Constitution of the National Women's Studies Association." *NWSA Journal* 14 (1): xix–xx. First published in 1977.

Neal, Mark Anthony. 1995. *New Black Man.* New York: Routledge.

Nemiroff, Greta Hoffman. 1978. "Rationale for an Interdisciplinary Approach of Women's Studies." *Canadian Woman Studies* 1 (1): 60–68.

Newell, William, ed. 1998. *Interdisciplinarity: Essays from the Literature.* New York: College Entrance Examination Board.

———. 2007. "Six Arguments for Agreeing on a Definition of Interdisciplinary Studies." *Association for Integrative Studies Newsletter* 29 (4): 1–4.

Newell, William, and William Green. 1998. "Defining and Teaching Interdisciplinary Studies." In *Interdisciplinarity: Essays From the Literature,* 23–24. New York: College Entrance Examination Board.

Newman, Jane O. 2002. "The Present and Our Past: Simone De Beauvoir, Descartes, and Presentism in the Historiography of Feminism." In *Women's Studies On Its Own,* edited by Robyn Wiegman, 141–73. Durham, NC: Duke University Press.

Nnaemeka, Obioma. 2003. "Nego-Feminism: Theorizing, Practicing, and Pruning Africa's Way." *Signs: Journal of Women in Culture and Society* 29 (2): 357–85.

Noble, Jean Bobby. 2006. *Sons of the Movement: FtMs Risking Incoherence in a Post-Queer Cultural Landscape.* Toronto: Women's Press.

Nussbaum, Martha. 1999. "The Professor of Parody." *New Republic* 22: 37–45.

O'Barr, Jean Fox. 1994. *Feminism in Action: Building Institutions and Community Through Women's Studies.* Chapel Hill: University of North Carolina Press.

Oldenburg, Ray. 1991. *The Great Good Place.* New York: Paragon House.

O'Reilly, Victoria. 1998. "Creating/Reclaiming Herstory in Concert: Twenty Years of Feminist Musical Research." In *Women's Studies in Transition,* edited by Kate Conway–Turner, 118–37. Cranbury: Associated University Presses.

Orr, Catherine M. 1997. "Charting the Currents of the Third Wave." *Hypatia* 12 (3): 29–45.

———. 1998. "Representing Women/Disciplining Feminism: Activism, Professionalism, and Women's Studies." Ph.D. dissertation, University of Minnesota.

———. 1999. "Tellings of Our Activist Pasts: Tracing the Emergence of Women's Studies at San Diego State." *Women's Studies Quarterly* 27 (3/4): 212–29.

Ortner, Sherry B. 1974. "Is Female to Male as Nature is to Culture?" In *Woman, Culture, and Society*, edited by Michelle Rosaldo and Louise Lamphere, 68–87. Stanford, CA: Stanford University Press.

Pecora, Vincent P. 2006. *Secularization and Cultural Criticism: Religion, Nation, & Modernity*. Chicago: University of Chicago Press.

Pellegrini, Ann. 1996. *Performance Anxiety: Staging Race, Staging Psychoanalysis*. New York: Routledge.

Pellauer, Mary. 1993. "The Moral Significance of Female Orgasm: Towards Sexual Ethics that Celebrates Women's Sexuality." *Journal of Feminist Studies in Religion* 9 (1-2): 161–82.

Penley, Constance. 1989. "Teaching in Your Sleep: Feminism and Psychoanalysis." In *The Future of an Illusion*, 165–84. Minneapolis: University of Minnesota Press. First published in 1986.

Phillips (Maparyan), Layli. 2006. *The Womanist Reader*. New York: Routledge.

Phillips, Lynn. 2000. *Flirting with Danger: Young Women's Reflections on Sexuality and Domination (Qualitative Studies in Psychology)*. New York: New York University Press.

Phoenix, Ann, and Pamela Pattynama. 2006. "Intersectionality." *European Journal of Women's Studies* 13 (3): 187–92.

Pitt, Alice. 1995. "Subjects in Tension: Engaged Resistance in the Feminist Classroom." Dissertation, OISE/University of Toronto.

———. 1996. "Fantasizing Women in the Women's Studies Classroom: Toward a Symptomatic Reading of Negation." *Journal for Curriculum Theorizing* 12 (4): 32–40.

———. 2003. *Play of Personal: Psychoanalytic Narratives of Feminist Education*. New York: Peter Lang.

Pollitt, Katha. 2009. "Amber Waves of Blame." *Nation* 288 (23): 10.

Pryse, Marjorie. 2000. "Trans/Feminist Methodology: Bridges to Interdisciplinary Thinking." *NWSA Journal* 12 (2): 105–18.

Puar, Jasbir. 2007. *Terrorist Assemblages: Homonationalism in Queer Times*. Durham NC: Duke University Press.

Queen, Carol. 2003. "The Queer In Me." In *Real Live Nude Girl: Chronicles of Sex-Positive Culture*, 10–15. San Francisco: Cleis Press.

Quinn, Rebecca Dakin. 1997. "An Open Letter to Institutional Mothers." In *Generations: Academic Feminists in Dialogue*, edited by Devoney Looser and E. Ann Kaplan, 174–82. Minneapolis: University of Minnesota Press.

Radicalesbians. 1970. "The Woman-Identified Woman." Documents from the Women's Liberation Movement: An On-line Archival Collection. Special Collections Library, Duke University. http://scriptorium.lib.duke.edu/wlm/womid/.

Ralston, Meredith L., and Edna Keeble. 2009. *Reluctant Bedfellows: Feminism, Activism and Prostitution in the Philippines.* Sterling: Kumarian Press.

Reger, Jo., ed. 2005. *Different Wavelengths: Studies of the Contemporary Women's Movement.* New York: Routledge.

Repko, Allen. 2008. *Interdisciplinary Research: Process and Theory.* Los Angeles: Sage.

Riley, Denise. 1988. *Am I That Name?: Feminism and the Category "Women" In History.* New York: MacMillan.

Ringrose, Jessica. 2007. "Troubling Agency and Choice: A Psycho-Social Analysis of Students' Negotiations of Black Feminist Intersectionality Discourses in Women's Studies." *Women's Studies International Forum* 30 (3): 264–78.

Robbins, Wendy, Meg Luxton, Margrit Eichler, and Francine Descarries, eds. 2008. *Minds of Our Own: Inventing Feminist Scholarship and Women's Studies in Canada and Québec. 1966–1976.* Waterloo: Wilfrid Laurier Press.

Robinson, Jean C. 2002. "From Politics to Professionalism: Cultural Change in Women's Studies." In *Women's Studies On Its Own,* edited by Robyn Wiegman, 202–10. Durham, NC: Duke University Press.

Rogers, Mary F., and C.D. Garrett. 2002. *Who's Afraid Of Women's Studies? Feminisms In Everyday Life.* Walnut Creek, CA: AltaMira.

Romero, Mary. 2000. "Disciplining the Feminist Bodies of Knowledge: Are We Creating or Reproducing Academic Structures?" In *NWSA Journal.* 12 (2): 148–62.

Roof, Judith. 1997. "Generational Difficulties: Or the Fear of a Barren History." In *Generations: Academic Feminists in Dialogue,* edited by Devoney Looser and E. Ann Kaplan, 69–87. Minneapolis: University of Minnesota Press.

Rosenberg, Sharon. 2004. "At Women's Studies Edge: Thoughts towards Remembering a Troubled and Troubling Project of the Modernist University." In *Troubling Women's Studies: Pasts, Presents, and Possibilities,* 195–239. Toronto: Sumach Press.

Rosenfelt, Deborah. 1984. "What Women's Studies Programs Do That Mainstreaming Can't." *Women's Studies International Forum* 7 (3): 167–75.

Rothenberg, Ellen. 2011. "Public Address." http://www.ellenrothenberg.com/public-address-about.html. Accessed June 9.

Rubin, David. 2005. "Women's Studies, Neoliberalism and the Paradox of the 'Political'." *Women's Studies for the Future: Foundations, Interrogations, Politics,* edited by Elizabeth Lapovsky Kennedy, and Agatha Beins, 245–61. New Brunswick, NJ: Rutgers University Press.

Rubin, Gayle. 1975. "The Traffic in Women: Notes on the 'Political Economy' of Sex." In *Toward an Anthropology of Women,* edited by Rayna Reiter, 157–201. New York: Monthly Review Press.

———. 1992. "Thinking Sex: Notes for a Radical Theory of the Politics of Sexuality." In *Pleasure and Danger: Exploring Female Sexuality,* edited by Carole Vance, 267–319. London: Pandora. First published in 1984.

Rupp, Leila, and Verta Taylor. 1987. *Surviving in the Doldrums: The American*

Women's Rights Movement, 1945 to the 1960s. Oxford: Oxford University Press.

Russo, Ann. 2006. "The Feminist Majority Foundation's Campaign to Stop Gender Apartheid." *International Feminist Journal of Politics* 8 (4): 557–80.

Rutenberg, Taly. 1983. "Learning Women's Studies." In *Theories of Women's Studies*, edited by Gloria Bowles and Renate Duelli-Klein, 72–78. New York: Routledge.

Sadli, Saparinah, and Marilyn Porter. 1999. "Importing/Applying Western Feminism: A Women's Studies Linkage Project." *Women's Studies International Forum* 22 (4): 441–49.

Sandoval, Chela. 1990. "Feminism and Racism: A Report on the 1981 National Women's Studies Association Conference." In *Making Face, Making Soul Haciendo Caras: Creative and Critical Perspectives by Feminists of Color*, edited by Gloria E. Anzaldúa. San Francisco: Aunt Lute Books.

———. 2000. *Methodology of the Oppressed.* Minneapolis: University of Minnesota Press.

Sands, Kathleen. 2008. "Feminisms and Secularisms." In *Secularisms*, edited by Janet R. Jakobsen, and Ann Pellegrini, 308–30. Durham, NC: Duke University Press.

Scanlon, Kyle. 2006. "Where's the Beef? Masculinities as Performed by Feminists." In *Trans/Forming Feminisms: Trans-Feminist Voices Speak Out*, edited by Krista Scott-Dixon, 87–94. Toronto: Sumach Press.

Schick, Carol, JoAnn Jaffe, and Ailsa M. Watkinson, eds. 2004. *Contesting Fundamentalisms.* Halifax: Fernwood.

Schuster, Marilyn, and Susan Van Dyne. 1985. *Women's Place in the Academy: Transforming the Liberal Arts Curriculum.* Lanham, MD: Rowman and Littlefield Publishers.

Scott, Joan Wallach. 1992. "Experience." In *Feminists Theorize the Political*, edited by Judith Butler and Joan W. Scott, 22–40. New York and London: Routledge.

———. 1999. "The Evidence of Experience." In *Feminist Approaches to Theory and Methodology: An Interdisciplinary Reader*, edited by Sharlene Hesse-Biber, Christina Gilmartin, and Robin Lydenberg, 79–99. New York: Oxford University Press.

———, ed. 2008. *Women's Studies on the Edge.* Durham, NC: Duke University Press. First published in 1997.

Scully, Diana, and Danielle M. Currier. 1997. *The NWSA Backlash Report: Problems, Instigators, and Strategies.* College Park, MD: National Women's Studies Association.

Sedgwick, Eve Kosofsky. 1985. *Between Men: English Literature and Male Homosocial Desire.* New York: Columbia University Press.

———. 1991. *Epistemology of the Closet.* Berkeley: University of California Press.

———. 2003. *Touching Feeling: Affect, Pedagogy, Performativity.* Durham, NC: Duke University Press.

Shaw, Susan, and Janet Lee, eds. 2009. *Women's Voices, Feminist Visions.* Columbus, OH: McGraw Hill.

Sheinin, Aaron Gould. 2009. "Legislators Back Off, Praise GSU Experts on Sex Issues." *Atlanta Journal and Constitution*. Feb. 10. http://www.ajc.com/news/content/metro/stories/2009/02/10/legislature_sex_experts.html.

Sherman, Julia, and Evelyn Torton Beck. 1980. *The Prism of Sex*. Madison: University of Wisconsin Press.

Shields, Stephanie. 2008. "Gender: An Intersectionality Perspective." *Sex Roles* 59 (5–6): 301–11.

Short, Kayann. 1994. "Coming to the Table: The Differential Politics of *This Bridge Called My Back*." *Genders* 20: 3–44.

Shohat, Ella, ed. 1998. *Talking Visions: Multicultural Feminism in a Transnational Age*. Cambridge, MA: MIT Press.

Shrewsbury, Carolyn M. 1987. "What Is Feminist Pedagogy?" *Women's Studies Quarterly* 15 (3/4): 6–14.

Showalter, Elaine. 1971. "Introduction: Teaching About Women." *Female Studies* (IV): iii–xiv.

Side, Katherine. 2005. "Standing Alone: Disciplining Women's Studies through Freestanding Graduate Programs." National Women's Studies Association Guide to Graduate Work in Gender and Women's Studies, 16–18. College Park, MD: National Women's Studies Association.

Siegel, Deborah L. 1997. "The Legacy of the Personal: Generating Theory in Feminism's Third Wave." *Hypatia* 12 (3): 46–75.

Smith, Andrea. 2008. *Native American and the Christian Right: The Gendered Politics of Unlikely Alliances*. Durham, NC: Duke University Press.

Smith, Barbara. 1982. "Racism and Women's Studies." In *All the Women Are White, All the Blacks Are Men, But Some of Us Are Brave: Black Women's Studies*, edited by Gloria T. Hull, Patricia Bell Scott, and Barbara Smith, 48–51. New York: The Feminist Press.

———, ed. 1983. *Home Girls: A Black Feminist Anthology*. New York: Kitchen Table, Women of Color Press.

Smith, Valerie. 1998. *Not Just Race, Not Just Gender: Black Feminist Readings*. New York: Routledge.

Snediker, Michael. 2009. *Queer Optimism: Lyric Personhood and Other Felicitous Persuasions*. Minneapolis: University of Minnesota Press.

The Social Justice Group at The Center for Advanced Feminist Studies, University of Minnesota, eds. 2000. *Is Academic Feminism Dead? Theory in Practice*. New York: New York University Press.

Soto, Sandra K. 2005. "Where in Transnational World are the Women of Color?" In *Women's Studies for the Future: Foundations, Interrogations, Politics*, edited by Elizabeth Lapovsky Kennedy, and Agatha Beins, 111–24. New Brunswick: Rutgers University Press.

"Southeastern Women's Studies Association." http//sewsa.nwsa.org. Accessed June 20, 2011.

Spelman, Elizabeth V. 1988. *Inessential Woman: Problems of Exclusion in Feminist Thought*. Boston: Beacon.

Springer, Kimberly. 2002. "Third Wave Black Feminism?" *Signs: A Journal of Women in Culture and Society* 27 (4): 1059–82.

Stacey, Judith. 1995. "Disloyal to the Disciplines: A Feminist Trajectory in the Borderlands." In *Feminisms in the Academy*, edited by Domna Stanton and Abigail Stewart, 311–29. Ann Arbor: University of Michigan Press.

Stake, Jayne E. 2007. "Predictors of Change in Feminist Activism Through Women's and Gender Studies." *Sex Roles* 57: 43–54.

Stanton, Domna C., and Abigail J. Stewart, eds. 1995. *Feminisms in the Academy*. Ann Arbor: University of Michigan Press.

Stimpson, Catharine R. 1975. "The New Feminism and Women's Studies," in *Women on Campus: The Unfinished Liberation*, edited by George W. Bonham, 69–84. New Brunswick, NJ: Change Magazine.

———. 1988. "What Matter Mind: A Theory About the Practice of Women's Studies. In *Where the Meanings Are: Feminism and Cultural Spaces*, 38–53. New York: Methuen. First published in 1973.

Stimpson, Catharine, Joan Burstyn, Domna Stanton, and Sandra Whisler. 1975. "Editorial." *Signs: A Journal of Women in Culture and Society* 1 (1): v–viii.

Stryker, Susan, Paisley Currah, and Lisa Jean Moore. 2008. "Introduction: Trans-, Trans, or Transgender?" *Women's Studies Quarterly* 36 (3 & 4): 10–22.

Tarrant, Shirra. 2006. *When Sex Became Gender*. New York: Routledge.

Taylor, Verta, Leila Rupp, and Nancy Whittier, eds. 2009. *Feminist Frontiers*. Columbus, OH: McGraw Hill.

Thomas, Clara. 2008. "Creating a Tradition of Women Writers and Feminist Literary Criticism." In *Minds of Our Own: Inventing Feminist Scholarship and Women's Studies in Canada and Québec, 1966–1976*, edited by Wendy Robbins, Meg Luxton, Margrit Eichler, and Francine Descarries, 43–50. Waterloo: Wilfrid Laurier Press.

Tong, Rosemarie. 1989. *Feminist Thought: A Comprehensive Introduction*. Boulder: Westview Press.

———. 1998. *Feminist Thought: A More Comprehensive Introduction*. Boulder: Westview Press.

Trans Entities: The Nasty Love of Papì and Wil. 2007. [Film] Directed by Morty Diamond.

Tringham, Ruth E. 1991. "Households with Faces: The Challenge of Gender in Prehistoric Architectural Remains." In *Engendering Archaeology: Women and Prehistory*, edited by Joan M. Gero and Margaret W. Conkey. Cambridge, MA: Basil Blackwell Press.

Tumang, Patricia Justine. 2002. "Nasaan ka anak ko? A Queer Filipina-American Feminist's Tale of Abortion and Self-Recovery." In *Colonize This! Young Women of Color on Today's Feminism*, edited by Daisy Hernández and Bushra Rehman, 370–81. Seattle, WA: Seal Press.

Turner, Caroline, Sotello Viernes, and Samueal L. Meyers, Jr. 2000. *Faculty of Color in Academe: Bittersweet Success*. Boston: Allyn and Bacon.

University of Victoria. 2007. "A Vision for the Future - Building on Strength: A Strategic Plan for the University of Victoria." http://web.uvic.ca/strategicplan/pdf/strategicplan.pdf.

Valentine, Gill. 2007. "Theorizing and Researching Intersectionality: A Challenge for Feminist Geography." *The Professional Geographer* 59 (1): 10–21.

Vance, Carol S., ed. 1992. *Pleasure and Danger: Exploring Female Sexuality.* London: Pandora Press. First Published 1984.

Vickers, Melana Zyla. 2005. "An Empty Room of One's Own: A Critical Look at the Women's Studies Programs of North Carolina's Publicly Funded Universities." The John William Pope Center for Higher Education Policy. Accessed February 11, 2011. http://popecenter.org/inquiry_papers/article.html?id=1549.

Walker, Alice. 1983. *In Search of Our Mothers' Gardens: Womanist Prose.* New York: Harcourt Brace Jovanovich.

Walker, Rebecca. 1992. "Becoming the Third Wave." *Ms.* 12: 39–41.

———. 1995. "Being Real: An Introduction." In *To Be Real: Telling the Truth and Changing the Face of Feminism*, edited by Rebecca Walker, xxix–xl. New York: Anchor Books.

Walkerdine, Valerie. 1990. *Schoolgirl Fictions.* New York: Verso.

Ward, Olivia. 2008. "Ten Worst Countries for Women." *The Toronto Star*, March 8. http://www.thestar.com/News/World/article/326354.

Warner, Michael. 1991. "Fear of a Queer Planet." *Social Text* 29: 3–17.

Washburn, Jennifer. 2005. *University, Inc.: The Corporate Corruption of Higher Education.* New York: Basic Books.

Weiler, Kathleen. 1991. "Freire and a Feminist Pedagogy of Difference." *Harvard Educational Review* 61 (4): 449–79.

Welch, Penny. 1994. "Is Feminist Pedagogy Possible?" In *Changing the Subject: Women in Higher Education*, edited by S. Davis, 149–62. London: Taylor and Francis.

———. 2006. "Feminist Pedagogy Revisited." *LATISS—Learning and Teaching in the Social Sciences* 3 (3): 171–99.

White, Christopher. 2009. "Sexuality Studies Under Attack!" *National Sexuality Research Center.* Accessed Feb. 12, 2009. http://nsrc.sfsu.edu/dialogues/users/Christopher.White/blog/sexuality-studies-under-attack

Wiegman, Robyn. 1999. "What Ails Feminist Criticism? A Second Opinion." *Critical Inquiry* 25: 362–79.

———. 2000. "Feminism's Apocalyptic Futures." *New Literary History* 31 (4): 805–25.

———. 2001. "Women's Studies: Interdisciplinary Imperatives, Again." *Feminist Studies.* 27 (2): 514–19.

———. 2002a. "Academic Feminism Against Itself." *NWSA Journal* 14 (2): 18–34.

———, ed. 2002b. *Women's Studies on Its Own: A Next Wave Reader in Institutional Change.* Durham, NC: Duke University Press.

———. 2002c. "The Progress of Gender: Whither 'Women'?" In *Women's Studies on Its Own*, 106–40. Durham, NC: Duke University Press.

———. 2005. "The Possibility of Women's Studies." In *Women's Studies for the Future: Foundations, Interrogations, Politics*, edited by Elizabeth L. Kennedy, and Agatha Beins, 40–60. New Brunswick, NJ: Rutgers University Press.

———. 2008. "Feminism, Institutionalism and the Idiom of Failure." In *Wom-

en's Studies on the Edge, edited by Joan Wallach Scott, 39–66. Durham, NC: Duke University Press. First published 1999.

Williams, Patricia J. 1991. "The Death of the Profane." In *The Alchemy of Race and Rights: Diary of a Law Professor*, 44–51. Cambridge: Harvard University Press.

Winnubst, Shannon. 2006. *Queering Freedom*. Bloomington: Indiana University Press.

Wise, Tim. 2001. "Is Sisterhood Conditional? White Women and the Rollback of Affirmative Action." *NWSA Journal* 10 (3): 1–26.

Women's Studies International Forum. 1991. "Special Issue: Reaching for Global Feminism in the Curriculum." 14 (4).

Women's Studies Quarterly. 1998. "Special Issue: Internationalizing the Curriculum: Integrating Area Studies, Women's Studies, and Ethnic Studies." 26 (3-4).

Woodhead, Linda. 2008. "Secular Privilege, Religious Disadvantage." *British Journal of Sociology* 59 (1): 53–58.

Yee, Shirley J. 1997. "The 'Women' in Women's Studies." *Differences: A Journal of Feminist Cultural Studies* 9 (3): 46–64.

Zemon Davis, Natalie, and Jill Ker Conway. 2008. "Feminism and A Scholarly Friendship." In *Minds of Our Own: Inventing Feminist Scholarship and Women's Studies in Canada and Québec, 1966–1976*, edited by Wendy Robbins, Meg Luxton, Margrit Eichler, and Francine Descarries, 78–88. Waterloo: Wilfrid Laurier Press.

Zimmerman, Bonnie. 2002. "Women's Studies, NWSA, and the Future of the (Inter)Discipline." *NWSA Journal* 14 (1): viii–xviii.

———. 2002. "The Past in Our Present: Theorizing the Activist Project of Women's Studies." In *Women's Studies on Its Own*, edited by Robyn Wiegman, 183–90. Durham, NC: Duke University Press.

———. 2005. "Beyond Dualisms: Some Thoughts about the Future of Women's Studies." In *Women's Studies for the Future: Foundations, Interrogations, Politics*, edited by Elizabeth Lapovsky Kennedy and Agatha Beins, 31–39. New Brunswick, NJ: Rutgers University Press.

Zinn, Maxine Baca, Lynn Weber Cannon, Elizabeth Higgenbotham, and Bonnie Thornton Dill. 1990. "The Costs of Exclusionary Practices in Women's Studies." In *Making Face, Making Soul* Haciendo Caras: *Creative and Critical Perspectives by Feminists of Color*, edited by Gloria E. Anzaldúa, 29–41. San Francisco: Aunt Lute Books.

Zinn, Maxine Baca, and Bonnie Thornton Dill. 1996. "Theorizing Difference from Multiracial Feminism." *Feminist Studies* 22 (2): 321–33.

About the Contributors

ANN BRAITHWAITE is Associate Professor and Director of Women's Studies at the University of Prince Edward Island. She is co-author of *Troubling Women's Studies* (2004), co-editor of *Atlantis: A Women's Studies Journal*, and former President of the Canadian Women's Studies Association/*L'association canadienne des études sur les femmes*. Her current research interests include thinking about disciplinarity and how definitions of Women's and Gender Studies are reflected in curricular decisions, and a new project tentatively titled *Women's Studies without Feminism*.

AIMEE CARRILLO ROWE is Associate Professor of Communication Studies at California State University, Northridge and author of *Power Lines: On the Subject of Feminist Alliances* (2008). She works with ethnographic, popular, literary, and performance-based texts in the fields of Women's Studies, Ethnic Studies, and Cultural Studies. Her current project, *Pasando Tiempo: Chicano/a Performance as Recovery*, traces how Chicana/o performance resists and rewrites U.S. assimilationist imperatives to generate multiple forms of recovery.

KARLYN CROWLEY is Associate Professor of English and Director of Women's and Gender Studies at St. Norbert College. She has published *Feminism's New Age: Gender, Appropriation, and the Afterlife of Essentialism* (2011) as well as articles in publications such as *Gastronomica* and *Stories of Oprah: The Oprahfication of American Culture* (2009). Her current research continues her interest in gender essentialism, spirituality, and alternative culture by analyzing natural childbirth and parenting practices.

ASTRID HENRY is Associate Professor of Gender, Women's, and Sexuality Studies and English at Grinnell College. She is the author of *Not My Mother's Sister: Generational Conflict and Third-Wave Feminism* (2004) and has chapters in a number of anthologies including *Different Wavelengths: Studies of the Contemporary Women's Movement* (2005) and *Catching A Wave: Reclaiming Feminism for the 21st Century* (2003). She serves on the Executive Council of the National Women's Studies Association. Her current book project is a study of contemporary memoirs by U.S. feminists.

MERRI LISA JOHNSON is Associate Professor and Director of the Center for Women's and Gender Studies at the University of South Carolina Upstate. She has edited or co-edited: *On the Literary Nonfiction of Nancy Mairs* (2011); *Third Wave Feminism and Television* (2007); *Flesh for Fantasy: Producing and Consuming Exotic Dance* (2006); and *Jane Sexes It Up: True Confessions of Feminist Desire* (2002). She has also published a memoir, *Girl in Need of a Tourniquet* (2010) and currently serves as President of the Southeastern Women's Studies Association.

WENDY KOLMAR is Professor of English and Director of Women's Studies at Drew University. She has served on the Governing Council and the Program Administration and Development Committee of the National Women's Studies Association and serves frequently as a program reviewer and consultant for WGS programs around the United States. She is currently working on the supernatural stories of the Anglo-Indian writer, Alice Perrin, and on the fourth edition of *Feminist Theory: A Reader*.

DIANE LICHTENSTEIN is Professor of English and former Chair of Women's Studies as well as of Interdisciplinary Studies at Beloit College. She co-edited a special issue of *Women's Studies Quarterly* (1999) focused on feminist activism and Women's Studies; and a cluster of essays on "locations" in the *NWSA Journal* (2005). She has also published *Writing Their Nations: The Tradition of Nineteenth-Century*

American Jewish Women Writers (1992) and articles on U.S. women writers as well as feminist collaborative leadership.

SUSANNE LUHMANN is Associate Professor of Women's Studies at the University of Alberta. She is a co-author of *Troubling Women's Studies: Pasts, Presents, and Possibilities* (2004) and is currently working on a book manuscript tentatively titled *Domesticating the Nazi Past: The Public Life of Familiar Memory.*

VIVIAN M. MAY is Associate Professor of Women's and Gender Studies at Syracuse University and is the author of *Anna Julia Cooper, Visionary Black Feminist* (2007). She has published articles in journals such as *Hypatia*, *African American Review*, *Callaloo*, and *NWSA Journal* and serves on the *Feminist Formations* board. She is working on a book, *Intersectionality: Theories, Histories, Practices*, to be published by Routledge, and she served as Co-Chair of the 2009 and 2010 National Women's Studies Association conferences.

LAYLI MAPARYAN is Associate Professor of Women's Studies and Associated Faculty of African American Studies at Georgia State University. She is the editor of *The Womanist Reader* (2006) and author of *The Womanist Idea* (2012). In 2009, she received a Contemplative Practice Fellowship from the Center for Contemplative Mind in Society. Currently, she is working with the University of Liberia, where she served in 2010 as a Fulbright Specialist, to help establish a Gender Studies Program.

MARTHA MCCAUGHEY is Professor of Sociology at Appalachian State University, where she also directed the Women's Studies Program. She is the author of *The Caveman Mystique: Pop-Darwinism and the Debates over Sex, Violence, and Science* (2008) and *Real Knockouts: The Physical Feminism of Women's Self-Defense* (1997). She edited the second edition of the *Women's Studies Program Administrators' Handbook* (National Women's Studies Association) and has served on the Southeastern Women's Studies Association Executive Committee.

SCOTT LAURIA MORGENSEN is Assistant Professor in the Department of Gender Studies at Queens's University. He is the author of *Spaces Between Us: Queer Settler Colonialism and Indigenous Decolonization* (2011) and co-editor of *Queer Indigenous Studies: Critical Interventions in Theory, Politics, and Literature* (2011). His current research projects examine the colonial biopolitics of global AIDS, racism and settler colonialism in Canadian queer politics, and histories of queer men in Women's and Gender Studies.

BOBBY NOBLE is Associate Professor of English and Sexuality Studies at York University. He has published *Sons of the Movement: FtMs Risking Incoherence in a Post-Queer Cultural Landscape* (2006) and *Masculinities without Men?* (2004), and co-edited *The Drag King Anthology* (2003). He is currently the Principal Investigator on a new, multi-year, funded study: The Feminist Porn Archive and Research Project.

CATHERINE M. ORR is Professor and Chair of Women's and Gender Studies at Beloit College. Her work has been published in *Women's Studies Quarterly*, *Hypatia*, *NWSA Journal*, and *Feminist Collections*. She served as National Conference Chair for the National Women's Studies Association (2006–08). Her research and teaching focuses on disciplinarity, feminist theorizing, whiteness, and popular culture. She enjoys thinking broadly about the productivity and limitations inherent in the life of institutions and disciplines, especially Women's and Gender Studies.

LAURA PARISI is Assistant Professor of Women's Studies at the University of Victoria. Her articles have appeared in journals such as *Politics and Gender*, *Journal of Human Rights*, and *Canadian Foreign Policy*. Her current research focuses on the gender mainstreaming practices of human rights and development non-governmental organizations. She recently served as the elected 2011 Program Chair for the Feminist Theory and Gender Studies Section of the International Studies Association.

ALISON PIEPMEIER is Associate Professor of English and Director of Women's and Gender Studies at the College of Charleston. She is the author of *Girl Zines: Making Media, Doing Feminism* (2009) and *Out in Public: Configurations of Women's Bodies in Nineteenth-Century America*

(2004) as well as co-editor of *Catching a Wave: Reclaiming Feminism for the 21st Century* (2003). She has served as Regional Representative and Elections Chair on the National Women's Studies Association Governing Council.

JENNIFER PURVIS is Associate Professor of Feminist Theory and Director of Women's Studies at the University of Alabama. She has written "Grrrls and Women Together in the Third Wave: Embracing the Challenges of Intergenerational Feminism(s)" (2004) and is currently working on a book manuscript focused on queer feminist futurity and alternative modalities of revolt across feminist "generations." She has served as the Southeast Regional Co-Chair of the National Women's Studies Association.

KATHERINE SIDE is Associate Professor and Head of the Department of Women's Studies, Memorial University of Newfoundland. Her research has been published in *NWSA Journal* and the *Journal of International Women's Studies*. She also publishes on human rights in Northern Ireland and the Republic of Ireland. She is President of the Canadian Women's Studies Association */L'association canadienne des études sur les femmes* and past holder of the Margaret Laurence Scholar in Residence in Gender and Women's Studies, Brandon University.

Subject Index